Issues in Monetary, Financial and Macroeconomic Adjustment Policies

Issues in Monetary, Financial and Macroeconomic Adjustment Policies

Edited by

Stuart Sayer

Blackwell
Publishing

First published 2005 by Blackwell Publishing Ltd

Library of Congress Cataloging-in-Publication Data has been applied for

ISBN 1-4051-2911-5

A catalogue record for this title is available from the British Library

Set in 10/12pt Times
by Integra Software Services Pvt. Ltd, Pondicherry, India
Printed and bound in the United Kingdom
by MPG Books Ltd, Bodmin, Cornwall

The publisher's policy is to use permanent paper from mills that operate a sustainable forestry policy, and which has been manufactured from pulp processed using acid-free and elementary chlorine-free practices. Furthermore, the publisher ensures that the text paper and cover board used have met acceptable environmental accreditation standards.

For further information on Blackwell Publishing, visit our website:
www.blackwellpublishing.com

CONTENTS

1

MONETARY, FINANCIAL AND MACROECONOMIC ADJUSTMENT POLICIES: AN OVERVIEW

Stuart Sayer

University of Edinburgh

1. Introduction

The survey articles that make up this volume cover a set of interconnecting topics: financial markets and economic development; financial crises; macroeconomic adjustment (e.g. in response to crises) and its impact on the poor; and the asymmetric effects of monetary policy and the zero bound to interest rates. While the topics clearly interconnect, they do not fit neatly into a standard sub-field of economics, as is reflected in the somewhat cumbersome title of this book. This appears to reflect a general trend in economic analysis and, more particularly, applied and policy analysis, which increasingly appears to transcend standard sub-field boundaries. A simple indication of this is the increasing difficulty of classifying articles in *Journal of Economic Literature* categories. One consequence of this trend is the need for researchers to keep abreast of a wider range of literature in a variety of sub-fields, highlighting the importance and usefulness of good survey articles.

2. Microfoundations, Fashion and Institutions

While finance, broadly defined, together with macroeconomic adjustment to financial crises, provides the common theme, several other common threads, which cast a more general light on applied economics and policy analysis, emerge from the surveys.

The first of these concerns *microfoundations*. The merits of deriving models or, at least, using models that are derivable, from 'sound' microfoundations is widely accepted among mainstream economists. Implementing this dictum effectively in applied contexts is, however, not an easy task. The microfoundations used need to be appropriate to enable the analyst to highlight the relevant issues. In the context of money and finance, this can be a difficult task. The standard micro framework of Arrow-Debreu has no room for money and only a very limited scope for finance. The Modigliani-Miller theorem makes finance largely an irrelevance. To create a role for money and restore the relevance of finance, frictions need to be introduced. But, what are the appropriate frictions? And, once identified, can they be modelled in a tractable way, which enables them to be integrated into a complete macroeconomic set up?

In the case of money some progress on this issue has been made in recent years (see Kocherlakota, 2002; Kiyotaki and Moore, 2002; Corbae *et al.*, 2002) but we remain some way from having an agreed, tractable and consistent microfounded model which can be used to analyse standard policy issues (see Wallace, 2001). As Yates contends (see footnote 12 in Yates' contribution), there is a sense in which money is not peculiar in this respect. The microfoundations of many other standard ingredients of macroeconomic models (e.g. firms, markets, and governments) can be questioned. Though the weakness of the microfoundations of money are, arguably, more problematic in a context, such as the zero bound to interest rates, where monetary policy is the focus of the analysis.

Our understanding of the microfoundations of finance and credit has, arguably, made greater progress in recent years, than that of money, by utilising a framework based on asymmetric information. This has enhanced our understanding of the operation of credit markets and credit rationing (e.g. Stiglitz and Weiss, 1981) and the role played by financial intermediaries (e.g. Diamond, 1991). Salvatore Capasso's contribution to this issue highlights a more recent literature, which shows how information asymmetries can give insight into the interrelation between financial markets and development. More generally, the asymmetric information approach to the analysis of credit markets sheds important light on the potential problems of traditional financial liberalisation, as explored in the contribution by Paul Auerbach and Jalal Uddin Siddiki. The removal of government restrictions on the operation of financial markets need not eliminate credit rationing and may encourage excessive risk-taking, producing a financial system that is vulnerable to shocks and crises. This link to the literature on financial crises is explored further in the contributions by Jan Breuer and Sweta Saxena. While a variety of insights from the related 'credit channel' literature are discussed, in the context of the transmission mechanism of monetary and other shocks, in the contributions by Pierre-Richard Agénor, Anna Florio and Tony Yates.

Agénor's survey raises a broader range of microfoundations issues. Agénor departs from the standard representative agent framework found in much of the macroeconomics literature in order to explore the consequences of macro-economic adjustment policies for the poor. *Inter alia*, his approach highlights the limitations of conducting a welfare analysis of macroeconomic policies in a framework which excludes consideration of their distributional consequences. Agénor also stresses the importance of labour markets for understanding the transmission mechanism in the developing world and the need for microfoundations to be sufficiently rich to capture the key features of both formal and informal sectors.

At a more general level, recognition that the microfoundations of the models we use are shaky, or possibly incomplete or inappropriate to the task at hand, provides a problem for the applied theorist or policy-maker. It is relatively easy to cast stones at workhorse models, but, as Tony Yates' writes 'Without an alter-native workhorse model, perhaps the best we can do is to proceed, but with a degree of caution, noting that our models and our conclusions built on them will be fraught with imperfections.'

A second common theme concerns the interaction between economic events and the development of economic models and analysis. This is highlighted, in particular, by Sweta Saxena's account of how succeeding generations of currency crises models have evolved to account for the changing nature of observed crises. But it is also apparent in the changing attention given to the 'liquidity trap', which largely disappeared from mainstream literature in the relatively high inflation era of the mid 1970s to mid 1980s, to reappear in the more recent era of relatively low inflation, prompted in particular by the recent experience of Japan.

In many respects it seems healthy that economic analysis responds and adapts to relevant real world issues. But it may, at least at times, indicate a less desirable tendency for economic analysis and/or policy to be driven by fads and fashion and 'throw the baby out with the bath water'. This tendency may, for example, be reflected by the McKinnon-Shaw prescription of financial liberalisation as a reaction to the excesses and apparent inefficiencies of traditional Keynesian and structuralist approaches to finance for development. There is a sense in which some strands of the traditional Keynesian and structuralist literatures lost sight of the benefits of the invisible hand, by overemphasising its weaknesses, while the advocates of financial liberalisation neglected the weaknesses which arise from, for example, frictions and information asymmetries. There does seem to be something of a tendency to throw out the Keynesian baby with its, albeit often dirty, bath water. As is to some extent reflected in the contributions by Auerbach and Siddiki and Florio, there can be valuable insights in the traditional and post-Keynesian literature and, perhaps even more so, in Keynes' own writings. It is encouraging to see some of these insights being rediscovered and re-presented in a modern better-microfounded guise.

Given the shaky nature of microfoundations, noted above, there is much to be said for pluralism, avoiding a neglect of the insights often found in the older literature even though it may not achieve modern standards of rigour. In an important sense, pluralism and robustness provide a way of hedging ones' bets and a basis from which to exercise what David Colander (1992) refers to as the 'lost art of economics', the all important judgements that are implicit in good applied economics and policy advice. This role for the 'art of economics' is also reflected directly in monetary policy-making in practice, with policy-makers eschewing the formal adoption of mechanical Taylor-like rules for instrument setting in favour of a more discretionary judgement-based approach (see Yates contribution and Svensson, 2003).

A further common thread, emphasised in particular in the contributions by Auerbach and Siddiki, and Breuer, is the importance of effective institutions and governance. As these authors argue there are a wide range of institutional factors that affect both the vulnerability of an economy to financial crises and the success or failure of financial liberalisation. These factors include: economic and financial rules and regulations, shareholder rights, transparency and supervision over the financial system, government distortions, legal origin, shareholder protection, property rights, and enforcement of contracts, alongside a range of political and sociological variables such as democracy and political instability, corruption, and social capital (Breuer). The increasing recognition of the importance of such institutional factors links to the broader literature on new political economy (see Sayer, 2000), which has seen rapid growth in recent years stimulated partly by theoretical developments but also by the availability of new and interesting data sets covering a range of political, governance and institutional issues (see Breuer's contribution and also Jain, 2001).

3. An Outline of the Contributions

Paul Auerbach and Jalal Uddin Siddiki provide a broad review of the theoretical and empirical literature linking the financial sector, financial liberalisation and economic development. They begin by exposing the limitations of traditional theoretical frameworks, which render finance more or less irrelevant and hence fail to provide an adequate basis for the analysis of the interplay between financial structure and economic development. They then turn to the more recent literature which builds an analysis of financial instruments and institutions on the foundation of information asymmetries. This richer literature, they argue, provides a better basis for analysing the weaknesses of simple-minded liberalisation measures, and highlights the importance of designing appropriate institutional structures to mitigate problems generated by asymmetric information. Their review of the empirical literature emphasises that, while studies confirm the importance of finance to economic development, they are indecisive about the effectiveness of the widely advocated policies associated with financial liberalisation.

Salvatore Capasso provides a more focused review of the asymmetric information literature, applied to financial contracts and their interrelationship with development. His review provides a detailed exposition of four core models, which indicate how differences in endowments and information distribution can give rise to different financial contracts. These contracts both affect, and are affected by, capital accumulation and growth, and capture the common features of evolving financial markets observed in many economies.

Jan Breuer turns to the literature on currency and banking crises, giving a broad overview of their history, which extends as far back as the Punic War between Rome and Carthage in 200 BC, before turning to the more modern analysis provided by first-generation through fourth-generation (or institutional) models. Breuer highlights the parallels to be found in the developing literatures on currency crises and banking crises, with second-generation currency crisis models building on the Diamond and Dybvig (1983) model of bank runs, and third-generation models merging together to provide 'twin crises' models. The third- and fourth-generation models also link to the literature on financial liberalisation, with poorly designed liberalisation measures, linked to weak financial governance and institutional structures, often identified as major causal factors. This under-lies the emphasis, noted above, placed by Breuer, and Auerbach and Siddiki, on the need for appropriately designed governance and institutional structures for financial liberalisation to succeed and the risks of financial crises to be limited.

Sweta Saxena highlights the distinctive features of first- through third-generation models of currency crises by graphically depicting the behaviour of the key economic variables in a number of illustrative cases for each model generation. The first-generation examples are drawn from Latin America in the 1970s and 1980s, the second-generation from Europe in 1992–93, and the third-generation from a range of Scandinavian, Asian and Latin American economies in the 1980s and 1990s. Saxena's survey also contains excellent short reviews of the literatures on herding, contagion, and (a form of) moral hazard, which are key features of standard currency crises models.

Pierre-Richard Agénor examines the effects on the poor of macroeconomic adjustment programmes, which might, for example, be introduced in response to financial crises. The motivation for this focus is the concern, backed by growing evidence, that economic and financial crises hurt the poor the most because they often lack the means (e.g. lack of assets and access to credit markets) to protect themselves against adverse shocks. At the same time the poor may also gain the most from effective adjustment programmes, which succeed in reducing inflation, interest rates and credit rationing. Following a summary of recent evidence on poverty in the developing world, Agénor explores this dynamic trade-off by considering the direct and indirect transmission channels by which macroeconomic policies affect the poor. He then constructs a model, incorporating the frictions typical of labour markets in the developing world, to explore more formally the important role played by the labour market in this transmission process. The penultimate section of Agénor's paper provides a brief overview of some of the existing empirical studies of the effect of macroeconomic adjustment on poverty, along with some new cross-country results, which highlight some of the issues raised earlier in the survey.

Anna Florio's survey turns its attention to monetary policy. She explores through a mix of case studies, econometric evidence and theory the asymmetric effects of monetary policy, highlighted by Friedman's remark that 'monetary policy was a string. You could pull on it to stop inflation but you could not push on it to halt recession. You could lead a horse to water but you could not make him drink' (Friedman, 1968, p. 1).

The book concludes with Tony Yates' detailed review of a particular aspect of this asymmetry, focusing on the implications of the 'zero' bound to nominal interest rates for the operation of monetary policy. Yates begins by considering whether the bound is literally at zero, before turning to the difficult task of assessing the risk of hitting this bound, and how this risk is affected by the operative inflation target, as well as other policy measures that it has been claimed might reduce this risk. Yates then provides a critical review of the main cures for the zero bound problem (i.e. alternatives to interest rate policy), which have been proposed: Gessell money or a 'carry tax'; money 'rains'; buying long bonds or shares to exploit the portfolio balance channel; devaluation of the exchange rate; selling options, which embody a promise not to raise rates in the future; and a conventional debt financed fiscal stimulus. Yates broad conclusion is that the 'cures' are uncertain and more risky than 'prevention'. Further since the risks of hitting the zero bound seem quite small anyway, it is possible that the typical inflation objectives of modern monetary regimes already embody adequate 'prevention insurance'.

References

Colander, D. (1992) The lost art of economics. *Journal of Economic Perspectives*, 6: 191–198.

Corbae, D., Temzelides, E. and Wright, R. (2002) Matching and money. *American Economic Review*, 92, 2: 67–71.

Diamond, D. (1991) Monitoring and reputation: the choice between bank loans and directly placed debt. *Journal of Political Economy*, 99: 689–721.

Diamond, D. and Dybvig, P (1983) Bank runs, deposit insurance and liquidity. *Journal of Political Economy*, 91, 3: 401–419.

Friedman, M. (1968) The role of monetary policy. *American Economic Review*, 58, 1: 1–17.

Jain, A. (2001) Corruption: a review. *Journal of Economic Surveys*, 15, 1: 71–121.

Kiyotaki, N. and Moore, J. (2002) Evil is the root of all money. *American Economic Review*, 92, 2: 62–66.

Kocherlakota, N. (2002) Money: what's the question and why should we care about the answer? *American Economic Review*, 92, 2: 58–61.

Sayer, S. (2000) Issues in new political economy: an overview. *Journal of Economic Surveys*, 14, 5: 513–526.

Stiglitz, J. and Weiss, A. (1981) Credit rationing in markets with imperfect information. *American Economic Review*, 71, 3: 393–410.

Svensson, L. (2003) What is wrong with Taylor rules? Using judgment in monetary policy through targeting rules. *Journal of Economic Literature*, XLI: 426–477

Wallace, N. (2001) Whither monetary economics? *International Economic Review*, 42 4: 847–869.

2

FINANCIAL LIBERALISATION AND ECONOMIC DEVELOPMENT: AN ASSESSMENT

Paul Auerbach and Jalal Uddin Siddiki

Kingston University

1. Introduction and Summary

The role of finance and financial institutions is central to contemporary debates surrounding strategies for economic development. In recent decades, the need to understand the role of financial allocation has taken on a renewed urgency, as international agencies such as the IMF and the World Bank have often indicated that financial liberalisation is a central aspect of the economic integration into the world economy for developing and post socialist economies. It is in this context that a new literature giving a significant place to the role of finance in economic development has emerged and become predominant (see Gibson and Tsakalotos, 1994; Fry, 1995, 1997; Levine, 1997). Much of the literature surveyed is concerned with issues at the macroeconomic level, though Levine (1997) gives extensive coverage to microeconomic allocation, which will be the focus of the present discussion.

Financial liberalisation implies a whole series of measures to bring the financial sector in line with that found in advanced capitalist, most especially Anglo Saxon countries. The near unanimity of international agencies in their call for financial liberalisation is not echoed in the academic literature. On the contrary, we find that every aspect of liberalisation is the subject of controversy from both a theoretical and empirical perspective. At the heart of these controversies is the role of finance in economic allocation and growth, to which we have devoted Section 2 of the survey. The relative neglect of this issue in the main stream of economics emerges from the presence of a 'classical dichotomy' between the real and financial sectors: a role for finance in allocation and growth is excluded by postulate. This separation of the real and financial sectors and the associated static approaches to the functioning of capital markets (the paradigm of the perfect capital market) and to financial efficiency have proved major obstacles to the development of a coherent approach to the role of finance and its institutional basis in economic allocation and growth. Nonetheless, there has developed a substantial literature on the issues of the optimality of 'free' capital market institutions and of the efficacious role of financial institutions in economic development. By contrast, the critique associated with Joseph Stiglitz emphasises the existence of problems of imperfect information and costly enforcement: financial markets are unlikely to work in the manner of those for 'chairs and tables' (Stiglitz, 1989, 1994; for a survey of the role of informational asymmetries in financial markets and economic growth, see Capasso, 2004).

In Section 3, the role of finance in economic allocation and growth is dealt with in the practical context of the contemporary debates surrounding financial liberalisation. From an analytical perspective, we first discuss the *locus classicus* of the literature supporting financial liberalisation, the McKinnon-Shaw model of the early 1970s. This model was used to justify the attack by international agencies on 'financial repression', a practice, especially common in developing countries, of maintaining government controls on interest rates. This practice was said to exert an adverse impact on saving, investment and the rate of economic growth, and would be alleviated by financial liberalisation. By contrast, neo-Keynesians have argued that financial liberalisation may well reduce effective demand and economic growth and increase instability in the financial system; Stiglitz, as noted in Section 2, suggests that what appears to be a financial liberalisation leading to a market clearing equilibrium may merely be a form of upward financial repression; neo-structuralist views note that, in developing countries, increases in saving in formal financial institutions as a result of financial liberalisation may merely be at the expense of unorganised money markets.

In Section 4, we review the empirical literature surrounding finance and economic development, and then that concerned with the efficacy of financial liberalisation. We believe it is a serious error to conflate these two literatures. While the first group of studies in general yields a strong positive relationship between the development of the financial sector and economic growth, the literature concerned with financial liberalisation yields mixed, if not contradictory outcomes. One convergent result is that the successful outcome of any liberalisation process appears to be closely linked to questions concerning the governance of the country under consideration. It is to these questions that we return in our conclusion.

2. The Role of Finance in Economic Allocation and Growth

2.1 Static Theory and the Neutrality of Money

An ambivalent attitude towards finance among economists concerned with economic development has persisted due to the fact that the main stream of economic theory, most certainly from the time of Adam Smith and David Ricardo, has focused on the role of 'real' factors in the determination of economic outcomes, including economic growth. It has been primarily this 'hard wiring' of the classical dichotomy into modern economic theory which has served as an obstacle to the analysis of the role of finance in economic development rather than, for instance, the opposition of Keynesian economists to a consideration of monetary factors.[1] During the early Cold War period, '[the] wider aspects of the role of financial development, and the part that might be played by improving capital markets, was scarcely mentioned' (Little, 1982, p. 110). This fact might seem somewhat surprising, given that in the context of economic rivalry with centrally planned economies, there was a powerful motivation for a justification for the role of financial allocation, since such forms of allocation were largely absent in the centrally planned system.[2] The 'real factors' emphasis of economic theory has, however, inhibited a coherent integration of the theoretical and practical considerations which surround the role of finance in microeconomic allocation and its effect upon economic growth.

The classical dichotomy postulates that finance, if it is not to obscure the role of these real factors, is to be seen as a diaphanous veil through which real outcomes may be viewed. A doubling or a halving of the amount of money in an economy will have its effect upon the general price level, but relative prices within the economy – the relationships between the prices of apples, labour and land – will stay the same: prices of every single good or service in this 'frictionless' economy will rise or fall by the same percentage as a result of this change in the stock of money. Since real outcomes in the economy – the allocation of goods and services – are dictated by relative prices, they will therefore be unaffected by changes in the stock of money. Changes in the stock of money will only affect the general price level – the monetary economy. This grand simplification greatly facilitates the analysis of monetary changes on the economy and has permitted the development of modern macroeconomics.

The implications of this presumption of monetary neutrality for other aspects of economic analysis were only fully brought home with the publication of the famous theorem of Modigliani and Miller (1958): in the context of the classical dichotomy and its associated perfect capital market, the value of a firm will not be contingent on its debt to equity ratio or (as subsequently proved) its dividend payout ratio. Over 40 years after the publication of the theorem, the economics profession has still not recovered from the shock of discovering that the standard presumption in economic theory of the presence of a perfect capital market implies that finance and financial variables can have no effect upon real economic outcomes in the business world. Thus, in a perfect capital market, the commonplace calculations made in the financial analysis of a firm – liquidity ratios, ratios of short and long term indebtedness to the term structure of assets, as well as the aforementioned debt to equity and dividend payout ratios, will have no effect on the fortunes of the firm. In the context of economic development, probity in the handling of financial affairs at the microeconomic level is often a central component of the advice offered to developing nations: a key aspect of main stream economic theory suggests that such matters are not worthy of consideration.[3]

Modern economic theory puts further obstacles before us if we wish to put forth the traditional arguments for the role of finance in the economy. The traditional arguments for the role of finance fall into two classes. First, finance and financial institutions increase the efficiency of the use of investment funds. But at the heart of modern economic theory is the presence in the economy of a state of competitive equilibrium, in which the economy's inputs, in conjunction with existing technology and ideas, are already being used optimally on the frontier of the economy's aggregate production function. Discussions concerning how societies can use their existing inputs more efficiently (e.g. Porter, 1990) are redundant in this context,[4] as are any notions that financial institutions can increase the efficiency of the use of investment funds in an economy. In addition, the statistical estimation techniques used in economics almost invariably presume that the economy's inputs are already being used efficiently on the frontier of the economy's production function, therefore making it difficult to test any propositions concerning the role of financial institutions in improving the efficiency of the use of inputs (see Aigner *et al.*, 1977 and Coelli *et al.*, 1998 for a survey).

The second class of arguments suggests a role for finance in increasing the rate of saving in the economy. This argument is reduced in significance by the original versions of neo-classical growth theory, which predict that financial variables only influence the level of income rather than the growth of income. The presence of diminishing returns to capital in neo-classical growth theory dictates that the long term growth rate in per capita income will not be enhanced by an increase in the level of investment (see Solow, 1956): as Lucas argued, 'a thrifty society will, in the long-run, be wealthier than an impatient one, but it will not grow faster' (Lucas, 1988, p. 10). Any increase in the rate of saving generated by financial institutions will therefore not affect the rate of growth. In the new, or endogenous growth theory, this problematic result is overcome by presuming that increased investment by one firm has spillover effects for other firms. As a result, increases in productivity are generated for the industry as a whole and hence economic growth can result from increased investment (Romer, 1986). A key implication of endogenous growth theory is that government financial policies directed at influencing the rate of saving and investment may affect the steady state rate of economic growth. Thus, the emergence of endogenous growth theory permits us analyse the impact of financial and investment policies on economic growth.

2.2 *The Static Ideal of a Perfect Capital Market*

A further difficulty in the application of economic theory to economic development is its static nature. Thus, the perfect capital market model serves the
important purpose in economic theory of setting a standard for how a capital
market *should* work. But, very much like the model of perfect competition for
goods to which it corresponds, the model proves of limited usefulness in the
context of economic development. In the perfect capital market model, the capital
market plays a passive role as a provider of funds. There is little room for the
dynamics of competition in the form of the development of new instruments for
savers, new mechanisms for the financing of projects and the extension of the
geographical domain of finance. Yet these factors are central to the evaluation of
the efficacy of a financial system and are an important aspect of the heuristic
justification for the role of finance to be found in Levine (1997) and others.

In a perfect capital market, there is a universal and uniform rate of discount
upon which all projects are judged, which emerges from the intersection of the
marginal disutility of saving and the marginal productivity of investment. Using
this model as an ideal, we shall see below that, as a rule,[5] a *too low* rate of
discount (r) will be linked to the defect of 'long termism', in which finance will be
found for projects yielding too low a rate of return or which are overly ambitious,
while a *too high* rate of discount will be linked to the defect of short termism.

There is a powerful presumption that a perfect capital market will have desirable, rational characteristics. With every project incorporating the same r into its
decision formula (with account having been taken of the riskiness of different
projects – not at all a trivial task), the capital market will disinterestedly rank
projects in terms of their contribution to net present value. By contrast, in the
days of central planning, a project from mathematicians at the University of
Craków for the design and sale of software that had excellent prospects for
generating a substantial stream of net cash flow would never have seen the light
of day. It is likely that it would have lost out to other projects with poorer
prospects for returns, but whose supporters had greater political clout – such as
the drilling of more coal mines, with a consequent loss of general efficiency.

A perfect capital market will use, without prejudice, the same measuring rod *r*
for the evaluation of all projects. Competitive forces will dictate that outcomes in
the market emerge under conditions of objectivity and anonymity, with a minimum gap between the borrowing and lending rate. Finance will be allocated to its
most highly valued use in society. The model of the perfect capital market is
important for setting a normative standard by which real life capital markets can
be judged though, as we shall see below, there are limitations to its use even in this
context. As a description of the workings of actual capital markets, however, it is
wholly inadequate.

2.3 *Financial Efficiency versus Financial Evolution*

Contemporary financial theory and its associated empirical research rests on the
presumption that financial markets are efficient.[6] But this notion of efficiency is

different from, and not to be confused with, the concept of capital market perfection discussed above. In the context of economic development this concept does not provide us with a meaningful framework in which to discuss changes in the efficacy and speed with which capital market institutions respond to profitable opportunities. Many of the central issues concerning the role of finance in economic development are thus excluded from consideration in the efficiency framework.

The doctrine of financial efficiency falls into three categories.[7] Weak form efficiency suggests it is impossible to make money on a consistent basis on financial markets solely by discerning trends in financial prices; with semi-strong efficiency, money cannot be made even with the use of publicly available information; in the case of strong form efficiency, financial markets are presumed to reflect the true state of affairs so accurately that money cannot be made even in the presence of privileged groups or insider information.

Of these forms of financial efficiency, by far the most interesting is the semi-strong form, since a real life approximation to weak form efficiency is a minimum prerequisite to a rationally functioning market, while strong form efficiency has never existed. The semi-strong form of efficiency asks the question – given the availability of public information about financial and business affairs, does the market absorb this information into the prices of financial assets with sufficient speed and accuracy that it is impossible to use this information on a consistent basis to 'beat the market' and make a positive return?

What we find, however, is that even this concept of financial efficiency is inadequate as a tool for the analysis of developmental trends in the financial sector. Since semi-strong form efficiency asks whether a market is efficient *given* the state of publicly available information, it may well be that, in this sense, the financial markets in the coffee houses of seventeenth century Britain were 'efficient' then, and that they are efficient today as well. The question begged, in this context, is how the expansion in the quantity and quality of publicly available information have changed the workings of the capital market, moving it perhaps closer in the direction of 'perfection', if we evaluate financial markets in static terms.

This expansion of information may have even greater significance in a dynamic context for the evolution of financial markets. The theory of financial market efficiency, since it postulates a *given* state of publicly available information, tends to obscure the dynamics of the *creation* of such information in different financial market systems and contexts and obscures the role of financial innovation and evolution (Auerbach, 1988, ch. 7). These changes can affect both saving and investment. Financial institutions and other actors can affect the context in which saving takes place by taking initiatives to attract more saving and by creating new and more attractive saving mechanisms and instruments; they can encroach on the domain of other financial institutions (e.g. banks moving into the sale of insurance), thereby increasing the range of choices available to savers. These institutions can also be innovative through the creation of new forms and terms of lending, including the creation of forms of money and near money such as credit cards (which can influence the rate of saving as well as investment), by the seeking out of new opportunities for lending (e.g. to smaller firms or new industries) and in the creation of innovative forms of finance (the bundling and securitisation of mortgages; equity based participation schemes).

Other forms of innovation may conflict with the traditional roles of financial institutions when they take the form of disintermediation – the by-passing of financial intermediaries in the raising of funds from the public. Thus, the use of equity finance and, in recent times, the growth of securitised forms of finance contest the central role of banks as a source of firm finance. Even these 'marketised' alternatives exist to a great extent because of the aggressive role played by investment banks and other financial institutions in creating them, as well as the initiatives taken by firms themselves to reduce the cost of finance.

Financial evolution also takes the form of geographical dispersion. While, at one level, finance and trade have always linked the peoples of the Eastern Hemisphere, the interpenetration of finance between countries and even within them is an on-going process. Financial evolution and innovation cannot be explained merely as a reflection of changes in the technology of transportation and communication. These changes, rather, evolve and interact with new attitudes to the conduct of business and finance, and gradually transform the whole environment in which economic decisions are made. No simple, systematic tendency can be detected in these changes (e.g. a movement from finance provided by institutions to financing in open markets), but after taking into consideration the retrogressive effects of war and differences in national histories, there is a long term tendency for business and financial affairs to be conducted more aggressively over time, and over an ever wider geographical domain.

The above claim might seem to put an optimistic gloss on the history of finance, with its presumption of an increasingly competitive and efficacious financial sector. But innovation in the domain of finance is not necessarily comparable to equivalent effects in the 'real' sector of the economy, and may have drastically different consequences. Savings in the 'real' sector in the control of inventories (stocks and work in progress) reflect a net rise in the productivity, and therefore in the real income, of the society as a whole. An equivalent innovation, which permits every enterprise in the economy to perform the same volume of transactions with only half of their present holdings of cash, generates no equivalent societal gain: the marginal cost to society of (fiduciary) money creation by the government is close to zero. On the contrary, an innovation which merely permits every firm to economise on its holdings of cash may merely reduce the liquidity of firms, so that this 'financial innovation' has merely contributed to the fragility of the economy.[8]

In general, innovation in the financial sector must be appraised differently from changes in other areas of the economy because of the special considerations which emerge in the context of macroeconomic regulation. The fact that the medium of exchange in modern economies is dominated by the issuances of banks and other privately owned profit making institutions makes for perpetual tension and difficulties: strong government commitments to back up the financial sector in a crisis can encourage, rather than prevent, risky behaviour; competition in this sector may exacerbate problems of pro-cyclical lending behaviour and instability. Political questions of regulation and control are thus particularly difficult and unavoidable in the financial sector.

2.4 *Financial Institutions and Economic Development*

The provision of finance is thus not merely a question of the presence of financial 'markets', but of institutions actively engaged in facilitating the operation of these markets. However, just as the paradigm of the perfectly competitive market long inhibited the development of the theory of the firm, so too has the static ideal of the perfect capital market inhibited the emergence of useful theories of financial institutions. There are two streams to the literature on financial institutions which are relevant to the question of financial liberalisation. There is an older literature which, on the whole, points to the efficacy of financial institutions as creative, entrepreneurial force in place of marketised arrangements. We consider this literature below. A more recent literature also emphasises the importance of financial institutions in economic development, often in the implicit context of the role played by financial liberalisation in promoting forms of 'financial deepening'.

In the more recent literature, financial institutions are seen to contribute to raising the efficiency of investment by providing the following three services (King and Levine, 1993a): first, financial institutions efficiently evaluate projects and select the most promising ones. Evaluating projects is costly and involves high fixed costs which are generally out of the range of individuals; specialised financial institutions develop cumulative experience in the evaluation of projects. Secondly, financial institutions pool household savings and mobilise them to finance the more promising projects. Thirdly, financial institutions share and diversify risks associated with innovation. We will use this framework to organise recent contributions to this literature, whose focus is largely on banks, and then consider the role of liquidity constraints and of stock markets.

First, financial institutions evaluate projects. The good reputation of borrowers acquired by their track records resulting from bank monitoring is important for eliminating widespread moral hazard (Diamond, 1991). Borrowers have two choices: either borrowing directly (issuing publicly traded bonds or commercial paper, without monitoring) and borrowing through a bank that monitors potential borrowers to eliminate problems of moral hazard. If moral hazard is sufficiently widespread, then new borrowers will begin their borrowing career by being monitored and later switch to issuing directly placed debt. The favourable track record acquired while being monitored will be useful in predicting future actions in the absence of monitoring. Reputation alone can eventually deal with the moral hazard problem, because the better reputation achieved over time implies that the adverse selection problem will become less severe.

Fama (1985) argues that there must be something special about bank loans, i.e. bank loans must be offering some special services or facilities to borrowers for which they are willing to pay higher interest rates than for issuing directly placed debt. He argues that contracting costs for bank loans are lower for individuals and small organisations than contracting costs for outside debt. Regular contacts by banks with small organisations and individuals give banks access to information on the credit worthiness of these organisations and individuals. Hence, it is cheaper for small organisations and individuals to give one agent (the banker) direct access to the organisation's decision processes than to produce the range of publicly available information that would make outside debt a viable means of financing.

The presence of information asymmetries affects the firm's issue-invest decision, which may explain some corporate financing choices (Myers and Majluf, 1984). Suppose a firm issues common stock to raise cash to undertake productive investment. Management is assumed to know more about the firm's value than potential investors. Investors interpret the firm's choice rationally. The management acts in the interests of existing shareholders, so if the new investment opportunities are profitable then managers would prefer internal sources of funds and prefer debt to equity if external financing is required. Managers would refuse to exploit new profitable investment opportunities by using risky securities to finance these projects unless the ability to issue low risk debt had already been used up. However, stockholders are better off *ex ante* when the firm carries sufficient slack to undertake potentially good investment opportunities. This slack can be built up by restricting dividends. The firm should not pay dividends if it has to recoup the cash by selling stock or some other risky security. If the manager has superior (insider) information, the issuance of new stock will reduce stock prices, other things being equal, while the issuance of debt will raise the stock price. An unstated implication of this result is that such a preference for debt financing will promote the role of bank loans, most especially in contexts in which banks possess insider information on potential borrowers.

Secondly, financial institutions mobilise savings to finance promising projects. Financial institutions must pass through a transitional period of learning. During this period, they supply funds and in the process learn about good projects (Lee, 1996). This learning is positively affected by the amount of loans disbursed by financial institutions. The greater the intensity and efficiency of a financial system, the more rapid the improvement in the flow of information. Thus, the higher the level of loans to firms, the more rapid will be the improvement in learning and economic growth. However, we note that this process is likely to be efficacious only if there is the possibility of competition among financial institutions: after all, governments and nationalised sectors should as well be able to 'learn by experience', but there is no obvious autonomous process generally postulated which forces them to *use* this experience in the future to raise efficiency.

It is also claimed that financial institutions can contribute to increasing efficiency by raising the quality or the level of accumulation of human capital, an essential growth enhancing factor in endogenous growth theory, by offering finance to financially constrained households (De Gregorio, 1996). We may note here that the financing of education – most especially higher education, is likely to be relevant only for the very top share of the income distribution in developing countries. In addition, it is traditionally recognised that free capital markets tend to underinvest in human capital because of the problems in indenturing future income streams. It is common practice, therefore, to use 'non market' forms of credit, such as government guaranteed loans, to subsidise students. Government intervention is particularly important in the presence of threshold effects in education, whereby a minimum literacy rate of 30–40% is a precondition for rapid economic growth (Azariadis and Drazen, 1990). This need for intervention follows from the fact that capital markets will tend to underinvest in education in early stages of economic development due to the presence of low literacy rates and spillover effects for education.

Furthermore, the presence of financial institutions will increase the fraction of investment which is directed to projects with high levels of social return (Greenwood and Jovanovic, 1990), since in the early stages of development, an economy is likely to possess a poor level of organisation and information concerning the range of potential productive activities. (This same argument has been used in defence of government planning.) Financial institutions act as 'monitoring stations', assembling information concerning investment opportunities and providing professional advice regarding productive investment projects and may thus add to the fluidity of investment by siphoning funds away from traditional venues and into new domains.

Thirdly, financial institutions share and diversify risks associated with innovation. Diamond (1984) develops the role of diversification undertaken by financial intermediaries pioneered in Leland and Pyle (1977). He assumes that there are N entrepreneurs with projects whose returns are distributed independently and identically and are independent of the market portfolio. All N bankers working in the intermediary can observe *ex ante* information concerning all N entrepreneurs. They face no group moral hazard problem since all bankers can observe each other's information and actions. Diamond shows that each banker's signalling decision is equivalent to that of a single entrepreneur signalling a project with a mean cost of $N\mu/N = \mu$ and variance $(1/N)^2 N\sigma^2 = \sigma^2/N$ (where σ is a constant). Diversification improves the expected utility of the agents in the intermediary (diversification is a decreasing function of variance), implying that diversified intermediation is potentially viable.

Diamond and Dybvig (1983) point to the ability of financial institutions to pool risk and thereby invest in projects which are productive, but of relatively longer term and therefore too illiquid for individual investors due to uncertainties about future liquidity demand. This ability of financial institutions to invest in these illiquid, but highly productive projects enhances the efficiency of investment and hence generates a rise in economic growth (Bencivenga and Smith, 1991). Bencivenga and Smith (1997) have further extended the work of Diamond and Dybvig (1983) to show that economic development will tend to generate specialisation in (financial) markets. The setting up of markets incurs costs. These costs are more affordable for societies on high levels of per capita income than for those where it is low. An increase in income raises the level of transactions through markets, which in turn reduces the average (or marginal) costs of transactions. These productivity gains lead to specialisation in market structures. Diamond (1984) also suggests that the fixed costs of acquiring information by every individual investor in a new investment will mean that financial institutions can economise on the duplication of research efforts.

For many projects, 'non-convexity' in investment is likely to prevail, i.e. there will be projects in which efficient operation involves a scale of funds which is unlikely to be forthcoming from an individual investor or entrepreneur (Greenwood and Jovanovic, 1990). Financial institutions pool individual funds and channel them into productive projects. Along with the quantity (saving and investment) and quality (efficiency) effects discussed above, financial institutions increase the proportion of saving that goes to investment (Pagano, 1993). That is, an increase in the activities of financial institutions raises competition among financial institutions and thereby reduces the leakage of investment caused by the commissions charged by financial institutions.

Increased liquidity may negatively affect economic growth by reducing saving: greater stock market liquidity may reduce uncertainty, which in turn reduces precautionary saving. Highly liquid stock markets may thus cause economic agents to reduce their saving (Arestis, *et al.*, 2001). In general, households face financial imperfections, i.e. liquidity constraints in financing future consumption. They are therefore more concerned about their future than would be the case without any liquidity constraints, causing households to save more for the future than they could otherwise (Jappeli and Pagano, 1994). When financial institutions can lend to households or firms, households may use credit to smooth their consumption over time, while firms will use it to finance production expenditure. Thus, a reduction in credit to households increases the rate of saving and there-fore the availability of credit to firms, implying the possibility of increasing output and growth. The positive impact of liquidity constraints on saving remains unchanged even in the presence of international perfect capital mobility[9] if the latter does not have any incremental impact on the availability of credit. How-ever, consider that there is an (exogenous) rise in the current income of the next generation, which increases their current and future income and their desired level of wealth (positive effects). Under such circumstances, the presence of perfect international capital mobility would reduce the severity of liquidity constraints, encouraging agents to borrow from abroad and save less (negative effects). The net impact on saving, depending on the relative strength of both effects, is unknown. Thus, in an open economy model, the net impact of economic growth on saving is undetermined. However, as explained earlier, liquidity constraints may reduce economic growth when they impose budgetary constraints on house-holds which reduce investment in human capital accumulation (De Gregori, 1996). Thus whether the liquidity constraint increases saving and economic growth depends on how credit is spent. More precisely, if credit is spent on consumption and unproductive investment, liquidity constraints may enhance growth by reducing unproductive expenditure. On the other hand, if credit is spent on increasing the quality of human capital, liquidity constraints reduce human capital formation and productivity growth (Buiter and Kletzer, 1992).

Stock market developments have proved to be an important part of both internal and external financial liberalisation in developed countries in the 1980s and 1990s. However, the literature on financial liberalisation pays little attention to stock markets due to the belief that the flow of funds from the household to the business sector through the stock market is negligible. Thus, stock markets are either considered unimportant or at best part of a slow, evolutionary process, and can thus be ignored. But recent data quoted in Arestis *et al.* (2001) show that stock market valuation grew from $2 trillion in 1982 to $4.6 trillion in 1986, $10 trillion in 1993 and $15.15 trillion in 1996, implying an average annual growth rate of 15%; emerging market capitalisation grew from less than 4 to 13% of total world capitalisation. Stock markets contribute to economic growth by facilitating specialisation, acquisition and dissemination (Diamond, 1984) and also reduce the cost of mobilising savings, thereby facilitating investment (Greenwood and Smith, 1997). Stock markets allow buyers and sellers to trade financial assets more quickly and cheaply, thereby increasing the accessibility of capital and thus contributing to economic growth.

In contrast with this positive view, it has been asserted that stock market development is unlikely to help in achieving quicker industrialisation and faster long term economic growth for the following reasons (Singh, 1997): first, stock market performance represents a poor guide to efficient investment allocation due to the inherent volatility and arbitrariness of stock market pricing. Secondly, stock market volatility caused by unfavourable economic shocks may exacerbate macroeconomic instability and reduce long term growth. Finally, stock market development may undermine an existing banking system which has been successful in the promotion of economic growth: in the cases of the post-war industrialisation of Japan, Korea and Taiwan, stock markets have played little role. Similarly, Germany and Italy have been able to achieve their post war economic success with little assistance from stock markets.

Indeed, in the older literature (Gerschenkron, 1962; Kindleberger, 1984) mentioned above, it is suggested that late developing economies such as Germany and Russia used highly centralised forms of banking and direct government involvement in place of the more marketised forms of finance to be found in the Anglo Saxon economies: these centralised administrative mechanisms were more efficient in the conservation of scarce skilled manpower than the sophisticated, marketised arrangements that exist in richer countries. Such centralised institutions were used *faute de mieux* as substitutes for the rich infrastructure of early developing economies. More recently, supporters of the form of financial system traditionally associated with Germany have used the language of contemporary economic theory to suggest its capacity to overcome many of the problems described in the section below: 'Bank intermediated finance is preferable to other forms of finance because of the potential ability of banks to overcome the problems of asymmetric information and moral hazard. Universal banks are not only specialized in screening and evaluating loan proposals; they also rely on economies of scope arising from their involvement with the loan applicant in other lines of business' (Black and Moersch, 1998, p. 1).

At the height of the boom in the Asian economies in the post war world, centralised financial arrangements were seen as playing an essential role in a strategy of rapid economic growth for developing countries through focused and co-ordinated development,[10] and not merely in the negative senses described above – a compensation for backwardness and a means of overcoming market imperfections. Bank directed finance as an alternative to market-based forms is not very fashionable at the moment, but is historically of great significance in the context, most especially, of developing countries. We return to these questions in the conclusion.

2.5 *Forms of Capital Market Failure*

Capital markets may well work inappropriately. They may evidence serious distortions simply because of the presence of monopoly power among financial institutions, be they the high street clearing banks in a rich country or the local money lender in a remote village in a poor one. But the paradigm of imperfect information and costly enforcement stands in contrast to the traditional debate on monopoly versus perfect markets and can explain the usurious rates associated with informal credit markets in developing countries without reference to monopoly (Hoff and Stiglitz, 1990). The monopoly power explanation of rural credit markets predicts that government intervention to provide institutional alternatives will bring about competition and reduce the usurious rates charged by traditional rural money lenders in developing countries. But empirical evidence for the last forty years has shown that government intervention has failed to drive traditional money lenders out of the market. It has been argued that observed high interest rates were a reflection of the presence of well nigh perfect credit markets that took into account the risks of default. However, neither the traditional monopoly nor the perfect market views can explain the continued coexistence of the formal and informal sectors, of credit rationing and the geographical segmentation of credit markets.

The McKinnon-Shaw hypothesis (to be discussed in Section 3) states that credit rationing mainly results from ceilings on interest rates, since these ceilings cause an under-supply of saving which generates an excess demand for credit. This hypothesis predicts that there would be no excess demand if interest rates were allowed to be determined by supply and demand. However, critics argue that market clearing is neither a law nor should be viewed as assumption necessary for competitive analysis in financial markets (Stiglitz and Weiss, 1981; Stiglitz, 1991). The prediction, Stiglitz and Weiss argue, that ceilings on interest rates cause credit rationing is based mainly on the unrealistic assumption that financial markets are the same as those for other goods, e.g. the 'markets for chairs and tables' and thus that the prices have neither sorting nor incentive effects. By contrast, they argue that lending rates – the prices of loans – help in distinguishing risky borrowers from safe ones, as only risky ones would be willing to borrow at high rates (sorting effects). In addition, high rates force borrowers to undertake high return projects in order to repay loans (incentive effects). Note that the rate of return and the probability of the success of a project are generally negatively correlated. Thus, interest rates convey a signal of the probability of default by borrowers.

The expected returns on risky projects to risk averse lenders are lower than those from safe projects. Thus, a safe borrower, unlike a risky one, would be unwilling to pay a high interest rate. Consequently, financial institutions maximising expected profits usually charge lower than equilibrium rates. In fact, financial institutions will decline to provide loans to borrowers who are willing to pay equilibrium rates, which would generally be higher in LDCs than the available rates. If, however, it is hypothetically assumed that banks charge market clearing rates, then borrowers will be forced to use the loans in high yielding, and therefore risky, projects in order to pay off the costs of the loans. Financial institutions avoid adverse selection and moral hazard problems[11] by avoiding high interest rates and risky borrowers. Hence, a loan market in equilibrium is generally associated with credit rationing.

In addition, the collection of strong collateral from risky borrowers, suggested by the McKinnon-Shaw school, does not eliminate adverse selection and moral hazard problems (Stiglitz and Weiss, 1981). The requirements of strong collateral force entrepreneurs without such collateral to start with small projects, which have relatively higher failure rates (Dunne and Hughes, 1994). Moreover, starting with the same level of equity, wealthier borrowers are the entrepreneurs who have taken risks and succeeded. Thus, wealthier borrowers are risk lovers and are able to provide strong collateral. Hence, taking strong collateral has two types of negative effects: first, it excludes potential entrepreneurs who are unable to provide strong collateral and secondly, it selects only wealthy borrowers who are risk lovers and hence, the probability of default for them is higher, ceteris paribus. Thus, a reduction in the debt-equity ratio of borrowers is not optimal if small projects have a high probability of failure.[12]

Furthermore, credit rationing prevails in equilibrium even when collateral in conjunction with interest rates is used optimally (Stiglitz and Weiss, 1992). Consider two types of loan contracts that banks can offer. One is denoted by F, which is associated with high interest rates and weak collateral. The other contract is G, and associated with low interest rates but strong collateral. Poor and rich borrowers buy F and G contracts, respectively. Banks would prefer F contracts as they yield high expected returns. Conversely, if banks offer G, they would be unable to offer high deposit rates, since a low lending rate is associated with G. Thus, both rich and poor borrowers have to accept F contracts as they do not have any other option. Therefore, a pooling equilibrium exists in which both risky and safe borrowers are offered the same loan contract. Similarly, if the supply of loans is less than the demand, some borrowers, regardless of whether they are poor or rich, fail to obtain loans through F contracts, while only some rich borrowers will be offered G contracts in order to cover the cost of funds. That is, there exists a separating equilibrium. Under both equilibria, credit may be rationed to differentiate borrowers, where lenders only know whether the borrowers are rich or poor, while the riskiness of the borrowers is unknown. Thus, the use of collateral with interest rates does not serve to allocate credit optimally. Consequently, the expected returns in Walrasian equilibrium are lower than those from some other contracts in which credit rationing exists. The probability of success and failure, which generally changes over the business cycle, also affects real interest rates, causing a violation of conventional macroeconomic presumptions that there is a pro-cyclical relationship between interest rates (i.e. returns on capital) and the marginal productivity of capital. More precisely, the probability of success (failure) of a project is higher when the economy is in boom (recession) and hence the proportion of total returns to an investment project captured by lenders varies over the business cycle. Thus, there is a rise in expected returns to lenders to safe projects and a fall in credit rationing when the economy is in boom, and vice versa.

Traditional theory predicts that an increase in the money supply reduces interest rates and increases investment and growth. By contrast, Stiglitz and Weiss (1992) argue that an increase in the money supply raises economic growth by increasing the availability of credit rather than by decreasing interest rates. An increase in the money supply will enable banks to offer more loans to poor borrowers, i.e. F contracts with high interest rates and weak collateral in our earlier example. This type of borrower is proportionately more excluded from obtaining loans when banks have inadequate funds, since these borrowers cannot meet the demand for high valued collateral. Thus, an increase in the money supply raises the capacity of lenders to extend new loans with high average lending rates to the high return projects which are generally undertaken by poor borrowers. Contractionary monetary policies reduce the availability of credit for poor borrowers and hence reduce average lending rates. This theoretical perspective is supported by the general finding that it is the availability of credit rather than its cost which is important in LDCs and by the fact that most of the available funds in, for instance, Bangladesh are taken by 'selective' big borrowers, with very little left for small ones (Siddiki, 1999). Thus, a rise in the money supply will increase loans to small borrowers who are willing to pay high interest rates, as is the case for the Grameen Bank of Bangladesh.[13]

2.6 Market Failure and Instability in Financial Markets

In many LDCs, the flow of information regarding borrowers and lenders is often manipulated against small depositors, with loans often granted to inefficient or even false investment projects undertaken by big borrowers. An uninterrupted flow of information and appropriate monitoring is important to avoid such manipulation. However, information flow and monitoring are costly processes and have public good characteristics: information collected by one financial institution can be used by others, and hence information and monitoring are under-supplied by competitive markets (Stiglitz, 1994; see also Stiglitz, 1989; for a survey, see Arestis and Demetriades, 1999). The absence of appropriate monitoring and information about the credit worthiness of borrowers or projects generates liquidity problems for financial institutions and creates instability in financial markets (Diaz-Alejandro, 1985).

Similarly, the lack of monitoring of banks creates an opportunity for the officials of banks to divert funds to their own use, which in turn damages the credibility of financial institutions and discourages depositors from using this medium. The resulting financial crises, including the bankruptcies of banks, have macroeconomic consequences by reducing the credibility of the banking system (Diaz-Alejandro, 1985). The government's role in circumventing financial crises or rescuing the financial system from a crisis is vital. A government assurance that it will protect the interests of depositors will help to increase the credibility of the financial system and hence depositors will avoid rushing to withdraw their money from banks. The moral hazard problem, however, indicates that there may be a high social cost to such policies.

Furthermore, the presence of large fixed costs in evaluating and monitoring borrowers or projects inhibits competition among financial institutions. Financial institutions prefer to establish long-run relationships with existing customers and keep their records of transactions and credit histories unknown to other financial institutions. This special knowledge is used to sell other products to existing customers. In other words, information regarding the behaviour of customers yields economies of scope which can be used in product diversification. Thus, a competitive market is sub-optimal and cannot generate functional and allocative efficiencies in the presence of scale economies (Gibson and Tsakalotos, 1994). Moreover, borrowers are generally as reluctant to change to a new bank as banks are to lend to new customers without knowing their credit histories. Thus, even when there are many lenders and borrowers, financial markets may well not behave in a competitive manner.

In conclusion, current analysis confirms an important role for finance in economic development. However, financial markets, have a range of particular characteristics, most especially those engendered by the presence of imperfect and asymmetric information. Thus, one may question the common presumption that, in the absence of monopoly power or inappropriate government interference, a market clearing price (i.e. the interest rate) will emerge in these markets that will prove optimal in all circumstances.

3. Financial Liberalisation: Analytical Aspects

3.1 *An Overview*

The broad theoretical issues discussed in Section 2 now emerge critically in the debates surrounding the liberalisation of the financial sectors of developing countries in the context of an increasing globalisation of financial affairs in general. Financial liberalisation implies a whole series of measures for the financial sector of a developing country in the direction of bringing practices in this sector in line with what is likely to be found in advanced capitalist, most especially

Anglo Saxon countries: privatisation of banks and other financial institutions; interest rate deregulation; relatively low reserve requirements for banks; the reduction or elimination of directed credit towards preferential or priority sectors or for government borrowing. How appropriate is this programme of reforms for the developing nations of the world?

The theory of the perfect capital market, which acts as a model and motivation for policies of financial liberalisation, also hints at a preference for Anglo Saxon market based forms of finance (e.g. stock markets) as opposed to financial systems of the traditional Japanese or German type, with their strong links between firms and financial institutions. Financial liberalisation in developing countries also involves, by implication, the opening up of the financial sector to the influence of financial affairs from abroad. Such policies may take two forms: a liberalisation of restrictions on the activities of domestic financial institutions and others in functioning internationally (e.g. a lifting of restrictions on the flow of capital abroad), and/or in an extension of the freedom accorded to foreign financial institutions and foreign nationals to function in the domestic financial environment. Financial liberalisation may also involve the introduction of common practice international standards in the disclosure requirements, auditing and operating procedures demanded of financial institutions.

Until the 1970s, governments' financial policies in LDCs may have been influenced by Keynesian and structuralist views. Such approaches advocated repressing the financial sector based on the belief that low levels of interest rates and the direction of credit towards priority sectors increased total investment and the rate of economic growth. Keynesian economists also tended to favour high levels of government expenditure to increase effective demand, which would in turn increase investment and economic growth (Bottomley, 1971). Lastly, financial policies undertaken by governments were often motivated by the notion that the financial sector is an 'easy' source of government revenues collected from monetary growth through seigniorage or inflation taxes. Thus, the financial sector in many developing countries was often characterised by ceilings imposed upon interest rates, high reserve requirements on commercial banks, the presence of directed or preferential credit policies and by inflation taxes.

It is in this context that McKinnon (1973) and Shaw (1973) argued against Keynesian and structuralist views, suggesting that financial repression exerts an adverse impact on saving, investment and the rate of economic growth and therefore advocated the liberalisation of the financial sector. We proceed below first to explore the McKinnon and Shaw hypothesis that economic growth rates are positively related to financial liberalisation. We then consider the views of the critics of financial liberalisation, including the post-Keynesian and neo-structuralist approaches and the controversy surrounding the writings of Joseph Stiglitz, in which it is argued that financial liberalisation is stagflationary and that government intervention is needed to avoid instability in financial markets.

3.2 *The McKinnon-Shaw Model*

McKinnon (1973) and Shaw (1973) argue that financial repression exerts an adverse impact on saving, investment and the rate of economic growth while financial liberalisation positively affects these factors.[14] Both models argue that the removal of ceilings on deposits results in positive real interest rates which increases saving, i.e. the availability of funds for investment, and economic growth. In these models, investment (I) is a negative function of real interest rates (r) while saving is positively influenced by r and rate of growth of national income (g):

$$I = I(r); \quad I_r < 0 \text{ and } S = S(r,g) \quad S_r > 0, \ S_g > 0$$

The impact of interest rate ceilings on savings and investment is explained in Figure 1. Real interest rates and saving are measured on the vertical and horizontal axes, respectively. $S(g)$ is the rate of saving, i.e. saving is positive function of economic growth (g) with $\ldots g_3 > g_2 > g_1$. Consequently, an increase in economic growth from g_1 to g_2 raises saving from $S(g_1)$ to $S(g_2)$, i.e. the saving curve $S(g_1)$ moves out to $S(g_2)$. In a free market without government controls on interest rates, the equilibrium, i.e. $S = I$, would be at E with real interest rate r_e and investment and saving equal to I_e.

Assume that the government has imposed a ceiling by setting the nominal interest rate, so that the real interest rate is r_1, which is lower than the rate in equilibrium r_e. With a controlled interest rate r_1, the level of saving is I_1, which is lower than both the equilibrium rate I_e and the demand for credit (I_3). Thus, investment is constrained by a lack of saving. With a ceiling on deposit rates and excess demand for investment, banks set lending rates at r_3. The lending institutions use margins $(r_3 - r_1)$ for non-price competition. Furthermore, there is an

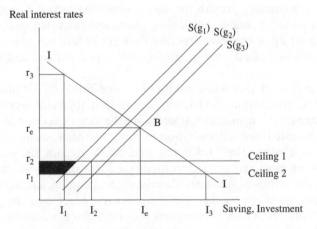

Figure 1. McKinnon-Shaw Hypothesis.

excess demand $(I_3 - I_1)$ for credit, which leads to credit rationing. Consequently, some profitable projects fail to obtain credit from financial institutions.

Ceilings on both lending and deposit rates thus distort the economy in the following ways (Fry, 1995, p. 26; 1997): first, the low level of interest rates encourages agents to increase present consumption, which reduces saving for future consumption below the socially optimal level. Second, depositors prefer to invest directly in low-yielding projects rather than accumulating money in banks, who would otherwise lend to more highly productive investors. Third, entrepreneurs choose more capital-intensive projects at the cost of labour-intensive ones, since the price of capital funds is lower than that which would exist with market determined interest rates. Fourth, entrepreneurs proceed with low-yielding projects which they would not want or could not afford to proceed with at market clearing interest rates. Fifth, a low level of income resulting from low lending rates discourages financial institutions from spending money on collecting information about projects or borrowers. Finally, financial institutions with externally determined interest rates will show a preference for low risk projects, since financial institutions are barred from charging the high risk premia associated with high return projects. Consequently, many projects which have returns lower than the threshold level of returns are selected. These projects would not have been taken up with market clearing rates.

Financial liberalisation in the form of removing or easing restrictions is thus seen to reduce inefficiency and to increase saving, investment and economic growth. Consider the case in which the government relaxes restrictions and consequently the interest rate rises to r_2 (Figure 1). Saving and investment increase to I_2 and economic growth to g_2. Projects which have returns higher than r_1 but lower than r_2 will no longer be undertaken, so that easing restrictions can be seen to increase the efficiency of investment and reduce credit rationing. Saving and investment increase to I_e and economic growth to g_3 when no restriction on interest rates is imposed and credit rationing disappears.

By contrast, financial repression in the form of governments' borrowing from the financial sector adversely affects investment and its efficiency, and economic growth (Schreft and Smith,1997; Roubini and Sala-i-Martin, 1992a). The main purpose of financial repression in LDCs is to raise government revenue (Roubini and Sala-i-Martin, 1992a). In countries with a high rate of tax evasion, the financial sector is a potential source of 'easy' resources for public budgets. Thus, governments in LDCs repress the financial sector by increasing monetary growth in order to finance their budget deficits. The resulting high inflation reduces the quantity and quality (i.e. efficiency) of investment and the rate of economic growth for a given level of saving. Thus, financial repression and economic growth are negatively related. However, the negative relationship between inflation and growth found by many studies is spurious, as the true cause of both the inflation and the slow growth (itself linked to inefficient investment) is the government budget deficit of the countries in question. Governments can further distort the financial sector by offering relatively high nominal interest rates on government bonds (Schreft and Smith, 1997). These high rates influence financial institutions or individuals to use a large proportion of their funds to buy government bonds in place of private capital investment, thus crowding out private investment.

3.3 *The Neo-Keynesian Critique*

In contrast with the McKinnon-Shaw approach, neo-Keynesian and post-Keynesian economists have argued that financial liberalisation can reduce effective demand and economic growth and increase instability in the financial system (Burkett and Dutt, 1991; Stiglitz, 1994; Taylor, 1983). The post-Keynesian approach contests the view that investment matches saving for a market determined equilibrium interest rate since the investment decision depends on many other factors such as expectations about future demand (i.e. 'animal spirits') and political stability. Saving, of course, in the Keynesian tradition, is primarily a function of income rather than interest rates. Thus, an increase in saving does not necessarily raise investment. Moreover, the presence of information asymmetries, externalities and economies of scale in the lending process causes market failures. These failures of the unregulated market can create financial instability.

The post-Keynesian theory of finance and economic growth predicts that financial liberalisation in a closed economy with excess capacity reduces aggregate demand and profits. This reduction in turn reduces saving, investment and economic growth (Burkett and Dutt, 1991; Gibson and Tsakalotos, 1994). Financial liberalisation in the form of interest rate deregulation has two opposing effects in the short-run. First, the positive effect: a rise in deposit rates influences agents to increase deposits and hence, there will be a rise in the supply of loans that reduces the lending rate and boosts investment and economic growth. Second, the negative effect: the increase in saving reduces aggregate demand and results in a decline in profits, saving, investment and output. Uncertainty, or a pessimistic view regarding future profits can further worsen the negative impact, so that the latter may predominate, with a resultant decline in saving, investment and economic growth. In the presence of long-run accelerator effects on investment, an increase in nominal interest rates in an economy with excess capacity raises the costs of borrowing which in turn raises prices, reduces real wages and aggregate demand (Dutt, 1991). Hence, there is a decline in saving, investment and capacity utilisation. The long-run negative impact is more persistent and severe than that in the short-run.

An increase in interest rates has further negative consequences (Gibson and Tsakalotos, 1994): first, it causes an appreciation in the real exchange rate, which exerts a negative impact on the tradable sector by making exports more expensive. The appreciation reduces exports and increases imports and hence induces a rise in the trade deficit. Secondly, a rise in interest rates may generate losses to a bank which is lending long term and borrowing on a short term basis. Banks cannot change lending rates on old credits during the agreed period when deposit rates go up after financial liberalisation. Thus, from the banks' point of view, the cost of funds is higher than the returns and banks therefore experience losses. Thirdly, an increase in interest rates raises government budget deficits in LDCs, since a significant proportion of deficits are financed by bank loans. Moreover, financial liberalisation in terms of a reduction in reserve requirements and relief from buying government bonds reduces tax revenues. The decline in government spending also reduces aggregate demand, which further exacerbates the negative impact of financial liberalisation on output and growth, since in LDCs high government budget deficits and the dependency of government revenues on inflationary taxes (seigniorage) are very common. In addition, the government is the main investor in education and other infrastructural development. Consequently, interest rate liberalisation will reduce government expenditures on education and other capital investment. Thus, the above arguments suggest that government budget deficits should be reduced before liberalising the financial sector.

3.4 *'Upward Financial Repression' and Instability in Financial Markets*

Assume that market clearing interest rates are non-positive or very low due to a low level of demand for investment funds. This low level of demand may be caused by depressed expectations and uncertainty about the future and/or either a preference for liquidity or for the accumulation of savings to make large purchases when access to credit markets is limited. Under such circumstances, saving may well take place even when interest rates are negative. Therefore, the setting of the real interest rate at a level above equilibrium by the government (termed upward financial repression) will cause an excess supply of funds, with the supply of investable funds higher than the demand derived from the stock of profitable investment opportunities (Beckerman, 1988). There is thus a problem in the setting of a market clearing rate here even in the *absence* of government intervention. Along with the arguments presented by Stiglitz (see Section 1), it is suggested here that what appears to be a financial liberalisation leading to a market clearing equilibrium may merely be a form of upward financial repression.

Financial institutions under such conditions face a dilemma, as they can neither lend deposits nor keep deposits to themselves. As is the case in many LDCs, banks may hesitate to lend, since there is an absence of profitable investment opportunities due to infrastructural underdevelopment and political instability: the probability of default is very high. The widespread default of bank loans in Bangladesh is a case in point. On the other hand, banks which become excessively liquid by not lending out deposits cannot make profits. Thus, 'upward financial repression' damages the stability of the financial system. Hellman *et al.* (2000) argue that financial liberalisation and the resulting high deposit rates are inconsistent with prudent bank behaviour and are systematically related to financial crises. Financial liberalisation boosts competition, which erodes profits and thus reduces bank franchise values. This fall in franchise values discourages banks from making good loans, generating a moral hazard problem. But increasing the capital requirements of banks to encourage them to internalise the adverse consequences of gambling may force them to hold inefficiently high amount of capital. Furthermore, with a freely determined market interest rate, banks still have excessive incentives to compete for deposits by offering higher rates. This competition among banks to offer high deposit rates may force banks to invest in risky assets. Thus, a financial liberalisation involving the freeing of deposit rate controls may generate a moral hazard problem. The imposition of higher capital requirements to combat this problem may well increase inefficiency.

3.5 Neo-structuralist Views

The McKinnon-Shaw School also argues that an increase in deposit rates reduces investment in unproductive assets, e.g. land and gold, and raises financial saving, investment and economic growth. This school has traditionally given little attention to the existence of unorganised money markets (UMMs) in LDCs, where a significant proportion of, especially, rural people are outside of the formal banking system (Ghatak, 1975). Formal financial institutions in LDCs are not 'user friendly' and poor borrowers cannot obtain loans due to their inability to provide the required collateral and to fulfil other formalities.

By contrast, poor borrowers can obtain loans from the UMMs with significantly less difficulty and thus use UMMs as their main source of funds. The UMMs are also more profitable to lenders as they usually charge relatively higher interest rates than formal financial institutions. Hence, the UMMs in the LDCs often act as substitutes for the formal banking system. A large volume of transactions are realised in the UMMs (van Wijenbergen, 1983; Taylor, 1983). UMMs can lend on a one for one basis and hence they are more efficient than formal financial institutions which, unlike to UMMs, pay a proportion of their deposits to the central bank.[15] Assume that economic agents hold the following three types of assets in their portfolios: time deposits, UMM (kerb market) assets and inflation hedges, e.g. land. Note that UMM assets are considered as productive assets, while inflation hedges are unproductive. Hence an increase in deposit rates influences agents to substitute time deposits for UMM assets. Time deposits have reserve requirements and hence the overall amount of credit in the economy falls when UMM assets are substituted for time deposits, causing a decline in investment and economic growth. Moreover, an increase in interest rates raises the costs of investment and hence, generates a rise in price level. Thus, interest rate liberalisation is stagflationary.

Neo-structuralists argue that 'non-institutional' lenders such as village money lenders, landlords or shopkeepers supply loans to small borrowers in the rural areas of developing countries – individuals who are unable to obtain loans from formal financial institutions. However, the interest rates charged by these non-institutional lenders are, as we have noted, high. These high interest rates are linked to a shortage of financial saving, at least partially due to the fact that a substantial proportion of the saving in the rural or peasant sector in many countries (e.g. India) takes the form of the hoarding of gold and jewellery. Thus, there is a pressing need for establishing more efficient financial intermediaries which can offer attractive financial products and thereby increase financial saving and hence bring about a reduction in interest rates (Myint, 1984, p. 58).

In summary, the McKinnon-Shaw approach argues that financial repression exerts an adverse impact on saving, investment and the rate of economic growth. Financial liberalisation positively affects these factors. The removal of ceilings on deposits results in positive real interest rates which increase saving, i.e. the availability of funds for investment, and economic growth. Critics of this approach point to information related problems such as moral hazard and adverse selection and to institutional considerations. In this context, it is suggested, financial liberalisation can often exacerbate the problems of developing countries in crisis.

4. Finance and Financial Liberalisation: Empirical Results

Below we distinguish between studies that consider the efficacy of finance in general for the facilitation of economic growth from those which deal with the success of financial liberalisation as a policy. As we have seen in Section 2, the two issues are quite distinct. It is conceivable that countries pursuing policies of financial repression might, if successful with these policies, register increases in their rates of economic growth compared with countries pursuing more liberalised policies. As a result of the higher rates of growth in these 'repressed' economies, their financial sectors (as measured, for instance, by the level of liquid liabilities to national income) could well end up being more developed than in liberalised economies.

4.1 Finance and Economic Development

Using cross-section data for 80 countries over the period 1960–89, King and Levine (1993b) show a highly significant positive relationship between the initial value of the ratio of liquid liabilities to GDP in 1960 and real per capita income. Demetriades and Hussein (1996) confirm the positive association between growth and initial financial development found by King and Levine, but argue that these results only represent a contemporaneous relationship and not a long term one: because financial indicators in a given country are correlated across time, they should be proxied by the level of current data rather than by initial ratios. An initial ratio may not embody important subsequent changes in the variable.

Ghatak (1997) examines the impact of financial development on economic growth in Sri Lanka during the period 1950–87. He concludes that interest rates and financial deepening (measured by real monetary growth) increase economic growth. Demetriades and Luintel (1996a) explore the relationship between financial policies and economic growth in Nepal during 1962–92. This study concludes that real per capita income is associated positively with financial deepening and negatively with bank branches. The negative relationship between per capita income and bank branches is said to reflect inefficiencies in financial intermediation for a given level of financial development. The authors also find that financial repression in the form of selective intervention has a positive impact on economic growth. In another extensive study using time-series techniques, Deme- triades and Hussein (1996) find that there have been stable long-run relationships between real per capita income and at least one of the key financial indicators in 13 out of 16 countries, most of which have followed or been following financial reforms. In these long-run relationships, financial variables positively affect real per capita income.

Using data for 85 developing countries from 1971 to 1995, Fry (1997) finds an 'inverted U shaped' relationship between the annual rate of economic growth and financial development measured by real interest rates. This result implies that too high or too low real interest rates are deleterious for economic growth: economic growth is maximised when interest rates are within the range of −5% to +15%. Similarly, using the Chilean and Korean experiences, Clarke (1996) suggests that the equilibrium interest rate is undefined and unstable, since the interest rate plays a dual role: it equilibrates saving and investment and also determines portfolio readjustment, including capital inflows. Portfolio readjustment causes fluctu- ations in interest rates. These fluctuations are intensified by the uncertainty and volatility of expected returns to investment and potential inflows of capital, all of which may distort the real exchange rate and increase the cost of borrowing.

Arestis et al. (2001) examine the relative impact of stock markets and banks on long-run economic growth in Germany, the USA, Japan, the UK and France. They find that both stock markets and banks have made important contributions to output growth in France, Germany and Japan, with the stock markets' con- tribution ranging from about one-seventh to one-third of the banks' contribution. These results are consistent with the view that bank based financial systems may be more able to promote long term growth than stock market based ones. In addition, the authors find a weak relationship between financial development and growth in the UK and the USA. The results also suggest that stock market volatility has negatively affected economic growth in France and Japan.

4.2 The Efficacy of Financial Liberalisation

Using both neo-classical and endogenous growth theory,[16] a large volume of empirical studies have been carried out to test the McKinnon-Shaw hypothesis. Findings supporting this hypothesis have concluded that policies in LDCs involv- ing high reserve requirements, inflation taxes and the imposition of ceilings on nominal interest rates have resulted in the repression of the financial sector in these countries and that more liberalised financial regimes are associated with faster economic growth. However, other studies have reached opposing conclu- sions. An examination of the whole empirical literature is beyond the scope of this survey. We therefore proceed to review only selected empirical studies, first, those focused on the central concerns of the McKinnon-Shaw hypothesis, and secondly those that deal with important peripheral considerations.

First, as tests of the 'core' hypotheses of the McKinnon-Shaw model, Roubini and Sala-i-Martin (1992b) have empirically examined the consequences of financial repression and whether inflation directly causes lower economic growth. The authors do not find any direct causal relationship between high inflation and low economic growth. Instead they find that financial repression tends to reduce the services the financial sector provides to the whole economy and, therefore, to reduce aggregate investment for a given level of saving. Thus, financial repression adversely affects long-run economic growth. In order to increase the revenue from money creation, governments of countries with high levels of tax evasion prefer to increase per capita real money by repressing the financial sector and creating high rates of monetary growth. As a result, high financial repression tends to be associated with high money growth, high inflation rates, high seigniorage and low economic growth. This association causes a spurious correlation between inflation and growth. They also examine whether the inclusion of financial variables into the Barro (1991) growth model can help explain low rates of growth in the Latin American region. Barro in his model includes regional dummies along with initial income, human capital, government expenditures and political instability. The Roubini and Sala-i-Martin (1992b) model includes financial repression[17] among the explanatory variables. Their results show a negative and statistically significant impact on economic growth for financial repression. In addition, the inclusion of financial variables causes the regional dummies for Latin American countries in the Barro model to be insignificant and improves the overall explanatory power (the value of R^2) of the model.

De Gregorio and Guidotti (1995) have also extended the Barro (1991) growth model by incorporating financial variables. The authors use the share of private sector credit as a percentage of GDP as an indicator of financial liberalisation since, they argue, the private sector channels resources more efficiently than publicly owned institutions. The authors find that financial liberalisation generally increases economic growth. This relationship is relatively stronger in low and middle income countries than in high income countries. The results also show that three-quarters of the effect of private sector credit on growth is channelled through efficiency gains. These gains are relatively higher in low and middle income countries than in high income countries. The authors argue that there is a weak relationship between financial liberalisation and growth in high income countries because financial liberalisation in these countries occurs to a large extent outside the banking sector. Thus, the level of private sector credit in the banking sector in developed countries fails to capture financial liberalisation. When De Gregorio and Guidotti (1995) used a panel data set for 12 Latin American countries for 1950–85, however, they found a robust and significant negative relationship between financial liberalisation and growth in Latin American countries. The authors concluded that, during the 1970s and 1980s, financial liberalisation without appropriate regulation in the Latin American region caused the financial sector to collapse, which exerted a negative impact on economic growth. These findings suggest that financial liberalisation may well be a necessary condition for the financial sector to improve economic growth, but will hardly prove sufficient.

Using a simultaneous equation model and data for 16 developing countries over 1970–88, Fry (1998) concludes that financial repression proxied by the square of the real interest rate and black market exchange rate premiums[18] reduces the investment to GDP ratio and export growth. The reduction in investment and export growth in turn reduces output growth rates. Output growth is also directly reduced by financial distortions, possibly through a reduction in the efficiency of investment.

Using panel cointegration analysis, Bandiera et al. (2001) examine the effect of the financial reform in the form of interest rate deregulation on aggregate private saving in eight developing countries where the nature and the phasing of financial liberalisation differ from country to country. The authors find mixed results. The impact of financial reform on saving is significantly negative for Korea and Mexico, positive for Ghana and Turkey, and with no clear effect discernible in Chile, Indonesia, Malaysia and Zimbabwe. The authors also find that, overall, the negative impact of financial liberalisation is greater than the positive impact, so that in aggregate, financial liberalisation reduces private saving.

Demetriades and Luintel (2001b) note that the case of South Korea contradicts the assertion of the McKinnon-Shaw hypothesis that interest rate ceilings and other financial restraints are deleterious to economic growth. They suggest a positive association between financial development, on the one hand, and the degree of state control over the banking system combined with mild repression of lending rates, on the other. They predict that severe financial repression negatively affects financial deepening, as in the case of India for 1961–91 (Demetriades and Luintel, 1996b, 2001a).[19] Their empirical results for 1956–94 in South Korea (Demetriades and Luintel, 2001b) show that government intervention in the financial system had positive effects on financial deepening. These results corroborate the neo-Keynesian and neo-structuralist view that government intervention in the financial sector can enhance economic growth by positively affecting financial development. The authors emphasise the need for a well functioning civil service and other relevant government institutions for the success of interventionist policies.

Second, there are important peripheral issues raised by financial liberalisation. An increase in officially controlled interest rates may not raise investment if the increase in bank deposits crowds out kerb market loans (van Wijnbergen, 1983). Changes in the officially controlled time deposit rate in South Korea have been found to be positively related to changes in the freely determined kerb market rate (Edwards, 1988). An increase in the time deposit rate in South Korea raises time deposits: most of the increased volume of time deposits comes at the expense of small kerb loans, which in turn causes kerb market rates to increase. This is an important effect, since both official and kerb markets rates are important determinants of aggregate investment. The rise in kerb market rates may be counterbalanced by the fact that increases in total available funds in the official segment caused by an increase in kerb market rates can positively affect real aggregate investment. Thus, the net effect of a change in the deposit rate in the official market depends on the relative strength of both effects. However, the official market is less efficient than the kerb market due to the reserve requirements associated with the official market. Thus, the net effect of an increase in official deposit rates tends to be negative.

Using a large sample of 53 countries over 1980–95, Demirgüç-Kunt and Detragiache (1998) explore the importance of a sound institutional environment for financial liberalisation to be effective. Their empirical results show that financial liberalisation is linked to financial fragility, especially in those developing countries where institutional development is weak. Financial liberalisation erodes bank monopolistic powers, suggesting an increased moral hazard to banks with a low franchise value, thereby tending to make banking crises more likely. They also find that financial development is positively correlated with output growth. Countries and time periods in which financial markets are liberalised, but have not experienced any banking crisis, will have higher levels of financial development than those in which markets are controlled. However, those countries and time periods which experience financial liberalisation along with a banking crisis have approximately the same level of financial development as those with neither of these. For all countries under consideration, the net effect on growth of financial liberalisation is not significantly different from zero. Thus, the institutional starting point for the economies concerned is of critical significance.

We may summarise the empirical results as follows. The empirical studies surveyed here suggest a positive causation between the development of a nation's financial sector and its overall economic development, confirming a view consistent with that of economic historians on the importance of financial development in Western Europe in its formative period.[20] The relationship between financial liberalisation and economic performance is far more ambiguous and does not substantiate the near unanimity of international agencies in their call for financial liberalisation. Perhaps the most suggestive result is that of Demirgüç-Kunt and Detragiache (1998), which stresses that the success or failure of a financial liberalisation programme is likely to be highly contingent on the level of institutional development in the countries concerned. It is to this issue which we return in our conclusion.

5. Conclusion: a Balance Sheet on Financial Liberalisation

There can be little doubt that the development of a nation's financial sector is concomitant, if not a prerequisite to, economic development in general. What can be said about the specific question of financial liberalisation?

Policies of financial liberalisation will, it is argued, permit the rate of saving and the efficiency of investment to increase by way of a rise in interest rates. Furthermore, the setting of market levels of interest rates should, in principle, promote the control of corruption in the banking sector, since it will mitigate the presence of cheap loans which can be handed out to selected borrowers.

The arguments above presuppose the existence of a competitive context for the making of loans. In the absence of competition, there is no obvious reason why liberalisation, resulting in an expansion of the range of financial resources in the private sphere, should be superior to government activity. Competition in the financial sector is important for efficiency as a process of *motivation* for lenders and borrowers to act efficiently. Competition among financial institutions will generate pressure to maximise returns on net worth, thus constraining the 'luxury' of lending corruptly to friends or relatives. Competition also acts as a generator of *informational signals* for lenders and borrowers, forcing lenders to explore and gather information about heretofore unknown sources of credit-worthy lending. These dynamic aspects of financial systems on the whole tend to point to favour the efficacy of the decentralised, marketised forms of finance which are associated with financial liberalisation, and yet the key justifications for financial liberalisation have remained those from the static, neo-Fisherian approach of the perfect capital market.

In general, competitive processes do not function in the absence of good information. Decentralised financial systems have a contradictory role in the *generation* of financial information. Marketised forms of finance, such as money raised from the public in a new share issue, tend to cause the disclosure of relatively more information than institutionalised forms of finance, such as bank lending (Benston, 1976). But there are limitations, even in principle, to the process by which markets will encourage the disclosure of more financial information through marketised forms of finance (the public issuance of debt or equity) rather than for institutionalised forms of finance, such as bank loans. The disclosure of information by a firm has 'public good' aspects – unless standards of disclosure are set by public authorities, financial institutions, the managers of firms and others trying to raise money from the public will always have the excuse that much information must be withheld, because disclosure will reveal competitive secrets to rivals. Thus, even in financial systems emphasising competitive, market-based activity, there are clear roles for government in the promotion of competition and the disclosure of financial information.

An important aspect of financial liberalisation is the loosening of the restrictions of the rights of foreign financial institutions and nationals to compete domestically in LDCs. Such policies may promote an increase in competition, but it has been suggested (Myint, 1984, ch 5) that an increase in the activities in LDCs of foreign financial institutions is of little benefit to small borrowers: foreign financial institutions target their funds to big borrowers, with small borrowers unable to meet the typical demands for the putting up of collateral in securing loans. In more positive terms, financial liberalisation may also be seen as part of a broader process of internationalisation. For financial institutions, this process may well entail the introduction of best practice international standards in disclosure requirements and in auditing and operating procedures (e.g. international 'best practice' would not permit the giving out of loans from a bank to its own directors[21]); this internationalisation of finance will also influence the rules and constraints under which non financial firms operate, most especially those attempting to procure finance from abroad.

The political economy of government intervention in the context of finance emphasises that, for instance, the prioritisation of loan funds for the purposes of promoting a strategy of economic development extends the scope for government corruption (Fry, 1997). Thus, financial liberalisation is seen by many of its supporters as having an important role in liberating economies from the 'grabbing hand' of government in financial affairs,[22] most especially in developing nations. But here is the paradox. While its supporters view financial liberalisation as a means of liberation from government corruption, the important results cited above of Demirgüç-Kunt and Detragiache (1998) suggest that the presence of adequate institutional structures are a prerequisite to a successful outcome to a financial liberalisation programme.

For critics of financial liberalisation, institutional considerations are also central. Many point to the historically unprecedented rapidity with which Japan and South Korea, among others, were transformed in the post war world using 'unorthodox' centralised methods of planning and finance (Amsden, 2001). A vital aspect of these historical processes were the presence of well run and efficacious (albeit authoritarian, in the case of South Korea) government institutions. The failures of the 'Asian Model' in recent years have stifled discussion of this topic even in academic circles, a disconcerting affirmation of the extent to which even academic writing is governed by current fashion.

In general, the quality of government intervention will be significantly influenced by the ability of the population to monitor government activity. Monitoring will be dependent upon (among other parameters), the level of democratic participation and legality in the country and population literacy (as emphasised in Sen, 1999). Even for those with a strongly anti-governmental position, there is an unavoidable role for governments in the creation of conditions in which financial market activity can take place effectively: the setting of standards and rules of behaviour for business activity and the creation of accounting and disclosure requirements to promote the generation of market information. By contrast, any reconstituted 'Asian model' which is to emerge will have to do so in the context of far greater public disclosure of economic information than has been practiced heretofore.

A second role for governments which also has broad acceptability is for intervention in conditions of market failure. But the range and limits of what constitutes 'market failure' is a central focus of controversy. The political economy literature has pointed to the potential costs to society of government intervention, most especially in the context of nations in which the institutions of civil society are weak. As we have seen, however, financial liberalisation is unlikely to eliminate the need for good governance by replacing government activity with an anonymous, competitive mechanism which efficiently allocates resources through the financial sector.

Acknowledgements

We would like to thank Professor Subrata Ghatak and two anonymous referees for their exemplary comments and suggestions.

Notes

1. Lucas excludes financial variables from his model and argues that '...the importance of financial matters is very badly over-stressed in popular and much professional discussions and so [I] am not inclined to be apologetic for going to the other extreme' (Lucas, 1988, p. 6).
2. The by-passing of questions of financial allocation in centrally planned economies may once again reflect the Ricardian heritage by way of the interpretation given to the economic formulations found in Marx's *Capital*, most especially the postumously published volume 2.
3. It is perhaps curious that the Modigliani-Miller conclusions came as such a surprise to the economics profession, since these results have always been implicitly presumed in the context of standard expositions of the microeconomics of the firm, in which only the 'real' factors governing costs and revenues have any effect upon outcomes. '...the predominance of the "perfect markets paradigm" in financial analysis...has been a major intellectual hurdle to the development of an analysis of banking and intermediation activities. In an ideal world of perfect capital markets...economic decisions do not depend in any way upon financial structure' (Lewis, 1991, p. 117); the orthodox view is elaborated in Fama (1980).
4. On this question, see Auerbach and Skott (1995).
5. This rule would apply in a strict way only for so-called normal projects in which there is a negative value for the initial outlay on the project (R_0) and positive values for all subsequent cash flows ($R_1...R_n$).
6. See Roll (1977). This result has not been superseded.
7. See Fama (1991).
8. It might be thought that such a saving of cash would increase the net supply of investable funds. But in a system of national fiduciary money, any such savings – increases in monetary velocity – are merely the equivalent of monetary creation, which can be done by governments at zero cost. By contrast, savings of non-fiduciary monies (e.g. silver) may increase national wealth by increasing net claims on foreign resources.
9. In an open small economy with perfect capital mobility, the interest rate is exogenous and is determined by international capital markets.
10. For the case of South Korea, see Amsden (1989).
11. The tendency for a biased selection in favour of risky borrowers is termed a *moral hazard* problem while the biased selection of risky projects is considered an *adverse selection* problem.
12. Note that the rate of delinquency in Bangladesh is much higher for big borrowers with strong collateral than is the case for small borrowers without collateral. These small borrowers without collateral often obtain loans from the Grameen Bank, while large borrowers receive loans from other financial institutions. Thus, the experience of Bangladesh tends to contradict the McKinnon-Shaw suggestion for the use of strong collateral in order to avoid adverse selection and moral hazard problems.
13. Small borrowers from the Grameen Bank of Bangladesh pay substantially higher interest rates than the rates available from conventional financial institutions. However, the delinquency rates are substantially lower than for conventional institutions (Siddiki, 1999).
14. Both the McKinnon and Shaw models argue that financial repression negatively affects saving, investment and economic growth. However, the transmission mechanisms

through which these negative effects work differ between these models. McKinnon postulates that investors have to accumulate money balances before investment takes place. Thus, in the McKinnon model, the demand for money and physical capital are complementary to each other. This complementarity hypothesis is based on the following two assumptions: (i) all investment is self-financed; (ii) investment expenditure is more indivisible than consumption expenditure. Under such circumstances, a high real deposit rate increases the accumulation of monetary balances, i.e. saving, and hence, a rise in the supply of funds for investment. The Shaw (1973) model, on the other hand, is based on the debt intermediation view, which asserts that the degree of financial sophistication which facilitates intermediation between savers and investors positively affects per capita income. This model predicts that financial liberalisation in the form of an increase in real deposit rates increases financial saving, which increases the capacity of the banking system as a loan provider. Hence, financial liberalisation increases the availability of funds for investment.

15. Note, however, that transactions involving financial institutions are likely to offer borrowers and lenders better legal protection and conditions of disclosure than are provided by UMMs. For the society as a whole, the formal sector has a greater potential for developing in a competitive direction than the highly localised arrangements involving UMMs.

16. Studies using neo-classical growth theory models to test the consequence of financial repression on economic growth may be of limited use: on *a priori* grounds, even if financial reform enhances the rate of investment, this will have no effect on the long term rate of growth in the neo-classical model. As we have indicated in Section 1, this has been a main motivation for the introduction of endogenous growth theory. Some studies surveyed here have made use of the latter approach (King and Levine 1993a, b).

17. A dummy is used to capture financial repression. This dummy takes a value one when the real interest rate is positive, two when it is negative but higher than minus 5%, three when less than minus 5%. Two dummies are also included to capture the extent of negativity. One of them takes a value one when the real interest rate is greater than minus 5%; otherwise it takes the value zero. The other dummy takes the value one when the real interest rate is less than minus 5%; otherwise it takes the value zero.

18. The difference between black market and official exchange rates as a percentage of official rates.

19. Comparable results are to be found in Daly and Siddiki (2002) for the period 1954–94.

20. Parker (1974); Gille (1970). But note the relative absence of financial considerations in Maddison (2001).

21. Loans in Bangladesh are mainly aimed at patronising socially and politically influential groups and individuals (Siddiki, 1999). Pressures from top executives and bribes are key determinants of obtaining loans from nationalised commercial banks in Bangladesh. These practices have caused the recovery of loans to be very low and have thereby created a default culture in Bangladesh.

22. A more general critique of government intervention may be found in Shliefer and Vishny (1998).

References

Aigner, D., Lovell, C. A. and Schmidt, P. (1977) Formulation and estimation of stochastic frontier production function models. *Journal of Econometrics* 6: 21–37.

Amsden, A. (1989) Asia's Next Giant: South Korea and Late Industrialization. Oxford: Oxford University Press.

Amsden, A. (2001) The Rise of 'The Rest': Challenges to the West from Late Industrializing Economies. Oxford: Oxford University Press.

Arestis, P. and Demetriades, P. O. (1997) Financial development and economic growth: assessing the evidence. Economic Journal 107: 783–799.

Arestis, P. and Demetriades, P. O. (1999) Financial liberalisation: the experience of developing countries. Eastern Economic Journal 25, 4: 441–457.

Arestis, P., Demetriades, P. O. and Luintel, K. B. (2001) Financial development and economic growth: the role of stock markets. Journal of Money, Credit and Banking 33: 16–41.

Azariadis, C. and Drazen, A. (1990) Threshold externalities in economic development. Quarterly Journal of Economics CV, 2: 501–526.

Auerbach, P. (1988) Competition. Oxford: Basil Blackwell.

Auerbach, P. and Skott, P. (1995) Michael Porter's inquiry into the nature and causes of the wealth of nations. In Groenewegen, J. and Pitelis, C. (eds), The Economy of the Future: Ecology, Technology and Institutions. Aldershot: Edward Elgar.

Bandiera, O., Caprio, G. and Honohan, P. (2001) Does financial reform raise or lower savings? World Bank, internet address: http://www.worldbank.org/research/interest/prr_stuff/working_papers/2062.pdf

Barro, R. J. (1991) Economic growth in a cross section of countries. Quarterly Journal of Economics 106: 407–444.

Beckerman, P. (1988) The consequences of 'upward financial repression'. International Review of Applied Economics 2, 1: 233–249.

Bencivenga, V. and Smith, B. (1991) Financial intermediation and endogenous growth. Review of Economic Studies 58: 195–209.

Bencivenga, V. and Smith, B. (1997) Financial markets in development, and the development of financial markets. Journal of Economic Dynamics and Control 21: 145–181.

Benston, G (1976) Corporate Financial Disclosure in the UK and the USA. New York: Saxon House.

Black, S. W. and Moersch, M. (1998) Introduction. In Black, S. W. and Moersch, M. (eds), Competition and Convergence in Financial Markets: The German and Anglo-American Models. Amsterdam: Elsevier.

Bottomley, A. C. (1971) Factor Pricing and Economic Growth in Underdeveloped Rural Areas. London: Crosby Lockwood.

Buiter, W. and Kletzer, K. (1992) Permanent international productivity growth differentials in an integrated global economy. NBER Working Paper No. 4220.

Burkett, P. and Dutt, A. K. (1991) Interest rate policy, effective demand and growth in LDCs. International Review of Applied Economics 5, 2: 127–154.

Capasso, S. (2004) Financial markets, development and economic growth: tales of informational asymmetries. Journal of Economic Surveys 18, 3: 267–292.

Clarke, R. (1996) Equilibrium interest rates and financial liberalisation in developing countries. Journal of Development Studies 32, 3: 391–413.

Coelli, T., Rao, D. S. P. and Battese, G.E. (1998) An Introduction to Efficiency and Productivity Analysis. Boston: Kluwer Academic.

Daly, V. and Siddiki, J. (2002) An empirical model for India: 1954–1994. European Research Studies Journal 6: 141–153.

De Gregorio, J. (1996) Borrowing constraints, human capital accumulation and growth. Journal of Monetary Economics 37: 49–71.

De Gregorio, J. and Guidotti, P. (1995) Financial development and economic growth. World Development 23, 3: 433–448.

Demetriades, P. and Hussain, K. (1996) Does financial development cause economic growth? Time-series evidence from 16 countries. Journal of Development Economics 51: 387–411.

Demetriades, P. and Luintel, K. (1996a) Banking sector policies and financial development in Nepal. *Oxford Bulletin of Economics and Statistics* 58, 2: 355–372.

Demetriades, P. and Luintel, K. (1996b) Financial development, economic growth and banking sector controls: evidence from India. *Economic Journal* 106: 359–374.

Demetriades, P. and Luintel, K. (2001a) The direct costs of financial repression: evidence from India. *Review of Economics and Statistics* 79, 2: 311–320.

Demetriades, P.O. and Luintel, K. (2001b) Financial restraints in the South Korean miracle. *Journal of Development Economics* 64: 459–479.

Demirgüç-Kunt, A. and Detragiache, E. (1998) Financial liberalization and financial fragility. International Monetary Fund Policy Working Paper 1917 (May).

Diamond, D. (1984) Financial intermediation and delegated monitoring. *Review of Economic Studies* 51, 3: 393–414

Diamond, D. (1991) Monitoring and reputation: the choice between bank loans directly placed debt. *Journal of Political Economy* 99: 689–721.

Diamond, D. and Dybvig, P. (1983) Bank runs, deposit insurance and liquidity. *Journal of Political Economy* 91, 3: 401–419.

Diaz-Alejandro, A. (1985) Good-bye financial repression, hello financial crash. *Journal of Development Economics* 19, 1&2: 1–24.

Dunne, P. and Hughes, A. (1994) Age, size, growth and survival: UK companies in the 1980s. *Journal of Industrial Economics* XLII, 115–140.

Dutt, A. K. (1991) Interest rate policy in LDCs: a post-Keynesian view. *Journal of Post Keynesian Economics* 13, 2: 210–232.

Edwards, S. (1988) Financial deregulation and segmented capital markets: the case of Korea. *World Development* 16, 1: 185–194.

Fama, E. (1980) Banking in the theory of finance. *Journal of Monetary Economics* 6: 39–57.

Fama, E. (1985) What's different about banks. *Journal of Monetary Economics* 15: 29–39.

Fama, E. (1991) Efficient markets II. *Journal of Finance* XLVI 5: December, 1575–1617.

Fry, M. (1995) *Money Interest, and Banking in Economic Development* (2nd edn). London: Johns Hopkins University Press.

Fry, M. (1997) In favour of financial development. *Economic Journal* 107: 754–77.

Fry, M. (1998) Savings, investment, growth, and financial distortions in Pacific Asia and other developing areas. *International Economic Journal* 12, 1: 1–24.

Gerschenkron, A. (1962) *Economic Backwardness in Historical Perspective*. Cambridge MA: Harvard University Press

Ghatak, S. (1975) Rural interest rates in the Indian economy. *Journal of Development Studies* 11: 190–201.

Ghatak, S. (1997) Financial liberalisation: the case of Sri Lanka. *Empirical Economics*, 22, 1: 117–31.

Gibson, H. and Tsakalotos, E. (1994) The scope and limits of financial liberalisation in developing countries. *Journal of Development Studies* 30, 3: 578–628.

Gille, B. (1970) Banking and industrialisation in Europe 1730–1914. In Cipolla, C (ed.), (1973), *The Fontana History of Western Europe Volume 3 – The Industrial Revolution*. Glasgow: Fontana/Collins.

Greenwood, J. and Jovanovic, B. (1990) Financial development, growth and distribution of income. *Journal of Political Economy* 98, 5: 1076–1107.

Greenwood, J. and Smith, B. D. (1997) Financial markets in development, and the development in financial markets. *Journal of Dynamics and Control* 21: 145–181.

Hellman, T. F., Murdock, K. and Stiglitz, J. (2000) Liberalisation, moral hazard in banking, and prudential regulation: are capital requirements enough? *The American Economic Review* 90: 147–165.

Hoff, K. and Stiglitz, J. (1990) Imperfect information and rural credit markets – puzzles and policy perspectives. *World Bank Economic Review* 4, 3: 235–250.

Jappeli, T. and Pagano, M. (1994) Savings, growth and liquidity constraints. *Quarterly Journal of Economics* 109, 1: 83–109.

Kindleberger, C. (1984) *A Financial History of Western Europe*. London: George Allen.

King, R. and Levine, R. (1993a) Finance, entrepreneurship, and growth: theory and evidence. *Journal of Monetary Economics* 32, 3: 513–542.

King, R. and Levine, R. (1993b) Finance and growth: Schumpeter might be right. *Quarterly Journal of Economics* 108, 3: 717–38.

Lee, J. (1996) Financial development by learning. *Journal of Development Economics* 50, 147–164.

Leland, H. E. and Pyle, D. H. (1977) Information asymmetries, financial structure and financial intermediation. *Journal of Money, Credit and Banking* 32, 2: 371–387.

Levine, R. (1997) Financial development and economic growth: views and agenda. *Journal of Economic Literature* XXXV, 688–726.

Lewis, M. K. (1991) Theory and practice of the banking firm. In Green, C. J. and Llewellyn, D. T. (eds), *Surveys in Monetary Economics*, vol. 2, 116–165. Oxford: Basil Blackwell.

Little, I. M. D. (1982) *Economic Development Theory, Policy and International Relations*. New York: Basic.

Lucas, R. E. (1988) On the mechanism of economic development. *Journal of Monetary Economics* 22: 3–42.

Maddison, A. (2001) *The World Economy: a Millennial Perspective*. Paris: OECD.

McKinnon, R. (1973) *Money and Capital in Economic Development*. Washington DC: Brookings Institution.

Modigliani, F. and Miller, M. (1958) The cost of capital, corporation finance and the theory of investment. *American Economic Review* 48: 261–297.

Myers, S. C. and Majluf, N. S. (1984) Corporate financing and investment decisions when firms have information that investors do not have. *Journal of Financial Economics* 13: 187–221.

Myint, H. (1984) *The Economics of Developing Countries* (5th edn). London: Hutchinson.

Pagano, M. (1993). Financial markets and growth: an overview. *European Economic Review* 37: 613–622.

Parker, G. (1974) The emergence of modern finance in Europe 1500–1750. In Cipolla, C. (ed.), *The Fontana History of Western Europe. Volume 2 – The Sixteenth and Seventeenth Centuries*. Glasgow: Fontana/Collins.

Porter, M. (1990) *Competitive Advantage of Nations*. London: Macmillan.

Roll, R. (1977) A critique of the asset pricing theory's tests. *Journal of Financial Economics* March, 129–176.

Romer, P. M. (1986) Increasing returns and long-run growth. *Journal of Political Economy* 94: 1002–1037.

Roubini, N. and Sala-i-Martin, X. (1992a) A growth model of inflation, tax evasion and financial repression. NBER Working Paper no. 3876, Cambridge MA.

Roubini, N. and Sala-i-Martin, X. (1992b) Financial repression and economic growth. *Journal of Development Economics* 39: 5–30.

Schreft, S. and Smith, B. (1997) Money, banking, and capital formation. *Journal of Economic Theory* 73: 157–182.

Sen, A. (1999) *Development as Freedom*. New York: Anchor.

Shaw, E. S. (1973) *Financial Deepening in Economic Activity*. New York: Oxford University Press.

Shleifer, A. and Vishny, R. (1998) *The Grabbing Hand*. Cambridge MA: Harvard University Press.

Siddiki, J. U. (1999) Economic liberalisation and growth in Bangladesh: 1974–95. PhD Thesis, Kingston University, England.

Singh, A. (1997) Financial liberalisation, stock markets and economic development. *Economic Journal* 107, May: 771–782.

Solow, R. M. (1956) A contribution to the theory of economic growth. *Quarterly Journal of Economics* 70: 65–94.

Stiglitz, J. (1989) Financial markets and development. *Oxford Review of Economic Policy* 5, 4: 55–68.

Stiglitz, J. (1991) Government, financial markets and economic development. Working Paper No. 3669, National Bureau of Economic Research, Inc., Cambridge, MA.

Stiglitz, J. (1994) The role of the state in financial markets. In Bruno, M. and Pleskovic, B. (eds), *Proceedings of the World Bank Conference on Development Economics*. World Bank, Washington D C.

Stiglitz, J. and Weiss, A. (1981) Credit rationing in markets with imperfect information. *American Economic Review* 71, 3: 393–410.

Stiglitz, J. and Weiss, A. (1992) Asymmetric information in credit markets and its implication for macro-economics. *Oxford Economic Papers* 44: 694–724.

Taylor, L. (1983) *Structuralist Macroeconomics: Applicable Models in the Third World*. New York: Basic Books.

van Wijnbergen, S. (1983) Interest rate management in LDC's. *Journal of Monetary Economics* 12: 433–452.

World Bank (1987, 1989) World Development Report. Washington DC.

3

FINANCIAL MARKETS, DEVELOPMENT AND ECONOMIC GROWTH: TALES OF INFORMATIONAL ASYMMETRIES

Salvatore Capasso

CNR-ISSM, Italy and University of Manchester

1. Introduction

The strong correlation between financial market development and economic growth is a well established fact which has received considerable attention by economists. Since the pioneering works by Gurley and Shaw (1955, 1960, 1967), Goldsmith (1969) and McKinnon (1973), a substantial volume of research has been devoted to verifying and understanding the existence of linkages between the real and financial sectors of economies. The direction in which financial markets have evolved over time, and the strong association of this development with capital accumulation and growth, present striking regularities and common features in many economies. In the initial stage of development, when income per capita is relatively low, financial intermediation is absent or very rudimentary. As capital is accumulated and income per capita increases, financial markets become more sophisticated with the emergence of financial intermediaries that grow in size and number, and the emergence of new and more complex forms of financial instruments (Goldsmith, 1969; King and Levine, 1993a, 1993b; De Gregorio and Guidotti, 1995). During these early stages of development, stock markets are relatively insignificant or completely absent, and bank intermediation is the predominant means by which savings are channelled to investment. As the economy continues to develop, however, stock markets begin to appear and subsequently expand in terms of both the number of firms listed and the total market capitalisation (Atje and Jovanovich, 1993; Demirgüç-Kunt and Levine, 1996a; Korajczyk, 1996; Levine and Zervos, 1996, 1998). The evidence also shows clearly that the development of stock markets is very often accompanied by an increase in real economic growth, suggesting the existence of strong two-way linkages between real and financial sector activity.

The importance of financial markets in the process of economic development has long been recognised by many economists. Schumpeter (1934) highlighted the role played by financial intermediaries in channelling resources towards more productive investments, while Bagehot (1873), and later Hicks (1969), provided further arguments for why financial development plays such a pivotal role in the economic system. To these authors, the development of financial markets, and institutions, was an essential prerequisite of the industrial revolution, expanding the opportunities for borrowing and lending that allowed firms to adopt new technologies and to take on riskier, but potentially higher-return, investments.

The central role played by competitive and well functioning financial markets in the developing process has been recognised by many policymakers, and strongly advocated by international agencies such as the IMF and the World Bank. Indeed, both the IMF and the World Bank often require, as an essential part of development programs, a significant process of financial liberalisation. Evidently, the idea is that financial liberalisation is a fundamental prerequisite for development and growth. However, as well documented by Auerbach and Siddiki (2004), if on the one hand, the evidence of the positive correlation between financial development and growth is a well known and unambiguous result, the sign of the impact of financial liberalisation on growth, as determined by empirical investigations, is unclear and debatable. Similarly, on theoretical grounds, as highlighted by Auerbach and Siddiki, the literature on financial liberalisation and growth provides controversial results.

While mainstream economists argue that financial liberalisation, in the form of interest rate ceiling removal, might spur development and growth via different channels – typically by encouraging savings and investments, by channelling more funds to financial intermediaries and to high-yielding projects and by discouraging investments in low-return projects (the so called McKinnon-Shaw hypothesis); new Keynesian and post Keynesian economists highlight the uncertain effect of financial liberalisation on growth. Indeed, for the latter the increase in the interest rate following interest rate ceiling removal may have a negative impact on aggregate demand and, ultimately, on growth.

Undoubtedly, the interrelationship between financial variables and real economic activity is a multifaceted and complex phenomenon which needs to be analysed in detail if ever to be understood. Very rarely financial markets work without frictions and impediments to the free transfer of resources. Those frictions are extremely important for the understanding of the mechanics behind real resource allocation and for the understanding of the relevance of financial development in the process of capital accumulation. In financial markets, for example, more than in any other market, the level of information asymmetry and the nature of information distribution among agents have significant relevance for resource allocation. In economies with informational asymmetries both the nature of financial contracts and the institutional setting crucially matter for investments and capital accumulation.

In spite of the above, it is only recently that economists have begun to construct fully-articulated theoretical models that are capable of explaining the complex interactions between real and financial development. According to Levine (1997), the recent literature on finance and growth may be regarded as following 'a functional approach' in search of possible connections between real and financial sector activity. For example, by pooling and diversifying risks, by increasing liquidity or by reducing monitoring costs, financial markets and institutions are believed to have a positive impact on growth because they divert investments towards more productive activities or increase the flow of savings (Greenwood and Jovanovich, 1990; Bencivenga and Smith, 1991; Saint-Paul, 1992; Blackburn and Hung, 1998). A common theme in this literature is the recognition that, in order for financial systems and institutions to play a role in the real allocation of resources, the equilibrium framework *à la* Arrow-Debreu needs to be modified by introducing some kind of market imperfection. Typically, these imperfections are associated with certain types of transaction costs or certain types of informational asymmetries that appear to be present in borrower-lender relationships. The basic idea is that financial markets can play a crucial role in improving the allocation of resources by alleviating or eliminating such frictions.

Among these frictions, the one theorists have employed more frequently in order to modify the Arrow-Debreu framework, is the assumption of informational asymmetries between borrowers and lenders. Under this assumption, the optimal financial contract presents peculiarities and features which strongly depend on the nature of the degree of informational problems and on the state of the economy. Furthermore, in this context banks and intermediaries come to play a crucial role since they can reduce the agency costs associated with the existence of private information. As a consequence, this framework provides a useful way to explain the endogenous development of the financial system and provide a different and more insightful account of the interaction between financial development and growth.

For these reasons a significant part of the literature has recently attempted to investigate the channels of interaction between real and financial variables by exploiting the microeconomic theory of optimal financial contracts under asymmetric information, and applying this theory to the macroeconomic level through the construction of dynamic general equilibrium models of the economy (Bernanke and Gertler, 1989; Bencivenga and Smith, 1993; Bose and Cothren, 1996, 1997; Blackburn and Hung, 1998; Boyd and Smith, 1996, 1998). These models are capable of interpreting the co-evolution of real and financial sector activity. On the one hand, financial development can affect growth by allowing a greater pooling of risks, increasing the quality of information, reducing monitoring costs or re-directing resources towards higher yielding projects. On the other hand, growth can affect the structure of the financial system by altering the incentives of financial institutions, changing the optimal financial arrangements of firms and providing more resources to pay for a more costly financial superstructure.

In what follows we present a broad, but selective, survey of this research, focusing on issues of finance and growth that arise from informational asymmetries between borrowers and lenders.[1] These studies provide an account of the joint endogenous determination of capital accumulation and the development of the financial system.

Because of the nature of these models, in which information asymmetries have macroeconomic consequences only because they have a microeconomic relevance, a detailed analysis of the functioning of these models at a micro level is required in order to fully grasp their working. It is for this reason that we choose to focus only on a few analytical frameworks, regarded as benchmark cases, to describe the possible channels of interactions between financial variables and capital accumulation and to capture the very general way of modelling finance and growth in this environment.

Specifically we select four frameworks which, for different reasons, can best outline interesting features about the issue of finance and growth. The first two of these studies hinge on the hypothesis of *ex ante* informational problems. These frameworks are able to explain general features of the development of financial markets, like the high degree of credit rationing or the scarce use of monitoring activity in underdeveloped economies. The last two of these studies are based on the hypothesis of *ex post* informational problems. These frameworks are able to shed light on more specific, but not less interesting, aspects of financial development, such as the evolution of corporate financing, and, for example, the development of stock markets. The four models are logically, and chronologically, connected since each stems, in some degree, from the previous.

As already stressed, in these models information asymmetries can affect capital accumulation only because they can affect the optimal financial contract between individuals or groups of individuals. The broad functioning of these models can be summarised by the following diagram:

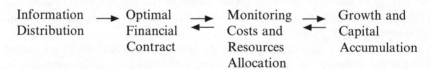

In section 2 we discuss models of finance and growth in which the nature of the financial contract between borrowers (firms) and lenders (households) is given. Typically, these models are based on *ex ante* informational asymmetries and the financial contract takes the form of a debt contract which is designed in such a way as to sort out different types of borrower through credit rationing. The benchmark framework is the one provided by Bencivenga and Smith (1993). In section 3 we discuss how these models have been extended to allow for endogenous changes in the contract structure. While debt continues to be the only mode of finance, firms optimally choose between contracts that involve rationing and contracts that involve screening, where this choice is affected by the level of real activity. The benchmark framework is the one provided by Bose and Cothren (1996, 1997).

Although studied extensively, the relationship between real and financial development continues to pose many questions for economists. One of the most notable of these is why it is only during the later stages of economic development that stock markets begin to emerge. In poor countries, such markets are almost non-existent, while in rich countries they are an essential part of the financial system. This suggests that, as economies develop, firms tend to change the method by which they acquire external funds, switching from indirect borrowing through bank intermediated debt finance, to more direct borrowing through the issue of equities and bonds. Sections 4 and 5 contain a discussion of some the latest research which extends the idea of endogenously determined financial structure further to the choice between debt and equity contracts when informational asymmetries arise *ex post*. This research seeks to explain the emergence and expansion of stock markets at late stages of economic development. The models we examine are those by Boyd and Smith (1996, 1998) (section 4) and Blackburn *et al.* (2004) (section 5). The last section contains some final comments.

2. Credit Rationing and Growth: Basic Considerations

One of the major problems that face investors is to determine the profitability and rate of return of the investment project that they are financing. Information about such outcomes is often very difficult or impossible to gather. As a consequence, investors either simply 'average' across the possible returns they might face, or try to separate a particular type of borrower and project by designing a financial contract with conditions that are unattractive to others. It has been widely argued (Rothschild and Stiglitz, 1976; Stiglitz and Weiss, 1981) that a common mechanism used by investors to sort out different types of borrower, and to reduce the adverse effects of informational frictions, is credit rationing. Undoubtedly, credit rationing is a widespread phenomenon that occurs in both developed and developing economies. To the extent that the majority of investments are financed through credit, then restrictions on the supply of credit provides an obvious link between the functioning of financial markets and economic growth. An example of this is presented by Bencivenga and Smith (1993) (hereafter B-S) in a model where lenders face different types of borrower with access to investment projects that have different rates of return.

Before turning to a more detailed description of the B-S model, it is useful to describe the very basic and common framework to all the models we examine.

The economy is inhabited by agents – borrowers and lenders – who live for two periods.[2] At the very beginning of the first period all young agents (or some) work and obtain a wage income. Once this is done, they access the credit market by supplying this income (lenders) or by demanding additional resources (borrowers). Still at the beginning of the first period, borrowers have access to a capital producing technology, and by employing the resources obtained in the credit market, they can produce capital. Capital takes one period to be produced and it will be available at the end of the first period. Once capital is produced, borrowers sell it in the market for output and repay the loan (we are at the beginning of the second period). Output is produced at the beginning of the second period by employing labour (supplied by the young generation of agents) and capital (produced in the previous period). All agents (borrowers and lenders) consume only in the second period. It is important to stress that issues of information asymmetries concern only the technology producing capital and not the technology to produce output, whose expected return is common knowledge.

In B-S, each borrower's expected return on the capital production technology (borrower's type) is private information and, therefore, unknown to lenders. Lenders only know they might face either a 'good' type (higher return) or a 'bad' type (lower return). Given that different borrower types have different costs of being denied a loan, lenders can use credit rationing as a means of revealing borrowers' identities. They do so by introducing a different probability of credit rationing (together with the other contractual elements: loan size and interest rate) in the contract. The contract for each type will be optimally designed in such a way as to be unattractive to the other type. The connection of finance with capital accumulation is easily explained by the fact that credit rationing restricts the amount of funds channelled towards investment and, therefore, it affects growth. The reverse causation, from growth to financial development, is explained by the fact that the cost to the lender of imposing a given amount of credit rationing (i.e. the form of the financial contract) depends on the return to capital and, therefore, on the level of real activity.

2.1 *Preferences and Technologies*

The economy consists of a constant population (normalised to 1) of two-period-lived agents belonging to overlapping generations. Each generation is identical in composition, with agents being separated at birth into two equal sized groups of borrowers and lenders. All agents are risk neutral and derive positive utility only from second period consumption.[3] Young lenders are endowed with one unit of labour which they supply inelastically to the market, earning the wage rate, w_t. This income can be lent to borrowers, or stored using a technology which yields one unit of output at time $t+1$ per unit stored at time t.

Young borrowers have no labour endowment, but they have access to a capital production technology which requires external funding to run. In the absence of such funding, young borrowers can run a home technology for producing output.[4] Borrowers consist of two types – a high risk (H) type (fraction λ of borrowers population) or a low risk (L) type (fraction $1 - \lambda$ of borrowers population). The capital production technology is such that, with probability p_i, $i = H, L$, $Q > 1$ units of capital are produced at time $t+1$ per unit of output invested at time t; with probability $1 - p_i$ the project fails and delivers zero units of capital. It is assumed that $1 \geq p_L > p_H \geq 0$. The home production technology requires no investment of resources and it delivers β_i units of output at $t+1$, with $\beta_i \leq 1$ and $\beta_L/p_L > \beta_H/p_H$. The latter inequality is extremely important for the workings of the model since it implies that different types of borrower face different costs of being denied credit. Indeed, it is because of this that lenders are able to sort out borrowers by announcing a probability that a borrower will be denied credit when applying for a loan. In other words, by choosing a probability of credit rationing for each of the two types of borrower, a lender can induce self selection and make each borrower reveal his own type. A necessary condition to separate borrowers is that 'bad' borrowers (the H type) have a higher alternative cost of being denied credit than the 'good' borrowers (the L type). This means that the return on the storage technology must be higher for L types than for H types: $\beta_L/Qp_L > \beta_H/Qp_H$.[5] To simplify matters, we assume that $\beta_H = 0$.

Production of output takes place in the second period of a borrower's life and requires a minimum level of the borrower's own capital. Thus, only those borrowers who have received a loan and have been successful in their capital production activity are able to produce output. Once output has been produced, borrowers repay lenders and consume what is left. A firm produces output according to the following function:

$$y_t = \bar{k}_t^{1-\theta} k_t^\theta L_t^{1-\theta}, 0 < \theta < 1; \tag{1}$$

where y_t denotes output, k_t denotes capital, L_t denotes labour and $\bar{k}_t$ denotes the average capital stock. Given (1) the marginal productivity of capital (the only accumulatable factor in the model) will be constant in equilibrium for a constant level of employment.[6] Nevertheless, this does not necessarily imply a positive long-run (endogenous) growth rate because capital is produced by a different technology. If this technology exhibits decreasing returns, then long-run growth will be zero.

With perfect competition in all markets, each factor will be paid its marginal productivity. Since $k_t = \bar{k}_t$ in equilibrium, it follows that the wage, w_t, and price of capital, ρ_t, are determined by:

$$w_t = (1 - \theta)k_t L_t^{-\theta}, \tag{2}$$

$$\rho_t = \theta L_t^{1-\theta}. \tag{3}$$

The possible impact of credit rationing in the model can be seen directly from (2) and (3). Given that the supply of labour is fixed (only lenders supply labour), and that the number of firms in any period depends on the number of borrowers financed in the previous period, the amount of labour per firm, and therefore the marginal productivity of capital, will depend on the amount of credit rationing (since this determines the number of borrowers eligible for loans).

2.2 The Credit Market

At the beginning of each period, a newly born borrower approaches a newly-born lender with a request for a loan to finance a capital project. With probability π_{it} the lender decides to fund the borrower and, simultaneously, fixes the terms of the financial contract, including the gross real rate of interest, R_{it}, and the loan size, q_{it}. With probability $1 - \pi_{it}$ the borrower is refused credit and is unable to secure a loan from any other lender.

In the absence of informational asymmetries (i.e. when a lender is fully informed about a borrower's type), the financial contract is easily determined. The interest rate would reflect the borrower's probability of failure and the project's expected rate of return such that a type H borrower would pay a higher rate of interest than a type L borrower. In this case there would be no need for credit rationing. In the presence of asymmetric information matters are more complicated. If a lender were to fix the interest rate applied to each type of borrower, then the contract designed for an L type borrower would also attract an H type borrower. As in Rothschild and Stiglitz (1976), this problem is resolved by introducing the possibility that a lender may deny credit to a borrower. This probability of credit rationing can induce a separating equilibrium through self selection.

Formally, a separating equilibrium is a financial contract that specifies, for each type of borrower, a rate of interest, a loan size and a probability of obtaining credit such that no lender has an incentive to deviate by offering a different contract, and that no borrower is better off by concealing her identity than by revealing it. If $(R_{it}, q_{it}, \pi_{it})$, $(i = H, L)$, denotes such a contract then the incentive constraints are

$$p_H \pi_{Ht}(Q\rho_{t+1} - R_{Ht})q_{Ht} \geq p_H \pi_{Lt}(Q\rho_{t+1} - R_{Lt})q_{Lt} \tag{4}$$

for a type-H borrower, and

$$p_L \pi_{Lt}(Q\rho_{t+1} - R_{Lt})q_{Lt} + (1 - \pi_{Lt})\beta_L \geq p_L \pi_{Ht}(Q\rho_{t+1} - R_{Ht})q_{Ht} \\ + (1 - \pi_{Ht})\beta_L \tag{5}$$

for a type-L borrower. Assuming that competition drives lenders' profits to zero, implying $q_{it}[p_i R_{it} + (1 - p_i)0] = q_{it}$,[7] the gross rate of interest charged to each type of borrower is given by

$$R_{it} = R_i = 1/p_i. \tag{6}$$

Hence $R_H > R_L$.

In order to be approached by a borrower, each lender must offer a contract that is not dominated by any other contract. In equilibrium, each lender will offer the same contract, obtained by maximising the borrower's expected utility. That is, each lender solves the problem:

$$\underset{R,q,\pi}{Max}\, p_i \pi_{it}(Q\rho_{t+1} - R_{it})q_{it} + (1 - \pi_{it})\beta_i \tag{7}$$

subject to (4), (5), (6) and the feasibility constraint $q_{it} \leq w_t$. This problem can be solved through intuition. Because the interest rate paid by high risk borrowers is higher than the interest rate paid by L type borrowers, no H type borrower has an incentive to reveal her identity and no L type borrower is ever motivated to conceal her identity (all other features of the contract being the same). Consequently, a lender needs to drive away H type borrowers from an L type contract by offering them the best conditions in terms of loan size and probability of credit rationing. Given that utility is increasing in q_{it} and π_{it}, the optimal solutions are the maximum values $q_{Ht} = w_t$ and $\pi_H = 1$. Once this H type contract is determined, the problem for the lender is to find the optimal L type contract. It is straightforward to show that the optimal loan size is again given by $q_{Lt} = w_t$, and that the incentive constraint, (4), is binding. Thus, the lender pushes the L type contract up to the point where an H type borrower is indifferent between revealing and not revealing her identity. The optimal probability of credit rationing is then determined as:

$$\pi_{Lt} = \frac{p_H Q \rho_{t+1} - 1}{p_H Q \rho_{t+1} - (p_H/p_L)}. \tag{8}$$

2.3 Capital Accumulation

The expression in (8) shows clearly that the probability of credit rationing is a function of the marginal productivity of capital, ρ_{t+1}. This is the sense in which the model predicts an influence of real economic activity on financial activity. It can also be shown that the reverse is true – that the marginal productivity of capital depends on the level of credit rationing. Recall that the number of firms producing output in each period depends on the number of firms that have not been credit rationed in the previous period. Recall also that the supply of labour is fixed, being equal to the fraction of lenders. It follows that the amount of labour per firm is given by:

$$L_t = \frac{1}{\lambda p_H + (1 - \lambda) p_L \pi_{Lt-1}}. \tag{9}$$

By virtue of (3), the marginal productivity of capital is then computed as:

$$\rho_{t+1} = \theta \left[\frac{1}{\lambda p_H + (1 - \lambda) p_L \pi_{Lt}} \right]^{1-\theta}. \tag{10}$$

Thus, the probability of credit rationing and the marginal productivity of capital are jointly determined by (8) and (10). This interdependence between real and financial activity translates into an interdependence between growth and financial activity. To see this, observe that, since only successful borrowers produce output in the second period of their lives, the amount of capital per firm at time $t+1$ is given by $k_{t+1} = Q w_t$. Given this, together with (2), it is possible to deduce the growth rate of capital as:

$$\frac{k_{t+1}}{k_t} = Q(1 - \theta)(\rho/\theta)^{-\theta/(1-\theta)} \tag{11}$$

where ρ_t has been substituted by the constant ρ.[8]

One can now understand the nature of the interrelationship between financial market activity and economic growth. An increase in the level of credit rationing (i.e. a decrease in π) has a positive impact on the marginal productivity of capital through (10), and, therefore, a negative impact on the rate of growth through (11). At the same time, changes in the growth rate can affect the level of financial activity in terms of the amount of credit rationing and the amount of resources transferred from savers to investors. These results show that, in a framework where investments are financed via credit, policies that exogenously reduce the level of credit rationing will have a positive impact on the rate of growth. On the other hand, it can be shown that policies designed to subsidise credit constrained agents can have adverse effects on growth and increase the amount of credit rationing by making adverse selection problems more severe.

3. Rationing versus Screening: Endogenising the Financial Structure

In the model of B-S credit rationing provides the means by which lenders can alleviate problems of adverse selection when they are confronted by borrowers of different unobservable types. While the amount of credit rationing both determines, and is determined by the level of real activity, the structure of financial contracts and the degree of asymmetric information are exogenously given: these contracts always take the form of debt contracts and are always expressed in terms of the same variables (the size of the loan, the interest payment on a loan and the probability of being denied a loan). In an extension of this framework, Bose and Cothren (1996, 1997) (hereafter B-C) allow lenders to solve problems of adverse selection not only through credit rationing, but also through screening, whereby a lender is able to spend resources on verifying a borrower's type. This gives rise to two types of contract – a rationing contract of the sort considered above, and a screening contract under which informational asymmetries are eradicated completely through the costly acquisition of information. Significantly, the optimal form of contract depends on the state of the real economy. In this way, changes in real economic activity affect not only the level of financial activity, but also the structure of the financial system.

In B-C, as in B-S, there is the same informational problem: the lender does not know if the borrower she is facing is a 'good' or a 'bad' borrower. In B-C, however, lenders can solve this problem by screening and verifying borrowers' type as well as by means of credit rationing. Screening, though, is costly and it might not be always optimal. The screening cost, in B-C's analysis, depends on the size of the loan and, more precisely, it is decreasing with the size of the loan. Under this assumption, for a low level of capital accumulation, when the size of the loan (i.e. the amount of funds intermediated in the credit market) is low, the screening cost is relatively high. For symmetric reasons, the cost of credit rationing is relatively low for a low level of capital accumulation, when the gross return on borrowers' projects is low. Subsequently, as the economy grows, and the size of the projects increases, it becomes more and more costly not to finance them. The result is that for a low level of development (low level of capital accumulation) the rationing contract might dominate the screening contract. As the economy develops, however, it might become optimal for lenders to offer a screening contract instead of a rationing contract. The transition from one contract to the other, and the evolution of the financial system, is endogenously determined by growth. In turn, as the economy moves from one financial regime to the other, a larger amount of resources might be freed and channelled to capital production (credit rationing decreases). This would explain the positive impact of financial development on growth.

3.1 *Preferences and Technologies*

The microeconomic framework is essentially the same as before. There is a unit mass of two-period-lived agents who belong to overlapping generations and who are divided into two equal sized groups of borrowers and lenders with preferences and technologies as described earlier. One difference from the previous framework is that lenders have access to a home production technology for producing capital, rather than a storage technology for preserving output.[9] This capital technology needs to be less productive than the borrowers' capital project if the latter is ever to be in use. Specifically, it is assumed that home production delivers $Q\varepsilon$ units of capital at $t+1$ per unit of output invested at time t, where $\varepsilon < 1$.

Output production is performed in the second period only by successful borrowers. The technology for output production is given by

$$y_t = k_t^\theta L_t^{1-\theta} \tag{12}$$

Assuming perfectly competitive factor markets, the profit maximisation conditions are

$$w_t = (1 - \theta)k_t^\theta L_t^{-\theta} \tag{13}$$

$$\rho_t = \theta k_t^{\theta-1} L_t^{1-\theta} \tag{14}$$

3.2 *The Credit Market*

As before, a borrower of type-i ($i = H, L$) who is granted credit runs the capital production technology which yields Q units of capital with probability p_i and zero units of capital with probability $1 - p_i$, where $p_L > p_H$. A borrower who is denied credit produces β_i units of output next period, where $\beta_L > \beta_H = 0$. Lenders have the opportunity to separate borrowers either by credit rationing, which occurs with probability $1 - \pi_{it}$, or by screening, which occurs with probability $1 - \phi_t$. For screening to be effective in preventing a borrower from trying to disguise his identity, a penalty must be incurred when a borrower is found to be lying. It is assumed that an H type borrower who applies for an L type contract faces the maximum penalty of being denied a loan if his identity is discovered. At the same time, it is also assumed that screening is costly for a borrower. In particular, screening requires a lender to spend δ units of output per unit lent. This implies that the loan size after screening is $w_t/(1+\delta)$.

As already discussed, in absence of any distortion or discriminatory features, an H type borrower will always try to imitate an L type in order to obtain a more convenient contract with a lower interest rate. However, this will not happen if the lender makes the L type's contract unattractive to the H type borrower by introducing either a high enough probability of credit rationing or a probability of screening.[10] This leaves the lender to solve two alternative problems. The solution to the first (the credit rationing contract) will involve the probability of credit rationing (together with the interest rate and loan size) that maximise L type borrower's expected utility:

$$\underset{R_L, q_L, \pi_L}{Max} \left\{ p_L \pi_{Lt} (Q\rho_{t+1} - R_{Lt}^r) q_{Lt}^r + (1 - \pi_{Lt})\beta_L \right\} \tag{15}$$

subject to the constraint that the H type borrower does not have the incentive to claim to be an L type,

$$p_H \pi_{Ht} (Q\rho_{t+1} - R_{Ht}^r) q_{Ht}^r \geq \pi_{Lt}\, p_H (Q\rho_{t+1} - R_{Lt}^r) q_{Lt}^r \tag{16}$$

and the constraint (zero profit constraint) that the expected return on the loan is at least equal to lender's alternative cost, $Q\varepsilon\rho_{t+1}$,

$$\pi_{Lt}(p_L R_{Lt}^r - Q\varepsilon\rho_{t+1}) q_{Lt}^r = 0 \tag{17}$$

The solution to the second (the screening contract) will involve the probability of screening, $1 - \phi_t$, (together with the interest rate and loan size) that maximise L type borrower's expected utility:[11]

$$\underset{R_L, q_L, \phi_t}{Max}\ \phi_t \left\{ p_L (Q\rho_{t+1} - R_{Lt}^n) q_{Lt}^n \right\} + (1 - \phi_t) p_L (Q\rho_{t+1} - R_{Lt}^s) q_{Lt}^s \tag{18}$$

subject to the constraint that the H type borrower does not have the incentive to claim to be an L type and lender's participation constraint (recall that screening costs δ units of output per unit lent)

$$p_H (Q\rho_{t+1} - R_{Ht}^n) q_{Ht}^n \geq \phi_t\, p_H (Q\rho_{t+1} - R_{Lt}^n) q_{Lt}^n \tag{19}$$

$$\phi_t \pi_{Lt}(p_L R_{Lt}^n - Q\varepsilon\rho_{t+1}) q_{Lt}^n + (1 - \phi_t)[p_L R_{Lt}^s - (1 + \delta)Q\varepsilon\rho_{t+1}] q_{Lt}^s = 0 \tag{20}$$

where the superscripts n and s denote the value of a variable in the case of non screening and screening respectively.

As in the previous model, a credit rationing contract involves the maximum amount of transferable funds, $q_{Lt}^r = w_t$, and a gross interest rate determined by the zero profit constraint in (17), $R_{Lt}^r = Q\varepsilon\rho_{t+1}/p_L$. However, it involves a probability of credit rationing – as determined by the incentive constraint in (16):

$$\pi_{Lt} = \pi = \frac{1 - \varepsilon/p_H}{1 - \varepsilon/p_L}, \tag{21}$$

which is fixed and no longer depends on the price of capital, as it did in B-S's framework (see eq. (8)). This is because of the assumption that lenders have access to a home production technology, instead of a storage technology. As a result, if capital accumulation affects financial market activity, this cannot be due to its effect on the amount of credit rationing.

Consider now the screening contract. The optimal strategy for lenders is to charge the L type borrower the minimum interest rate, $R^s_{Lt} = 0$, when screening takes place and the maximum interest rate, $R^n_{Lt} = Q\varepsilon\rho_{t+1}/\phi_t p_L$, when screening does not take place. As usual, the loan size is set equal to its maximum level in each case, $q^n_{Lt} = w_t$ and $q^s_{Lt} = w_t/(1 + \delta)$. The probability of screening, like the probability of credit rationing, is determined by the binding incentive constraint in (19):

$$\phi_t = \phi = 1 - (1/p_H - 1/p_L)\varepsilon. \tag{22}$$

Having characterised each type of financial contract, it is now possible to identify the conditions under which one of them will be preferred to the other. By simply comparing borrower's expected utility under the rationing contract, $(q^r_{Lt}, R^r_{Lt}, \pi_L)$, and the screening contract, $(q^s_{Lt}, q^n_{Lt}, R^s_{Lt}, R^n_{Lt}, \phi_t)$, it is easy to show that the latter contract dominates the former if

$$\beta^*_t \equiv Q w_t \rho_{t+1}(p_L - \varepsilon)/(1 + \delta) > \beta_L. \tag{23}$$

It is now clear how the structure of the financial system is endogenous in the model and influenced by real economic activity. According to (23), the prevalence of one contract over the other depends on the marginal productivity of capital and the wage rate. In particular, a larger value of either of these variables makes the screening contract more preferable. For example, when the marginal productivity of capital is high, the gross return from the project is large and rationing is more costly. Since both the marginal product of capital and the wage rate are functions of the capital stock (see eq. (13) and (14)), then the optimal choice of contract depends ultimately on the process of capital accumulation to which we now turn.

3.3 Capital Accumulation

It is possible to show that $\beta^*_t < \beta_L$ is more likely at low levels of capital, in which case only rationing takes place. Conversely, $\beta^*_t > \beta_L$ is more likely at high levels of capital, in which case only screening occurs. When $\beta^*_t = \beta_L$ lenders randomise between the two contracts implying the co-existence of rationing and screening. These results accord with the empirical evidence in the sense that a higher level of credit rationing is typically observed in poorer economies. At the same time the amount of capital accumulation depends on the prevailing contract regime since the amount of resources transferred as loans, and invested in capital production, is different under each regime.

Under a rationing contract, the total amount of capital produced at time $t+1$ is equal to the capital produced by borrowers who are not rationed plus the capital produced by lenders who have refused to give loans and invested their income in the home production of capital instead. Thus,

$$k_{t+1} = 0.5[\lambda p_H + (1 - \lambda)p_L\pi]Qw_t + 0.5[(1 - \pi)(1 - \lambda)]Q\varepsilon w_t \qquad (24)$$

Under a screening contract, the total amount of capital is equal to the capital produced by borrowers who are screened and not screened (lenders do not use their home production technology in this case). Hence,

$$k_{t+1} = 0.5[\lambda p_H + (1 - \lambda)\phi p_L + (1 - \phi)(1 - \lambda)p_L/(1 + \delta)]Qw_t \qquad (25)$$

A comparison of (24) and (25) reveals that the capital accumulation path under screening is higher than the capital accumulation path under rationing. This implies that when the economy switches from one financial regime to the other, there is a jump in the rate of growth.

In summary, the model predicts that the structure of the financial market both determines, and is determined by, the level of real economic activity. At low levels of activity, a financial regime based on rationing prevails. At high levels of activity, a regime based on screening is preferred. Transition from one regime to the other is characterised by an increase in the growth rate and the use of both rationing and screening as devices to alleviate problems of asymmetric information.

4. From Debt Contracts to Equity Contracts: the Emergence of Stock Markets

The incentive problems encountered in the previous models arise from the existence of *ex ante* asymmetric information about the characteristics of borrowers: lenders are unable to observe directly whether a borrower is a high risk type or a low risk type. Another kind of incentive problem arises when there is *ex post* asymmetric information about the returns on borrowers' investment: that is, when lenders are unable to observe directly the outcomes of projects. In this case, lenders face problems of moral hazard, rather than problems of adverse selection. The main implication of this is that lenders must monitor, or verify, the claims of borrowers about project returns when contractual repayments are not honoured. Since verification is costly, a lender will find it optimal to engage in verification only in a limited set of possible contingent states. As shown by the vast literature on the issue (Townsend, 1979, Diamond 1984, Gale and Hellwig 1985, Williamson 1986, 1987a, 1987b), the optimal solution to a standard costly state verification (CSV) problem, where agents are risk neutral and monitoring costs do not depend on project returns, is always a debt contract, whereby the loan repayment is predetermined and independent of the actual profitability of the investment. Intuitively, a security that involves a fixed repayment (such as debt) allows the creditor to avoid the cost of monitoring under some contingencies. Monitoring takes place only when the project's return is not high enough to repay the creditor, a state which is referred to as a bankruptcy state. By contrast, other forms of securities for which the loan repayment is a function of the project's profitability (such as equity) are not optimal since they always require monitoring whatever the state.

In what follows we summarise the analyses by Boyd and Smith (1996, 1998) (henceforth Bo-S) who modify the standard CSV framework in such a way as to provide an account of why firms find it optimal to acquire external finance through the issue of equity rather than the issue of debt.

The working of the model is the following. Borrowers have access to two alternative projects for producing capital. The first project has a higher expected return which is known to the lender. The actual return on the project, however, is unobservable to outsiders. If the lender wants to verify the result of production, she must incur in a cost which is decreasing in the price of capital (the interest rate). The second project has a lower expected return, but the actual return on this project is costlessly observable to the lender. Bo-S show that the way the lender optimally finances the two projects is radically different. More precisely, while the unobservable project is optimally financed through a debt contract, the observable project is optimally financed through equity issue. The dependence of the equity-debt choice on growth is easily explained. For low level of capital accumulation, when the interest rate is high, the monitoring cost is relatively low. As a consequence, agents use more intensively the unobservable technology. This, in turn, implies that debt finance is more widespread than equity finance. As capital accumulates, and the price of capital decreases, the monitoring costs increase and the unobservable technology becomes less and less profitable. As a result, the economy will show a larger fraction of equity finance. This process explains the emergence of stock markets at later stages of economic development.

4.1 *Preferences and Technologies*

The basic features of the economy are the same as before. Population is a unit mass of two-period-lived agents, half of whom are lenders (households), and half of whom are borrowers (firms). In the first period, households have one unit of labour endowment which they supply to final output producers, while firms have access to an investment project from which capital is produced. Unlike the previous models, however, all borrowers are the same, implying the absence of any *ex ante* informational asymmetries. Instead, there are *ex post* informational asymmetries due to the stochastic nature of project returns which are observable only to borrowers.

The basic challenge is to develop a valid macroeconomic framework that is capable of explaining why the issue of equity might be optimal given the contrary prediction of the CSV paradigm. This is accomplished by assuming that firms have access to two types of capital production technology. Specifically, it is assumed that firms are able to divide their total investment, i_t, between a publicly observable project, i_t^o, and a privately observable project, i_t^u, (i.e. $i_t = i_t^o + i_t^u$). Only by spending a fixed amount of output, γ, can lenders observe the return on the latter; otherwise, the return on this technology is unobservable. Both technologies are stochastic: the observable technology delivers x units of capital at time $t+1$ per unit of output invested at time t, where $x \in \{x_1, x_2, \ldots x_N\}$ denotes an iid stochastic variable, with $p_n \equiv \text{prob}(x = x_n)$ and expected value $\hat{x} = \Sigma x_n p_n$; the unobservable technology delivers ω units of capital at time $t+1$ per unit of output invested at time t, where $\omega \in [0, \Omega]$ has the p.d.f. $g(\omega)$ and an expected value $\hat{\omega} = \int_0^\Omega \omega g(\omega) d\omega$. As in B-C, lenders have access to a home capital production technology whereby one unit of output invested at t yields r units of capital at $t+1$. The expected returns on these three technologies are assumed to satisfy $\hat{\omega} > \hat{x} > r$. Evidently, the unobservable technology must have a higher expected return than the observable technology since its use implies a higher cost associated with acquiring information. The relatively low return on the safe technology means that this technology will only be used as a residual investment and accessed when the others are not available.[12]

Production of output takes place in the second period of a borrower's life according to

$$y_t = k_t^\theta L_t^{1-\theta} \qquad (26)$$

As usual, it is assumed that all markets are perfectly competitive, so that the price of labour and the price of capital satisfy

$$w_t = (1 - \theta) k_t^\theta L_t^{-\theta} \qquad (27)$$

$$\rho_t = \theta k_t^{\theta-1} L_t^{1-\theta} \qquad (28)$$

4.2 The Credit Market

In the present set-up, a financial contract needs to specify the size of the loan, the state in which monitoring will occur (and will not) and the amount of repayment in each of these states. It is clear that the repayment in a non-monitoring state can be made contingent only on the return on the observable technology: denote this repayment by $b_t(x)$. By contrast, the repayment in a monitoring state can be made contingent on the return on the observable as well as the unobservable technology: denote this repayment by $R_t(\omega, x)$. It is also evident that these states – denoted $N(x_t)$ for non-monitoring state and $M(x_t)$ for monitoring state – will themselves be determined by the return on the observable technology. The contract is designed by borrowers who choose the allocation of the total investment taken as given, $\bar{i}$, between the two technologies, $z_t = i_t^o / \bar{i}$ (and $1 - z_t = i_t^u / \bar{i}$) (both of which are observable by lenders), together with the repayments and the verification states. In order to be accepted by a lender, the contract must not be dominated by any other contract. Thus, a borrower designs a contract which maximises his own expected utility, and which is incentive compatible and feasible.[13] The role of incentive compatibility is to induce the borrower to tell the truth about the return on the project and to declare a state of bankruptcy only when such a state actually occurs. For this to be accomplished, the repayment in the bankruptcy state must be always greater than the repayment in the non bankruptcy state:

$$R_t(\omega, x) \le b_t(x) \ \forall \ \omega \in M_t(x) \tag{29}$$

In other words, if the latter is not in place then the borrower has the incentive to lie, and always to claim bankruptcy, even when this has not occurred.

The feasibility constraint requires that the repayment in each state is no higher than the actual return from the project:

$$R_t(\omega, x) \le \rho_{t+1}[z_t x + (1 - z_t)\omega], \tag{30}$$
$$b_t(x) \le \rho_{t+1}[z_t x + (1 - z_t)\omega]. \tag{31}$$

We can now state borrower's problem. This will consist in the determination of the optimal repayment in the two states, R_t and b_t, as well as of the optimal relative use of the two technologies, z_t, in order to maximise the expected return on the investment, $\rho_{t+1}[z_t \hat{x} + (1 - z_t)\hat{\omega}]$, less the expected repayment to the lender per unit invested:

$$\max_{i,R,b,z} i_t \rho_{t+1}[z_t \hat{x} + (1 - z_t)\hat{\omega}]$$
$$-i_t \left[\sum_n p_n \int_{\omega \in M_t(x_n)} R_t(\omega, x_n) \, g(\omega) d\omega + \sum_n p_n \int_{\omega \in N_t(x_n)} b_t(x_n) \, g(\omega) d\omega \right] \tag{32}$$

subject to (29), (30), (31) and the lender's zero profit constraint:

$$i_t \left[\sum_n p_n \int_{\omega \in M_t(x_n)} R_t(\omega, x_n) \, g(\omega) d\omega + \sum_n p_n \int_{\omega \in N_t(x_n)} b_t(x_n) g(\omega) d\omega \right]$$
$$= r\rho_{t+1} + \gamma \sum_n p_n \int_{\omega \in M_t(x_n)} g(\omega) d\omega. \tag{33}$$

where $\gamma \sum_n p_n \int_{\omega \in M_t(x_n)} g(\omega) d\omega$ is the expected monitoring cost and $r\rho_{t+1}$ lender's alternative cost.

The solution of the above problem implies the following. Since monitoring is costly, a borrower will always try to avoid the bankruptcy state whenever possible. Thus, a borrower will always make the repayment in the non-bankruptcy state, $b_t(x)$, if the return on the project allows him to do so. If not, then the borrower will declare bankruptcy and the lender will monitor. For a given realised return on the observable technology, x_n, and a given repayment, $b_t(x_n)$, the return on the unobservable technology, ω, will determine whether a borrower can meet the repayment or not. It can be shown that, for a given x_n, the minimum return on the unobservable technology for which bankruptcy can be avoided is defined implicitly by (31) under equality: $b_t(x_n) = \rho_{t+1}[z_t x_n + (1 - z_t)\tilde{\omega}_{nt}]$. In other words, for a given x_n, a borrower will go bankrupt if $\omega_t < \tilde{\omega}_{nt}$. Under certain assumptions, this minimum value of ω is independent of the realised x_n. This result is important since it indicates that the optimal repayment, $b_t(x_n)$, can be subdivided into two components: a fixed component, $\rho_{t+1}(1 - z_t)\tilde{\omega}_t$, which does not depend on the observable project's return, and a variable component, $\rho_{t+1}z_t x_n$, which does depend on this return. A natural interpretation of these components is to view the former as a debt payment and the latter as an equity payment. In general, therefore, it is optimal for a firm to issue both debt and equity to finance its investments. Exactly how much of each security is issued depends on the proportion of investment allocated to the observable technology, z_t, and proportion allocated to the unobservable technology, $1 - z_t$. Significantly, these proportions change with changes in the level of capital accumulation, as discussed below.

4.3 *Capital Accumulation*

The optimal allocation of investment between observable and unobservable technologies depends on the expected monitoring cost, expressed in terms of units of capital. As such, this allocation will change if the price of capital changes, as it does during the process of development. Specifically, it can be shown that z_t increases along the path of capital accumulation. Intuitively, as capital is accumulated, the price of capital falls which increases the perceived cost of bankruptcy so that borrowers find it optimal to use less of the unobservable technology and more of the observable technology. This translates into a greater use of equity relative to debt. The capital accumulation path is determined specifically by recalling that the amount of capital available in each period is given by the capital produced from the observable and unobservable technologies of borrowers plus the capital produced from the home technology of lenders. Thus, the aggregate stock of capital at time $t + 1$ is

$$K_{t+1} = 0.5\bar{i}[z_t\hat{x} + (1 - z_t)\hat{\omega} - r] + 0.5rw_t \tag{34}$$

While the effect of capital accumulation on financing choice is unambiguous (i.e. firms tend to issue more equity and less debt), the reverse effect of the financial regime on growth is less clear. On the one hand, a more intensive use of the observable technology (associated with the issue of equity) reduces the resources spent on monitoring, thereby stimulating growth. On the other hand, since the observable technology has a relatively low expected return, a greater use of it tends to slow down growth.

5. More on the Development of the Stock Market. Multiple Enforcement Problems and Firm's Optimal Capital Structure

The emergence of equity markets at later stages of economic development and the strong positive correlation between stock market development and economic growth represent a well known empirical result. Yet, empirical studies have not been able to establish the exact causal relationship which could go either way. Blackburn *et al.* (2004) (B-B-C hereafter) provide an account of the possible two-way linkages between stock market development and economic growth, and an alternative interpretation of the development of equity markets. To these authors, the emergence of equity contracts is the result of lenders' attempts to solve multiple enforcement problems when a firm's choice of investment project and level of effort devoted to that project are private information. Capital accumulation can influence the development of equity markets because it can affect the degree of control of the lender over these choices. The analysis is based on a principal-agent framework in which the borrower-firm (the agent) has access to an array of different projects, each with an expected return that depends on the risk of the project itself and on the amount of effort that the borrower exerts. The lender (principal), who has the task of designing the optimal financial contract, cannot directly control the firm's effort, but, he has the option to either impose his own choice of project at a cost, or to leave this choice up to the borrower. The optimal financial contracts under these two alternative circumstances are not the same. When the lender chooses the project, the optimal financial contract is a typical debt contract. When the firm chooses the project, the optimal financial contract is a mixture of debt and equity. The reason for this is that when the choice of project is imposed by the lender, a fixed repayment (debt contract) is sufficient to induce the optimal level of effort by the firm. By contrast, when the choice of project is left up to the borrower, a fixed repayment is not enough to induce the best effort level, nor the best choice of project: in this case, part of the payment must be a function of the actual return (equity payment) in order to induce the borrower to exert the optimal effort level.

The optimal choice of contract depends essentially on the cost to the lender of taking charge of project selection. In B-B-C this cost is represented by the wage the lender is forgoing by not supplying his labour in the market, and by spending, instead, his time in selecting and imposing the project choice on the borrower. At low levels of capital accumulation, when the return to labour is relatively low, and so is the wage rate, this cost is low and the debt contract dominates. As the economy develops, and the wage rate prevailing in the market goes up, the cost of imposing the project choice increases until it eventually becomes optimal for the lender not to interfere directly in this choice: the financial contract will involve both debt and equity. Nevertheless, an equity market might never appear if the economy reaches a steady state before the switch in the financial system occurs. If a switch does take place, then the economy jumps from a low capital accumulation path to a high capital accumulation path so that growth is temporarily stimulated. The reason is that less resources are wasted in the economy for project selection. This could give an account of the positive impact of stock market development on growth.

5.1 *Preferences and Technologies*

The economy is inhabited by an infinite sequence of two period lived overlapping generations of agents. Population is constant and normalised to 2. Half of the population consists of borrowers (firms) and half of lenders (households). Young lenders are endowed with one unit of labour which is supplied inelastically to the market. Young borrowers have access to a risky capital producing technology which requires external resources. Suppliers of such funds are young lenders. The return on the capital producing technology depends on borrower's effort, $h_t \in (0,1)$, as well as, on which specific project, $x_t \in \Re_+$, is chosen. In particular, by investing i_t units of output at time t, this technology delivers, at time $t+1$, $x_t i_t^\alpha h_t^\beta$ (where α, $\beta \in [0,1]$; $\alpha+\beta<1$) units of capital with probability $p(x_t) = e^{-\sigma x_t} (\sigma > 0)$, and 0 units of capital with probability $1 - p(x_t)$.[14]

Each young borrower, who is endowed with one unit of effort (or entrepreneurial time), can alternatively employ all, or a fraction, of this effort in the capital producing technology or into a home technology to produce output. The home technology does not require external resources and it delivers $\phi(1 - h_t)$ units of output at time $t+1$ when it runs together with the capital production technology, or ϕ_0 units of output (in this case $h_t = 1$) when the capital production technology is not undertaken, with $\phi > \phi_0$ due to knowledge spillovers.[15] The output foregone on the home technology represents the borrower's alternative cost of supplying effort in capital production.

All old borrowers produce output by employing capital and labour according to the production function

$$y_t = \bar{k}_t^\theta k_t^{1-\theta} L_t^\theta, 0 < \theta < 1. \tag{35}$$

Once more, it is worthwhile to outline that even if there is a positive externality in output production, the model will not be able to display an endogenous rate of growth since the technology to produce capital exhibits decreasing returns.

Assuming perfectly competitive markets, each factor of production will be paid its marginal product and, therefore,

$$w_t = \theta k_t L_t^{\theta-1}, \tag{36}$$

$$\rho_t = \rho = (1 - \theta)L^\theta. \tag{37}$$

5.2 *The Credit Market*

At each point in time the credit market opens and each young borrower approaches a young lender for a loan. The repayment on the loan can take either the form of debt, d_t – a fixed sum independent of the project's return – or equity, s_t – a repayment which depends on the project's return – or a combination of the two. The lender designs the financial contract in order to motivate the borrower to exert the maximum level of effort, h_t, and to choose the optimal project, x_t. Both the effort and project choices are not observable. However, the lender has the possibility to reduce this double enforcement problem by directly choosing the project. This is costly since it requires a fixed amount of lender's working time, $1 - \eta$, and it involves the consequent loss of foregone wage income. Therefore, as one can easily anticipate, the lender's optimal alternative of directly or indirectly enforcing the choice of the project will depend on the wage rate and, ultimately, on the level of capital accumulation. Moreover, since each of these alternatives involves a different financial contract, the prevailing financial contract will depend on the level of capital accumulation too.

Interestingly, B-B-C show that when the lender decides to directly enforce the choice of the project, the repayment will only be in the form of debt. On the contrary, when the lender controls indirectly the choice of the project, the optimal repayment will be a mixture of debt and equity. In order to understand the reasons behind these results, it is worthwhile to summarise the problems faced by the lender.

The lender knows that the borrower will choose the effort and the project in order to maximise her own utility function. Therefore, for a given payment schedule, borrower's reaction functions read

$$h_t = \arg\max e^{-\rho x_t}(1 - s_t)(rx_t i_t^\alpha h_t^\beta - d_t) + \phi(1 - h_t) \tag{38}$$

$$x_t = \arg\max e^{-\rho x_t}(1 - s_t)(rx_t i_t^\alpha h_t^\beta - d_t) + \phi(1 - h_t) \tag{39}$$

Moreover, the borrower will not undertake the production process unless the contract does guarantee at least what she can get by not running the project, ϕ_0:

$$e^{-\rho x_t}(1 - s_t)(rx_t i_t^\alpha h_t^\beta - d_t) + \phi(1 - h_t) \geq \phi_0 \tag{40}$$

Under the circumstance of direct enforcement of the project's choice, the lender's problem will be to maximise his own expected utility function:

$$\underset{s_t, d_t, x_t}{Max}\, e^{-\rho x_t}[s_t(rx_t i_t^\alpha h_t^\beta - d_t) + d_t] \tag{41}$$

s.t. the incentive constraint on effort, (38), the rationality constraint, (40) and the non negativity constraints. On the other hand, if the choice of the project is left up to the borrower, the problem will be:

$$\underset{s_t, d_t}{Max}\, e^{-\rho x_t}[s_t(rx_t i_t^\alpha h_t^\beta - d_t) + d_t] \tag{42}$$

s.t. the incentive constraints on effort and project, (38), (39), the rationality constraint, (40) and the non negativity constraints. The solution to the first maximisation problem involves a repayment in the only form of debt ($s_t = 0$ and $d_t > 0$). Vice versa, the second maximisation problem involves a repayment in the form of both debt and equity ($s_t > 0$ and $d_t > 0$). Intuitively, since the level of effort is a decreasing function of equity issue, it is always optimal for lender to reduce as much as possible the equity payment. This can be done when lender controls directly the choice of the project, since the debt payment is sufficient to obtain the optimal level of effort. On the contrary, if both the choice of effort and project are left up to the borrower, by fixing equity payment to zero, the only debt payment is not sufficient to determine the optimal values of both effort and project. In this case, therefore, the optimal contract will involve a positive equity payment.

5.3 Stock Market Development

Controlling the project delivers a contract very close to the first best.[16] However, controlling the project is also costly and, therefore, it is not necessarily optimal for the lender to opt for such an alternative. By comparing the lender's expected utility under the two cases, we can establish when one contract dominates the other. If the lender decides to enforce the choice of the project, part of his labour income is foregone and the amount of loanable funds is reduced to $i_t = \eta w_t$. On the the other hand, not controlling the project will allow the lender to transfer to the borrower all of his wage, $i_t = w_t$. Since the wage rate is a function of the capital accumulated in the economy, enforcement costs, and the prevalence of one contract over the other, ultimately depend on the level of capital in the economy. As B-B-C show, at low levels of capital, when wage income is low, the cost of controlling the project is low and the debt-only contract dominates (one-enforcement problem). As capital is accumulated, and the wage income increases, the cost of enforcing the project choice goes up, and it might be so high that the lender finds it optimal to leave the choice of the project up to borrower. In this case the prevailing contract is a mixed debt-equity contract (two-enforcement problem). Hence, it is possible to determine a critical level of capital, k^c, below which the financial system is characterised by the prevalence of debt. As the economy reaches this critical level of capital the equity market emerges. It could also be the case that the equity market never appears. This occurs if the economy reaches the steady state before the critical level of capital is reached. This could explain the existence of financial traps with low level of capital and an under-developed financial system with no equity markets.

In migrating from one financial regime to the other, the economy moves to a higher capital accumulation path. There will be a temporary increase in the rate of growth of output and capital per capita which, eventually, will converge towards the long run equilibrium value (which is zero). The transition to a higher accu-mulation path can be easily explained. When the system switches to a financial system with two enforcement problems (and an equity market), the total amount of resources transferred and invested in capital production increases since there is no loss of resources in the process of direct enforcement. Hence, the model is able to provide an explanation for the positive impact of equity market development on the real rate of growth.

6. Final Considerations

Is financial development only a side-show of the process of economic development, or does it play a crucial role in the determination of real resource allocation?

In the last decades a new and deep wave of interest on this issue has stimulated many theoretical investigations. Mainly, these studies have aimed at the determination of the channels through which financial development could interact with economic growth and capital accumulation. Backed by a very strong support of the empirical evidence, which shows that the development of financial markets, instruments and institutions is strongly linked with economic development, economists have tried to analyse the possible mechanisms of interaction between the real and the financial side of the economic systems. Notwithstanding the huge efforts, this research has answered only to few questions, and many others issue needs to be addressed. The strong ties between financial development and growth cannot be fully understood if not within a clear theory of how agents interact in an environment where information are not uniformly distributed and where new financial instruments and markets evolve as a consequence of those distortions.

On the wake of the developments of the literature on asymmetric information and optimal financial contract, a new path of research has been initiated and is currently under development. These studies give an account of the co-evolution of real and financial markets on the basis of solutions to problems of adverse selection and moral hazard between investor and firm-borrower.

Our objective, here, was to determine the common features of these recent studies, in order to point out the marginal value added by this research to the large literature on finance and growth and, more importantly, possible future developments. By following the most recent research developments, we discuss four frameworks which show, mainly, that the assumptions regarding the nature of informational asymmetries between agents are extremely important in the determination of the possible interrelationship between financial market structure and the process of capital accumulation. It is very intuitive to argue that adverse selection can generate credit rationing and reduce the amount of funds channelled towards investments (Bencivenga and Smith, 1993), or it can induce screening, and, therefore, reduce the amount of investments through monitoring costs (Bose and Cothren, 1997). It has also been verified that simple or more complex form of moral hazard can induce agents to develop new form of contracts and securities; the development of equity markets is one very significant example (Boyd and Smith, 1998; Blackburn, Bose, Capasso, 2004).

From the above exercise, one can understand that the development of financial markets is a multifaceted and complex process, difficult to explain in its integrity. Further research needs to point towards more specific and detailed issues if it wants to capture the main features of the strong ties between financial development and economic development.

Notes

1. There are several studies which broadly survey the literature on finance and growth: Pagano (1993) and Levine (1997), to quote some among others. However, our objective differs from that of these studies in two major respects. One is that we focus on that specific part of the literature on finance and growth – not yet organically examined – which focuses on the assumption of information asymmetry; the other is that we provide a detailed microeconomic analysis of these models in an attempt to outline the common methodological approach followed by this literature.
2. The two-period structure greatly simplifies the analysis since it allows separation between the phase of capital production (which usually is subject to information frictions) from that of output production.
3. This assumption implies that all income is saved. Thus, the possible effects of financial activity on growth do not derive from factors concerning the choice of the optimal consumption/saving ratio.
4. This assumption is important to the extent that it determines the alternative cost of being credit rationed.
5. Note that this condition is more restrictive than simply assuming a more efficient storing technology for L type borrowers, $\beta_L > \beta_H$, since $p_L > p_H$.
6. The assumption of constant returns to scale is a common assumption in this class of models since it simplifies the analysis considerably. Indeed, the financial contract is designed in the first period by taking as given the price of capital which, instead, is determined in the second period. As a consequence, if the latter is given and it does not depend on the amount of capital produced, then there are no problems of dynamic inconsistency.
7. That is the expected return on the loan must equal the return on the storing technology.
8. It is straightforward to verify that the expression in (11) is also the rate of growth of output per firm and the rate of growth of total output. It may be verified that an equilibrium with a constant rate of growth requires a constant price of capital, $\rho_t = \rho$ and, therefore, a constant level of credit rationing, $\pi_{Lt} = \pi$. In the case where there were no informational asymmetries, the rate of growth would be maximum since there would be no rationing, $\pi = 1$.
9. As in the previous model, this gives the alternative cost to lending and it determines the rate of interest on the loan.
10. The H type borrower who reveals her type will obtain the best contract given lender's alternative cost. That is, she will get the highest amount of loan, $q_{Ht} = w_t$, the interest rate $R_{Ht} = Q\varepsilon\rho_{t+1}/p_H$ and she will not be credit rationed, $\pi_H = 1$.
11. It is not optimal to screen always since screening is costly. What the lender does in the screening contract is to announce a probability that a borrower claiming to be L type will be monitored.
12. It follows that the size of the investment in the stochastic technologies needs to be bounded and the amount of savings must exceed this limit in order to have the safe one in use at each point in time.
13. The fact that it is the borrower (rather than the lender) who chooses the contractual terms does not imply any formal difference in the analysis. The reason is that, since lender always receives zero profit, the contract is solved by determining the maximum utility for the borrower.

14. Therefore, the riskiness of the technology is a function of the project, x_t. One can easily verify that, other things being the same, the expected return on the technology is a concave function of the project.
15. In other words, when the home technology runs together with the main project it is more productive, for example because the borrower acquires further skills.
16. The 'first best' refers to a situation in which both effort and project are observable.

References

Atje, R. and Jovanovic, B. (1993) Stock markets and development. *European Economic Review* 37: 632–640.

Auerbach, P. and Siddiki, J. U. (2004) Financial liberalisation and economic development: an assessment. *Journal of Economic Surveys* 18, 3: 231–265.

Bagehot, W. (1873, 1962 edition) *Lombard Street*. Homewood IL: Richard D. Irwin.

Becsi, Z and Wang, P. (1997) Financial development and growth. *Economic Review, Federal Reserve Bank of Atlanta*, 46–62.

Bencivenga, V., Smith, B. and Starr, R. M. (1996) Equity markets, transactions costs, and capital accumulation: an illustration. *World Bank Economic Review* 10, 2: 241–265.

Bencivenga, V. R. and Smith, B. (1991) Financial intermediation and endogenous growth. *Review of Economic Studies* 58: 195–209.

Bencivenga, V. R. and Smith, B. (1993) Some consequences of credit rationing in an endogenous growth model. *Journal of Economic Dynamics and Control* 17: 97–122.

Bernanke, B. and Gertler, M. (1989) Agency costs, net worth, and business fluctuation. *American Economic Review* 79: 14–31.

Blackburn, K. and Hung, V. (1998) A theory of growth, financial development and trade. *Economica* 65: 107–124.

Blackburn, K., Bose, N. and Capasso, S. (2004) Financial development, financial choice and economic growth. *Review of Development Economics*, forthcoming.

Bose, N. and Cothren, R. (1996) Equilibrium loan contracts and endogenous growth in the presence of asymmetric information. *Journal of Monetary Economics* 38: 363–376.

Bose, N. and Cothren, R. (1997) Asymmetric information and loan contracts in a neo-classical growth model. *Journal of Money, Credit, and Banking* 29: 423–439.

Boyd, J. and Smith, B. (1996) The coevolution of real and financial sectors in the growth process. *World Bank Economic Review* 10: 2, 371–396.

Boyd, J. and Smith, B. (1998) The evolution of debt and equity markets in economic development. *Economic Theory* 12: 519–560.

De Gregorio, J. and Guidotti, P. (1995) Financial development and economic growth. *World Development* 433–448.

Demirgüç-Kunt, A. and Levine, R. (1996) Stock market development and financial inter-mediaries: stylized facts. *World Bank Economic Review* 10: 2, 291–321.

Diamond, D. (1984) Financial intermediation and delegated monitoring. *Review of Economic Studies* 51: 393–414.

Gale, D. and Hellwig, M. (1985) Incentive-compatible debt contracts: the one-period problem. *Review of Economic Studies* 52: 647–663.

Goldsmith, R. Y. (1969) *Financial Structure and Development*. New Haven CT: Yale University Press.

Greenwood, J. and Jovanovic, B. (1990) Financial development, growth, and the distribution of income. *Journal of Political Economy* 98: 1076–1107.

Gurley, J. G. and Shaw, E. S. (1955) Financial aspects of economic development. *American Economic Review* 45: 515–538.

Gurley, J. G. and Shaw, E. S. (1960) *Money in a Theory of Finance*. Washington DC: Brookings Institute.

Gurley, J. G. and Shaw, E. S. (1967) Financial structure and economic development. *Economic Development and Cultural Change* 15: 257–268.

Hicks, J. (1969) *A Theory of Economic History*, Oxford, Claredon Press

King, R. and Levine R. (1993a) Finance and growth: Schumpeter might be right. *Quarterly Journal of Economics* 108: 717–737.

King, R. G. and Levine, R. (1993b) Finance entrepreneurship, and growth: theory and evidence. *Journal of Monetary Economics* 32: 513–542.

Korajczyk, R. (1996) A measure of stock market integration for developed and emerging markets. *World Bank Economic Review* 10, 2: 267–289.

Levine, R. (1991) Stock markets, growth and tax policy. *Journal of Finance* 46: 1445–1465.

Levine, R. and Zervos, S. (1996) Stock market development and long-run growth. *World Bank Economic Review* 10, 2: 223–239.

Levine, R. and Zervos, S. (1998) Stock markets, banks and economic growth. *American Economic Review* 88: 537–557.

Levine, R. (1997) Financial development and economic growth: views and agenda. *Journal of Economic Literature* XXXV, 688–726.

McKinnon, R. I. (1973) *Money and Capital in Economic Development*. Washington DC: Brookings Institution.

Pagano, M (1993) Financial markets and growth: an overview. *European Economic Review* 37: 613–622.

Rothschild, M. and Stiglitz, J. (1976) Equilibrium in competitive insurance markets: an essay on the economics of imperfect information. *Quarterly Journal of Economics* 90: 629–650.

Saint Paul, G., (1992) Technological choice, financial markets and economic development. *European Economic Review* 36: 763–781.

Schumpeter, J. (1934) *The Theory of Economic Development*. Leipzig, Cambridge MA: Harvard University Press

Stiglitz, J. and Weiss, A. (1981) Credit rationing in markets with imperfect information. *American Economic Review* 71: 393–410.

Townsend, R. (1979) Optimal contracts and competitive markets with costly state verification. *Journal of Economic Theory* 21, 2: 265–293.

Williamson, S. D. (1986) Costly monitoring, financial intermediation and equilibrium credit contracting. *Journal of Monetary Economics* 18: 159–179.

Williamson, S. D. (1987a) Costly monitoring, loan contracts, and equilibrium credit rationing. *Quarterly Journal of Economics* 102: 135–145.

Williamson, S. D. (1987b) Financial intermediation, business failures, and real business cycles. *Journal of Political Economy* 95: 1196–1216.

4

AN EXEGESIS ON CURRENCY AND BANKING CRISES

Janice Boucher Breuer

University of South Carolina

1. Introduction

The record of economic development and growth across countries, even looking back to the early 1900s, shows that currency crises are as commonplace and socio-economically diverse as banking crises. Often times, the two go hand in hand. Eichengreen and Bordo (2002) find that between 1973 and 1997, the frequency of twin crises (banking and currency crises) is about equal to the frequency of banking crises. For countries that experience financial crises – currency or banking crises or both, the economic losses can be large and disruptive with recovery times of 2–4 years.[1] The human toll exacted is not only financial and economic, but social, emotional, and political. Indonesia is one example.

In many episodes of financial crises, banking and currency problems are present together. That banks act as intermediaries for domestic and foreign currency transactions may, in part, explain their relationship. For this reason, it seems worthwhile to survey literature on the two in tandem. Currency and banking crises have some characteristics in common and may be causally related. Kaufman (1999, p. 4) notes that 'banking and currency crises both involve an actual or potential depreciation in the value of claims.' Both bank and currency markets deal in finance and intangibles. For both markets, soundness of and confidence in the market are important. Transactions in both markets can involve a time dimension. Finally, banks borrow and lend in domestic and foreign currency. Marion (1999) points out that banking and currency crises are attacks on price-fixing policies. For exchange rates, the price of domestic currency is fixed against foreign currency; for bank deposits, the rate of exchange between coin and currency and demand deposits is fixed by the required reserve ratio.[2]

Broadly speaking, financial crises are similar to wartimes to the extent that they heighten uncertainty in nearly all types of transactions, relationships, and decision-making. Information and incentive problems are exacerbated. The permeating pall of uncertainty cast by crises raises their costs and lengthens their duration. At the same time, crises reveal institutional, political, and economic weaknesses that may themselves contribute to crises in the first place. In the Chinese language, the character representing 'crisis' means 'danger and opportunity'. It may seem unsympathetic to suggest that crises present opportunity, but they present opportunity for building reforms that can strengthen a country and reduce the likelihood it will suffer crises again.[3] Trite statements like these however belie the cohesion, commitment, effort, endurance, and will necessary to establish change. Experience with many Asian, Eastern European and former Soviet economies as well as with advanced countries such as Japan demonstrates that the pace of reform can be slow, stymied, and subject to civil unrest.

Because crises interfere with progress on economic growth, it seems natural that recent research on economic growth is being used as a springboard for understanding crises. Beginning with the seminal work of Barro (1991) who showed that countries with political instability are likely to experience lower rates of economic growth, the nexus between law, politics, sociology, and economics in understanding success in economic growth are being studied. Factors like trust, democracy, corruption, property rights, social cohesion, and the rule of law are being considered for their contribution to economic growth.[4]

Not surprisingly, the latest developments in the literature on financial crises – currency and banking crises – are beginning to highlight the role played by 'social capital', 'social infrastructure', or 'institutions'.[5] Answers like 'budget and current account deficits', 'hyperinflation', 'depletion of foreign reserves', 'contagion', and 'overlending/overborrowing' offered by earlier models beget deeper questions. What institutional factors set the stage for hyperinflation, foreign reserve loss, inconsistent policy and/or excessive borrowing and lending? These are important questions coming from a new and different perspective that are beginning to be asked. Answers to these and related questions will likely set the stage for governance, anticorruption, financial regulation and supervision policy measures being considered by the IMF and World Bank.

The remainder of the paper is organized as follows. The defining characteristics of currency and banking crises and a summary overview of twentieth century experience with them are discussed in Section 2 The historical development of the literature on crises up through, what I call, fourth-generation models, is set out in Section 3. A brief digression relating institutions is also contained in this section. The empirical work on crises is reviewed in Section 4. Policy options for preventing or mitigating crises are surveyed in Section 5 and directions for future research appear in Section 6.

2. Currency and Banking Crises

2.1 Identifying Currency Crises

Currency crises get their name because they show up as a 'crisis' overtly marked by a steep, sustained drop in a currency's value. The steep decline in the currency value is the identifying characteristic of a currency crisis. However, a currency crisis is defined as a 'crisis' because of the ensuing negative economic effects. These include recession and unemployment; banking and business failures; inflation; reductions in investment, and losses in wealth. Less obvious is a heightened level of uncertainty in business and other transactions. Currency crises can be devaluations brought about by governmental action or forced by private market speculators, or an outcome of the two. Currency crises are ordinarily defined with regard to some type of fixed exchange rate though they need not be. For example, the sustained dollar appreciation during 1981–85 might be considered a currency crisis for the USA.

What are called 'currency crises' today were called 'balance of payments crises' forty years ago. Whatever the name, they are first and foremost defined (or perhaps recognized) by the drop in currency value. This first condition is considered necessary in defining a currency crisis. Frankel and Rose (1996) in identifying episodes of currency crises take the drop in the currency value to be 25% devaluation combined with a 10% increase in the rate of it. The second condition, not used alone in identifying a currency crisis but rather as secondary, is a rapid depletion of foreign reserves. Kaminsky and Reinhart (1999) use a weighted average of a country's devaluation and foreign reserve loss. A tertiary condition used in identifying a currency crisis is central bank action to increase overnight interest rates. Eichengreen *et al.* (1996) use a weighted average of these three measures.

Though the onset of a currency crisis is demarcated by a steep and sustained drop in a currency's value, it need not be the initiating factor. Imagine a world with one currency. Crises of exchange (payment) between two countries could still arise. Crises of exchange could arise because of hyperinflation or because of balance sheet problems for the government, corporate, and/or banking sector. So, the line demarcating when a currency crisis occurs is an identifying point, and not necessarily a starting point.

2.2 Identifying Banking Crises

Systemic banking crises (or banking sector distress) are defined to be insolvency of the banking system. Insolvency occurs when asset values fall short of liabilities. That is, capital turns negative. An alternative definition recognizes a high ratio of nonperforming loans to assets. Because of difficulty in measuring solvency for the banking system and because some cutoff criteria are necessary, the identification of banking crises is based on one or more of four generally accepted measures used by researchers in dating crises. According to Demirguc-Kunt and Detragiache (1997) these are: (1) ratio of nonperforming assets to total assets in the banking system exceeds 10%; (2) the cost of a rescue operation was at least 2% of GDP; (3) the episode involved large scale nationalization of banks; and (4) extensive bank runs took place or other emergency measures were enacted by the government. These criteria are often also combined with anecdotal information as to the onset of banking crises collected by various government agencies.

Similar to the discussion of identifying currency crises, the four criteria merely serve as the identification point for banking crises and not necessarily their starting point. That is, the four features reveal a banking crisis but not what started it. As with currency crises, banking crises also carry in their wake the same negative outcomes as currency crises. However, tumult in the banking system wrought by a banking crisis is more disruptive than a currency crisis alone. Kaufman (1999) finds that the loss in output and recovery time for banking crises is worse than for currency crises. Bordo and Shwartz (2002) also find the loss in output for banking crises to be more severe than for currency crises.

2.3 *Similarities with Sovereign Debt Crises*

While currency and banking crises have received top billing in the literature since the mid-1990s, it would be remiss not to mention the sovereign debt crises of the 1980s and their similarities with currency and banking crises. Sovereign debt crises share aspects of currency and banking crises together. A sovereign debt crisis occurs when a national government is unable to pay interest or principal on its government-issued debts to foreign, private creditors due to a shortage of foreign reserves. This is similar to a banking crisis except that it is now a public rather than a private institution that is insolvent. As with insolvency of private banks, the insolvency of the government interferes with its ability to borrow and lend. Sovereign debt crises also result in currency crises because the shortage of foreign reserves in addition to the ensuing capital flight strains the ability to maintain a fixed exchange rate. Many aspects of the sovereign debt crises of the 1980s appear in the Asian financial crisis except with the Asian crisis unproductive borrowing originated with the private sector rather than the government.

2.4 *Historical Experience with Crises*

The twentieth century experience with financial crises may be the most often studied but they are by no means the first. Crises related to money and inflation date back to 200 BC. According to Davies (2002), during the second Punic War between Rome and Carthage (218–201 BC), Roman rulers debased their coinage to pay troops and this led to inflation. He also notes that the practice of debasing is carried out by later emperors such as Nero (54 AD) and Constantine (313 AD) and that Diocletian (301 AD) imposed direct controls on prices and wages to help contain inflation. As well, the exchange of foreign currency is not a twentieth century or even nineteenth century phenomenon. 'Money changers' have provided a service of exchanging one currency for another since, at least the times of Jesus Christ.

The historical record of currency and banking crises dating back to the 1880s is substantively reviewed in Bordo *et al.* (2001) which provides, in large part, the basis for the discussion below. Bordo *et al.* consider four regimes: the Gold Standard (1880–1913), the interwar years (1913–39), the Bretton Woods era (1940–71) and the post-Bretton Woods era (1972–98) across which they examine crises.[6] Data on 21 countries is available from 1880 to 1971 and for the most recent period, 56 countries are covered. Crises are measured as zero-one events so that the magnitude, of say, a devaluation or banking system insolvency, is not under consideration. However, statistics on the frequency, duration, and associated output losses of crises are provided.

2.4.1 *Historical Record on Currency Crises*

Table 1 presents summary statistics culled from Bordo *et al.* (2001) on experience with currency crises. During the Gold Standard, the 21 countries considered span Europe, Scandinavia, and North and South America. For the 21 countries considered over the 34 year period, 11 had currency crises. There are 22 currency crises in all, five of which occur with banking crises. From 1909 to 1913, there are no currency crises.

For the interwar years, there are no currency crises from 1913 to 1919. Spanning the two periods then is an 11 year period between 1909 and 1919 void of any currency crises. From 1920 to 1939, there are 48 currency crises and all countries experience a currency crisis at least once. Of the 48 currency crises, 16 occur jointly with banking crises.

From 1940 to 1971, there is a six-year period absent of currency crises lasting from 1940 to 1946. The Bretton Woods agreement was signed in 1944 establishing par values of currencies against the US dollar which was convertible to gold at \$35 an ounce. For the same 21 countries examined earlier, there are 45 currency crises, 12 of which occur in 1971, the *de facto* end year of the Bretton Woods agreement. All countries save Japan experience at least one currency crisis. There is one incidence of a currency crisis coincident with a banking crisis – Brazil. (In fact, that is the only incidence of a banking crisis, too).

Table 1. Summary Statistics of Currency Crises, 1880–2002.

Regimes	Periods	Number of currency crises
Gold Standard	1880–1913	22
Interwar years	1913–1919	0
	1920–1939	48
Bretton Woods era	1940–1971	45
Post-Bretton Woods era	1972–1998	162
	1999–2002	7[a]

Source: Bordo *et al.* (2001).

Note[a]: I will discuss the specifics behind the summary statistics without presenting the complete data from the Tables in Bordo *et al.* (2001). The interested reader should consult Bordo *et al.* (2001).

For the 1972–98 period covered by Bordo *et al.* (2001) 56 countries are considered, spanning all continents but Antarctica and the Artic. No currency crises are reported during the first three years. Subsequently, there are 162 counts of currency crises, experienced at least once by all countries save Germany, Hong Kong, and Taiwan.

The record on currency crises shows there is little immunity from them. Currency crises befall industrialized, emerging, and developing countries. They are spread across the world and not localized to a specific region. Some are scattered over time and some clustered at points in time.

2.4.2 *Historical Record on Banking Crises*

Table 2 presents statistics on banking crises culled from Bordo *et al.* (2001) which relies on Caprio and Klingebiel (1996, 1999) for data covering 1980s–90s. Banking crises selected for study are systemic crises only. Twenty-one countries are included for the 1880–1971 period and 56 countries for the 1972–98 period.

Over the 1880–1913 period, there are thirty banking crises. No banking crises occur after 1908 and no crises occur for six countries. Of the 30 crises, five are joint with currency crises.

The 1919–39 period begins with a quiet spell – there are no banking crises until 1920. Spanning the two time periods, then, is an 11 year period between 1909 and 1919 in which there are no banking crises. Over this same time span, no currency crises are recorded, either. After 1919, there are 47 banking crises, sixteen of which are concurrent with currency crises. Australia and the UK are the only countries immune to banking crises.

The period 1940–71 is distinguished from the others by the absence of any banking crisis except one occurring in Brazil in 1963. Indeed, by this time, countries had established central banks and their function as lender of last resort had, in many cases, already been tried and tested. Also, during this time, regulation over the domestic banking systems was more restrictive than subsequently and capital flows were low and restricted. These factors may have helped prevent overly risky domestic lending and capital-flight led banking crises.

Table 2. Summary Statistics of Banking Crises, 1880–2002.

Regimes	Periods	Number of banking crises
Gold Standard	1880–1913	30
Interwar years	1913–1919	0
	1920–1939	47
Bretton Woods era	1940–1971	1
Post-Bretton Woods era	1972–1998	60
	1999–2002*	3

Source: Bordo *et al.* (2001);
* based on Caprio and Klingebiel (2003).

Recorded for the period 1972–98 and 56 country panel are 60 banking crises of which 17 are joint with currency crises. Thirteen of the 56 countries have no banking crisis. Eight of these are European countries and two (Austria and Belgium) experience neither a currency crisis nor a banking crisis. Banking crises do not appear until 1976. Combined with the previous sample, there is thus a 37 year period over which only one banking crisis is recorded.

The historical record on banking crises shows some large spans of time virtually free of banking crises. Outside of these time spans, there is nearly one banking crisis reported every year. The record also shows that as with currency crises, banking crises breach socioeconomic and geographical barriers.

3. Models of Currency and Banking Crises

A review of the literature on currency and banking crises finds they share a parallel development. First-generation models of currency crises are based on macroeconomic fundamentals and speculation. This is true of banking crises, too. Second-generation models of currency and banking crises introduce speculation based on self-fulfilling expectations that need not be tied to fundamentals. Third-generation models of currency crises use an overborrowing/overlending paradigm where their relationship to activities in the banking system is introduced. These models emphasize incentives and opportunities that invite lending and borrowing for overly risky or unproductive projects. Third generation models of banking crises are also developed with the same paradigm except that activities in the currency market are introduced. Third generation models consider 'twin crises' as opposed to currency or banking crises independently.

Current thinking on currency and banking crises, what I call fourth-generation models, considers the role of institutional factors. In these models, factors like politics (voting, checks and balances, etc); civil order including rule of law, trust, ethnic tensions, culture, social norms; property rights; legal origin; and types of governance be it over the financial sector or the trade sector, etc. are important determinants of economic outcomes. These variables are important because they impact information, uncertainty, and transactions costs and can affect the efficiency of decision-making.

Another parallel aspect of the development of the literature on currency and banking crises is that their development is in response to actual experience. First-generation models were developed in response to the sovereign debt crisis of Latin America of the 1980s, second-generation models to the European ERM crisis (1992–93) and Mexican crisis (1994–95), and third-generation models to the Asian crisis (1997–98) (see Saxena, 2004). Likewise, the banking crisis literature has evolved following historic experience with crises beginning with bank runs in the nineteenth century, asset mismatch problems, on to the effects of deregulation and deposit insurance, asset price cycles, and over-lending as in the case with Japan.

A final parallel aspect of the development of the currency and banking crisis literature is the empirical methods used to investigate and predict currency crises.

Studies of both types of crises typically use multinomial probit models (because of the zero-one definition of crises) and event studies. Forecasting models ('early warning indicators') are also commonly developed because of the obvious desire to avoid future crises by predicting when they will happen.

3.1 *First, Second, and Third Generation Models of Currency Crises*

The earliest models of currency crises belong to Salant and Henderson (1978), Krugman (1979), and Flood and Garber (1984).[7] Agenor *et al.* (1991) and Blackburn (1993) review these models. The models begin with a fixed rate (no band) regime and mobile capital. These are essentially models of balance of payments crises instigated by government budget deficits funded by the central bank. In these models, persistent increases in the money supply (and related inflation) deliver a speculative attack. Speculators recognize that the exchange rate commitment cannot be maintained in the face of the money supply increase and so they sell the currency that is in excess. Their action forces devaluation as the central bank's foreign reserves become dangerously low. Connolly (1986) and Krugman and Rotemberg (1990) extend these models to a crawling peg regime and a fixed rate with band.

First generation models explain currency crises by poor domestic macroeconomic conditions such as large, recurring budget deficits monetized by the central bank; hyperinflation; and large, recurring current account deficits and their attendant depletion of foreign reserves. All of these conditions can incite a speculative attack on the currency. These types of models were used to explain the sovereign debt crisis of Latin America in the 1980s but they also explain instances of poor macro-management as in the case of the USA during the latter years of the Bretton Woods agreement.

First generation models also point out that external macroeconomic conditions can set the stage for a crisis as in Dooley (1997).[8] A rise in the real interest rate of developed countries can trigger large, sustained capital outflows from emerging and developing countries that drains their foreign reserves.

Second generation models have been developed by Obstfeld (1994) and Calvo (1995), Eichengreen *et al.* (1996), and Cole and Kehoe (1996). Flood and Marion (1998) and Rangvid (2001) provide reviews. These models are non-linear models that emphasize that speculative attacks can occur in the absence of poor macroeconomic fundamentals. Crises can arise out of self-fulfilling attacks. In these models, herding behavior, information cascades, and contagion play a role (see Saxena, 2004, and Pericoli and Sbraca, 2003, for a survey). A belief by speculators that current policy is inconsistent with sound long run economic fundamentals or that it cannot be sustained in the future can bring about an attack even while current fundamentals remain sound. An example of policy inconsistency would be maintenance of a fixed exchange rate in the face of unemployment that is trending upward. Speculators are smart enough to realize that the political cost of maintaining the peg at the expense of dealing with future increases in unemployment is too high. So, they recognize devaluation is a likely, eventual outcome.

Prisoner's dilemma mentality sets in. Speculators know devaluation is likely, they just don't know when. Not wanting to be left the last to act, they sell domestic currency now. Herding ensues and a full-scale speculative attack emerges even before unemployment becomes a problem.

Second-generation models were introduced to explain the European Exchange Rate Mechanism (ERM) and Mexican crises. These crises did not appear to be instigated by macroeconomic fundamentals but by inconsistent policy and political events. In Europe, Britain, France, Italy, and Sweden suffered currency crises because of policy inconsistent with long run maintenance of their peg to the German mark. Also, referenda on monetary union (referred to as the 'Maastricht Treaty') were rejected by the Dutch and narrowly passed by the French. These events raised concerns that fixity could even be maintained in the future despite macroeconomic fundamentals that were sound. In Mexico, assassinations of two government officials, (one a candidate for presidency) and uprisings in the Chiapas raised concerns about continuance of economic reforms, progress, and capital inflows.

The Asian crisis motivated the development of third-generation models. Third-generation models explicitly make a connection between the banking and international currency markets. Indeed, the Asian crisis has been called a 'financial crisis' because it involved widespread banking and currency claim problems. That banking and currency crises would be coterminous seems obvious. Yet, early models of the interaction between problems in the banking and international sectors by Diaz-Alejandro (1985) and Velasco (1987) received scant attention until the Asian crisis was well underway. Diaz-Alejandro (1985), writing about the Chilean experience and Velasco (1987), writing about the southern cone countries warned of the dynamic feedback between banking problems and currency crises. Likewise, models of the sovereign debt crisis could have served as a warning about the consequences of over-borrowing whether public or private.

Relative to first and second generation models, the Asian crisis seemed to be an anomaly. Macroeconomic fundamentals were strong – annual growth rates were high, inflation rates were low, budget deficits were low, current account deficits were manageable, capital inflows were strong, and political stability reigned. However, these statistics obscured a burgeoning problem in the banking sector – bad loans to domestic borrowers and unhedged, short-term borrowing from foreign banks. The bad loan problem was considered to be an outcome of incentives and opportunities for 'too much lending'.

First, liberalization of capital controls raised the level of capital inflows to emerging market economies and this meant the capacity to lend (by both banks and the government) to the domestic sector widened. Necessarily, this would mean higher risk loans would be made (see Auerbach and Siddiki, 2004). Second, given the massive capital inflows, opportunities for graft and corruption ('crony capitalism') widened. This meant more loans were made for ill-founded projects. Third, domestic financial liberalization, particularly with regard to interest rate controls, meant more competition across banks. Increased competition meant some banks were more willing to gamble by making riskier loans with upside potential that could substantially increase their profitability and market share. Fourth, deposit insurance provided to banks by government deposit insurance schemes and also provided to foreign lenders through the IMF encouraged domestic banks to make riskier loans than they would have absent the insurance. This is referred to as the 'moral hazard' problem. These four factors are by no means mutually exclusive and one or more were present in the Asian crisis.

Numerous contributions to third-generation models of currency crises have been made by Calvo (1995), Goldfajn and Valdes (1997), Miller (1996), Sachs *et al.* (1996), McKinnon and Pill (1998), Chang and Velasco (1998), Krugman (1998), Corsetti *et al.* (1998), Buch and Heinrich (1999), Kim and Lee (1999), Allen and Gale (2000), Burnside *et al.* (2000), Schneider and Tornell (2000), and Dekle and Kletzer (2001).[9] Wei and Wu (2001) make a related contribution modeling borrowing arising from crony capitalism.

3.2 *First, Second, and Third-generation Models of Banking Crises*

The taxonomy I use to review the development of models of banking crises is the same I use for models of currency crises. Thus, I consider first, second, and third-generation models of banking crises. I will later consider fourth-generation models, too. Though models of banking crises have not elsewhere been organized this way, I choose this structure because of the parallels I mentioned earlier that I see in the development of these two topics.

First-generation models of banking crises use the experience of the Great Depression as a starting point as in Mishkin (1978). In these models, poor macroeconomic conditions that recognizably may result in consumer defaults and business failures and in turn lead to banking problems incite a speculative attack on bank deposits. Given macroeconomic weakness, bank customers speculate that banks do not or will not have the cash available to meet their withdrawals. Consequently, customers run to the bank to withdraw all their deposits believing that if they are the first to act, they will be paid back in full. Unfortunately, a herd of customers emerges and indeed the ability of the bank to completely satisfy the cash withdrawals fails. The outflow of deposits in turn forces the bank's closure.

Flood and Garber (1984) and Diamond and Dybvig (1983) are the seminal works on banking crises modeled as a self-fulfilling attack on bank deposits. Their work can be categorized as a second generation model because the attack can occur in the absence of weak macroeconomic or banking conditions. Attacks in these models can be triggered when speculators recognize that current policy aimed at one objective will likely be traded off to secure another objective. Interestingly, Diamond and Dybvig's model provided the basis for the development of second generation models of currency crises.

Third generation models of banking crises are 'credit cycle' models that characterize a boom-bust nature inherent in borrowing and lending. Gavin and Hausmann (1996) and Kiyotaki and Moore (1997) are the seminal works. In these models, banking crises originate with the asset side of a bank's balance sheet. During economic booms, lending becomes profligate for a few reasons: (1) during boom times when real estate and stock market values are increasing rapidly, banks are willing to finance larger loans owing to the increased value of collateral backing the loan; and (2) the rise in the value of equities owned by banks (in banks able to acquire shares in corporations) enables them to make more loans. When a bust comes, the depression in collateral and equities value impedes the bank's ability to make loans on the same order of magnitude. A credit crunch ensues which can reverberate throughout the economy making it more likely that loan defaults will increase and a crisis ensue.

Third-generation models contrast to the first and second generation models where events on the liabilities (deposits) side perpetrate the crisis. They share some features of first-generation models because poor macroeconomic conditions are the banks undoing, so to speak. However, in third-generation models, the failure of banks to understand the credit risk they are undertaking as well as to monitor their loans and use due diligence during boom times contributes to the crises. Third-generation models of banking crises have actively been used in the development of third-generation models of currency crises that explicitly recognize the interaction between the banking system and currency markets.

3.3 *Fourth-generation Models of Financial Crises*

In keeping with the taxonomy I have been using to organize the development of the literature on banking and currency crises, I next introduce what I call 'fourth-generation' models. I group banking and currency crises together and refer to them as 'financial crises'. For fourth generation models, answers like budget and current account deficits, hyperinflation, self-fulfilling attacks, excessive borrowing and lending, and the like beget deeper questions. What institutional factors set the stage for hyperinflation, foreign reserve loss, herding, and inconsistent policy? In these models, economic and financial rules and regulations, shareholder rights, transparency and supervision over the financial system, and government distortions are emphasized. Also considered are legal variables such as legal origin, shareholder protection, property rights, enforcement of contracts, political variables such as democracy and political instability, and sociological variables such as corruption, trust, culture, ethnicity, and the like.[10] The development of fourth-generation models of financial crises is in the very early stages and so there remains much work that can be done. However, before discussing fourth-generation models, an overview of institutions seems useful.

3.3.1 *A Digression on Institutions*

What are institutions? According to Lin and Nugent (1995), institutions are defined broadly as 'a set of humanly devised behavioral rules that govern and shape the interactions of human beings, in part by helping them to form expectations of what other people will do'.

Implicit in this definition is the notion that uncertainty is prevalent in interactions. In fact, uncertainty is featured to some degree or another in every transaction and every decision.[11] Whether obvious or not, uncertainty is attempted to be overcome, reduced, or its effects shared through legal structures, social norms, rules of the game, or an accepted modicum of trust. These are what Rodrik (1999) refers to as 'non-market institutions'. He says '...the market economy is necessarily 'embedded' in a set of non-market institutions'. In Hall and Jones (1999) terminology, this would be 'social infrastructure' and in Knack and Keefer's (1997) terminology 'social capital'. Because currency and financial markets are particularly subject to uncertainty, the role of institutions may be that much more important to them, especially if crises are to be avoided or their prevalence at least minimized. In fourth-generation models of financial crises, institutions that facilitate a well-functioning currency and banking system are explored.

3.3.2 *Fourth-generation/Institutional Models of Financial Crises*

Theoretical, institutional models of financial crises are few and far between at present despite media speak and empirical studies which make claims that financial governance, corruption, and implicit or accepted legal practices are contributing factors. Claims that 'institutions matter' stem from accounts of events that took place during the Asian crisis as well as the swell of evidence from empirical research on economic growth demonstrating the importance of institutional features in macroeconomic outcomes. See Hall and Jones (1999), Temple and Johnson (1998), Acemoglu *et al.* (2002), Rodrik *et al.* (2002) and Alesina *et al.* (2002). As well, research at the IMF has begun to take into account financial structure, legal regime, and macro institutional indicators recognizing that these affect economic decision-making and thus vulnerability to crises. Because of the paucity of theoretical, institutional models and the fact that most of them have emerged to explain the Asian crisis, my discussion in this section will address twin-crises (or financial crisis) style models.

One recent contribution to institutional modeling of crises is Johnson *et al.* (2000) who use a version of Jensen and Meckling's (1976) agency model. In the agency model, the potential conflict of interest between managers and shareholders leads to the possibility of stealing (misappropriation, corruption) and ex ante, gives rise to monitoring, screening, and covenants placed on managers. La Porta *et al.* (1998) point out that different financial, contractual arrangements such as shareholder versus creditor rights and poor enforcement of those rights can matter to the likelihood that a conflict will arise. In Johnson *et al.* weak corporate governance engenders a higher probability of stealing which leads investors to speculate that asset values are overstated which in turn leads them to withdraw funds. As this happens, asset values decline. Johnson *et al.* reason the model can also explain reductions in currency value using the same story.

Rajan and Zingales (1998) argue that in relationship-based economies where contracts are poorly enforced, capital inflows are likely to be shorter term. This is because foreign investors, realizing the potential for malfeasance and misappropriation in such a system, are only willing to commit funds short-term. Consequently, such countries are more prone to financial crises when beset by adverse shocks. Rajan and Zingales use the Asian crisis as an example. Agenor and Aizenman (1999) also develop a model to explain the Asian crisis. In their model, banks play a central role but face enforcement and verification costs associated with loans. Their model is motivated by the observation that weaknesses in legal infrastructure contribute to financial crises. They show a debt overhang may emerge in response to higher enforcement and verification costs or an expected negative shock to output. Chan-Lau and Chen (1998) develop a model of a financial intermediary who lends the deposits of foreign lenders to domestic borrowers. However, since lending is subject to costly loan monitoring, intermediaries may choose not to intermediate when monitoring costs are high. This suppresses capital inflows. An increase in the strength of economic fundamentals makes the intermediary willing to intermediate without monitoring so that capital inflows (in turn lent domestically) now increase. However, since no monitoring was undertaken, investment projects receiving loans become riskier. When a negative shock occurs, capital outflows materialize and a crisis ensues.

Aside from the models mentioned above, there are a number of theoretical models not specifically developed for financial crises that could nevertheless be adapted as foundations for them. I include in these models Acemoglu and Verdier's (2000) model of inefficient policies and institutions as the outcome of political power, Shleifer and Vishny's (1993) model of corruption, and models of shirking, product liability, and risk and insurance. These models all make central a potential conflict of interest which I view as essential to modeling crises.

4. Empirical Studies of Financial Crises

In this section, I choose to cover empirical work on financial crises dated 1996 or later. The date serves as a 'rebirth' of the literature on currency (or balance of payments) and banking crises. Prior to it and by comparison, relatively few articles were published on these topics. Subsequently, work begins to appear spurred by the onset of numerous currency and banking crises, some of them contemporaneous, and many of them intertwined with issues of economic growth. I focus the first section below almost entirely on 'twin crises/financial crises' (and hence largely on third generation models) and pay minor attention to related work that considers separately, currency or banking crises.[12] In the second section, I review empirical studies of institutional models of banking and currency crises.

4.1 Empirical Studies of Twin Crises/Third-generation Models

Fanfare on the joint occurrence of currency and banking crises owes to Kaminsky and Reinhart (1999) who coined the term 'twin crises'. Their work explores crisis endogeneity and finds that in liberalized financial markets, banking crises tend to precede currency crises but that there is feedback between the two.[13] They also find some common causes of crises in weakening fundamentals and that twin crises tend to be more severe in terms of their economic effects than currency or banking crises, separately, a result echoed by Kaufman (1999) and Bordo *et al.* (2001). Kaminsky and Reinhart (1999) find a bunching of banking crises in the 1980s and 1990s while the number of currency crises per year over the period remains about the same. They posit that financial liberalization and high real interest rates in the USA as well as contagion could be the explanation.

They investigate crises using two techniques. The first is an event study showing the time series behavior of fifteen macroeconomic variables eighteen months prior to the crisis (currency, banking, or twin) and 18 months afterward, relative to 'tranquil' times. The second is a scoring method, which essentially locates crisis indicators as being ones that minimize the noise-to-signal (false positives) ratio. Their investigation finds that a financial shock, be it financial liberalization or capital account liberalization, generates a boom-bust cycle. Since they find weak macroeconomic fundamentals contribute to crises, they offer that it would be hard to characterize them as self-fulfilling. They also state that history offers lessons – recent crises share commonality with earlier crises in Latin America and Europe, a finding supported by Kamin (1999). In closely related work, Glick and Hutchinson (1999) find that twin crises are more common in financially liberalized emerging markets and that banking crises appear a leading indicator of currency crises. They conclude that openness of the capital account alongside liberalized financial markets spells crisis vulnerability.

Bordo *et al.* (2001) analyze 120 years of financial history and find that crisis frequency has doubled since 1973. However, they find little evidence that crises have grown more severe in terms of output losses or duration. Blame for crises, conceded in numerous other papers, is capital account openness and bailout systems. Indeed, they find banking crises are less likely when capital controls are in place although they find the reverse for currency crises. They also mention that currency crises tend to be exacerbated when the fixed exchange rate commitment is credible and insurance against exchange rate risk is provided. These conditions may lead to large foreign currency exposures by banks.

Corsetti *et al.* (1998) provide an exhaustive, detailed account of the factors, complexities, and interactions involved in precipitating the Asian crisis. These factors range from current account and budget deficits to real exchange rates to excessive bank lending and financial fragility as well as political instability. The paper largely points out that abundant investment projects, many of which turned out to be unprofitable due to cronyism or government intervention, excited capital inflows because of implicit guarantees of insurance either at the domestic or international level. Aided by capital account liberalization, strong capital inflows expanded opportunities for domestic lending. In the wake of domestic financial deregulation, domestic lenders pursued riskier projects. Such 'overlending' eventually precipitated a crisis as macroeconomic conditions soured and loans became nonperforming. Similar in spirit is Corbett and Vines (1999) and Yoshitomi and Ohno (1999).

All in all, shared characteristics of empirical studies of twin crises are that they: (1) rely on banking crisis data from Demirguc-Kunt and Detragiache (1997) and

Caprio and Klingebiel (1999); (2) identify currency crises dates using a few accepted practices; (3) are cross sectional; (4) focus on the 1970s-97 period; (5) use event studies or probit estimation; (6) typically provide estimates of duration and output losses associated with the crises; and (7) concentrate most on the Asian crisis.

Coincident conclusions from empirical studies of twin crises are that: (1) a vicious spiral between banks and the currency market can exacerbate banking and currency crises; (2) domestic financial liberalization encourages more risky lending by banks; (3) capital account liberalization makes a country more vulnerable to crises because of the reverse possibility that outflows in mass may occur; (4) domestic deposit insurance schemes and bailout provisions by the international community contribute to risky lending and add to vulnerability; (5) unhedged, short-term foreign exchange liabilities of banks contribute to the vicious spiral; (6) procrastination in adjusting a peg invites a large scale attack; (7) industrial policy by the government through directed lending makes the banking system vulnerable to crisis; (8) relationship lending (e.g. chaebols or cronyism) undermines the stability of banks; (9) twin crises are more severe in terms of output losses than currency or banking crises separately; (10) twin crises are more prolonged than currency or banking crises separately; and (11) twin crises afflict developing and emerging countries more so than industrial countries.

4.2 *Empirical Studies of Institutional Models/Fourth Generation Models*

Antecedents to the literature on what I have called 'fourth-generation models of financial crises' figure prominently over the past decade in the literature on economic growth. Recent empirical contributions (along with continuing controversy) come from Alesina *et al.* (2002), Acemoglu *et al.* (2002), and Rodrik *et al.* (2002). Acemoglu *et al.* conclude 'it appears that weak institutions cause volatility through a number of microeconomic, as well as macroeconomic, channels'.

Since the work of Schumpeter (1911), Gurley and Shaw (1955), and McKinnon (1973), it has been generally accepted that financial development contributes to economic growth.[14] Likewise, the virtues a stable currency can confer on an economy have long been acknowledged.[15] The Gold Standard and the Bretton Woods System as much as European Monetary Union was motivated by a desire to achieve gains a stable currency would bring. The observation of many developing and emerging countries 'fear of floating' is telling.[16] While it may seem a bit premature to say that the latest research has moved beyond investigating the link between 'credit and growth' and 'exchange rate system and economic performance' to the institutions that support a stable financial system, inclusive of the exchange rate regime, this is the tack I will take.[17] I believe empirical research into the effect of 'institutions' broadly speaking (i.e financial, economic, political, legal, and social) on financial (and other) outcomes will afford insight into the preconditions for crises.

I group the papers on institutions below as relating to: (a) currency crises and (b) banking crises.[18]

4.2.1 *Currency Crises and Institutions*

The bridge from third to fourth-generation models of currency crises comes through recognition, and by now acceptance, that financial liberalization measures, be they deregulation of the domestic financial sector or removal of capital controls, and that deposit insurance schemes, whether provided by the domestic government or international community, alter the incentive structure of transactions and thus redound to financial outcomes. Indeed, some third-generation models include measures of these variables in their analysis (Kaminsky and Reinhart, 1999; Aziz *et al.*, 2000).

Keeping in mind the definition of institutions given by Lin and Nugent (1995), as 'a set of humanly devised behavioral rules that govern and shape the interactions of human beings, in part by helping them to form expectations of what other people will do', there are a diverse set of variables that have been (and can be) explored for their significance to crises. In Mulder *et al.* (2002), (hereafter, MPR), these variables include macro institutional indicators, indicators of legal regimes, and corporate governance standards. MPR argue that the impact of macro institutional indicators and indicators of the legal regime affect the quality of the lending decisions and thereby the incidence of crises. Likewise, corporate governance standards affect the soundness of private sector transactions and may also indicate how involved the government is in business transactions.

The macro institutional and corporate governance variables used in MPR are in fact balance sheet indicators largely related to characteristics of public and private debt. These variables are 'institutional' in the sense that they provide more detail than with previously used measures of debt. For example, they have measures of the maturity structure of overall debt rather than an aggregate measure. This is a step in the right direction although it begets the question, what institutions influence the maturity structure of debt.[19] The more obvious institutional variables included in their work are indexes of: legal origin, creditor rights, shareholder rights, contract enforcement, and accounting standards all from La Porta *et al.* (1998). MPR undertake an event study as well as a probit estimation to consider the role of these factors in currency crises. They find that in addition to traditional variables like the current account deficit and overvaluation are corporate financial leverage, share of corporate leverage that is borrowing from banks, overall indebtedness of corporate and banking sectors in relation to exports, the ratio of public debt to total debt (macro institutional detail, which could also be a policy regime variable) and shareholder rights.

The issue of shareholder rights and other governance issues in crisis vulnerability are also studied in Johnson *et al.* (2000). Their work focuses specifically on the Asian Crisis. They find that many measures of governance such as corruption and rule of law are significant in regressions explaining currency crises. They also find the effectiveness of protection of shareholder rights impacts the size of the currency depreciation, better than standard macroeconomic factors. Table 3 of their paper presents the set of corporate governance variables they use. These

include: judicial efficiency, corruption. rule of law, enforceable minority shareholder rights, anti-director rights, creditor rights, and 1990 accounting standards.

4.2.2 Banking Crises and Institutions

Institutional studies of banking crises (banking sector distress) are becoming more
abundant, in part due to the development and accessibility of the Demirguc-Kunt
and Detragiache (1997) and Caprio and Klingebiel (1999) datasets on banking
crises in conjunction with the development and accessibility of the detailed dataset
provided by Barth, Caprio, and Levine (2001) on financial regulatory and supervisory systems around the world. Also, events in Japan and pains experienced by
their banking system have motivated interest in banking crises. The range of
'institutional' factors considered across the studies discussed below is wide.

Banking sector fragility (and bank performance) is exhaustively studied by
Barth et al. (2002) who undertake a study of the banking systems of 107 countries
using measures of regulation and supervision gathered in their earlier work. They
examine whether a host of regulations on capital adequacy, supervisory power,
regulations on mixing banking and commerce, and government ownership of
banks, to name a few, affect bank fragility. They conclude (p. 40) that 'regulatory
and supervisory practices that (1) force accurate information disclosure; (2)
empower private sector corporate control of banks; and (3) foster incentives for
private agents to exert corporate control work best to promote bank performance
and stability'. In a related paper, Barth et al. (2002), consider whether the
structure, scope, or independence of bank supervision affects bank profitability.
They find preliminary evidence that suggests little effect of the structure of supervision on bank profitability and suggest that these factors may be more important
for bank safety and soundness as well as development of the banking system.

An early and often-cited study by Demirguc-Kunt and Detragiache (1997) finds
that banking crises may be adversely impacted, not only by poor macro fundamentals, but by deposit insurance schemes as well as weak law enforcement.
Hutchison (1999) finds that financial liberalization predicts banking crises and
draws implications for European Monetary Union. Bongini et al. (1999) investigate CAMEL[20] variables, bank size, and the role of 'connections' in bank distress
and closure during the Asian crisis using bank-specific data. They find that
CAMEL variables do reasonably well in predicting distress, that big financial
institutions are more likely to become distressed but less likely to be closed, and
that when it comes to connections, whether with industrial groups or influential
families, the probability of distress is higher. Mehrez and Kaufmann (1999)
consider the effects of transparency (lack of pure information) on banking crises
in financially liberalized markets. A lack of transparency, which manifests as
uncertainty, can lead to poor lending decisions, which are the basis for the crisis.
Empirically, they find that financial liberalization increases the chance of crisis
up to five years later and that following liberalization, countries with low
transparency are more likely to suffer banking crises. Since they measure transparency from an index of corruption, it is also possible that corruption is the

determining factor in banking crises. Related to the role of information in banking crises is Keefer (2001). Keefer (p. 16) argues that 'government policies play a
significant role in determining whether banks choose prudent or imprudent
strategies'. As such, government policies can impact the magnitude of crises (as
measured by their fiscal cost). Keefer goes further and asks 'what impacts government policies?' He suggests more 'policy distortions' arise when there are fewer
veto players and when voters are less informed. He finds that the cost of banking
crises are lower with more informed voters, a larger number of veto players, and
how close elections are to the time of crisis.

   Eichengreen and Arteta (2000) undertake a comprehensive review of the literature on banking crises and offer a list of leading suspects in banking crises.
According to Eichengreen and Arteta (2000, p. 3), these are: 'lending booms,
the exchange rate regime, destabilizing external factors, precipitous financial
liberalization, inadequate prudential supervision, and weaknesses in the legal
and institutional framework'. However, they go on to say that there is no consensus on these factors, in part due to divergent time frames, country groups, and
explanatory variables used in the studies. They investigate whether a weaker
institutional environment, proxied by an index of law and order and reliability
of contract enforcement leads to greater risks of financial liberalization. Their
evidence on this score is fragile and they argue for more research in this area.[21]

5. Policy for Dealing with Financial Crises

The international financial crisis that spread from Asia to Russia and continues to
threaten Latin America has induced policymakers and economists around the
world to reconsider the international financial architecture. This includes international institutions, national policies the role of regulatory agencies, and international agreements that govern activity in the international monetary and
financial markets. Hence, what types of reforms should be adopted are among
the most important global policy issues of this decade. The policy agenda for
dealing with financial crises fall into four broad categories – (1) control of
financial flows; (2) functions of a lender of last resort; (3) governance; and (4)
surveillance. Control of financial flows is two-pronged and deals with domestic
finance and international capital flows. Lender of last resort functions address the
need and reach of the IMF and other organizations that bail out insolvent
countries as well as central banks that do the same with respect to domestic
banks. Governance deals with regulation and supervision of financial systems as
much as with information provided by banks and countries. Improvements in
regulation and supervision alone cannot help mitigate financial system risk.
Accurate, timely information on the status of banks and the fiscal and monetary
affairs of countries is needed, too. Surveillance aims at understanding the complex of vulnerabilities that may predispose a country to banking and/or currency
crises. Surveillance necessarily depends on the quality of information provided by
financial institutions and countries. Debate surrounds each of these agenda items

and the ability to manage financial crises and prevent them in the future remains uncertain.

5.1 *Control of Financial Flows*

Since most crisis countries experienced large capital inflows before the crisis and large capital outflows after, much attention has focused on capital controls as a tool of crisis prevention. Actually, there are many different types of capital control measures, with different consequences, often varying with circumstances as much as the nature of the instruments. Capital controls could be placed on any type of outflow or only on short-term capital outflows. Alternatively, taxes on short-term capital inflows and outflows could be imposed. Different exchange rates could be applied to capital account transactions. Capital controls may be used temporarily to limit capital flow volatility when vulnerability to a crisis seems evident, or to influence the volume or composition of inflows. Of course, the effects of specific capital controls may change over time and could become quite different from what may have been intended.

Many economists are still skeptical of controls on capital flows and there is no clear conclusion about the best capital controls for preventing financial crises. While Malaysia's use of capital controls has been heralded as a successful example of the effective use of capital controls, an understanding of other conditions that were present in Malaysia, institutional or otherwise, needs to be assessed before the contributory role they may have played in yielding a successful outcome can be rightly claimed.

Mishkin (1999), for example, argues that capital controls have the undesirable feature that they may block funds from entering a country that will be used for productive investment opportunities. Although these controls may limit the fuel supplied to lending booms through capital flows, over time they produce substantial distortions and misallocation of resources as households and businesses try to get around them. Corsetti *et al.* (1998) study strategies to recover from the crisis. They focus on the role of the IMF in dampening or exacerbating the impact of the crisis. They also discuss the case for limiting international capital mobility as a crisis management strategy. They find that in fact, the cases for controls on both short-term capital inflows, especially during a crisis and capital outflows, especially in the aftermath of a currency crisis appear much more controversial in the ongoing academic and policy debate. In other words, there are still a large number of controversial and unresolved issues concerning the arguments in favor of capital controls.

According to Edwards (1999), the rapidly growing popularity of controls on capital inflows as a device for minimizing external vulnerability is rooted in a misreading of the recent history of financial crises, especially on Latin American experiences. Mishkin (2001) also argues that although capital flows did contribute to the crisis, they are a symptom rather than the underlying cause, suggesting exchange controls are unlikely to be a useful strategy to avoid future crises. In his view, encouraging prudential controls could be thought of as a form of capital controls. For example, banks might be restricted in how fast their borrowing could grow and this might have the impact of substantially limiting capital inflows.

Domestic financial liberalization measures have also been pointed to in explaining the onset of banking crises. The argument goes that when domestic financial liberalization measures (such as the freeing of interest rates from government control, reducing reserve requirements, allowing participation in the securities market, etc.) takes place within a financial system where transparency, oversight, capital adequacy, and other regulatory and supervisory issues have not been considered, poor decisions by bank management may be engendered. The competitive nature of banking that emerges when freed from government control can lead to overextension of bank loans and promises to depositors that cannot be kept (see Auerbach and Siddiki, 2004). Likewise, in countries where corruption is widespread and business gets done through bribes, the whole issue of sequencing of policies and practices becomes important. In addition, domestic financial liberalization can contribute to 'overborrowing' from abroad and thus contribute to banking and currency crises.

5.2 *Lender of Last Resort*

Another hot topic of debate over the prevention of financial crises is whether an international lender of last resort should become part of the global financial architecture. Indeed, Fischer (1999) and others argue that the International Monetary Fund (IMF) has increasingly played the important role of a crisis manager and an international lender of last resort by lending to the crisis countries. But, the net benefits reaped from having an international lender of last resort are not agreed. Many of the arguments herein are the same arguments applied to a domestic lender of last resort. The benefits come in the prevention of bank runs and the avoidance of panics and contagion on a global scale. Financial instability can be averted. The costs are the moral hazard arguments that a lender of last resort can perversely encourage risk taking (on a global scale) by providing insurance to the banking system.

Mishkin (1999) finds that in the aftermath of the Asian Crisis, one of the lessons learned is that, in the case of emerging market countries, there is a strong rationale for having an international lender of last resort. However, in order to avoid creating excessive moral hazard that supports financial instability, an international lender of last resort has to impose appropriate conditionality on its lending. Other conditions may be required as well to ensure that the benefits of an international lender of last resort outweigh the costs.

Jeanne and Wyplosz (2001) find that after building a model of an emerging economy that is vulnerable to international liquidity crises, an international lender of last resort can, in principle, help cope with financial crises by providing hard currency to cash-strapped countries. They find that to be effective, the size of the intervention by an international lender of last resort will depend on how its resources are used by the domestic authorities. On the other hand, Williamson

(2000) finds that procedures for sovereign debt restructuring, including roll-overs and write-downs, are necessary complements to an international lender of last resort. According to Kumar *et al.* (2000), they find the need for an effective lender of last resort for sovereign states and the procedures for sovereign debt restructuring are important because they can help cope with global financial crises.

In a related paper, Aizenman (2002) provides a brief summary of the various proposals for preventing financial crises induced by financial opening. One of these proposals is to restrict the involvement of institutions like the IMF, World Bank and banking deposit insurances because by subsidizing sovereign borrowing, they may induce moral hazard problem. Furthermore, a less aggressive strategy to provide greater stability is the imposition of reserve requirements on lenders and/or borrowers, including the possibility of capital adequacy requirements that are linked to bank's portfolio risk. The Basel Accord II is a move in this direction.

5.3 *Governance*

'Good governance' has become a buzzword in policy debates over the prevention of financial crises. I interpret 'good governance' as policies, rules, guidelines, practices, and other institutions that reduce uncertainty in transactions. Given my interpretation, 'governance' covers a range of topics from data dissemination at the country level to disclosure and transparency of the financial and non-financial corporate sectors. It includes regulatory and supervisory issues related to the financial and corporate sectors as well as accounting standards. It also includes issues related to management incentives in financial and non-financial businesses and the avoidance of corruption in the private and public sector.

Properly designed, measures of good governance will serve to increase information and reduce uncertainty in transactions. For the banking and foreign exchange markets, good governance can thus help avoid crises. There is much on the agenda and much work remains. Spurred by the financial crises of the 1990s, the Bank for International Settlements, the IMF and the World Bank, along with the national governments of many countries are already considering or re-considering the significance of governance to soundness of the financial system.

Given each country's institutional structure, a uniform set of 'good governance' measures should not be expected but rather circumstance-dependent measures that take into account a country's specific institutional factors relating to law, politics, finance, economics, culture, and the like. For example, it may not be appropriate to suggest that allowing bank participation in real estate activities helps reduce risk in the banking system. It may depend on the extent of government involvement in the construction industry and the pervasiveness of corruption in the economy.

5.4 *Surveillance*

While crisis prevention depends, in part, on establishing domestic and international financial liberalization measures, lender of last resort functions, and good governance that reduce risks, being prepared for a crisis can help moderate its scope. Surveillance measures aim at 'seeing crises' on the horizon so action can be taken to avoid or, at least, lessen their size. The 'Financial Sector Assessment Program' (FSAP), a joint project established in 1999 between the IMF and World Bank is doing just that. A series of 'macroprudential indicators' is being designed to help assess vulnerability to crises so that they can be prevented.[22]

6. Concluding Remarks and Directions for Future Research

This sojourn covering currency and banking crises began by noting their similarities, summarizing historical experience with them, and addressing their consequences. A review of the theoretical and empirical literature on currency and banking crises up through fourth-generation/institutional models was provided and overview of the current policy debate for dealing with financial crises was broached.

I end with a wish to encourage more research on institutions and financial crises. Indeed, that is the direction I see current research going. Borrowing and synthesizing from the literature on economic growth that institutions matter comes research on institutions as they relate to many aspects of the financial system – crises, financial depth, financial development, financial efficiency, profitability, and so on. In my view, 'institutions' are significant in how they help cope with (or worsen) uncertainty. Since I see risk and uncertainty as in part arising from a conflict of interests between transacting parties, I think a great deal of research effort could be directed at understanding sources of potential conflict of interests between transacting parties and how institutions either reduce or widen the spread.

The potential for a conflict of interest is present in nearly all business and financial transactions, even outside of the principal-agent paradigm where it is most obvious. The relationship between firms and domestic banks, domestic banks and foreign banks, firms and foreign investors, domestic governments and foreign investors, domestic governments and a foreign governments, domestic governments and domestic agents, domestic banks and foreign aid providers, and even buyers and sellers can each be framed with a conflict of interest in mind.

To be sure, many outcomes are inherently conditioned on a potential conflict of interests. Institutions, be they contracts, rules, regulations, methods of supervision and oversight, accepted practices, peer pressure, culture, laws, or other incentives are implicitly or explicitly conditioned to minimize the potential conflict of interests. In future research, I would hope 'conflict of interests' would be at the core of theoretical and empirical work on institutions as they relate to any economic outcome, not just banking and currency crises. Many new databases have recently become available that quantify 'institutional' aspects across countries that will help promote research in this area.[23]

Finally, I offer a sample of questions related to institutions and the financial system. They are: (1) what mix of institutions is associated with a lower probability of financial crises? (2) what institutions tilt lending toward the short-term rather than the long term? (3) what institutions encourage malfeasance by borrower or lender? (4) what institutions affect the 'project composition' of borrowing? (5) what institutions contribute to asset price bubbles? (6) what do historic examples of institutional change offer in the way of understanding their economic effects? I hope these questions inspire further research.

Acknowledgements

Support generously provided by Center for International Business Education and Research, University of South Carolina, Columbia, SC. Thanks to Pattama Shimpalee for data assistance and help with Section 5.

Notes

1. See Eichengreen and Bordo (2002), Tables 7–9.
2. The coin and currency/demand deposit exchange rate based on the required reserve ratio (or high powered money) is implicitly altered by deposit insurance and lender of last resort capabilities of the central bank. Likewise, IMF lending implicitly alters the going market value of the foreign currency exchange rate.
3. Drazen and Grilli (1993, p. 598) argue that 'from a dynamic prospective, crises and emergencies may be welfare-improving and hence desirable'.
4. See Lin and Nugent (1995), Mauro (1995), Knack and Keefer (1997), Temple and Johnson (1998), Hall and Jones (1999), Acemoglu *et al.* (2002), and Rodrik *et al.* (2002). The current research programs of the World Bank, the IMF, and the NBER also attest to the importance of the new direction.
5. The foundation for these studies is the work Douglas North and Mancur Olson had been advancing since the 1970s that emphasizes institutions are the framework within which economic transactions transpire. As such, the design of the institutions may impact the outcome of the economic transactions by altering the transactions themselves.
6. I hesitate to call the period after 1971 the 'floating rate era' given the fact that many non-industrialized countries continued to maintain fixed or semi-fixed rates.
7. Footnote 1 in Flood and Marion (1998) spells out the details.
8. Dooley's (1997) model also has aspects of third-generation models.
9. Coincidentally, McKinnon and Pill builds on Gavin and Hausmann (1996) who develop a model of *banking* crises based on overlending.
10. Table 1 in Frankel (2002) summarizes similar questions regarding balance of payments/currency crises.
11. Arrow (1972, p. 357) says 'Virtually every commercial transaction has within itself an element of trust, certainly any transaction conducted over a period of time'. Fukayama (1995) points out institutions, broadly speaking, affect transactions costs.
12. Kaufman (1999) also offers a review.
13. Kaminsky and Reinhart pay tribute to Diaz-Alejandro (1985), Velasco (1987), Calvo (1995), Goldfajn and Valdes (1995) and Miller (1996) whose work also addresses banking and currency crises, together.
14. Levine (1997) offers an historical review of the development and findings of this literature. Auerbach and Siddiki (2004), in a companion article in this issue, provide a more recent and wide-ranging survey.

15. Reinhart and Rogoff (2002) offer a new perspective. Their reclassification of exchange rate arrangements shows that, excluding 'freely falling' currencies, the inflation and GDP growth records of countries that float or observe some degree of fixity is not very different over the period 1970–2001 (see Charts 9 and 11).
16. See Calvo and Reinhart (2002).
17. I should point out that empirical studies of currency and/or banking crises that introduce a 'financial liberalization' variable or 'capital account liberalization' variable are introducing one level of institutional variables already.
18. There also exists a literature relating institutions to financial sector development. See La Porta *et al.* (1998), Guiso *et al.* (2000), Calderon *et al.* (2001), Stulz and Williamson (2001), Beck *et al.* (2002), and Claessens and Laeven (2002).
19. This question has been posed elsewhere by Diamond and Rajan (2000) and Miller (1997). The answer to it is surely important given that many developing and emerging countries have access only to short-term debt of, in many cases, five-years or less. Given theoretical work related to sunk costs, start up costs, gestation of investment, and so on, it would seem that without access to longer-term debt, developing and emerging countries may be consigned to be crisis-prone with the scope of entrepreneurial ventures constricted by time-to-payoff.
20. CAMEL stands for: *C*apital Adequacy, *A*sset Quality, *M*anagement, *E*arnings, and *L*iquidity Management.
21. Paolera and Taylor (2003) compare Argentina's crisis of 1929 and 2001 and find a common thread: 'the interaction of a weak, undisciplined, or corruptible banking sector, and some other group of conspirators from the public or private sector that hasten its collapse'.
22. See Hilbers (2001).
23. These databases include, Alesina *et al.* (2002) 'Fractionalization', Reinhart and Rogoff's (2002) database on exchange rate arrangements, Kaufmann *et al.*'s (2002) database on measures of governance, Barth *et al.*'s (2001) 'The regulation and supervision of banks around the world', Beck *et al.*'s database on financial development and structure, La Porta *et al.*'s (1998) database on legal origin, Heritage Foundation's 'Indices of freedom', International Country Risk Guide, the World Bank's 'World Business Environment Survey', the World Bank's 'Database of Political Institutions', and the 'World Values Survey'.

References

Acemoglu, D. and Verdier, T. (2000) The choice between market failures and corruption. *American Economic Review* 90: 194–211.

Acemoglu, D., Johnson, S., Robinson, J. and Thaicharoen, Y. (2002) Institutional causes, macroeconomic symptoms: volatility, crises, and growth. NBER Working Paper 9124.

Agenor, P.-R., Bhandari, J. S. and Flood, R. P. (1991) Speculative attacks and models of balance of payments crises. NBER Working Paper 3919.

Agenor, P.-R. and Aizenman, J. (1999) Financial sector inefficiencies and coordination failures: implications for crisis management. NBER Working Paper 7446.

Aizenman, J. (2002) Financial opening: evidence and policy options. University of California – Santa Cruz. Working Paper.

Alesina, A., Devleeschauwer, A., Easterly, W., Kurlat, S. and Wacziarg, R. (2002) Fractionalization. NBER Working Paper 9411.

Allen, F. and Gale, D. (2000), Financial contagion. *Journal of Political Economy* 108: 1–33.

Arrow, K., (1972). Gifts and exchanges. *Philosophy and Public Affairs* I: 343–62.

Auerbach, P. and Siddiki, J. U. (2004) Financial liberalisation and economic development: an assessment. *Journal of Economic Surveys* 18, 3: 231–65.

Aziz, J., Caramazza, F. and Salgado, R. (2000) Currency crises: in search of common elements. IMF Working Paper 00/6, 7.

Barro, R. J. (1991) Economic growth in a cross section of countries. *Quarterly Journal of Economics* 106: 407–43.

Barth, J. R., Caprio, G., Jr. and Levine, R. (2001) *The regulation and supervision of banks around the world: a new database.* World Bank.

Barth, J. R., Caprio, G., Jr. and Levine, R. (2002) Bank regulation and supervision: what works best? NBER Working Paper 9323.

Barth, J. R., Nolle, D. E., Phumiwasana, T. and Yago, G. (2002). A cross-country analysis of the bank supervisory framework and bank performance. Economic and Policy Analysis Working Paper 2002–2.

Beck, T., Demirguc-Kunt, A. and Levine, R. (1999) *A New Database on Financial Development and Structure.* World Bank.

Beck, T., Demirguc-Kunt, A. and Levine, R. E. (2002). Law, endowment, and finance. NBER Working Paper 9089.

Blackburn, K. and Sola, M. (1993) Speculative currency attacks and balance of payments crises. *Journal of Economic Surveys* 7: 119–144

Bongini, P., Claessens, S. and Ferri, G. (1999) The political economy of distress in East Asian financial institutions. World Bank, mimeo.

Bordo, M. and Schwartz, A. (2002) Charles Goodhart's contributions to the history of monetary institutions. NBER Working Paper No. 8717.

Bordo, M., Eichengreen, B. Klingebiel, D. and Martinez- Peria, S. M. (2001) Is the crisis problem growing more severe? *Economic Policy* 24: 51–82.

Buch, C. M. and Heinrich, R. P. (1999) Twin crises and the intermediary role of banks. *International Journal of Finance and Economics* 4: 313–323.

Burnside, C., Eichenbaum, M. and Rebelo, S. (2000) *Prospective deficits and the Asian crisis.* World Bank.

Calderon, C., Chong, A. and Galindo, A. (2001) Structure and development of financial institutions and links with trust: cross-country evidence. Inter-American Development Bank Working Paper #444.

Calvo, G. (1995) Varieties of capital-market crises. University of Maryland. Working Paper,

Calvo, G. and Reinhart, C. (2002) Fear of floating. *Quarterly Journal of Economics* 117: 379–408.

Caprio, G. and Klingebiel, D. (1996) Bank insolvencies: cross-country experience. Policy Research Working Paper 1620. World Bank.

Caprio, G. and Klingebiel, D. (1999) Episodes of systemic and borderline financial crises. World Bank. mimeo.

Chan-Lau, J. A. and Chen, Z. (1998) Financial crisis and credit crunch as a result of inefficient financial intermediation with reference to the Asian financial crisis. IMF.

Chang, R. and Velasco, A. (1998), Financial fragility and the exchange rate regime. NBER Working Paper No.6469.

Claessens, S. and Laeven, L. (2002) *Financial Development, Property Rights, and Growth.* World Bank.

Cole, H. and Kehoe, P. (1996) A self-fulfilling model of mexico's 1994–1995 debt crisis. *Journal of International Economics* 41: 309–30.

Connolly, M. B. (1986) The speculative attacks on the peso and the real exchange rate: Argentina, 1979–81. *Journal of International Money and Finance* 5: 117–30.

Corbett, J. and Vines, D. (1999) Asian currency and financial crises: lessons from vulnerability, crisis, and collapse. *World Economy* 22: 155–177.

Corsetti, G., Pesenti, P. and Roubini, N. (1998) What caused the Asian currency and financial crisis? Part I and II. NBER Working Paper No.6833 and 6844.

Davies, G. A. (2002) *A History of Money from Ancient Times to Present Day*, 3rd edn. Cardiff. University of Wales Press.

Dekle, R. and Kletzer, K. M. (2001) Domestic bank regulation and financial crises: theory and empirical evidence from East Asia. NBER Working Paper 8322.

Demirguc-Kunt, A. and Detragiache, E. (1997) *The Determinants of Banking Crises: Evidence from Developed and Developing Countries*. World Bank.

Diaz-Alejandro, C. F. (1985) Good-bye financial repression, hello financial crash. *Journal of Development Economics* 19: 1–24.

Diamond, D. W. and Rajan, R. G. (2000) Banks, short-term debt and financial crises: theory, policy implications, and applications. NBER Working Paper 7764.

Diamond, D. W. and Dybvig, P. H. (1983) Banks runs, deposit insurance, and liquidity. *Journal of Political Economy* 91: 401–419.

Dooley, M. P. (1997) A model of crises in emerging markets. NBER Working Paper No. 6300.

Drazen, A. and Grilli, V. (1993) The benefits of crisis for economic reforms. *American Economic Review* 83: 598–607.

Edwards, S. (1999) On crisis prevention: lessons from Mexico and East Asia. NBER Working Paper No. 7233.

Eichengreen, B. and Arteta, C. O. (2000) Banking crises in emerging markets: presumptions and evidence. University of California, Berkeley, mimeo.

Eichengreen, B. and Bordo, M. (2002) Crises now and then: what lessons from the last era of financial globalization. NBER Working Paper No. 8716.

Eichengreen, B., Rose, A. and Wyplosz, C. (1996) Contagious currency crises. NBER Working Paper No. 5681.

Fischer, S. (1999) On the need for an international lender of last resort. *Journal of Economic Perspectives* 13: 85–104.

Flood, R. and Garber, P. (1984) Collapsing exchange-rate regimes: some linear examples. *Journal of International Economics* 17: 1–13.

Flood, R. and Marion, N. (1998) Perspectives on the recent currency crisis literature. IMF Working Paper WP/98/130.

Flood, R. and Marion, N. (2002) A model of the joint distribution of banking and currency crises. IMF, mimeo.

Frankel, J., (2002) Promoting better national institutions: the role of the IMF. panel discussion at Third Annual IMF Research Conference, Washington, DC. forthcoming in *IMF Staff Papers*.

Frankel, J. and Rose, A. K. (1996) Currency crashes in emerging markets: an empirical treatment. *Journal of International Economics* 41: 351–366.

Fukayama, F. (1995) *Trust: Social Virtues and the Creation of Prosperity*. New York: Free Press.

Gavin, M. and Hausmann, R. (1996) The roots of banking crises: the macroeconomic context. In R. Hausmann and L. Rojas-Suarez (eds), *Banking Crises in Latin America*. Baltimore MD: Johns Hopkins University Press, pp. 27–63.

Glick, R. and Hutchison, M. (1999) Banking and currency crises: how common are twins? University of California-Santa Cruz, mimeo.

Goldafajn, I. and Valdes, R. (1997) Balance of payments crises and capital flows: the role of liquidity. Central Bank of Chile, Working Paper 11.

Guiso, L., Sapienza, P. and Zingales, L. (2000) The role of social capital in financial development. NBER Working Paper 7563.

Gurley, J. G. and Shaw, E. S. (1955) Financial aspects of economic development. *American Economic Review* 45: 515–38.

Hall, R. E. and Jones, C. I. (1999) Why do some countries produce so much more output per worker than others? *Quarterly Journal of Economics* 114: 83–116.

Hilbers, P. (2001) The IMF/World Bank Financial Sector Assessment Program. *Economic Perspectives*. Electronic Journal of the U.S. Department of State.

Hutchison, M. M. (1999) Determinants of European banking distress: evaluating the risks from EMU and financial integration. University of California-Santa Cruz, mimeo.

Jeanne, O. and Wypolosz, C. (2001) The international lender of last resort: how large is enough? IMF Wokring Paper WP/01/76.

Jensen, J. and Meckling, W. (1976) Theory of the firm: managerial behavior, agency costs, and ownership structure. *Journal of Financial Economics* 34: 305–60.

Johnson, S., Boone, P., Breach, A. and Friedman, E. (2000) Corporate governance in the Asian financial crisis. *Journal of Financial Economics* 58: 141–86.

Kamin, S. (1999) The current international financial crisis: how much is new? *Journal of International Money and Finance* 18: 501–514.

Kaminsky, G. and Reinhart, C. (1999) The twin crises: the causes of banking and balance-of-payments problems. *American Economic Review* 89: 473–500.

Kaufman, G. G. (1999) Banking and currency crises and systemic risk: a taxonomy and review. Federal Reserve Bank of Chicago. Working Paper 99–12.

Kaufmann, D., Kraay, A. and Zoido-Lobaton, P. (2002) Governance matters II. World Bank. Policy Research Working Paper 2772.

Keefer, P. (2001) When do special interests run rampant? Disentangling the role of elections, incomplete information, and checks and balances in Banking Crises. World Bank.

Kim, Y. J. and Lee, J.-W. (1999) Overinvestment, Collateral lending, and economic crisis. Center for International Development, Harvard University. CID Working Paper 4.

Kiyotaki, N. and Moore, J. (1997) Credit cycles. *Journal of Political Economy* 105: 211–48.

Knack, S. and Keefer, P. (1997) Does social capital have an economic payoff? A cross-country investigation. *Quarterly Journal of Economics* 112: 1251–88.

Krugman, P. (1979) A model of balance of payment crises. *Journal of Money, Credit, and Banking* 11: 311–25.

Krugman, P. and Rotemberg, J. (1990) Target zones with limited reserves. NBER Working Paper 3418.

Krugman, P. (1998) What happened to Asia? Mimeo, MIT.

Kumar, M. S., Masson P. and Miller, M. (2000) Global financial crises: institutions and incentives. IMF Working Paper WP/00/105.

La Porta, R., Lopez-de-Silanes, F., Shleifer, A. and Vishny, R. W. (1998) Law and finance. *Journal of Political Economy* 106: 1113–55.

Levine, R. (1997) Financial development and economic growth: views and agenda. *Journal of Economic Literature* 35: 688–726.

Lin, J. Y. and Nugent, J. B. (1995) Institutions and economic development. In J. Behrman and T. N. Srinivasan, eds, *Handbook of Economic Development*, vol. 3A. Amsterdam: North-Holland.

Marion, N. (1999) Some parallels between currency and banking crises. Dartmouth University, mimeo.

Mauro, P. (1995) Corruption and growth. *Quarterly Journal of Economics* 110: 681–713.

McKinnon, R. I. and Pill, H. (1998) International overborrowing: a decomposition of credit and currency risks. Stanford University, mimeo.

McKinnon, R. I. (1973) *Money and Capital in Economic Development*. Washington, DC: Brookings Institute.

Mehrez, G. and Kaufmann, D. (1999) Transparency, Liberalization, and Financial Crises. World Bank.

Miller, V. (1996) Speculative currency attacks with endogenously induced commercial bank crises. *Journal of International Finance and Money* 15: 385–403.

Miller, V. (1997) Political instability and debt maturity. *Economic Inquiry* 35: 12–27.

Mishkin, F. (1996) Understanding financial crises: a developing country perspective. NBER Working Paper No. 5600.

Mishkin, F. (1978) The household balance sheet and the Great Depression. *Journal of Economic History* 38: 918–37.

Mishkin, F. (1999) Lessons from the Asian crisis. *Journal of International Money and Finance* 18: 709–723.

Mishkin, F. (2001) Financial policies and the prevention of financial crises in emerging market countries. NBER Working Paper No. 8087, Cambridge, MA: NBER.

Mulder, C., Perrelli R. A. and Rocha, M. D. S. (2002) New strategies for currency crises early warning systems: a balance sheet approach. IMF Working Paper.

Obstfeld, M. (1994) The logic of currency crises. *Cahiers Economiques et Monetaires*, Bank of France, 43: 189–213.

Paolera, G. della and Taylor, A. M. (January 2003) Gaucho banking redux. NBER Working Paper 9457.

Pericoli, M. and Sbracia, M. (2003) A primer on financial contagion. *Journal of Economic Surveys* 17: 571–608

Rajan, R. G. and Zingales, L. (1998) Which capitalism? Lessons from the East Asian crisis. *Journal of Applied Corporate Finance* 11: 40–48.

Reinhart, C. and Rogoff, K. S. (2002) The modern history of exchange rate arrangements: a reinterpretation. NBER Working Paper 8963.

Rangvid, J. (2001) Second generation models of currency crises. *Journal of Economic Surveys* 15: 613–646

Rodrik, D. (1999) Institutions for high-quality growth: what they are and how to acquire them. Speech delivered at IMF Conference on Second Generation Reforms.

Rodrik, D., Subramanian, A. and Trebbi, F. (2002) Institutions rule: the primacy of institutions over geography and integration in economic development. NBER Working Paper 9305.

Sachs, J., Tornell, A. and Velasco, A. (1996) Financial crises in emerging markets: the lessons from 1995. *Brookings Papers on Economic Activity* 16: 147–215.

Salant, S. and Henderson, D. (1978) Market anticipation of government policy and the price of gold. *Journal of Political Economy* 86: 627–48.

Saxena, S. C. (2004) The changing nature of currency crises. *Journal of Economic Surveys* 18, 3: 321–50.

Schneider, M. and Tornell, A. (2000) Balance sheet effects, bailout guarantees, and financial crises. NBER Working Paper 8060.

Schumpeter, J. A. (1911) *The Theory of Economic Development*. Cambridge, MA: Harvard University Press.

Shleifer, A. and Vishny, R. W. (1993). Corruption. *Quarterly Journal of Economics* 108: 599–617.

Stulz, R. and Williamson, R. (2001) Culture, openness, and finance. NBER Working Paper 8222.

Temple, J. and Johnson, P. A. (1998) Social capability and economic growth. *Quarterly Journal of Economics* 113: 965–90.

Velasco, A. (1987), Financial crises and balance of payments crises. *Journal of Development Economics* 27: 263–83.

Wei, S.-J. and Wu, Y. (2001) Negative alchemy: corruption, composition of capital flows, and currency crises. NBER Working Paper 8187.

Williamson, J. (2000) The role of the IMF in a reformed global financial architecture. Institute for International Economics, mimeo.

Yoshitomi, M. and Ohno, K. (1999) Capital account crisis and credit contraction. Asian Development Bank, Working Paper 2.

5

THE CHANGING NATURE OF CURRENCY CRISES

Sweta C. Saxena

University of Pittsburgh

1. Introduction

Currency crises that have been observed in recent years are not a new phenomenon – they date back to the gold standard era. However, the main features of the crises in Latin America in the 1970s and early 1980s are quite different from the crisis in Europe in 1992. Theoretical literature has evolved over time to account for the changing nature of these crises. While many theoretical and empirical papers have been written about various episodes of these crises, the change in their mechanism over time has not been demonstrated well. This paper fills the gap in the literature by graphically depicting the main features of these crises. Such a visual analysis should allow the reader to better understand and follow the changes in the mechanisms over time.

In the analysis of these currency crises, we note two common features, namely, a fixed exchange rate regime and capital flight and speculative attack. While this paper summarizes much of the literature on currency crises, data is restricted to the first and second generation models and the models of twin crises.[1,2] The rest of the paper is organized as follows. Section 2 discusses the first generation models' application to Latin America. Section 3 unfolds the European crisis of 1992. Section 4 presents the stylized facts from the twin crises literature. The next three sections summarize the literature on herding, contagion and moral hazard, respectively. Section 8 concludes.

2. First Generation Models and Latin America

The literature on currency crises began with the works of Krugman (1979) and Flood and Garber (1984). These papers have now come to be known as the *First Generation Models of currency crises*.[3] They typically depict the scenario of the Latin American countries in the 1970s and early 1980s, where the collapse of the exchange rate regime occurs under the monetization of budget deficits that depletes the foreign exchange reserves of the central bank. The sudden collapse comes about due to perfectly mobile capital that moves to maintain the uncovered interest parity. In a perfect foresight version of the first generation models, instantaneous capital flows ensure that there are no jumps in the exchange rate that would represent a profit opportunity for speculators. When the shadow value of the exchange rate crosses the fixed rate, there is a sudden loss of reserves, an increase in interest rates and the currency begins to depreciate.

Figures 1–5 depict the main characteristics of the first generation crises in Latin America in the 1970s and early 1980s. Budget deficits (mostly exceeding 8–10% of GDP) were financed by soaring growth rates of money and domestic credit. High current account deficits along with massive capital outflows accompanied the loss of foreign exchange reserves and/or an increase in interest rates. The exchange rate eventually depreciated. This is illustrated for the Bolivian crisis from 1982 to 1985, the Brazilian crises in 1983, 1986 and 1989–90, the Chilean crisis from 1971 to 1974, Peruvian crises in 1976 and 1987 and the Uruguayan crisis in 1982.

Although theoretical models explain the empirical occurrence of these crises in a straightforward manner, they suffer from some obvious weaknesses. First, the rule of deficit financing assumed is very rigid, even though it is not sustainable in the long run. Second, while the investors are actively maximizing the returns on their assets, the government is too passive – it knows that the central bank is losing reserves, and hence it can and should abandon parity before exhausting all reserves, but it chooses not to do so. Lastly, theoretical models imply that the exchange rate will adjust smoothly when the exchange rate regime shifts from a fixed to a flexible one. In reality, countries experience quick, unexpected and huge devaluations.[4] The perfect information postulate in these models prohibits discrete jumps in the exchange rate, but uncertainty, as introduced by Krugman (1979) and Flood and Garber (1984), may not be sufficient to explain the big devaluations that follow the crises. In Krugman (1979), incomplete knowledge on the part of the investors about how much of its reserves the government is willing to use to defend the exchange rate produces the possibility of alternating balance of payments crises and recoveries of confidence. In Flood and Garber (1984), uncertainty in domestic credit creation produces the same cycles of crises and recoveries.[5]

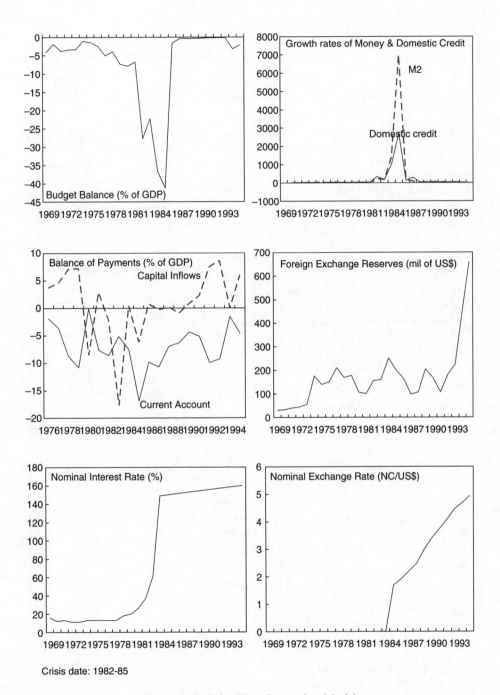

Figure 1. Bolivia: First Generation Model.

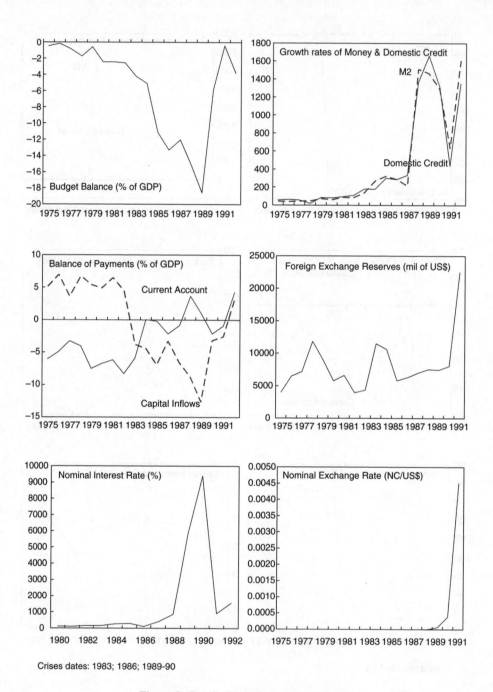

Figure 2. Brazil: First Generation Model.

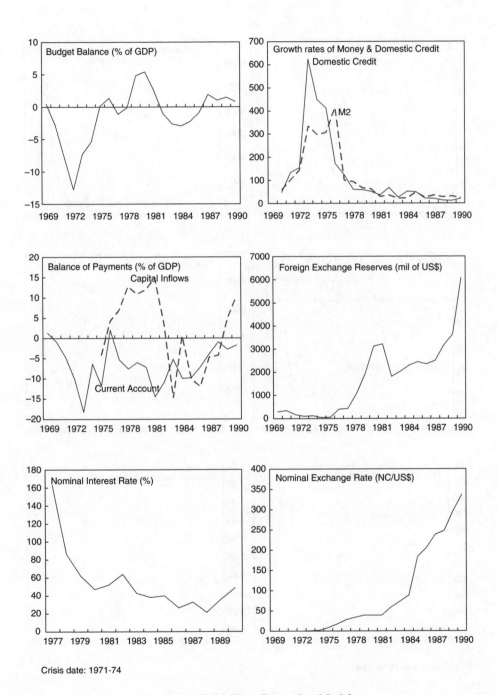

Figure 3. Chile: First Generation Model.

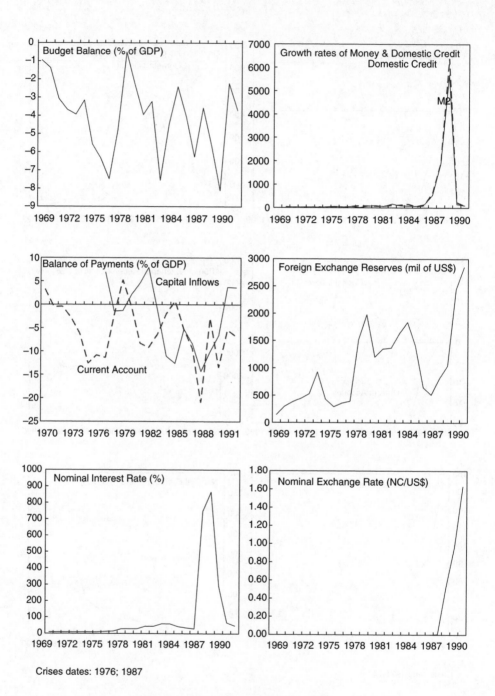

Crises dates: 1976; 1987

Figure 4. Peru: First Generation Model.

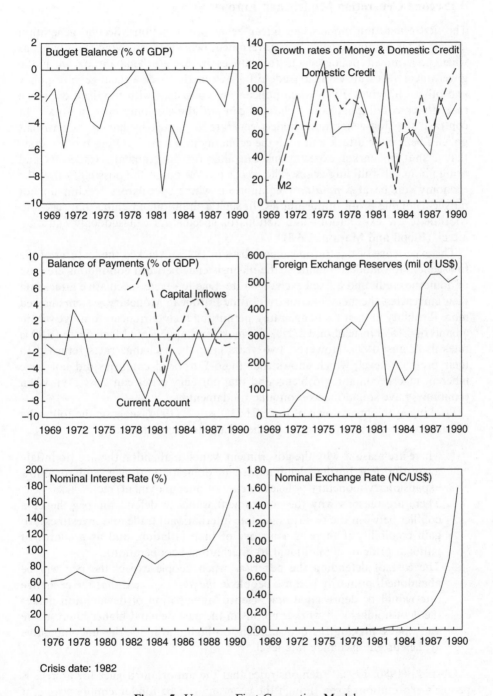

Figure 5. Uruguay: First Generation Model.

3. Second Generation Models and Europe

The first-generation models had linear behavioral functions. Second-generation models focus on non-linearities in government behavior – studying what happens when government policy reacts to changes in private behavior or when the government faces an explicit trade-off between the fixed exchange rate policy and other objectives. Even when policies are consistent with the fixed exchange rate, attack-conditional policy changes can *pull* the economy into an attack. In contrast, the first-generation models generate an attack by having inconsistent policies before the attack and *push* the economy into a crisis. Other models show that a shift in market expectations can alter the government's trade-offs and bring about self-fulfilling crises. The newer models admit the possibility that the economy can be at a *no-attack* equilibrium where speculators see but do not pursue available profit opportunities. In such a situation, anything that serves to coordinate the expectations and actions of speculators can suddenly cause an attack (Flood and Marion, 1998).[6]

The experience of the European countries in 1992–93 lacked the features of the first-generation models – namely, the inconsistency between continuous creation of domestic credit and a fixed exchange rate. Due to severe speculative attacks on their currencies, the member countries of the European Monetary System allowed more flexibility in their exchange rates, permitting their currencies to move within a band of ±15% instead of ±2.25% for most Exchange Rate Mechanism (ERM) rates in August 1993. However, two years later the exchange rates returned to their pre-crisis level, which shows that these European countries did not have inherent macroeconomic problems and that currency crises can arise even when economies have sound macroeconomic fundamentals.

Looking at the breakdown of the ERM, Obstfeld (1994) suggests the following features of the crises experienced by these European countries:

1. There are reasons why the government wants to abandon the peg (to inflate away the debt burden denominated in domestic currency, and to follow expansionary monetary policies in case of unemployment, etc).
2. There are reasons why the government wants to defend the peg, hence a conflict between the two (to facilitate international trade and investment, to gain credibility if there is a history of high inflation, and as a source of national pride or commitment to international cooperation).
3. The cost of defending the peg rises when people expect the peg will be abandoned, primarily because people *in the past* expected that the exchange rate would be depreciated *now*. Hence, anticipation of devaluation makes the debt-holders and worker unions in the past demand higher interest rate and wages, making the debt-burden too high and industries uncompetitive at the current exchange rate level.

Obstfeld (1986, 1996a)[7] demonstrates that the important trigger for a crisis is people's expectation. Even though the economy can be fundamentally strong, if people expect a devaluation in the near future, they could put enormous pressure on the central bank by converting their domestic currency to foreign currency before the devaluation. If a sufficient number of people proceed as such, the central bank could run out of foreign reserves, necessitating a devaluation. In this case, the crisis is self-fulfilling. Often the models that emphasize the above characteristics are called *Second Generation Models of currency crises*.

In addition, these models show that the timing of the crisis is indeterminate because that too depends on people's expectations. In the indeterminate range, the economy could certainly face *an attack* if a large trader can take a massive position against the fixed exchange rate (like George Soros did against the British pound in 1992). But if the foreign exchange market consists of many small, credit constrained traders and no large trader, then without anything to coordinate their expectations and actions, the investors cannot mount an attack of sufficient size to move the economy from a *no-attack* to an *attack equilibrium*. Hence, the economy can maintain a fixed exchange rate indefinitely unless something coordinates expectations and actions to cause an attack (Flood and Marion, 1998).

Figures 6–10 demonstrate the crisis that hit Europe in 1992–93. In the wake of German Unification in 1989, Germany's fiscal policy became expansionary, which was counteracted by the Bundesbank's contractionary monetary policy as seen in the rise in interest rate (to prevent inflation). With perfectly mobile capital across the European borders, unfavorable interest differentials with Germany led to outflow of capital from the rest of Europe. In order to maintain the balance of payments equilibrium, the European countries had to raise their interest rates. This would have normally been appropriate, except that all the countries were in a cyclical downturn at that time. Speculators believed that it would be too costly for governments to maintain the peg by raising interest rates, in the face of recession and high unemployment levels. Hence, the speculative attack.

As can be seen in the figures, budget deficits before the crisis were low (less than 5% of GDP). None of these countries had burgeoning current account deficits, like the Latin American countries in the first generation models. Fixed exchange rate under the ERM, along with positive inflation differentials with Germany, led to real appreciation of exchange rates,[8] which made these economies uncompetitive. Recession or cyclical downturn, along with rising interest rates, led the speculators to believe that the governments would not be able to maintain their respective pegs. This led to speculative attacks on the British pound, Italian lira and French franc, which later spread to other countries.[9]

While these models emphasize multiple equilibria, Krugman (1996) disputes such indeterminacy of the speculative attacks and suggests that timing of the crisis can be determined by tracing the deteriorating fundamentals. In responding to Krugman's criticism, Kehoe (1996) and Obstfeld (1996b) point out that the new crisis models do not assert that every fixed exchange rate regime must be subject to a self-fulfilling crisis, and that while it is argued that a self-fulfilling crisis can occur even though a fixed exchange rate can be sustained in the absence of speculation, there is no denial that deteriorating fundamentals can lead to a crisis and can eliminate multiple equilibria and indeterminacy of timing of a crisis. Furthermore, a speculative attack may have nothing to do with the long-run

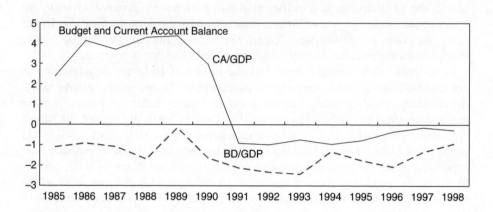

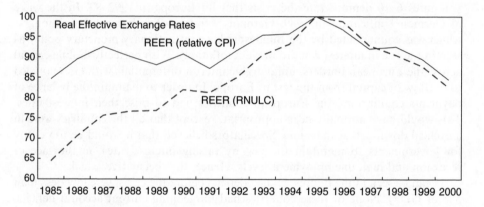

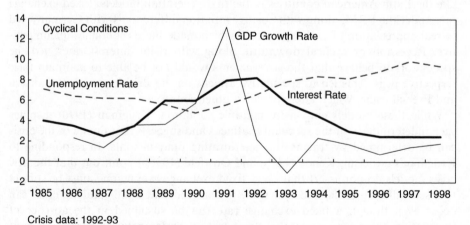

Figure 6. Germany: Second Generation Model.

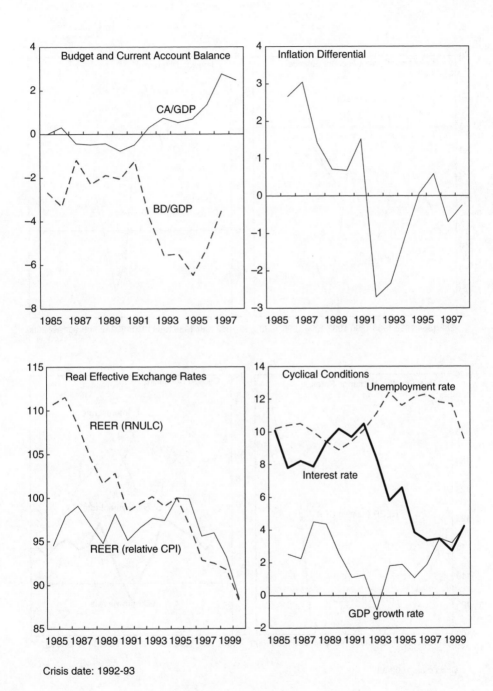

Crisis date: 1992-93

Figure 7. France: Second Generation Model.

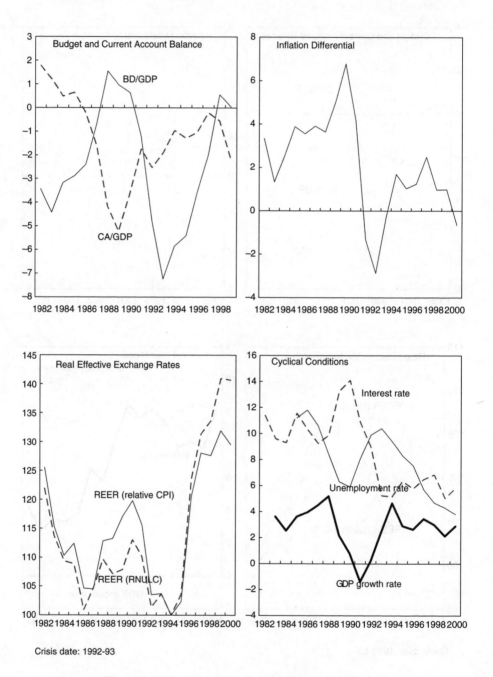

Figure 8. United Kingdom: Second Generation Model.

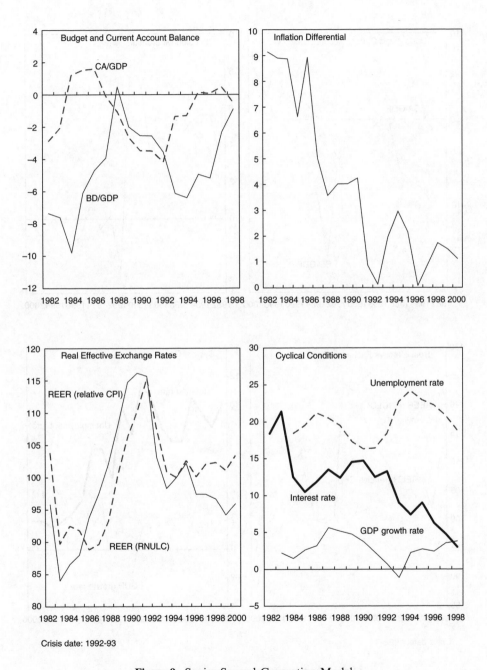

Figure 9. Spain: Second Generation Model.

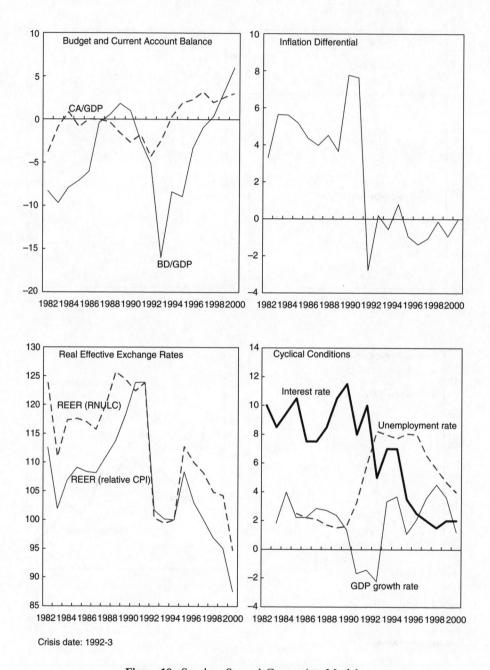

Figure 10. Sweden: Second Generation Model.

sustainability of a fixed exchange rate regime if it occurs in the face of some temporary problems faced by an economy, as was clearly witnessed by the European economies.

4. Models of Twin Crises

The newer generation models emphasize the importance of the financial sector and capital flows in currency crises, hence, the term *twin crises*. The frequent occurrence of twin crises (Nordic countries in 1990s, Turkey in 1994, Venezuela, Argentina and Mexico in 1994, Bulgaria in 1996, and Asian countries in 1997) has led academicians and policymakers to analyze the causes and causation of these crises.

1. Stoker (1995) and Mishkin (1996) argue that a *balance of payments crisis leads to a banking crisis*. According to Stoker, an external shock in the face of a fixed exchange rate leads to loss of reserves. If this loss of reserves is not sterilized, then a speculative attack is followed by a period of abnormally high interest rates leading to a credit crunch, increased bankruptcies and financial crisis. Mishkin argues that devaluation could weaken the position of the banks if they have foreign currency denominated liabilities.
2. However, Diaz-Alejandro (1985), Velasco (1987), Calvo (1995) and Miller (1995) argue that *banking crises lead to balance of payments crises*. The argument is that central banks print money to bailout financial institutions and hence lose their ability to maintain the prevailing exchange rate commitment.
3. But Reinhart and Vegh (1996) and Kaminsky and Reinhart (1999) suggest that the *two crises have some common causes* – an example of 'perverse' dynamics of an exchange rate-based inflation stabilization plan. Since prices are slow to converge to international levels, the exchange rate appreciates markedly. Initially, the boom in imports and economic activity is financed by borrowing abroad. This leads to a widening of current account deficits and financial markets infer that the stabilization program is unsustainable, hence the currency is attacked. The increase in bank credit during the boom is financed by foreign borrowings, such that when capital flows out and the asset market crashes, it leads to the collapse of the banking system as well. McKinnon and Pill (1996), Goldfajn and Valdes (1997) and Chang and Velasco (1998) show that the intermediating role of the banking sector (which creates liquidity problems later on) can make the boom-bust cycles more pronounced, leading to the collapse of the currency and the banking sector.[10]

The stylized facts that these models tend to explain are that banking crises are highly correlated to currency crises, capital inflows increase steadily before the crisis and fall sharply during the crisis and banking activity (intermediation) increases some time before the collapse. In particular, Kaminsky and Reinhart (1999) show that:

1. During the 1970s, when markets were highly regulated, there was no apparent link between the balance of payments (BOP) and banking crises. The two crises became more entwined in the 1980s following the liberalization of financial markets across many parts of the world. Their results show that the collapse of a currency deepens the banking crisis, activating a vicious spiral.
2. While banking crises often precede BOP crises, their results point to common causes. Both crises are preceded by recessions or below-normal economic growth, in part attributed to a worsening of terms of trade, an overvalued exchange rate (affecting exports negatively) and the rising cost of credit. A shock to financial institutions (possibly financial liberalization and/or increased access to international capital markets) fuels the boom phase of the cycle by providing access to financing, but leaves the economy vulnerable as the unhedged foreign liabilities of the banking system rise.
3. They show that crises (external or domestic) are typically preceded by a multitude of weak and deteriorating economic fundamentals and the incidence of crises where the economic fundamentals were sound are rare (as Krugman argues). Compared with single crises, the economic fundamentals tended to be worse, the economies were considerably more frail, and the crises (both banking and currency) were far more severe for the 'twin' crises.

Figures 11–16 demonstrate the occurrence of the twin crises in Latin American, European and Asian economies in the 1980s and 1990s. Financial indicators (M2 multiplier, ratio of M2 to reserves, domestic credit as a percentage of GDP, bank deposits, lending-deposit ratio and interest rates) rise rapidly before the crisis. The excessive liquidity fuels growth in the economy. Since domestic inflation is higher than the world inflation, the real exchange rate appreciates, which, along with a deterioration in the terms of trade, leads to current account deficits[11] and squeezes profit margins, leading to bankruptcies, increase in non-performing loans, deepening of the economic contraction and banking sector problems. This reveals the weaknesses in the economy and leads to capital outflows. Under the fixed exchange rate regime, the peg is initially defended by the loss of foreign exchange reserves and/or high interest rates. But eventually the currency collapses, bringing down the booming banking sector. These stylized facts are depicted for the Chilean crisis of 1981–83, the Danish crisis of 1987–90, the Indonesian and the Korean crisis of 1997, the Norwegian crisis of 1988–91, and the Venezuelan crises of 1989 and 1993–94.

5. Herding

The bank run literature provides a similar explanation of currency crises – *herd behavior*. Herding, which is an example of an information cascade, is said to exist when individuals tend to choose actions similar to previous actions chosen by other individuals. In other words, with herding effects, individuals tend to move in conformity, and a small shock to society could lead to a mass shift in the actions of people. In some special cases, people choose to give up their private

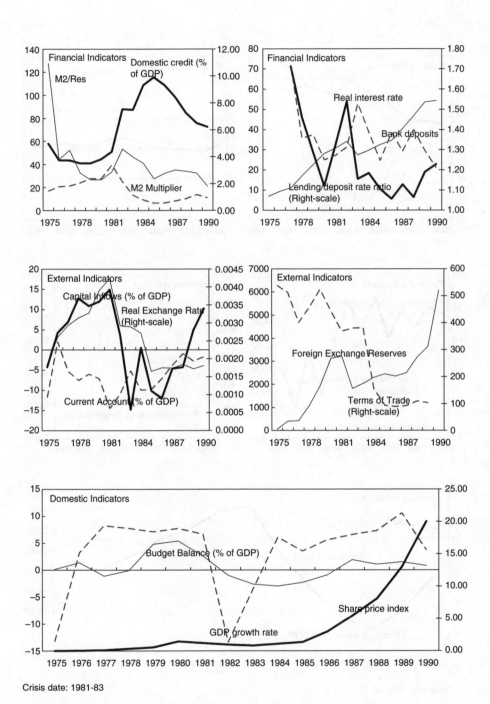

Figure 11. Chile: Twin Crises.

Crisis date: 1981-83

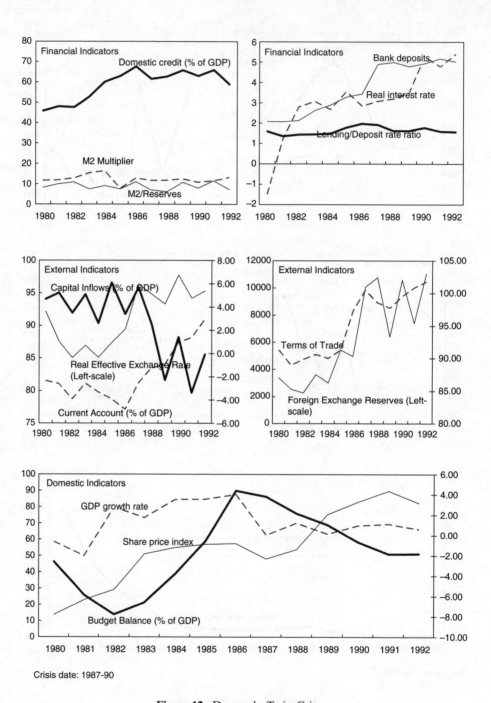

Figure 12. Denmark: Twin Crises.

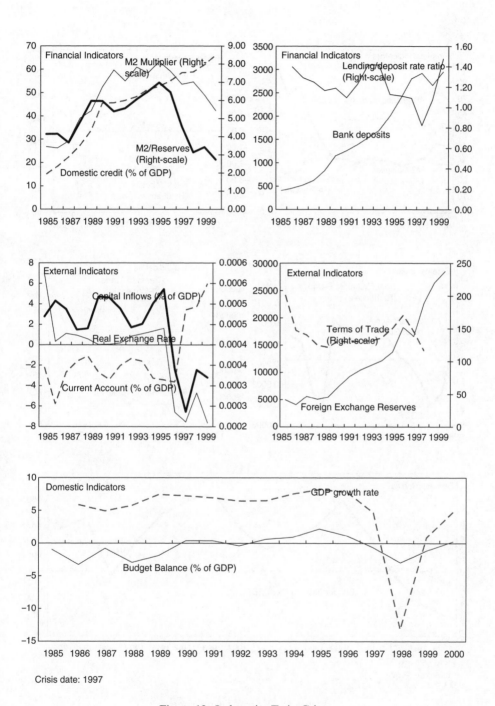

Figure 13. Indonesia: Twin Crises.

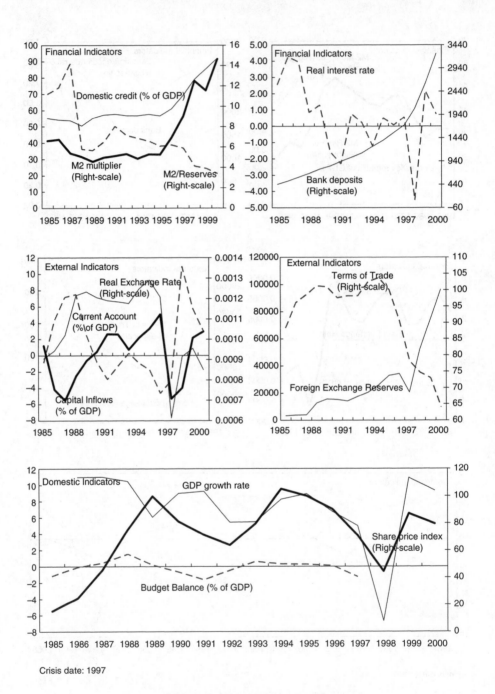

Figure 14. Korea: Twin Crises.

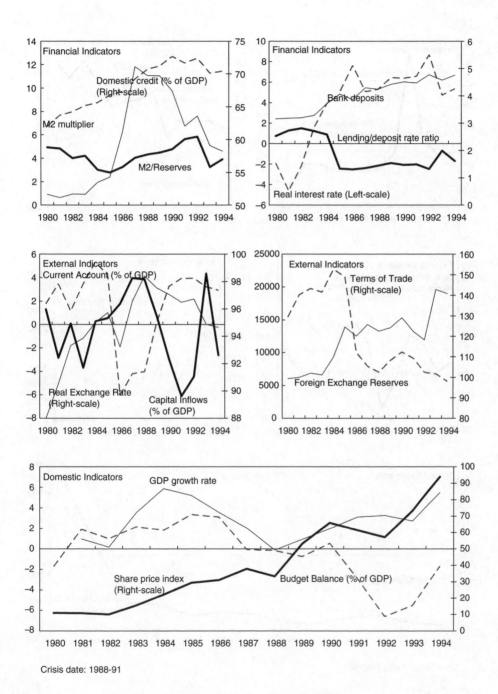

Figure 15. Norway: Twin Crises.

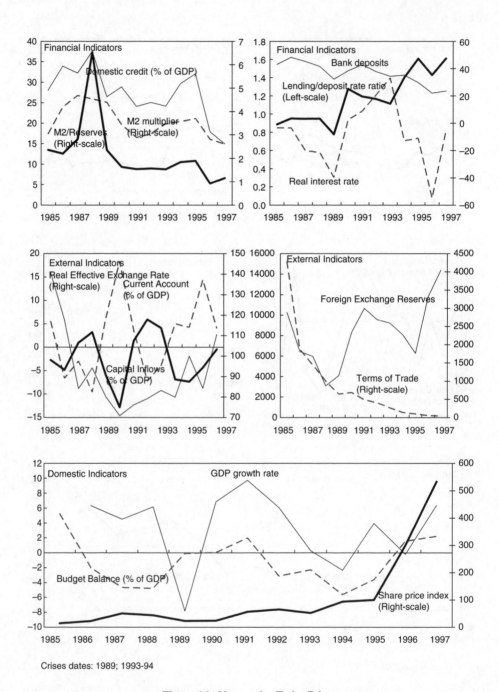

Crises dates: 1989; 1993-94

Figure 16. Venezuela: Twin Crises.

information or signals they possess and follow the actions of others, even though the private information or signals they have would suggest they should act otherwise.

A famous example is Keynes' beauty contest.[12] Earlier work includes the papers by Leibenstein (1950) on bandwagon effects. Recently, more rigorous models have been suggested to explain herd behavior.[13] Here we focus on a number of models that have been used to explain investment behavior.

Froot *et al.* (1992) show that speculators with short horizons may herd on the same information, trying to learn what the other informed traders know. These could lead to multiple equilibria, and herding speculators may even choose to study information that is completely unrelated to fundamentals. So, the large perceived penalty for missing a bull market leads managers to follow the pack even if fundamentals do not warrant it; conversely, the penalty of losses during the bear market are lower as all other managers are losing money as well.[14]

Krugman (1998a) suggests similar reasons why herding might occur. First, there is a *bandwagon effect*, which is driven by the awareness that investors have private information – where investors ignore their own information and thrive on the information of other investors. Suppose that investor 1 has special information about the Thai real estate market, investor 2 has special information about the financial conditions of the banks and investor 3 has information about the internal discussions of the government. If investor 1 gets some negative information, he may sell, since that is the extent of his information; if investor 2 learns that 1 has sold, he may sell also even if his own private information is neutral or slightly positive. And investor 3 may end up selling even if his own information is positive because the fact that 1 and 2 have sold leads him to conclude that both may well have received bad news, even when in fact they have not. Krugman argues that bandwagon effects in markets with private information create a sort of 'hot money' that at least sometimes causes foreign exchange markets to overreact to news about national economic prospects. Second, much of the money invested in crisis-prone countries is managed by agents rather than directly by principals – so *principal-agent problems* arise. To the extent that money managers are compensated based on comparison with other money managers, they may have strong incentives to act alike even if they have information suggesting that the market's judgement is in fact wrong.

Chari and Kehoe (1997) link debt-default actions of the governments to herding behavior. In their model, investors have private information about the state of the economy and have a prior notion about the competence of the government. The credibility of the government is built on its ability to pay its debts – the government is competent if it could repay foreign debt in a crisis state. If the prior that the government is competent is either very high or very low, then the investors ignore their private information and either lend or don't lend, respectively. If the prior is in the intermediate range, the possibility of herding arises. In this range, capital flows are very sensitive to small pieces of information and hence volatile.

Although herding is a type of distortion, where certain massive actions by some individuals can hurt the economy, these actions could be entirely rational from individuals' points of view.[15] Such rational behavior occurs when there are payoff externalities (payoffs to an agent adopting an action increases as the number of agents adopting that action increases) or principal-agent problems (managers have an incentive to hide in the herd so that their actions cannot be evaluated).

The above models usually assume sequential actions by individuals, so that those who take actions later will observe what actions others have taken previously. Calvo and Mendoza (1998) introduce a model in which herding can exist even when individuals have simultaneous decision-making. They find that with informational frictions, herding behavior may become more prevalent as the world capital market grows. With globalization, the cost of collecting country-specific information to discredit rumors increases and managers, facing reputational costs, choose to mimic the market portfolio. Hence, small rumors can induce herding behavior and move the economy from a *no attack* to an *attack equilibrium*.

Of course, as Flood and Marion (1998) argue, in many cases, herding could explain some part of the currency crises, but not the whole. First, individuals are less likely to ignore their own or new information in a world where they can adjust their strategies continuously to new information. Second, where strategic interactions are important, the cascade story is unsatisfactory, because the potential capital gains arising from the action of one agent do not depend on actions chosen by others.

6. Contagion

Another way crises propagate is through *contagion*. The currency crises of the 1990s have consisted of three regional waves: the ERM crisis (1992–93), the Latin American crisis (1994–95) and the Asian crisis (1997–98). The issue of contagion explains how seemingly different countries can experience the same crisis.[16]

Contagion could be explained in terms of real linkages between the countries: a crisis in country A worsens the fundamentals of country B. For example, suppose Thailand and Malaysia export the same products in the world markets. Hence, a Thai devaluation would depress Malaysian exports, and could push Malaysia past the critical point that triggers a crisis. In Europe, there was an element of competitive devaluation: depreciation of the pound adversely affected the trade and employment of France, and increased pressure on the French government to abandon its peg to the deutschemark.

In addition to trade, there could be direct financial linkages as well. Financial institutions in the home country may have a credit exposure or equity stakes in corporations, financial institutions, or real estate in the neighboring countries. A crisis in the neighboring country could then spillover by causing weakness in the home country's financial sector. This seems to explain the propagation of the crisis from Russia to Brazil. The investors liquidate holdings in one part of their portfolio due to losses in another part.

However, Krugman (1998a) argues that trade links in Asia and Europe were weak[17] and in Latin America nil. Mexico is neither an important market nor an important competitor for Argentina; why, then, he asks, should one crisis have triggered another? He offers two rational explanations for contagion between seemingly unlinked economies, as noticed by Drazen (1999). First, countries are perceived as a group with some common, but imperfectly observed characteristics. For example, Latin American countries share a common culture and therefore, a 'Latin temperament'; but the implications of this temperament for economic policy may be unclear. Once investors have seen one country with that cultural background abandon the peg under pressure, they may revise downward their estimates of the willingness of other countries to defend their parities – i.e., 'wake up call'. That is what happened in the case of the Asian Crisis. There was no news – just re-examination and re-evaluation of the already existing information because countries with similar background gave up the parity. Second, the political commitment to a fixed exchange rate itself is subject to herding effects. This was clearly the case in Europe – once Britain and Italy left the ERM, it was politically less costly for Sweden to abandon the peg to the deutsche mark than it would have been had Sweden devalued on its own.

However, not all contagion is negative. During the wave of optimism that followed the Mexican and Argentine reforms in the early nineties, countries that had done little actual reform, like Brazil, were also lifted by the rising tide. The apparent myopia of markets about Asian risks seems to have been fed by a general sense of optimism about Asian economies in general (as emphasized by Radelet and Sachs (1998)).

7. Moral Hazard

The final explanation for currency crises is the problem of *moral hazard*, as proposed by Krugman (1998b) and Corsetti *et al.* (1998) for the Asian crisis. Moral hazard can occur under asymmetric information because borrowers can alter their behavior after the transaction has taken place in ways that the lender regards as undesirable. In financial markets, however, moral hazard could occur in the absence of asymmetric information; i.e., moral hazard arises from the possibility that investor behavior will be altered by the extension of government guarantees that relieve investors of some of the consequences of risk taking.

Krugman (1998b) considers the case of over-guaranteed and under-regulated financial intermediaries. Since these institutions are not risking any capital ex-ante, and have the liberty to walk away at no personal cost in case of bankruptcy, the economy engages in excessive investment. This economy is made worse by globalization, due to its increasing access to the world capital market. If it did not have access to the world capital market, then excessive investment demand would show up as high rates of interest, and not as excessive investment. But access to the world market allows the moral hazard in the financial sector to translate into real excess capital accumulation.

Corsetti *et al.* (1998) also recognize moral hazard as a source of over-investment, excessive external borrowing and current account deficits. Unprofitable projects and cash shortfalls are re-financed through external borrowing as long as foreign creditors lend to domestic agents against future bail-out revenue from the government. The government deficits need not be high before the crisis, but refusal of foreign creditors to re-finance the debt (knowing that the government's stock of foreign reserves is below a critical minimum) forces the government to mediate and guarantee the outstanding stock of external liabilities. The government could either raise sufficiently large revenues from explicit taxation or it might have recourse to seigniorage revenues (printing money). In the former case, the financial crisis doesn't coincide with an exchange rate collapse. In the latter case, expectation of inflationary financing leads to expectation about exchange rate depreciation, which creates a wedge between domestic and international interest rates, causing the currency to collapse.

In fact, the argument of moral hazard is not only applicable to the intermediaries, but extends to governments as well. Proponents of moral hazard argue that the IMF creates a bailout for governments or investors in the event of a crisis. However, Radelet and Sachs (1998) do not see the Asian crisis as a result of carelessness on the part of investors who were confident of a bailout, knowing that only the state-owned enterprises can be bailed out in the event of a crisis. According to Radelet and Sachs, if creditors feared the risk of a crisis in Asia, then the spread on Asian bonds should have increased, but it did not. If creditors felt an increasing risk of a government-led bailout, then ratings of long term government bonds should have gone down, but they did not either. A large part of the investment went into the risky equity market, and bank loans went to the non-financial corporate sector, where a direct government bailout was least possible. Creditors had been aware of weak bankruptcy laws and ineffective judicial systems in Asia. Hence, the foreign investors lent because they anticipated these economies would perform well, and not because they believed that they would be bailed out.

8. Conclusion

This paper attempts to fill the gap in the literature by clearly demonstrating how the nature of currency crises has changed over time. The paper graphically presents the stylized facts for the first and second generation models of currency crises and also on twin crises. The crises in the 1990s have been more frequent and more severe when compared to the crises of the earlier decades. A frequently advanced reasoning is 'globalization' and immediate transfer of news due through developments in information technology. Clearly, crises have been a result of poor and problematic policies (as in the first generation models) as well as of mere expectations of speculators (second generation models). In this globalized world, where information transfers so fast, it is in the interest of the policymakers to follow prudent macroeconomic policies in order to avoid speculative activity. Countries need to make timely assessments of the stance of their policies, for example, Germany should have realized early enough the mayhem its tight monetary policy would cause for other nations and should have abandoned that policy. Or policymakers should realize that fixed exchange rates in the face of huge budget deficits and open capital accounts are an invitation to speculative attacks. In fact, Levy-Yeyati and Sturzenegger (2003) find that less flexible exchange rate regimes are associated with slower growth and greater output volatility for developing countries. Hence, emerging market economies should move towards more flexible exchange rates (not necessarily free floats) and/or should even consider selective capital controls on inflows to change the composition of the flows towards longer maturity (as in Chile). In the absence of good macroeconomic policies, time and again, countries have and will continue to be punished by the markets.

Acknowledgements

I would like to thank Sherri Barrier and Alexis Haakensen for excellent research assistance and Deniz Atasoy, Brandon Tracy and Sandra Williamson for editorial suggestions. This paper draws on my survey with Kar-yiu Wong. The usual disclaimers apply.

Notes

1. The dates of all crises are taken from Kaminsky and Reinhart (1999).
2. In order to conserve space, we only show data for 5–6 episodes of crises for each generation model. The longer version of the paper is available upon request from the author.
3. See Blackburn and Sola (1993) for a more extensive survey.
4. The exchange rates in Figures 1–5 do not show discrete devaluations because the data is period-averaged and is annual.
5. These models differ from Obstfeld (1996a), which introduces the cost to holding foreign currency.
6. See Rangvid (2001) for a more extensive survey of second generation models.
7. Obstfeld (1996a) introduces the cost of holding foreign currency which was missing from Krugman (1979) and Flood and Garber (1984).
8. Note: RNULC stands for real effective exchange rates based on normalized unit labor costs.
9. Refer to Buiter et al. (1998) for a day-to-day description of the European crisis.
10. These are open-economy versions of the classic Diamond-Dybvig (1983) model of bank runs, where uninsured demand deposit contracts are able to provide liquidity but leave the banks vulnerable to runs.
11. This trend gets reversed most of the time following the depreciation of the exchange rate.
12. In a beauty pageant, a judge picks the girl that he thinks others will pick, rather than the one he considers to be the most beautiful.
13. See, for example, Banerjee (1992), Bikhchandani et al. (1992), and Froot et al. (1992).
14. As Krugman (1998a) puts it: 'I feel worse if I lose money in a Thai devaluation when others don't, than I will if I lose the same in the general rout'.
15. Refer to Devenow and Welch (1996) for a summary on rational herding literature.
16. Refer to Kaminsky et al. (2003) for a discussion of 'fast and furious' crises, where some crises induce contagion effects, while others do not. See Pericoli and Sbraca (2003) for a survey of financial contagion.

17. A mere devaluation in the case of Europe would not have meant a unilateral increase in exports, as the European trading partners were all in a recession or at least in a downturn.

References

Banerjee, A. (1992) A simple model of herd behavior. *Quarterly Journal of Economics* CVII(3): 797–817.

Bikhchandani, S., Hershleifer, D. and Welch, I. (1992) A theory of fads, fashion, custom, and cultural change as informational cascades. *Journal of Political Economy*, 992–1026.

Blackburn, K. and Sola, M. (1993) Speculative currency attacks and balance of payments crises. *Journal of Economic Surveys*, 7: 119–144.

Buiter, W., Corsetti, G. and Pesenti, P. (1998) *Financial Markets and European Monetary Cooperation: The Lessons of the 1992–93 Exchange Rate Mechanism Crisis*, Japan-U.S. Center Monographs on International Financial Markets, Cambridge University Press: Cambridge.

Calvo, G., (1995) Varieties of capital market crises. Mimeo, University of Maryland.

Calvo, G. and Mendoza, E. (1998) Rational herd behavior and the globalization of securities markets. Mimeo, University of Maryland.

Cerra, V. and Saxena, S. C. (2002) Contagion, monsoons and domestic turmoil in Indonesia: a case study in the Asian crisis. *Review of International Economics* 10(1): 36–44.

Chang, R. and Velasco, A. (1998) Financial crises in emerging markets: a canonical model. Federal Reserve Bank of Atlanta Working Paper, 98–10.

Chari, V. V. and Kehoe, P. (1997) Hot money. National Bureau of Economic Research Working Paper 6007, Cambridge MA.

Corsetti, G., Pesenti, P. and Roubini, N. (1998) Paper tigers? A model of the Asian crisis. Mimeo, New York University.

Devenow, A. and Welch, I. (1996) Rational herding in financial economics. *European Economic Review* 40: 603–15.

Diaz-Alejandro, C. (1985) Good-bye financial repression, hello financial crash. *Journal of Development Economics* 19, 1–2: 1–24.

Drazen, A. (1999) Political contagion in currency crises. NBER Working Paper 7211, Cambridge MA.

Eichengreen, B., Rose, A. and Wyplosz, C. (1996a) Contagious currency crises: first tests. *Scandinavian Journal of Economics* 98(4): 463–84.

Flood, R. and Garber, P. (1984) Collapsing exchange rate regimes: some linear examples. *Journal of International Economics* 17: 1–17.

Flood, R. and Marion, N. (1998) Perspectives on the recent currency crisis literature. IMF Working Paper WP/98/130

Froot, K., Scharfstein, D. and Stein, J. (1992) Herd on the street: informational inefficiencies in a market with short-term speculation. *Journal of Finance* 47(4): 1461–84.

Goldfajn, I. and Valdes, R. (1997) Capital flows and the twin crises: the role of liquidity. IMF Working Paper WP/97/87.

Kaminsky, G., Lizondo, S. and Reinhart, C. (1997) Leading indicators of currency crises. IMF Working Paper WP/97/79.

Kaminsky, G. and Reinhart, C. (1999) The twin crises: the causes of banking and balance of payments problems. *American Economic Review* 89(3): 473–500.

Kaminsky, G., Reinhart, C. and Vegh, C. (2003) The unholy trinity of financial contagion. *Journal of Economic Perspectives* 17(4): 51–74.

Kehoe, T. J. (1996) Comments on Krugman (1996). In *Macroeconomics Annual*. Cambridge MA: NBER, pp. 378–392.

Krugman, P. (1979) A model of balance-of-payments crises. *Journal of Money, Credit and Banking* 11(3): 311–325.

Krugman, P. (1996) Are currency crises self-fulfilling? In *Macroeconomics Annual*. Cambridge MA: NBER: 345–378

Krugman, P. (1998a) Currency crises. Mimeo, MIT.

Krugman, P. (1998b) What happened to Asia? Mimeo, MIT.

Leibenstein, H. (1950) Bandwagon, snob, and veblen effects in the theory of consumers' demand. *Quarterly Journal of Economics* 64(2): 183–207.

Levy-Yeyati, E. and Sturzenegger, F. (2003) To float or fix: evidence on the impact of exchange rate regimes on growth. *American Economic Review* 93(4): 1173–93.

McKinnon, R. and Pill, H. (1996) Credible liberalization and international capital flows: the overborrowing syndrome. In Takatoshi Ito and Anne Krueger (eds), *Financial Deregulation and Integration in East Asia*. Chicago: Chicago University Press, pp. 7–42.

Miller, V. (1995) Central bank reaction to banking crises in fixed exchange rate regimes. Mimeo, Université de Quebec à Montreal.

Mishkin, F. (1996) Understanding financial crises: a developing country perspective. In *Annual World Bank Conference on Development Economics*. Washington DC: World Bank, pp. 29–62.

Obstfeld, M. (1986) Rational and self-fulfilling balance of payments crises. *American Economic Review* 76(1): 72–81.

Obstfeld, M. (1994) The logic of currency crises. *Banque De France, Cahiers Economiques et Monetaires* 43: 189–213.

Obstfeld, M (1996a) Models of currency crises with self-fulfilling features. *European Economic Review* 40: 1037–47.

Obstfeld, M. (1996b) Comment on Krugman (1996). In *Macroeconomics Annual*. Cambridge MA: NBER, pp. 393–403.

Pericoli, M. and Sbracia, M. (2003) A primer on financial contagion. *Journal of Economic Surveys* 17: 571–608.

Radelet, S. and Sachs, J. (1998) The East Asian financial crisis: diagnosis, remedies, prospects. Mimeo, Harvard Institute for International Development.

Rangvid, J. (2001) Second generation models of currency crises. *Journal of Economic Surveys* 15: 613–646.

Reinhart, C. M. and Vegh, C. (1996) Do exchange rate-based inflation stabilizations sow the seeds of their own destruction? Mimeo, University of Maryland and UCLA.

Sachs, J., Tornell, A. and Velasco, A. (1996) Financial crises in emerging markets: the lessons of 1995. *Brooking Papers on Economic Activity* 1: 147–217.

Salant, S. and Henderson, D. (1978) Market anticipation of government policy and the price of gold. *Journal of Political Economy* 86: 627–48.

Saxena, S. C. and Wong, K.-y. (1999) Currency crises and capital controls: a selective survey. Mimeo, University of Pittsburgh and University of Washington.

Stoker, J. (1995) Intermediation and the business cycle under a specie standard: the role of the Gold Standard in English financial crises, 1790–1850. Mimeo, University of Chicago.

Velasco, A. (1987) Financial and balance of payments crises. *Journal of Development Economics* 27: 263–93.

Appendix 1. Data Source.

Series	Source
Nominal Exchange Rate	IFS line ae; rf
Real Effective Exchange Rate (based on CPI)	IFS line rec
Real Effective Exchange Rate (based on RNULC)	IFS line reu
Total Foreign Reserves Minus Gold	IFS line 11.d
Reserve Money	IFS line 14
Consumer Price Index	IFS line 64
Bank Deposits	(IFS line 24 + IFS line 25)/IFS line 64
Domestic Credit	IFS line 32
M2 measure of money supply	IFS line 34 + IFS line 35
Discount Rate	IFS line 60
Treasury Bill Rate	IFS line 60C
Deposit Rate	IFS line 60L
Lending Rate	IFS line 60P
Exports	IFS line 70
Imports	IFS line 71
Terms of Trade	(IFS line 74/IFS line 75)*100
Current Account Balance	IFS line 78ald
Capital Inflows	IFS line 78bjd + IFS line 78cad
Budget Balance	IFS line 80
GDP	IFS line 99b
GDP Volume	IFS line 99bvr
Unemployment Rate	IFS line 67R
Share Price	IFS line 62

6

MACROECONOMIC ADJUSTMENT AND THE POOR: ANALYTICAL ISSUES AND CROSS-COUNTRY EVIDENCE

Pierre-Richard Agénor

The World Bank Washington DC

1. Introduction

Understanding and assessing the poverty and distributional effects of macroeconomic adjustment programs remain issues of considerable importance for economists and policymakers alike. A key reason for this is the growing evidence that economic and financial crises hurt the poor the most, because they often lack the means to protect themselves from adverse income and employment shocks. The poor lack assets (such as land and bank deposits) and often have no direct access to credit markets (or face prohibitive borrowing costs when they do), to smooth the impact of these shocks. For the very poor, unfavorable shocks may be large enough to result in actual declines in consumption, bringing it down below subsistence levels and exerting a detrimental effect on their longer term nutrition and health prospects. Moreover, due to the lack of education and marketable skills, the poor tend to be less mobile (across sectors and regions) than better-educated workers and are therefore often unable to switch jobs and capitalize on available employment opportunities. Finally, indirect sources of income and public transfers other than unemployment benefits may decline during crises, because during such episodes the ability of relatives (or local communities) to engage in resource sharing and income redistribution may be reduced, while at the same time governments may be forced to adjust drastically their fiscal accounts with across-the-board cuts in expenditure.

There is also growing recognition of the fact that assessing the impact of adjustment programs on the poor may entail *dynamic trade-offs*. In particular, it is now well recognized that the large budgetary cuts that have been associated in some cases with stabilization efforts have fallen to a significant extent on transfers to households and other types of social expenditure, thereby worsening the plight of lower-income groups in the short term. At the same time, however, it is also well understood that these groups tend to be the ones most adversely affected by rapid inflation, credit rationing, and high interest rates, in part because of the effect of these variables on private sector activity and employment. To the extent that fiscal austerity leads to a durable reduction in the rate of inflation, greater access to credit by private firms, and lower borrowing rates, the poor may benefit from government spending cuts in the longer run. It is therefore important to carefully evaluate the net benefits (in present value terms) that such trade-offs entail in designing adjustment programs.

Despite the importance of these issues, however, the evidence examining the impact of adjustment programs (and macroeconomic policies in particular) on the poor remains relatively limited. Various country- (or region-) specific studies have been published in recent years, but they often remain highly descriptive when it comes to assessing the effect of macroeconomic and other structural variables on poverty. In addition, although it is well recognized that the poor often generate a sizable share of their income from wage employment, the role of the labor market in the transmission of macroeconomic policy shocks to lower-income groups (particularly those located in the urban sector) has not been fully explored in analytical and empirical models. Understanding this role is all the more important given the peculiarities and imperfections (which often result from government intervention) that often characterize the labor market in developing countries.

The present study attempts to contribute to the current debate at three levels. First, it provides an analytical overview of the various transmission channels of macroeconomic policy to the poor, dwelling in the process on the most recent analytical and empirical literature in this area. Second, it provides a formal analysis of the role of the labor market in the transmission of policy shocks to the urban poor, taking into account the type of distortions often observed in the developing world. Although the model is used to examine only the effect of a particular shock, it is sufficiently general to serve a variety of purposes. Third, it provides some new, quantitative evidence on the effect of macroeconomic factors on poverty, based on cross-country regressions.

The remainder of the paper is organized as follows. Section II provides a brief review of the recent evidence on poverty in developing countries. The various channels through which macroeconomic policies affect the poor are discussed in Section III. Both direct and indirect effects (through, for instance, inflation, aggregate demand, income distribution, and macroeconomic volatility), are analyzed. The role of the labor market is also discussed in general terms. Section IV develops an analytical framework that captures in a more formal way the role of the urban labor market in the transmission mechanism of macroeconomic policy shocks. The model incorporates several important and well-documented features of the labor market in developing countries, such as efficiency wages, a large informal sector, labor market segmentation, a heterogeneous and imperfectly mobile labor force, and wage flexibility in the informal economy.[1] The impact and steady-state effects of an increase in taxes – a typical measure in adjustment programs – are also examined. Section V provides cross-section econometric evidence on the impact of macroeconomic and structural variables on poverty, including the degree of openness, school enrollment rates, real exchange rate depreciations, macroeconomic volatility, income inequality, and asymmetric movements in income levels and output growth. Finally, Section VI summarizes the main results of the analysis and elaborates on its policy implications.

2. Poverty: A Brief Overview

It is now well recognized that poverty is a multidimensional concept, encompassing not only insufficient income but also lack of access to adequate health services and sanitation, a high degree of illiteracy, and deprivation of basic rights and security (see World Bank, 2000). These dimensions of human deprivation interact in many important ways; for instance, improvements in health conditions lead to higher productivity and enhance the ability of workers to increase their incomes. Nevertheless, the focus of this brief overview will be limited to income poverty.

Figure 1 shows the evolution of poverty in various regions of the developing world during the period 1987–98. The indicator displayed is the headcount index (the proportion of individuals or households earning less than a given absolute level of income, or poverty line), which measures the *incidence* of poverty.[2] Extreme poverty (defined as living on less than $1 per day) is shown on the left-hand side, whereas relative poverty (defined as the share of people living on less than $2 per day) is shown on the right-hand side. Both indicators depict a similar picture. The incidence of poverty is the highest in South Asia and sub-Saharan Africa. In sub-Saharan Africa, poverty has in fact increased slightly. Indeed, following a significant improvement in living standards during the 1970s and 1980s, extreme poverty declined only slowly in the developing world during the 1990s. The share of the world population living on less than $1 a day fell from 28% in 1987 to 23% in 1998, but the number of poor people remained roughly constant as the population increased. The share of people living on less than $2 per day (a more relevant threshold for middle-income economies such as those of East Asia and Latin America) showed roughly similar trends. At the same time, progress in alleviating poverty has been far from even across regions; in fact, apart from East Asia, little progress has been achieved during the period in reducing poverty rates. Between 1987 and 1998, poverty rose rapidly in Eastern Europe and Central Asia, and continued to rise (albeit at a relatively low rate) in sub-Saharan Africa. In East Asia, the proportion of people in poverty (both extreme and relative) declined dramatically during the same period, despite the

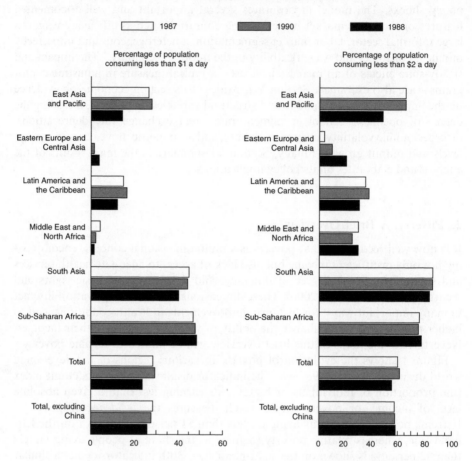

Figure 1. Developing Countries: Poverty Measures.

Source: World Bank.

fact that the 1997–98 financial crisis slowed progress considerably. But in South Asia, where a significant propotion of the world's poor live, progress has been much less significant. And in Latin America, although the share of the population in poverty fell during the 1990s, the absolute number of poor people increased to 181 million (of which 90 million live in extreme poverty) in 1998, as a result of population growth (Wodon et al., 2001).

2.1 Rural and Urban Poverty

The recent evidence also suggests that the distribution of the poor between rural and urban areas varies considerably across regions. This is particularly well illustrated by comparing Latin America and sub-Saharan Africa. In a country like Chile, for instance, poverty is evenly distributed between rural and urban areas (Anríquez et al., 1998). By contrast, in sub-Saharan Africa, the poor tend to be concentrated in rural areas. According to the data compiled by Sahn et al. (1997, ch. 2), for instance, the share of the national poverty rate accounted for by rural areas in the late 1980s and early 1990s was 66% in Gambia, 72% in Ghana, 90% in Kenya and Tanzania, 88% in Madagascar, 98% in Malawi, and 71% in Zambia.[3] According to World Bank estimates, three-fourths of the poor in Côte d'Ivoire in 1995 were located in rural areas (World Bank, 1997, p. 11). At the same time, in many countries in sub-Saharan Africa – where both population and urbanization growth rates tend to be relatively high, compared to other regions of the developing world – the regional distribution of poverty in the past few years has been substantially affected by rapid rural-to-urban migration. In several cases, urban poverty, although not as severe as it is in rural areas, has become a major source of public concern. In Ghana for instance, the rural poverty rate was 34% in 1992, whereas the urban poverty rate was 26.5% (Canagarapajah and Mazumdar, 1997). Although rural poverty declined sharply between 1987 and 1992, little progress was achieved in reducing urban poverty during that period.

The sources of income of the rural poor and the urban poor also differ significantly. The rural poor in many countries in sub-Saharan Africa, for instance, are predominantly self-employed and continue to rely on direct earnings from agricultural production as their main source of income – although income from salaried employment and self-employment in small enterprises have become important in some countries.[4] The data compiled by Sahn et al. (1997) indicate that in countries like Côte d'Ivoire, Ghana, Guinea, Madagascar, and Tanzania, more than 90% of the rural workers were self-employed in the early 1990s, reflecting the predominance of own-account agriculture and, to a much lesser extent, small and micro enterprises in manufacturing and services. By contrast, the urban poor are typically self-employed workers in very small enterprises in the informal (nonwage) sector; but their incomes tend to fluctuate in response to changes in activity in the formal economy, because of the ease of entry in the informal sector and the degree of mobility of the labor force between the two sectors.

The distribution of poor households between rural and urban areas has important implications for studies aimed at assessing the effect of short-term stabilization policies on poverty. Income characteristics suggest, for instance, that the rural poor may be less vulnerable, and the urban poor more vulnerable, to some types of macroeconomic policy shocks. The reason is that, unlike the urban poor, the rural poor can cushion the impact of an adverse shock to income on consumption by adjusting the share of their agricultural output that they keep for themselves.[5] At the same time, the urban poor tend to benefit more than the rural poor from food subsidies. Thus, large cuts in government subsidies may have a larger effect on the urban poor. This reasoning would suggest that studies focusing on the effects of macroeconomic adjustment on the poor may need to analyze separately the behavior of urban and rural poverty rates, with macroeconomic variables possibly playing a less significant role in the former case.

2.2 *Poverty, Growth, and Inequality*

Figures 2 and 3 show the relationship between growth (as measured by the annual rate of change of real GNP per capita) and two measures of poverty during the 1990s: the headcount index (defined in the previous section) and the poverty gap

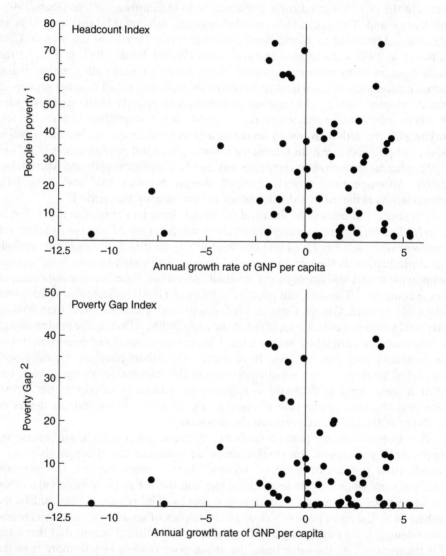

Figure 2. Developing Countries: Growth and People in Absolute Poverty (in percent).

Source: Table 4 in World Bank, *World Development Report* (2000/2001). [1]Proportion of the population earning US$1 or less a day, various survey years. [2]Poverty gap at US$1 or less a day, various survey years.

Note: Sample consists of 54 countries for which data are provided in the *World Development Report*.

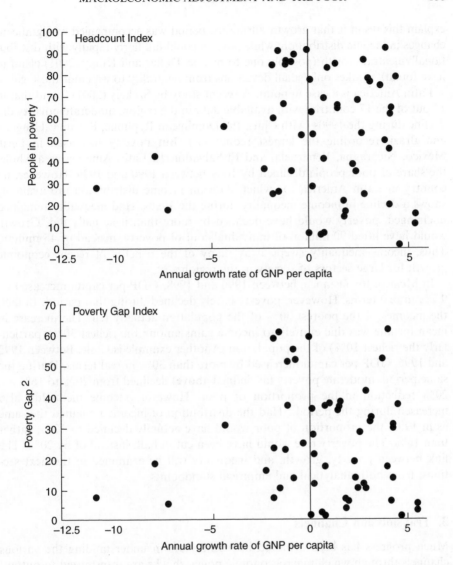

Figure 3. Developing Countries: Growth and People in Relative Poverty (in percent).

Source: Table 4 in World Bank, *World Development Report* (2000/2001). [1]Proportion of the population earning US$2 or less a day, various survey years. [2]Poverty gap at US$2 or less a day, various survey years.

Note: Sample consists of 54 countries for which data are provided in the *World Development Report*.

index (defined as the average shortfall of the income of the poor with respect to the poverty line, multiplied by the headcount index), which measures the *depth* of poverty. Both extreme and relative poverty measures are used. The figures show no obvious pattern in the relation between growth and poverty. One reason that may explain this result is that growth during the period was accompanied by significant changes in income distribution: while poverty could fall fairly rapidly with distributionally-neutral growth (possibly one to one, as Dollar and Kraay (2001) claim to have found), it takes only small deviations from neutrality to wipe out those gains.

Latin America is a case in point. A recent study by Székely (2001) found that in 12 out of the 17 countries with available data in the region, moderate poverty did decline during the 1990s (with Chile, the Dominican Republic, Panama, Uruguay and Brazil recording the largest reductions). But poverty increased in Peru, Mexico, Nicaragua, Venezuela, and El Salvador. In Latin America as a whole, the share of poor people declined by 10% between 1990 and 1999. However, no country in Latin America for which data on income distribution are available shows a decline in income inequality during the 1990s. Had inequality remained unchanged, poverty would have declined by more than it actually did. Growth would have lifted 90 million of individuals out of poverty, instead of 45 million. Thus, income inequality swept away many of the benefits of recent economic growth for large sectors of society in the region.

In Mexico, for instance, between 1996 and 1998, GDP per capita increased by 9.7% in real terms. However, poverty barely declined during that period. In fact, the incomes of the poorest 30% of the population actually fell. The increase in mean income was due entirely to income gains among the richest 30% (particularly the richest 10%) of the population. Another example is Chile. Between 1992 and 1996, GDP per capita increased by more than 30% in real terms. During the same period, moderate poverty (as defined above) declined from 20% to 16% – a 20% reduction in the proportion of poor. However, income inequality also increased during the period.[6] Had the distribution of income remained the same as in 1992, the proportion of poor would have actually declined to 10%, rather than 16%. The poverty rate would have been cut in half, instead of by 20%. The link between poverty, growth, and inequality will be examined in the next sections, from both analytical and empirical standpoints.

3. Transmission Channels

Much progress has been achieved in recent years in understanding the various channels through which macroeconomic policy shocks are transmitted to output, employment, wages, and prices in a developing-country context (for an overview, see Agénor and Montiel, 1999). Several of these channels are relevant for understanding the impact of macro shocks on the poor, in both rural and urban areas. This section identifies these various channels, dwelling on a distinction between direct and indirect effects.

3.1 Direct Effects

The most direct channels through which macroeconomic adjustment programs affect the poor are public sector layoffs and freezes on the wage bill, cuts in government expenditure on transfers and subsidies, and increases in public sector prices.[7]

3.1.1 *Wage freeze, Layoffs, and Spending Cuts*

Fiscal consolidation often take the form of cuts in real wages in the public sector (for instance, by freezing the nominal wage bill in a context of non-zero inflation) and laying off employees. Wage cuts and layoffs may raise directly the poverty rate, particularly in the absence of a safety net (such as a government-run unemployment benefits scheme) or if they occur during periods of low activity (and thus low demand for labor). A cut in current transfers to low-income households reduces their resources directly, whereas a reduction in subsidies on goods and services (such as basic food items and gasoline) that are consumed by the poor lowers their purchasing power.[8] Both measures may worsen poverty by forcing households to reduce consumption, with the effect of the latter depending on the expenditure pattern of the poor and their ability to dissave (or borrow) to offset the negative income shock. As noted earlier, to the extent that the urban poor benefit more from transfers and subsidies to begin with, urban poverty rates may increase proportionately more.

However, there are various factors suggesting that assessing the effect of macro-economic policy on the poor by looking only at aggregate indicators of public expenditure may be misleading. First, there is empirical evidence that social expenditure (including spending on education and health) benefits disproportionately upper-income households. For instance, Camargo and Ferreira (2000) found that in Brazil, social expenditures are to a large extent appropriated by the middle classes and the rich. Li *et al.* (1999), in a study based on a relatively large group of developing countries, found that the share of the richest income quintile in public spending on education, at 28%, was more than double that of the poorest income quintile (13%). Similar results were obtained by Castro-Leal *et al.* (1999) for a group of African countries. And in many Latin American countries, social security and social safety nets have long been 'reserved' for the relatively small group of workers in the formal sector and government employees. In such conditions, large cuts in social expenditure may have little impact on the poorest of the poor.

Second, it may be argued that a wage freeze or layoffs of low-productivity workers, to the extent that they lower overall government expenditure and reduce pressures for monetization of the fiscal deficit, may lower inflation and therefore generate an indirect benefit for the poor (see below). The net welfare effect in present value terms, therefore, is ambiguous because of conflicting effects on (current and future) income. Third, in addition to the *level* effect associated with reductions in public expenditure, there may be a *compositional* effect: the share of social spending in total government expenditure may actually increase at the same time that overall spending is being cut.[9] Moreover, transfers and subsidies may fall both as a percentage of GDP and as a percentage of total government expenditure without any adverse effect on poverty if, at the same time, improved targeting of social spending takes place – thereby improving the flow of resources actually reaching the poor. Indeed, in some adjustment programs, expenditure reforms have entailed a redirection of health and education expenditures toward basic/preventive health care and primary education (which benefits the poor more than secondary or tertiary education), and an improvement in the targeting of social safety nets – notably by transforming generalized transfers to households into more specific transfers to the very poor.

Clearly, expenditure reallocation continues to be a major issue in the design of adjustment programs – particularly, at the present time, in countries where debt relief, and associated fiscal savings, create new opportunities for reform and improved targeting. The lack of political influence of the poor, and pressures exerted by more powerful interest groups, may well continue to represent major stumbling blocks to pro-poor reallocations. But the point, nevertheless, is that in cases where fiscal consolidation occurs in such a way that it benefits the poor, the net effect of adjustment may be beneficial – even if the overall level of public expenditure falls.

3.1.2 *Increases in Public Sector Prices*

Increases in prices of goods and services produced by the public sector – such as utilities and other types of public services, such as toll roads – often figure prominently in macroeconomic and structural adjustment programs, particularly when large fiscal imbalances prevail at the inception of the program and public enterprises provide large transfers to the government. Because they reduce the purchasing power of the poor (just like cuts in subsidies do), they hurt them directly. By how much poverty rises will depend ultimately on the consumption-expenditure pattern of the poor and their ability to 'smooth' consumption through dissavings and borrowing. Once again, however, if the increase in public sector prices leads to a lower fiscal deficit and reduced inflationary pressures, the net effect on the poor may be positive in the medium term.

3.2 *Indirect Effects*

Indirect effects of macroeconomic policy on the poor operate through changes in aggregate demand and output (assuming that excess capacity exists initially) and employment in the private sector; changes in the rate of economic growth; changes in inflation and the relevant expenditure price deflator for the poor; changes in the real exchange rate; macroeconomic volatility; and distributional effects.[10] In addition, output and employment effects associated with stabilization policies may be asymmetric – imparting some degree of 'hysterisis' to the behavior of poverty rates.

3.2.1 *Aggregate Demand and Employment*

Macroeconomic adjustment programs affect aggregate demand and employment (and thus poverty) through various channels. The first category of effects results from reductions in transfers and subsidies (as noted earlier), and cuts in government expenditure other than wages and salaries. In particular, cuts in capital spending (which have longer-run effects as well, as discussed below) have often been large in practice, due to the difficulty of compressing the wage bill. By reducing aggregate demand and the demand for labor, everything else equal, these reductions in public expenditure may increase poverty.

The second category of effects through which macroeconomic policy affects aggregate demand operates through changes in private spending. Specifically, there are several channels through which lower public spending can lead to a *reduction* in private expenditure:

- If public investment and private sector investment are complementary (particularly with regard to public investment in infrastructure, as the evidence for developing countries gathered by Agénor and Montiel (1999) suggests), a cut in public investment outlays – in addition to its direct effect on aggregate demand noted earlier – may reduce the productivity of the private capital stock at the margin, and thus reduce private expenditure and aggregate demand.
- An increase in direct taxation aimed at reducing fiscal imbalances, such as an increase in tax rates on wages or profits, may reduce private expenditure on consumption and investment, by reducing expected income and the net rate of return on capital.
- Restrictive credit and monetary policies may lower private expenditure on consumption and investment, either directly (if credit availability effects are important) or by raising interest rates (which translate also into a higher cost of capital).[11]

However, there are also several channels through which public expenditure cuts can lead to *higher* private expenditure:

- As implied by Ricardian equivalence, a reduction in public expenditure (such as a cut in capital spending, as noted earlier) may lead to an equal reduction in perceived future tax liabilities by the private sector, owing to lower financing needs to retire public debt. The present value of future disposable income will increase, resulting in an increase in current private spending. The net effect of a reduction in public spending on aggregate demand would thus be ambiguous.[12]
- The fall in domestic activity associated with a reduction in public spending at the original level of prices and interest rates could also lead to an increase in private expenditure. Suppose that the initial drop in income leads to a reduction in the demand for money, thereby creating excess supply on the money market. If nominal interest rates adjust downward immediately to maintain portfolio equilibrium, interest-sensitive components of aggregate demand would tend to increase, if inflation does not fall in the exact same proportion. Alternatively, if interest rates are slow to adjust, the excess supply of money may cause households to increase current spending in order to lower their real holdings of money balances (real balance effect). The net, general equilibrium effect on aggregate demand would, again, be ambiguous.
- Even in the absence of a real balance effect, the reduction in financing requirements by the public sector may reduce the cost, or increase the

availability, of bank credit to the private sector, thereby increasing private spending and the capacity to produce (if production was, to begin with, constrained by the ability to finance working capital needs).

● If prices are flexible, or if the cut in public spending was foreseen at the time that currently prevailing nominal wage contracts were agreed upon, the domestic price level could fall sufficiently to increase private spending, thereby mitigating the impact of the cut in public spending on total aggregate demand.

The foregoing discussion suggests, therefore, that the effects of macroeconomic adjustment on poverty operating though changes in aggregate demand are less clear-cut than is often thought. Although there are various channels through which such policies may reduce aggregate demand and worsen poverty (by reducing the level of activity and employment), there are also channels through which they may lead to an increase in aggregate demand and lower unemployment. Moreover, to the extent that reductions in aggregate demand associated with macroeconomic policy also lead to a fall in inflationary pressures (as discussed below) they may also benefit the poor.

3.2.2 Economic Growth

Macroeconomic policies may affect the poor not only through their impact on the *level* of output but also its *growth rate* over time. There are several channels through which this can occur. Sustained reductions in transfer payments from the public sector to the poor may have an adverse effect not only on the level of income of the poor but also on their propensity to save. In turn, lower savings rates may affect negatively the growth rate of output, as emphasized in endogenous growth models (see Agénor, 2000, ch. 11).[13] Similarly, to the extent that cuts in public sector investment (particularly in infrastructure) may reduce private investment through a complementarity effect, as indicated earlier, they may lower the rate of economic growth. Tax increases encourage evasion and the shifting of activities to the informal economy – so much so that the net impact may be a fall in revenue. As can be inferred from the analysis in Loayza (1996), which dwells on Barro (1990), the loss in tax revenue may reduce in the longer run the government's capacity to invest in infrastructure and thus lower the rate of economic growth if, again, there is complementary between public and private capital formation. In all these cases, by reducing the economy's growth rate, macroeconomic adjustment may have an adverse impact on poverty.

At the same time, however, the lower inflation rates that tend to be associated with macroeconomic adjustment may increase growth rates through their effect on the level and efficiency of investment, as documented in a number of analytical and empirical studies (see, for instance, Choi *et al.*, 1996). Moreover, to the extent that adjustment reduces the degree of macroeconomic volatility (as discussed later), it may also have a positive effect on growth.

3.2.3 *Inflation and Expenditure Deflators*

The poor are more vulnerable to inflation than higher-income groups as a result of a variety of factors:

- Their income (wages or income from self-employment) is often defined in nominal terms, and they often do not benefit from indexation mechanisms. In periods of high inflation, therefore, the purchasing power of their resources may fall dramatically.[14]
- They have few inflation hedges – few real assets, such as land, and usually no indexed financial assets – with which to insulate themselves from the effect of price increases.
- Their holdings of cash balances are subject to the inflation tax, which, although not usually accounted for in standard measures of poverty, could have a significant negative effect on the welfare of the poor.[15]

All three factors suggest that inflation stabilization would benefit the poor proportionately more than upper-income groups. However, a number of mitigating factors should be taken into account. First, because the poor allocate a large share of their income (or own production, if they are self-employed in agriculture) to subsistence, what matters is not so much the movement in the overall level of prices but rather the behavior of the prices of the goods and services that the poor consume (that is, a properly-weighted expenditure deflator). If, for instance, basic staple foods account for a large share of expenditure of low-income households, and if the prices of these commodities are kept under control, disinflation may have little impact on the poor. Second, to the extent that disisnflation is accompanied by a sharp drop in aggregate demand and employment (as discussed earlier), the excess supply of labor may lead, everything else equal, to further downward pressure on wages and a worsening of the plight of the poor. Finally, even if reducing inflation has desirable effects in the longer run, the short-run effect may be to worsen poverty if (as also noted earlier) fiscal adjustmtent takes the form of extensive cuts in social programs. Thus, as indicated in the introduction, there may be a dynamic trade-off, which suggests that it is the *net* present value of a reduction in inflation that needs to be assessed, in order to determine if stabilization from high inflation is indeed beneficial to the poor.

The situation is, in fact, more complicated than that, because lower inflation also contributes indirectly to growth, as shown empirically in studies such as those of Bruno and Easterly (1998) and Sarel (1996).[16] Higher growth rates increase the level of income per capita, and the higher level of income tends to lower measured poverty rates, in the absence of adverse shifts in inequality (see below). As noted earlier, inflation may affect growth rates through its impact on the level and efficiency of investment. More specifically, suppose that inflation drives a wedge between the marginal returns to real and financial capital. It thus distorts production incentives. The elimination of this distortion increases both the level and the rate of growth of output. In the model developed by Gylfason (1998) – in which both real and financial capital are used as inputs in the production process – increased price stability improves the efficiency with which capital is utilized, and thus increases the full-employment level of output in the long run; this represents a fairly conventional static output gain. But lower inflation also increases the rate of economic growth in the presence of constant returns to (broad) capital, as emphasized in the new endogenous growth literature (see, for instance, Easterly, 1993). This dynamic gain can be substantial in practice, as suggested by the simulations performed by Gylfason (1996).[17] Thus, by lowering the level of inflation (and possibly the variability of inflation, as discussed below) and improving the allocation of resources, macroeconomic adjustment promotes growth, thereby enhancing its long-term benefits to the poor.

3.2.4 *Real Exchange Rate*

The combination of exchange rate, fiscal, and monetary policies implemented in macroeconomic adjustment programs often aims at achieving a depreciation of the real exchange rate, in order to foster a reallocation of resources toward the tradables sector. In turn, a real depreciation may affect poverty (and income distribution) through two main channels:

- A real depreciation – brought about either through a nominal depreciation or a fall in the price of nontradable goods – favors consumers of nontradables (such as food, housing and retail services) in general, and the urban poor in particular. However, in practice, a real depreciation is often implemented through a nominal depreciation, which also raises the domestic price of imported goods. To the extent that such goods are consumed by the poor, there is a negative income effect that may offset, at least in part, the relative price effect.
- A real depreciation tends to foster a reallocation of resources toward agricultural export activities, raising the income of export-crop farmers and rural households (see Dorosh and Sahn, 2000).[18] In countries where the poor are predominantly located in rural areas, a real depreciation will therefore raise incomes and reduce poverty.

However, there are other offsetting supply-side effects of a real exchange rate depreciation that must also be taken into account. Because resources are reallocated toward the tradable sector, the demand for labor in the nontradable sector may fall; lower employment and nominal wages (in the presence of downward rigidity of prices) may translate into a fall in real wages and a higher incidence of poverty. In particular, if the urban poor are also producers of nontraded goods (as is the case in the informal sector), the economy-wide benefit of a reduction in rural poverty may be highly mitigated and aggregate poverty may well increase.

The real exchange rate depreciation that often accompanies macroeconomic adjustment programs (at least in their initial stages) may also bring about indirect effects on poverty. For instance, it has been noted that a real depreciation can lead to an increase in the user cost of capital in the tradable sector, because capital goods (machinery and equipment) are often imported in developing countries (Lora and Olivera, 1998). This tends to lower investment in fixed capital and, as a result of complementarity, to reduce the demand for skilled workers. To the extent that skilled and unskilled labor are net substitutes (as the evidence suggests for many countries), the demand for unskilled workers may increase, raising employment and average income of the poor, thereby reducing the incidence of poverty. However, to the extent that the real depreciation is accompanied (or brought about) by a trade liberalization program that features a sharp reduction in tariffs, one may get the exact opposite results: the user cost of imported capital goods may fall significantly in net terms – thereby leading to an increase in the demand for skilled labor, a fall in unskilled employment, and an increase in poverty. Finally, if the real exchange rate depreciation is brought about by a nominal devaluation, and if the economy is a net importer of intermediate inputs (such as oil), the real depreciation will also represent a negative supply-side shock which may reduce the demand for labor (even in the tradables sector) – so much so that the net effect may be a contraction in output, an increase in unemployment and a higher incidence of poverty. The possibility that a nominal devaluation can be contractionary through adverse supply-side effects has indeed been noted in a number of analytical and empirical studies (see Agénor and Montiel, 1999, ch. 8).

3.2.5 Macroeconomic Volatility

A high degree of macroeconomic volatility is a well-documented feature of the economic environment in developing countries (see Agénor and Montiel, 1999, ch. 1). Such volatility results very often from external factors (such as sharp changes in a country's terms of trade or fluctuations in world interest rates, due to abrupt changes in market sentiment) but is also sometimes policy-induced, in part as a result of the absence of rules-based policymaking and the propensity to adopt 'stop-and-go' policies. In turn, macroeconomic volatility can affect the poor through the following channels:

- Investment and growth. Volatility tends to distort price signals and the expected rate of return for investors; in the presence of irreversibility effects (see Dixit and Pindyck, 1994), the decision to wait may lead to lower private investment and lower growth rates. Nonlinearities generated by capital market imperfections may also lead to significant effects of volatility on investment (Aizenman and Marion, 1999).
- Precautionary savings. The propensity to save for both rich and poor households may increase if macroeconomic volatility translates into higher income uncertainty or an increased probability of facing borrowing constraints in 'bad times' (as in Agénor and Aizenman, 2000). However, higher savings may also increase resources available for financial intermediaries to lend to potential investors, thereby stimulating growth; the net effect on poverty is thus a priori ambiguous.

- Credit market effects. A higher degree of macroeconomic volatility may heighten the perceived risk of default by lenders, and either increase the incidence of credit rationing or lead to a higher risk premium and borrowing rates for private firms (see Agénor and Aizenman, 1998). This may have an adverse effect on labor demand and the poor.
- Distributional effect. This effect may itself result from changes in inflation (see below).

Several studies have recently focused on the impact of macroeconomic volatility on growth. Bleaney (1996), for instance, in a cross-section study covering the period 1980–90, found that macroeconomic instability (particularly when measured by the fiscal balance and the degree of volatility of the real exchange rate) has a significant negative effect on the rate of economic growth and possibly also a negative effect on investment.[19] Rodrik (1998) obtained similar results for sub-Saharan Africa. Evidence for Latin America also suggests that macroeconomic volatility has tended to worsen income distribution and increase poverty in the region (Londoño and Székely, 1997).[20] Overall, therefore, the foregoing discussion suggests that macroeconomic adjustment, to the extent that it results in greater macroeconomic stability, may well lead to higher growth rates and reduce the incidence of poverty.

3.2.6 Distributional Effects

As noted in the previous section, the impact of growth on poverty can be highly mitigated by changes in income distribution. In general, large differences may exist between countries rergarding the extent to which growth (even when it is distribution-neutral) will affect poverty. Under distribution-neutrality, the higher the extent of initial inequality, the lower the poor gain from growth – a smaller share of total income implies a smaller absolute gain from a given increase in total income. However, in practice growth is not always distribution neutral. Indeed, the evidence reviewed by Bruno, Ravallion, and Squire (1998) suggests that and that changes in distribution can indeed have a large impact on poverty. They estimate that, holding mean income constant, a 1 percentage point increase in the Gini index is typically associated with roughly a 4 percentage point increase in the proportion of the population living on less than $1 a day. There is also a growing analytical literature suggesting that initial distribution matters to the extent and nature of subsequent growth (see, for instance, Galor and Zeira, 1993). This link can operate through credit market constraints, which limit the ability of the poor to invest in acquiring skills and may therefore tend to perpetuate poverty.

Another channel through which inequality may affect growth is through changes in macroeconomic volatility. Ramey and Ramey (1995) found that greater volatility of the growth rate tends to reduce the average rate of growth – an effect that may in part be due to its deterring effect on physical and human capital accumulation. More recently, Breen and Garcia-Penalosa (1999), using a cross-section of 80 developed and developing countries, found that income inequality is positively correlated with aggregate volatility, measured by the standard deviation of the annual growth rate of output.

Several explanations have been put forward to account for the adverse impact that inequality may have on macroeconomic volatility and ultimately on growth. Alesina and Perotti (1996) argued that high inequality may lead to political instability, which may in turn results in high macroeconomic volatility and lower growth. Aghion *et al.* (1999, pp. 1628–30), by contrast, argued that there is a direct effect of inequality on macroeconomic fluctuations. Inequality in (initial) resources leads to inequality in access to investment opportunities across individuals in the presence of capital market imperfections – as a result, for instance, of collateral requirements. This can generate persistent and large cyclical fluctuations in credit and investment (as individuals increase borrowing during booms and reduce it during recessions) that are detrimental to growth because of unexploited opportunities to invest in high-yield projects.

An important question is, then, what accounts for changes in income distribution? Figure 4 displays the correlation between the Gini coefficient and real GDP per capita for the sample of developed and developing countries included in the study of Dollar and Kraay (2001). The figure suggests a 'clustering' pattern – higher-income developed countries, in general, tend to have lower inequality than developing countries. At the same time, within the group of developing countries, the relationship

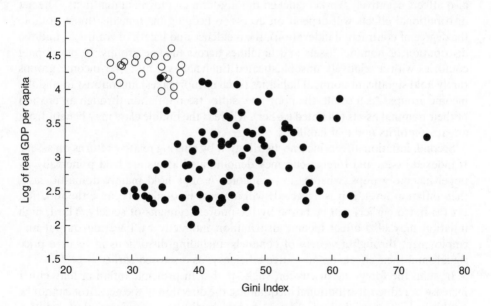

Figure 4. Gini Index and Per Capita Real GDP (annual averages, various periods).

Source: Dollar and Kraay (2001) and World Bank.

Note: The list of countries includes both industrial and developing countries (countries in transition are excluded from the Dollar-Kraay sample). The light-colored circles represent industrial countries.

appears to be positive – a relationship that is consistent with the view that higher inequality is conducive to a higher aggregate propensity to save, higher rates of capital accumulation, and higher growth rates. However, recent formal econometric studies (such as Barro, 2000) have been unable to find a robust relation between per capita income and inequality. In particular, the hypothesis of a Kuznets curve, an inverted U-shape relation between income levels and inequality, appears to be fragile (see also Fields (2001) and Fishlow (1995)). There is stronger evidence that changes in income inequality are related to investment in human capital – and thus to borrowing constraints, as noted earlier. As argued by Londoño and Székely (1997, 2000), in particular, the worsening in income inequality observed in Latin America in recent years appears to have been the result of growing inequalities in educational opportunities and inadequate access to credit markets.

High and variable inflation may also explain large changes in the distribution of income and wealth; such effects may be of considerable importance in evaluating the costs and benefits of macroeconomic adjustment programs. In general, changes in income distribution are the result of two categories of factors: the allocation of assets (both real and financial) and their relative rates of return. Inflation affects income distribution through both channels. First, it affects the relative values of different assets and liabilities. By lowering the real value of both nominal assets and liabilities, unanticipated inflation, in particular, favors debtors and holders of real equity over lenders and owners of nominal assets. In the absence of indexation, it also affects negatively workers locked in long-term employment contracts. The net distributional effects will depend on access to hedging instruments (most notably the degree of contractual indexation), the incidence and length of contracts, and the distribution of nominal assets and liabilities across income groups. In developing countries with a relatively unsophisticated financial system, lower-income groups rarely hold significant nominal liabilities (such as mortgages), in contrast to middle-income groups. As a result, the poor may suffer from inflation through an erosion of their nominal assets (as noted earlier), whereas the middle class may benefit from an erosion of its nominal liabilities.

Second, inflation affects income distribution by altering relative returns on assets. If indexed assets and foreign-currency denominated assets are held principally by upper-income groups, whereas lower-income groups hold mainly domestic cash, then inflation (even if it is expected) will increase inequality, because the inflation tax (as noted earlier) will be borne by the poorer segments of society. Third, high inflation may also affect income distribution indirectly by lowering output and employment through a variety of channels, including distortions in relative price signals and their effects on allocative efficiency, as discussed earlier.

In sum, the foregoing discussion suggests that in principle inflation may either increase or reduce distributional inequalities; the direction of the net effect cannot be established *a priori*. Indeed, Figure 5, which displays the correlation between inequality (as measured by the Gini index) and inflation for the group of developed and developing countries included in the data compiled by Dollar and Kraay (2001), does not show any obvious association between the two variables – beyond the clustering pattern observed in Figure 4. However, several formal empirical studies

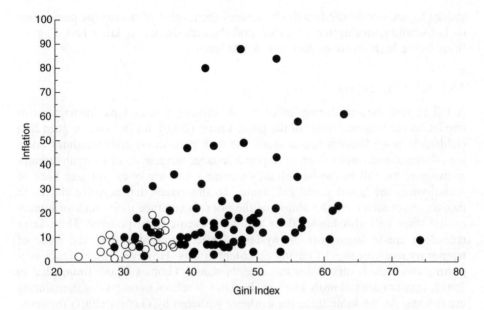

Figure 5. Gini Index and Inflation (annual averages, various periods).

Source: Dollar and Kraay (2001) and World Bank.

Note: The list of countries includes both industrial and developing countries (countries in transition are excluded from the Dollar-Kraay sample). The light-colored circles represent industrial countries.

found that inflation tends indeed to increase inequality. Bulir (2001), in particular, found that the adverse effect of inflation on income distribution is highly significant at high inflation levels. In such conditions, macroeconomic adjustment, by lowering mean inflation and its variability, may well have a very significant effect on poverty, through a reduction in income inequality.

3.3 *Asymmetric Effects of Cycles and Crises*

A growing body of empirical evidence suggests that cyclical downturns and economic crises may have an asymmetric effect on poverty: recessions or sharp output contractions may increase poverty rates significantly, whereas expansions tend to have a more limited effect. To the extent that the austerity measures that are often at the core of macroeconomic adjustment programs lead to adverse, short-run movements in output, asymmetric effects may mitigate significantly the longer-run benefits of adjustment for the poor. It is thus important to understand the sources of asymmetry. Following Agénor (2001a), five main classes of explanations can be distinguished. The first dwells on parents' decisions regarding their children attending school; the second is based on asymmetric changes in expectations and confidence factors; the third relies on a 'credit crunch' at the firm level, with rationing induced by either adverse selection problems or negative shocks to net worth; the fourth emphasizes the impact of borrowing constraints on household consumption behavior; and the fifth dwells on 'labor hoarding' by firms facing high turnover costs for skilled labor.

3.3.1 *Schooling Effects*

A fall in real income during an economic downturn may have an irreversible impact on the human capital of the poor. Lustig (2000), for instance, argued that children in poor families (particularly the very poor ones) are sometimes taken out of school and put to work in response to large adverse shocks – in an attempt to mitigate the fall in the household's income – but are often not sent back to school when the 'good times' roll again. To the extent that negative shocks to income affect adversely the ability of the poor to enhance their stock of human capital, they will also hinder their ability to escape from poverty. Thus, large recessions create some sort of 'hysteresis' effect on poverty, in the sense of temporary negative shocks having persistent effects. However, the evidence supporting this view is mixed; for instance, Neri and Thomas (2000) found that in Brazil, children are not more likely to drop out of school in recessions than during expansions. At the same time, the evidence gathered by Gaviria (2001) for seven Latin American countries suggests that it is the lower middle-class households (rather than the poor households) that are more likely to cut back on human capital investments in response to adverse income shocks.

3.3.2 *Expectations and Confidence Factors*

Consumers and firms may be more pessimistic during recessions than they are optimistic during expansions, and immediate prospects may matter more during downturns than future prospects. If consumers and firms worry more about the overall economic outlook and the economy's likely direction in a downturn, a positive output shock – induced by, say, a relaxation of credit constraints or an increase in government spending – may have a smaller impact (and thus be less effective) on private spending decisions during recessions than during booms. In addition, if the perceived degree of uncertainty about future profitability rises during recessions, firms may be less willing to invest – even after a large positive shock to aggregate demand. The reason, of course, is the 'option value' associated with waiting for the uncertainty to dissipate (Dixit and Pindyck, 1994). If output and labor demand become less responsive to positive shocks during a recession, the initial increase in poverty induced by higher unemployment may be difficult to reverse.

3.3.3 *Adverse Selection, Net Worth, and the Credit Market*

Recessions may be accompanied by high or increasing interest rates because an economic slowdown may raise the risk of bankruptcy. This may lead banks to raise the premium that they charge over and above the cost of funds, as shown for instance by Agénor and Aizenman (1998). An increase in the perceived risk of default may also lead to a tightening of credit constraints if lenders are unwilling to lend to riskier borrowers, as implied by adverse selection models of the credit market (see, for instance, Jaffee and Stiglitz, 1990). The tightening of credit constraints may magnify the impact of the initial recession on borrowing and spending, through both demand- and supply-side effects. The resulting fall in labor demand and thus the effect on poverty may also be compounded. If expansions are not characterized by an equivalent reduction in the perceived risk of default, adverse selection problems may impart an asymmetric bias to output shocks.[21]

A related argument that may explain a credit crunch in an economic downturn is based on net worth effects. A collapse in asset prices (e.g. real estate or equity prices) may lead to a sharp drop in the value of the collateral against which firms borrow. To the extent that firms (particularly small and medium-size ones) have limited alternatives to secure loans, banks may curtail credit because of the drop in value of assets that they can seize in case of default, possibly affecting smaller firms the most. A lower level of credit (or a higher risk premium) will, again, reduce output and employment, and eventually increase the incidence of poverty. An asymmetric effect may result from the fact that, after the crisis, economic uncertainty may remain high, expectations may remain pessimistic at least for a while, entailing as a result a slow recovery in asset prices.

3.3.4 *Borrowing Constraints and Household Consumption*

Credit constraints operating at the household level may also represent a source of asymmetry in the response of poverty to output shocks. If such constraints become binding during recessions – as a result of adverse selection, or net worth effects, because household wealth may be also adversely affected by sharp drops in asset prices – they may hamper the ability of households to smooth consumption.[22] The available evidence suggests indeed that risk-sharing and consumption smoothing remain highly imperfect in developing countries. The poorest households are typically those least insured against shocks because of their inability to accumulate assets and because, as noted earlier, asymmetric information problems and high transactions costs may completely preclude access for them to private market insurance or credit mechanisms to smooth income fluctuations. As a result, consumption smoothing through borrowing and lending is simply not feasible. Poor households may then have no option but to engage in either sub-optimal labor allocation decisions (such as forcing children to quit school and work, as noted earlier), or to let consumption fluctuate as much as income – with possibly detrimental longer-run effects on productivity.

3.3.5 *The 'Labor Hoarding' Hypothesis*

Recessions may also worsen poverty through an asymmetric effect on employment and productivity (see Agénor, 1999, 2001a). In a downturn, unskilled workers (among which the poor tend to be concentrated) are often the first to lose their jobs as firms 'hoard' their skilled labor force because of the existence of relatively higher turnover costs (hiring, training and firing costs) associated with the use of that category of labor. The incentive to do so is greater the more transitory the shock is perceived to be. Firms are therefore off their (skilled) labor demand curve during recessions, and skilled workers' wages are higher than their marginal product. When the expansion phase comes, the priority for firms is often to recoup the productivity losses and foregone profit opportunities incurred during the down-turn. If the degree of complementarity between skilled labor and physical capital is high (as the evidence suggests), they may increase fixed investment significantly and substitute away from unskilled labor. This, in turn, may produce a strong degree of persistence in unskilled unemployment and poverty over the course of the business cycle.

3.4 *The Role of the Labor Market*

The thrust of the foregoing discussion is that there are a variety of channels – with possibly offsetting (direct and indirect) effects – through which macroeconomic adjustment affects poverty. The importance of each of these channels will depend, of course, on the institutional and structural characteristics of individual economies. A key underlying theme of the discussion, however, is that the labor market is a crucial element in understanding the link between macroconomic adjustment and poverty. The poor often generate a significant share of their income from labor services. The way the labor market operates conditions the employment and wage outcomes of many specific policy decisions that are part of adjustment programs. There are, of course, more general reasons than poverty itself for focusing on the role of the labor market in the process of macroeconomic adjustment. Whether or not a devaluation leads to a reduction in the current account deficit, for instance, depends largely on the extent to which real wages are flexible downward. And labor market distortions may affect the productivity of all categories of workers, skilled and unskilled, thereby affecting the incomes of all types of households (rich and poor) and the economy's overall growth rate. Nevertheless, because of their precarious condition, the poor are likely to be particularly affected by labor market imperfections that hinder an efficient allocation of resources.

As noted earlier, for studies focusing on the role of short-term macroeconomic factors on poverty in developing countries, understanding the dynamics of the urban labor market is crucial. In this respect there are a number of important institutional characteristics of this market that need to be considered.[23] In general, the urban labor market can be divided into a formal segment (which includes, on the demand side, large private enterprises and the public sector) and an informal segment, which is characterized by ease of entry, a high degree of wage flexibility, and the absence of enforcement of labor regulations.[24] Because formal employment in many developing countries (in both Latin America and sub-Saharan Africa) has increased only slowly in recent decades, whereas urban migration has been exten-sive, informal urban employment has increased dramatically in size. In Kenya, for instance, the share of the informal sector in employment outside agriculture is currently about 60%. In Ghana, between 1980 and 1990, employment in the formal sector declined significantly, despite a substantial increase (by 50%) of the non-agricultural labor force. Estimates by Canagarapajah and Mazumdar (1997, p. 45) suggest that much of the expansion in the labor force was absorbed by the informal sector, whose size increased from 36 to 45% of the total (agricultural and non-agricultural) labor force. In Bangladesh, 90% of the labor force is in the informal (nontraded) sector, mainly in rural areas. In Latin America, informal sector employment accounted for 57.4% of total employment in 1996, nearly 6 percentage points more than in 1990. For the region as a whole, the expansion in the number of informal sector jobs during the same period accounted for 80% of the net increase in employment (Lora and Olivera, 1998, p. 10). Figure 6 suggests that the size of the urban informal sector tends to be inversely related with the level and rate of growth of GDP per capita. There is also some evidence that the size of the informal sector is related to the tax burden; Figure 7 suggests indeed that both the share of overall tax revenue in GDP and the share of direct taxes in GDP are inversely related with the share of urban informal sector employment.

Empirical studies indicate that workers in the formal sector typically have higher levels of education than those employed in the informal sector. In part this is because formal sector firms use more advanced technologies, which require workers with higher levels of skills (and sometimes considerable on-the-job training) to be operated. Higher wages allow firms to reduce turnover costs for highly-skilled workers. A study of the manufacturing industry in Kenya, for instance, found a very significant effect of firm size on wages (Bigsten and Horton, 2001), even after controlling for (observable) labor quality differences and working conditions. In addition to reducing labor turnover, firms may be willing to pay more to enhance productivity, attract better workers, or maintain loyalty and morale, in line with various forms of efficiency wage theories (see Agénor, 1996, 2000). The evidence also suggests that the urban poor (who provide mostly unskilled labor) are disproportionately employed in the informal sector. In Chile, for instance, 30% of employment in the total population was informal in 1994; it was 45% amongst the poor (Anríquez et al., 1998). Estimates for sub-Saharan Africa are much higher. Thus, 'disguised' unemployment often characterizes the urban informal labor market. Other evidence indicates that open unemployment is also important in many developing countries, affecting both skilled and unskilled workers. This suggests that the extent of labor mobility between the formal and the informal sectors, although quite high, may not be perfect at least in the short run – thereby limiting the 'shock-absorbing', or countercyclical, role of the informal sector. The next section presents a macroeconomic model with a labor market structure that captures several of the characteristics highlighted above and analyzes the impact of fiscal adjustment on poverty.

4. Macroeconomic Policy, the Urban Labor Market, and Poverty

Dwelling on the above observations, this section presents a macroeconomic model of a small open developing economy that provides a useful framework for the

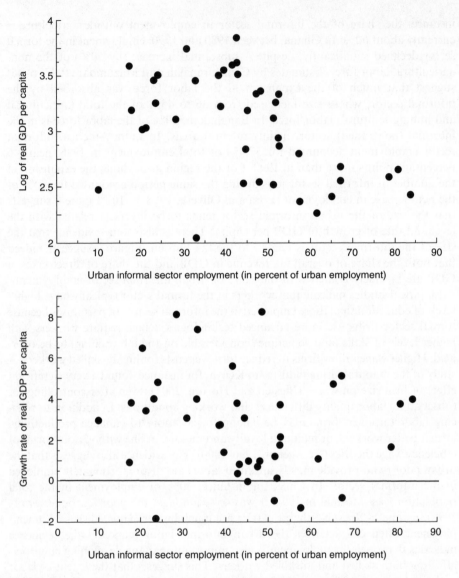

Figure 6. Developing Countries: Informal Sector and Per Capita Real GDP (averages).

Source: World Bank and International Labor Organization.

Note: The list of the countries is Argentina (1990–95), Bangladesh (1993), Benin (1992), Bolivia (1990–96), Botswana (1985, 1996), Brazil (1990–95), Cameroon (1993), Chile (1990–95, 1997), Colombia (1984,1986,1988,1990–95), Costa Rica (1990–95), Cote d'Ivoire (1996), Ecuador (1990–97), Ethiopia (1996), Gambia (1992–93), Ghana (1997), Guatemala (1987, 1989), Honduras (1990–95), India (1993), Indonesia (1995), Iran (1996), Jamaica (1996), Kenya (1992–95), Madagascar (1995), Mali (1989, 1996), Mauritius (1992), Mexico (1990–96), Morocco (1988), Niger (1995), Pakistan (1992), Panama (1990–95), Paraguay (1990–96), Peru (1984, 1986–87, 1989–97), Philippines (1988, 1995), South Africa (1995), Sri Lanka (1985), Tanzania (1990–91, 1995), Thailand (1988, 1990–95), Tunisia (1981), Uganda (1993–94), Uruguay (1990–97), Venezuela (1990–97), Zambia (1993).

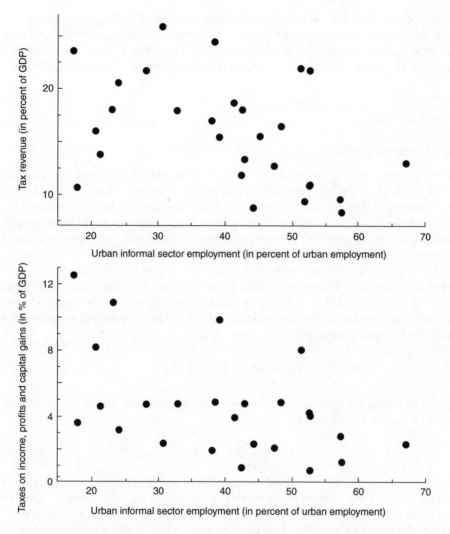

Figure 7. Developing Countries: Informal Sector Size and Tax Revenue (averages).

Source: World Bank and International Labor Organization.

Note: The list of the countries is Argentina (1990–95), Bolivia (1990–96), Botswana (1985, 1996), Brazil (1990–95), Cameroon (1993), Chile (1990–95, 1997), Colombia (1984, 1986, 1988, 1990–95), Costa Rica (1990–95), Cote d'Ivoire (1996), Ecuador (1990–97), India (1993), Indonesia (1995), Iran (1996), Kenya (1992–95), Madagascar (1995), Mauritius (1992), Mexico (1990–96), Morocco (1988), Pakistan (1992), Panama (1990–95), Paraguay (1990–96), Peru (1984, 1986–87, 1989–97), Philippines (1988, 1995), South Africa (1995), Sri Lanka (1985), Thailand (1988, 1990–95), Tunisia (1981), Uruguay (1990–97), Venezuela (1990–97).

analysis of the role of the labor market in the transmission of macroeconomic policies to the poor.[25] Three categories of agents are assumed to operate in the economy considered: firms, households (or workers), and the government.[26] The nominal exchange rate is fixed. The economy consists of two major segments, the formal economy and the informal sector. The capital stock in each production sector is fixed within the time frame of the analysis. The labor force is also fixed and consists of skilled and unskilled workers; within each group, workers are identical.

4.1 Basic Structure

4.1.1 The Formal Sector

Production in the formal economy consists of an exportable good and requires both types of labor. For simplicity, total output of exportables is assumed to be sold abroad.[27] The price of exportables is fixed on world markets; the demand for exportables is infinitely elastic at that price, and output is supply-determined. Setting the world price of exportables to unity implies that the domestic price of exports is equal to the nominal exchange rate, E.

Let Y_X denote the production of exportables, n_S and n_U employment levels of skilled and unskilled labor (measured in natural units) in that sector, and e the level of effort provided by a typical skilled worker. The level of effort provided by an unskilled worker is constant and normalized to unity for simplicity. Assuming a Cobb-Douglas production technology yields[28]

$$Y_X = (en_S)^\alpha n_U^{1-\alpha}, \quad 0 < \alpha < 1. \tag{1}$$

Generalizing the specification developed by Agénor and Aizenman (1999), the effort function is defined as

$$e = 1 - \Lambda\left(\frac{\Omega}{w_S^c}\right)^\gamma, \quad 0 < \Lambda < 1, \ \gamma \geq 0, \tag{2}$$

where w_S^c denotes the *consumption wage* for skilled workers in the exportables sector, and Ω the worker's reservation wage. Equation (2) indicates that an increase in skilled workers' consumption wage relative to their reservation wage raises the level of effort. Effort is also concave in w_S^c. If effort is independent of relative wages ($\gamma = 0$), or if the consumption wage is continuously equal to the reservation wage, $e = 1 - \Lambda$.[29]

Whereas skilled workers determine the level of effort on the basis of the consumption wage that they face, producers set instead the *product wage*, w_S. Suppose that the consumer price index is a weighted, geometric average of the price of imported goods, E – assuming that the foreign-currency price of these goods is normalized to unity – and the price of nontradables, P_N:

$$P = E^{1-\delta} P_N^\delta, \quad 0 < \delta < 1, \tag{3}$$

where δ measures the share of home goods in total expenditure.

Let $z = E/P_N$ denote the relative price of imports in terms of nontradables; z will be referred to in what follows as the real exchange rate. By definition, therefore, $P = z^{-\delta}E$, so that

$$w_S^c = z^\delta w_S. \tag{4}$$

A binding minimum wage for unskilled workers is in place in the formal economy. For a given level of the minimum wage, firms in the formal sector determine employment levels and the product wage earned by skilled workers so as to maximize profits and minimize the cost of skilled labor in efficiency units. Formally, let w_m be the real minimum wage (measured in terms of the price of exportables) earned by unskilled workers in the formal sector. Assuming that firms incur no hiring or firing costs, the firm's decision problem is thus

$$\max_{n_S, n_U, w_S} \Pi_X = \left\{ [1 - \Lambda(\frac{\Omega}{z^\delta w_S})^\gamma] n_S \right\}^\alpha n_U^{1-\alpha} - w_S n_S - w_m n_U,$$

with z and w_m taken as given.

The first-order conditions for this optimization problem are:

$$\alpha(\frac{n_U}{e n_S})^{1-\alpha}[1 - \Lambda(\frac{\Omega}{z^\delta w_S})^\gamma] = w_S, \tag{5}$$

$$(1 - \alpha)(\frac{n_U}{e n_S})^{-\alpha} = w_m, \tag{6}$$

$$\alpha(\frac{n_U}{e n_S})^{1-\alpha} n_S(\frac{\partial e}{\partial w_S}) = \alpha\gamma\Lambda(\frac{n_U}{e n_S})^{1-\alpha}(\frac{n_S}{w_S})(\frac{\Omega}{z^\delta w_S})^\gamma = n_S. \tag{7}$$

The first two conditions equate the real net marginal product of each category of labor to the relevant real wage. The third determines skilled workers' wage so as to ensure that the level of effort is optimal. It can be re-written as

$$\alpha\gamma\Lambda(\frac{n_U}{e n_S})^{1-\alpha}(\frac{\Omega}{z^\delta w_S})^\gamma = w_S,$$

which can be equated with condition (5) to give

$$(1 + \gamma)\Lambda(\frac{\Omega}{z^\delta w_S})^\gamma = 1,$$

so that

$$w_S = \frac{[(1 + \gamma)\Lambda]^{1/\gamma}\Omega}{z^\delta} = \theta(z, \Omega), \quad \theta_z < 0, \theta_\Omega > 0. \tag{8}$$

Equation (8) indicates that the efficiency wage for skilled workers is negatively related to the real exchange rate and positively to the opportunity cost of effort.

For a given level of the reservation wage, a depreciation of the real exchange rate induced by a fall in the price of nontradables increases the consumption wage and raises the level of effort – allowing firms to reduce the equilibrium product wage.

The demand functions for labor can be derived from the above equations as:

$$n_S^d = n_S^d(\bar{\omega}_S; \bar{\omega}_m), n_U^d = n_U^d(\bar{\omega}_S; \bar{\omega}_m). \tag{9}$$

These equations indicate that an increase in the product wage for either category of labor reduces the demand for both of them, as a result of gross complementarity.

Substituting these results in equation (1) and using (8) yields the supply function of exportables:

$$Y_X^s = Y_X^s(\bar{\omega}_S; \bar{\omega}_m) = Y_X^s(\overset{+}{z}; \bar{\omega}_m). \tag{10}$$

4.1.2 The Informal Economy

Firms in the informal economy produce a nontraded good, which requires only unskilled labor and is used only for final consumption. The price of this good is flexible, and adjusts to equilibrate supply and demand.

Technology for the production of the nontraded good in the informal sector is characterized by decreasing returns to labor:

$$Y_N = n_N^\eta, \quad 0 < \eta < 1, \tag{11}$$

where Y_N denotes output of home goods, and n_N the quantity of labor employed in the informal economy. Producers maximize profits given by $z^{-1}Y_N - \omega_N n_N$, where $\omega_N < \omega_m$ denotes the real wage in the informal sector, measured in terms of the price of exportables.[30] Profit maximization yields the familiar equality between marginal revenue and marginal cost, $\omega_N = Y_N'/z$, from which labor demand can be derived as

$$n_N^d = (\frac{\omega_N z}{\eta})^{1/(\eta-1)}, \quad n_N^{d\prime} < 0, \tag{12}$$

where $\omega_N z$ measures the product wage in the informal sector. Substituting equation (12) in (11) yields the supply function of informal sector goods:

$$Y_N^s = (\frac{\omega_N z}{\eta})^{\eta/(\eta-1)}, \quad Y_N^{s\prime} < 0. \tag{13}$$

4.1.3 Households

There are two categories of households in the economy: an 'upper-income' household, which consists of all workers (skilled and unskilled) employed in the formal economy, and a 'low-income' household, which consists of all workers employed in the informal sector.[31] The key difference between upper- and low-income households is that the former group pays income taxes, saves a non-zero fraction of its current disposable income, and accumulates wealth in the form of a tradable interest-bearing bond, whereas the latter group pays no taxes and spends all of its income. Both categories of households supply labor inelastically and consume, in addition to the nontraded good produced in the informal sector, an imported good which is imperfectly substitutable for the home good.

Consider first the upper-income household. Its income consists of total output of exportables, Y_X^s, and interest income on holdings of traded bonds, i^*B^*, where i^* is the world interest rate (assumed constant) and B^* the foreign-currency value of these holdings.[32] Total consumption expenditure, c_R, depends positively on both disposable income and current wealth:

$$c_R = \alpha(Y_X^s + i^*B^* - T) + vB^*, \quad 0 < \alpha < 1, \; v > 0, \tag{14}$$

where T denotes lump-sum taxes (measured in terms of the price of exportables) paid by the upper-income household.[33]

If all savings are invested in interest-bearing assets, the flow of savings or the stock of foreign bonds held by the upper-income household evolves over time according to

$$\dot{B}^* = Y_X^s + i^*B^* - T - c_R,$$

that is, using (14):

$$\dot{B}^* = (1 - \alpha)(Y_X^s + i^*B^* - T) - vB^*. \tag{15}$$

The upper-income household consumes imported goods (in quantity c_R^I) as well as home goods (in quantity c_R^N). Assuming a Cobb-Douglas sub-utility function, the allocation of total consumption expenditure among these goods is given by

$$c_R^I = (1 - \delta)c_R, \quad c_R^N = \delta z c_R, \tag{16}$$

where δ, as indicated earlier, measures the share of home goods in expenditure.

Resources of the low-income household (measured in terms of exportables) consist of income generated in the informal economy, $z^{-1}Y_N^s$. All income is spent on consumption, c_P:

$$c_P = z^{-1}Y_N^s. \tag{17}$$

Assuming for simplicity an allocation rule across consumption goods that is similar to the upper-income household's yields

$$c_P^I = (1 - \delta)c_P, \quad c_P^N = \delta z c_P. \tag{18}$$

4.1.4 *The Market for Informal Sector Goods*

The equilibrium condition of the market for informal sector goods can be written as:

$$Y_N^s = c_R^N + c_P^N.$$

Using equations (13), (16) and (18), this condition becomes

$$Y_N^s(\omega_N z) = \delta z(c_R + c_P),$$

which can be re-written as, using (17):

$$Y_N^s(\omega_N z) = \frac{\delta}{1 - \delta} z c_R. \tag{19}$$

4.1.5 *The Informal Labor Market*

The demand for labor in the informal sector is derived from profit maximization and is given by equation (12). Determining the supply of labor involves two steps. First, in line with the 'luxury unemployment' hypothesis, skilled workers who are unable to obtain a job in the formal sector are assumed to prefer to remain unemployed rather than seek employment in the informal economy.[34] Second, the supply of unskilled workers in the formal sector, n_U^s, is assumed to change gradually over time as a function of wage differentials across sectors. Wage and employment prospects are formed on the basis of prevailing conditions in the labor market. Thus, denoting by n_U^p the constant number of unskilled workers in the labor force, the supply of labor in the informal sector, $n_U^p - n_U^s$, is also given at any point in time. The equilibrium condition of the labor market in the informal economy can consequently be written as

$$n_U^p - n_U^s = n_N^d(\omega_N z). \tag{20}$$

With wages in the informal sector adjusting continuously to equilibrate supply and demand for labor, this equation yields:[35]

$$\omega_N = \omega_N(\overset{-}{z}, \overset{+}{n_U^s}), \quad \partial \omega_N / \partial z = -1, \tag{21}$$

which indicates that a depreciation of the real exchange rate has an exact offsetting effect on the market-clearing wage. The reason is that, with labor supply constant, labor demand cannot change – which in turn requires the product wage, $\omega_N z$, to remain constant. An increase in the number of workers seeking employment in the formal economy has a positive effect on the market-clearing wage.[36]

Migration flows are determined by expected income opportunities, along the lines of Harris and Todaro (1970).[37] The expected wage in the formal economy is equal to the minimum wage weighted by the probability of being hired in the exportables sector. Assuming that hiring in that sector is random, this probability can be approximated by the ratio of currently employed workers to those seeking employment, n_U^d/n_U^s. The expected wage in the informal economy is simply the going wage, because there are no barriers to entry in that sector. Thus, the supply of unskilled workers in the formal sector evolves over time according to

$$\dot{n}_U^s = \beta\left\{\frac{\omega_m n_U^d}{n_U^s} - \omega_N\right\}, \quad \beta > 0, \tag{22}$$

where β denotes the speed of adjustment. Implicit in the above formulation is the assumption that workers employed in the informal sector do not engage in on-the-job search. As suggested by Agénor (1999), this assumption can be motivated by the existence of informational inefficiencies. The labor market in many developing countries is characterized by the absence of institutions capable of processing and providing in a timely manner relevant information on job opportunities to potential applicants – particularly those with low levels of qualifications. As a result, job search for unskilled workers in the formal sector often requires, literally speaking, waiting for employment offers at factory gates.

4.1.6 *Government*

The government consumes only imported goods and finances its expenditure through lump-sum taxes collected on the upper-income household:[38]

$$T = g_I, \tag{23}$$

where g_I denotes the foreign-currency value of government imports.

4.2 *Long-Run Equilibrium*

The dynamic structure of the model is derived in Appendix A.[39] As shown there, the dynamics of the model can be formulated in terms of the size of the unskilled labor force seeking employment in the formal economy, n_U^s, and the upper-income household's holdings of traded bonds, B^*. A key feature of the model is that, as implied by equation (22), in the long run the unskilled wage ratio – the ratio of wages earned by unskilled workers in the formal and informal sectors – must be equal to the inverse of the unskilled employment ratio in the formal economy:

$$\omega_m/\tilde{\omega}_N = \tilde{n}_U^s/\tilde{n}_U^d. \tag{24}$$

This equation indicates that, as long as the minimum wage exceeds the informal sector wage (as required here to avoid a corner solution), unskilled unemployment will emerge in equilibrium. As shown in Appendix A, in addition to condition (24), in the steady state the current account must be in equilibrium. From the steady-state solutions of B and n_U^s, the equilibrium values of the 'short-run' variables, the real exchange rate and the real wage in the informal economy, can be derived.

The steady-state equilibrium of the model is depicted in Figure 8. The locus BB gives the combinations of B^* and n_U^s for which bond holdings remain constant, whereas the locus LL depicts the combinations of B^* and n_U^s for which the size of the unskilled labor force seeking employment in the formal sector does not change over time. Stability (as discussed in Appendix A) requires LL to be steeper than BB. The steady-state equilibrium obtains at point E. If the economy's initial position is at, say, point A – characterized by a negative differential between the expected wage in the formal and the informal sectors, and a current account deficit – the transition toward the steady state will be characterized by a fall in the size of the unskilled labor force seeking employment in the formal sector and a reduction in holdings of foreign bonds (the economy must dissave to finance the external imbalance). Beyond point A' (located on LL), the expected income differential turns positive, because the continuous inflow of workers in the informal sector that occurs during the first phase of adjustment puts downward pressure on wages there. The supply of unskilled labor to the formal economy therefore begins to increase. Holdings of foreign bonds continue to decline, however, until the steady-state position is reached at E.

A graphical illustration of the partial, long-run equilibrium of the labor market, adapted from Agénor (1999, 2002), is presented in Figure 9. Panel A depicts the demand functions for labor in the formal sector. The demand curve for skilled labor, n_S^d, is downward-sloping, because it is negatively related to ω_S, the wage earned by skilled workers. Skilled unemployment is given in Panel A by the distance between the fixed supply of skilled labor, n_S^p, and the equilibrium point on the demand curve (point G). The demand curve for unskilled labor, n_U^d, is also downward-sloping because of gross complementarity between skilled and unskilled labor. Curve HH in Panel B depicts the relationship between the (long-run) supply of unskilled workers in the formal sector, n_U^s, given by equation (24), and employment of unskilled workers in the formal economy, n_U^d. It is derived by using the market-clearing condition (21) – taking z as given – to eliminate ω_N in (24). HH has a positive slope that is greater than unity, as implied by the assumption that $\omega_m > \omega_N$. The difference between point B (located on the 45-degree line) and B' (located on HH) gives unskilled unemployment. Curve VV is given by $n_U^p - n_U^s$; it is thus a linear transformation of HH. It determines the supply of labor (and thus actual employment) in the informal economy (point B''). Given the labor demand curve in the informal sector, n_N^d, the market-clearing wage is determined at point C in Panel C. The positive relationship between the skilled workers' wage and the informal sectorwage – obtained by combining (8), (21), and (24) – is displayed as curve WW in Panel D. Thus, unemployment of

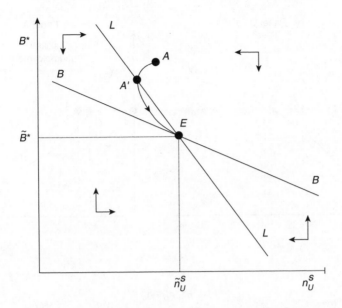

Figure 8. Steady-State Equilibrium.

both categories of labor – 'quasi-voluntary' unemployment of skilled workers and 'wait' unemployment of unskilled workers – prevails in equilibrium.[40]

4.3 *Fiscal Adjustment, Employment, and the Poor*

The model developed in the previous section can be used to analyze the labor market and poverty effects of a variety of macroeconomic policy shocks that have often been part of adjustment programs implemented in developing countries. For illustrative purposes, this paper limits itself to an analysis of the impact and steady-state effects of an increase in lump-sum taxes. This experiment also helps to illustrate the fact that fiscal austerity is not necessarily detrimental to the poor (even in the short run), once general equilibrium effects are properly accounted for.

4.3.1 *Steady-State Effects*

As shown in Figure 10, a rise in lump-sum taxes T leads in the long run to a reduction in the stock of foreign bonds held by the upper-income household and an increase in the supply of unskilled labor in the formal sector. The new equilibrium is at E', located at the intersection of the new curves $B'B'$ and $L'L'$. Intuitively, the rise in T has two effects. The first is that it dampens consumption of informal sector goods by the upper-income household. At the initial level of supply of these goods (that is, at the initial values of the real exchange rate and the product wage in that sector), the real exchange rate must depreciate. The second effect results from the fact that an increase in taxes also lowers private

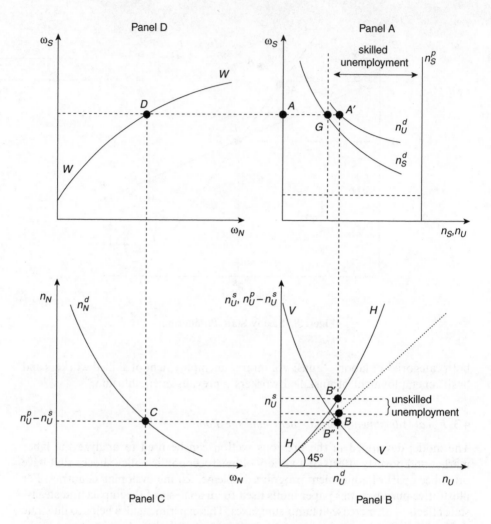

Figure 9. Labor Market Equilibrium.

Source: Agénor (2002).

spending on imports, whereas the real exchange rate depreciation stimulates exports. Both effects tend to create a current account surplus, at the initial level of the stock of foreign bonds held by the upper-income household. But for the current account to be in equilibrium in the long-run interest receipts on foreign bonds must fall to offset the improvement in the trade balance. And because the world interest rate does not change, this can happen only through a reduction in the stock of foreign bonds held by the rich.

The depreciation of the real exchange rate lowers skilled workers' efficiency wage in the formal sector, thereby raising the demand for both categories of

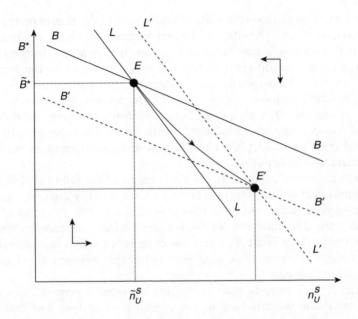

Figure 10. Increase in Lump-Sum Taxes.

labor. The increase in labor demand raises the probability of employment in the formal economy and thus expected income there. This tends to increase the supply of unskilled labor in the formal economy. Because the demand for skilled labor rises, the long-run effect of the shock is a reduction in the unemployment rate of skilled workers. Whether unemployment of unskilled workers rises or falls would seem to be a priori ambiguous; both the supply of, and the demand for, unskilled labor rise in the formal economy. As shown in Appendix A, however, it can be established that demand rises by more than supply in relative terms; the net outcome is thus a reduction in the *rate* of unemployment of unskilled labor in the urban formal sector. The fall in labor supply in the informal sector puts upward pressure on the market-clearing wage $\tilde{\omega}_N$ – thereby outweighing the negative effect of the real depreciation.[41] The product wage there ($\tilde{\omega}_N\tilde{z}$) unambiguously rises, which brings about the required reduction in labor demand. Thus, informal sector wages move in the same direction as output in the formal economy, whereas output and employment move in opposite directions in both sectors.

4.3.2 *Transitional Dynamics*

The transitional dynamics associated with the increase in taxes are also illustrated in Figure 10. The impact effects operate in the same direction as the long-run effects described earlier: a reduction in consumption of domestic and imported goods by the upper-income household, a real depreciation, a fall in skilled workers' wages, and an increase in the demand for both categories of workers. The rise in labor demand raises the probability of employment (and thus expected income) in the formal economy. The effect of the real depreciation on the product wage in the informal economy is now completely offset by a *reduction* in the real wage there; as a result, the differential between expected wages in the formal and informal sectors unambiguously rises – thereby raising on impact the flow of labor in the formal economy ($\dot{n}_U^s(0) > 0$). The reason why the initial movements in z and ω_N exactly offset each other is that n_U^s cannot change on impact. As a result, the product wage in the informal sector, $z\omega_N$, cannot change either, as can be inferred from equation (20). Thus, output and employment in the informal sector remain also constant on impact.

Although output of exportables rises as a result of the fall in skilled workers' wage, the net effect of the increase in taxes is a reduction in income and savings by the upper-income household, and thus a decumulation in holdings of foreign bonds ($\dot{B}_0^* < 0$). Over time, the adjustment process leads the economy monotonically from point E to point E', where the current account is in equilibrium, the flow of savings is again zero, and expected wages between the formal and informal sectors are equal.

What happens to poverty rates during the adjustment process? Suppose that the legal minimum wage is used as the official poverty line, and that average income in the informal sector, Y_N^s/n_N^d, is less than ω_m at all times (given (11) and (12), this implies that $\omega_N z/\eta < \omega_m$). Suppose also that the unemployed earn an (imputed) income from own production that is less than ω_m. The headcount index measure of poverty, I_H, can thus be defined as the number of workers employed in the informal sector, plus unemployed workers in the formal economy (skilled and unskilled), divided by the size of the labor force, n:

$$I_H = \frac{1}{n}\left\{n_N^d + (n_S^p - n_S^d) + (n_U^s - n_U^d)\right\},$$

or equivalently, given that $n = n_S^p + n_U^s + n_N^d$:

$$I_H = 1 - \left(\frac{n_S^d + n_U^d}{n}\right).$$

On impact, as indicated earlier, the supply of unskilled labor in the formal economy remains constant, and employment in the informal sector does not change, because the product wage there remains constant. Thus, poverty falls as a result of the increase in the demand for both skilled and unskilled labor in the exportables sector. This is also the case in the long run. The analysis therefore helps to illustrate an important point that was alluded to earlier in less formal terms: fiscal austerity does not necessarily have an adverse effect on the poor, neither in the short or the long run. The reason is that the poverty effects of macroeconomic policies in a typical developing-country context operate through complex channels involving changes in aggregate demand and supply in the formal and informal sectors, as well as changes in relative prices and wages. Once these general equilibrium effects are accounted for, as was done here, macroeconomic adjustment may well benefit the poor by stimulating employment – even while exerting downward pressure on wages.

5. Empirical Evidence

The thrust of the foregoing discussion is that it is usually difficult to draw clear-cut theoretical conclusions regarding the overall effect of macroeconomic variables on poverty, as a result of conflicting effects – operating either simultaneously or at different moments in time. Empirical studies are thus important to assess whether net effects are positive or negative. This section begins by reviewing some recent studies. It then presents some new econometric results for a cross-section of countries.

5.1 Factual, Econometric, and Simulation Studies

Existing studies analyzing the effect of macroeconomic factors on poverty consist of three main types: factual, econometric, and macro-simulation studies. Some of the factual studies focusing on Latin America have suggested, for instance, that the poverty impact of expenditure policies adopted in the context of stabilization (and structural adjustment) programs during the 1980s has often been negative.[42] Another factual study that attempts to assess the effect of macroeconomic adjustment on poverty in sub-Saharan Africa is by Demery and Squire (1996). They use the macroeconomic policy index developed by the World Bank to do so.[43] They found that improvements in macroeconomic management (as captured by changes in the policy index) are associated with a decline in the incidence of poverty. More specifically, Demery and Squire find that for the six African countries that they consider – Côte d'Ivoire, Ethiopia, Ghana, Kenya, Nigeria, and Tanzania – poverty fell in countries that improved their macroeconomic policy regime and deteriorated in the one case (Côte d'Ivoire) in which it did not.[44] A depreciation of the real exchange rate was a key factor in the macroeconomic adjustment process; it also affected favorably rural incomes, benefitting the poor both directly and indirectly. In general, however, factual empirical studies aimed at assessing the link between macroeconomic adjustment programs and poverty face an important hurdle, namely, the fact that they typically do not consider 'counterfactual' scenarios. Too often the process of adjustment is blamed for the increase (or reduction) in poverty, without considering what would have happened in the absence of adjustment.

Among the econometric studies, Cardoso et al. (1995) and Amadeo and Neri (1997) have found that inflation and unemployment have an adverse effect on poverty in Brazil. Amadeo and Neri (1997), in particular, found that although inflation implies lower per capita income for all deciles of the distribution of income in Brazil, its effect on per capita earnings is lower for the upper-income households. Put differently, inflation has a larger effect on earnings of the poor than on average per capita income. The use of time-series data in a single-country context is an important avenue of future research in the analysis of the role of macroeconomic factors in the determination of poverty rates. Romer and Romer (1998), for instance, used time-series technique to investigate the short- and long-run effects of monetary policy on poverty and found that these effects go in opposite directions. Their evidence for the United States shows that a cyclical boom (and lower unemployment) created by an expansionary monetary policy is associated with improved conditions for the poor in the short run. Their cross-section evidence from a large sample of countries, however, shows that low inflation and stable aggregate demand growth are associated with lower poverty in the long run. Both the short- and long-run relationships are quantitatively large, statistically significant, and robust. But because the cyclical effects of monetary policy are inherently temporary, they concluded that monetary policy that aims at low inflation and stable aggregate demand is the most likely to permanently improve conditions for the poor. Agénor (2001a) used a vector autoregression approach to analyze the extent to which output shocks have an asymmetric effect on the poor in Brazil, while being simultaneously controlling for changes in the minimum wage and unemployment. This type of study should be further developed to include (vector) error-correction models, so as to distinguish, among the determinants of poverty, between long-run factors (such as the degree of inequality and the level of public expenditure on education and health) and short-term macroeconomic factors.

Some other studies have used simulation techniques to examine the effect of macroeconomic policy shocks on poverty. In particular, several recent papers focusing on sub-Saharan Africa have used computable general equilibrium (CGE) models for this purpose. Subramanian (1996), for instance, evaluated the impact of government policies (as well as external shocks) on poverty in Cameroon. Sarris (1996) examined the effects of various macroeconomic policy shocks (a 20% devaluation, an increase in public investment spending financed by a corresponding reduction in public current expenditure, and a reduction in public sector employment) in a CGE model for Tanzania. All shocks in his study resulted in short-term declines in real income for the rich and the poor alike. However, losses for the non-poor were significantly higher than the losses incurred by the poor (rural and urban), reflecting the losses in implicit rents. In the longer term, with output growth rates increasing and inflation falling, income gains were significant for both the poor and middle-income households. Other studies include Bourguignon et al. (1991) and Lofgren (2001).

A limitation of many existing CGE models, however, is that the treatment of the labor market, and more specifically wage formation mechanisms, often do not capture the complex intersectoral relationships that are observed in practice. The structure of the labor market has a major impact on the transmission of macroeconomic shocks and adjustment policies to economic activity, employment, and relative prices; but applied policy models have often captured only a narrow set of its features – such as an economy-wide rigid minimum wage (see for instance Maechler and Roland-Host, 1995). As illustrated in the analytical model presented earlier, for instance, feedback effects between formal and informal sector wages play a critical role in the transmission process of macroeconomic shocks in a context in which efficiency considerations (or turnover costs) matter in the determination of formal sector wages. Existing models have paid insufficient attention to the macroeconomic implications of alternative sources of labor market segmentation, differences in wage formation across various labor categories, inter-sectoral wage rigidity (as opposed to aggregate wage rigidity), and feedback effects between relative prices and wage decisions by price-setting firms. All of these features have important implications for understanding the impact of policy and exogenous shocks on poverty. Labor market segmentation, in particular, tends to restrict labor mobility and can be associated with persistent wage differentials, as noted earlier; these, in turn, may prevent the reallocation of resources necessary to cope with external and policy-induced shocks. Again, because the poor in many developing countries generate a significant fraction of their income from labor services, accounting explicitly for the complexity of the labor market is crucial for understanding the impact of pretty much any type of shock on poverty in the short and medium run.

A detailed treatment of the labor market is a key feature of the Integrated Macroeconomic Model for Poverty Reduction (IMMPA) developed by Agénor, Izquierdo and Fofack (2002) and Agénor, Fernandes, and Haddad (2002). Another characteristic of IMMPA is that it accounts explicitly for the channels through which various types of public investment outlays affect the economy. Economists and policymakers have long recognized that different forms of public investment can have different effects on output and employment, but the channels through which alternative forms of public spending operate have seldom been incorporated explicitly in applied macroeconomic models used for development policy analysis. In IMMPA, investment in infrastructure (or, rather, the stock of public capital in infrastructure) affects directly the level of production in the private sector – and thus the marginal productivity of primary factors employed in that sector – whereas public investment in education has a direct impact on the decision to acquire skills. This effect operates in addition, of course, to movements in relative wages across skill categories and the initial level of individual wealth, which acts as a constraining factor in the presence of credit constraints. IMMPA also allows an analysis of the poverty and distributional effects of policy and exogenous shocks in two ways: first by calculating a set of indicators (for income distribution) based directly on the simulation results of the macro component; second, by linking these simulation results to a household expenditure survey. There are various country applications under way, most notably for Brazil, Cameroon, Morocco, and Senegal. Many fruitful lessons on the impact of adjustment on the poor are likely to emerge from them.[45]

5.2 Cross-Country Econometric Evidence

This section presents, in a cross-country empirical framework, some preliminary results on the relationship between macroeconomic factors and poverty in developing countries.[46] The macroeconomic variables examined include several of the variables discussed earlier: public expenditure, inflation, income levels and output growth, and the real exchange rate. In addition, several structural variables are also considered. The estimation method is a OLS with fixed effects. As discussed in Appendix B, the sample is relatively small (19 countries, and at most 52 observations).

Specifically, the dependent variable is the poverty rate (*POV*), measured by the headcount index for the population as a whole. The 'basic' set of explanatory variables used in the regressions are defined as follows (see Appendix B for more precise definitions):[47]

- *INFL* is the inflation rate in consumer prices;
- *ILLITY* is the youth illiteracy rate in percent of the adult population, which aims to capture the level of education of the labor force;
- *LHOSPITAL* is the log of hospital beds per 1,000 persons, which measures overall health conditions;
- *GDPPC* is GDP per capita at PPP exchange rates, which captures the level of economic development;
- *REALGR* is the annual growth rate of GDP per capita, measured at PPP exchange rates, which can be viewed as either a proxy for the rate of return on investment, or as a measure of cyclical movements in output;
- *REALEX* is the annual rate of change of the real effective exchange rate (defined such that an increase is a depreciation);
- *URBAN* is the relative share of the urban population in proportion to total population;
- *CTOT* is the rate of change of the terms of trade;
- *VREALXL* and *VINFL* are measures of macroeconomic volatility, which consist of rolling standard deviations of the real exchange rate and inflation;
- *OPEN* is the ratio of the sum of imports and exports of goods and services in percent of GDP, and aims to capture the degree of commercial openness.

The previous discussion suggests that inflation should have a positive effect on poverty. An increase in the illiteracy rate is expected to be positively correlated with poverty, whereas an improvement in health indicators should be inversely related to poverty. Both the level of GDP per capita and its rate of growth are expected to be negatively correlated with the poverty rate. The effect of a real exchange rate depreciation is in general ambiguous; it is likely to lead to a reduction in poverty if it benefits small farmers in the tradable sector, as is the case in many low-income developing countries. A higher rate of urbanization also has in general an ambiguous effect on aggregate poverty; to the extent that rural-to-urban migration translates into greater access to public services in urban areas, it may lower poverty; but to the extent that inflows of workers in the urban sector lead to an excess supply of labor in the informal sector and lower wages there, it may increase poverty. An improvement in the terms of trade may reduce poverty if it represents an increase in the relative price of agricultural commodities (thereby benefiting small farmers in rural areas) or a fall in the price of imported consumption goods (benefiting mostly households in urban areas). An increase in macroeconomic volatility (associated with output shocks, inflation, or fluctuations in the real exchange rate) is expected to increase poverty, possibly through its adverse effect on growth, as discussed earlier. Finally, the degree of openness has a priori an ambiguous effect on poverty. To the extent that trade openness increases exposure to external shocks, or if greater access to imported capital goods leads firms to substitute away from unskilled labor in the production process, it may increase poverty; but to the extent that it gives greater access to foreign intermediate inputs and foreign technology, it may end up benefitting the poor.

Table 1 summarizes some of the basic empirical results. They indicate that changes in the terms of trade, the urbanization ratio, the illiteracy rate and the volatility of inflation do not have a statistically significant impact on poverty.[48] By contrast, inflation has in general a significant, adverse effect on poverty, in line with the earlier results reported by Agénor (1999) and Easterly and Fischer (2001). A greater degree of openness tends to reduce poverty significantly, as is the case for the number of hospital beds (which has the correct sign and is significant in several regressions). Both the level of real GDP per capita and its growth rate have the expected negative sign and are highly significant in almost all regressions. The rate of depreciation of the real exchange rate has a strong, negative effect on poverty, which is consistent with the view that improvements in the relative price of tradables benefit farmers producing exportables in the agricultural sector. The volatility of the real exchange rate is also highly significant, indicating that macroeconomic instability has an adverse impact on poverty – possibly through its effect on income distribution, as noted earlier. Finally, the fixed effects (which are not reported here to save space) are all statistically significant, suggesting that country-specific factors are important in determining the behavior of poverty rates.

Table 2 extends the analysis in Table 1 to account for the possibility of asymmetric output shocks in both the level of real GDP per capita and its growth rate. Specifically, observations on the level and growth rate of GDP per capita are split into two sub-samples. In both cases, two dummy variables, *DUMMYPOS* and *DUMMYNEG*, are created; for the level of GDP per capita, the first is equal to 1 times *GDPPC* when *GDPPC* at period t is higher than *GDPPC* at time $t-1$ (and 0 otherwise), and the second is equal to 1 times *GDPPC* when *GDPPC* at period t is lower than *GDPPC* at time $t-1$. For the growth rate, the first is equal to 1 times *REALGR* when *REALGR* is positive (and 0 otherwise), and the second equal to 1 times the absolute value of *REALGR* when *REALGR* is negative (and 0 otherwise). The results show first that all the variables that were significant in Table 1 remain so; in particular, real exchange rate depreciations, a higher degree of openness, and better health conditions tend to lower poverty, whereas inflation and macroeconomic volatility tend to increase it. The results also show that there is no evidence of asymmetric effect of the level of GDP per capita on poverty: both variables have coefficients that are significant and statistically indistinguishable. By contrast, positive growth rates of output have no statistically significant effect on poverty, whereas higher negative growth rates affect significantly and

Table 1. Developing Countries with the number of observations greater than or equal to two: Determinants of the Poverty Rate (OLS with fixed effects).

	Dependent variable: headcount poverty index							
	(1)	(2)	(3)	(4)	(5)	(6)	(7)	(8)
INFL	0.092 (1.999)	0.135 (2.345)	0.056 (1.491)	0.149 (2.270)	0.083 (1.596)	0.073 (1.569)	0.072 (1.624)	0.138 (2.404)
ILLITY	0.254 (0.971)	—	0.008 (0.034)	0.153 (0.547)	0.154 (0.612)	—	—	—
LHOSPITAL	-0.120 (-1.174)	-0.164 (-1.874)	—	-0.188 (-1.934)	-0.091 (-1.092)	-0.083 (-0.738)	-0.070 (-0.981)	-0.167 (-1.906)
GDPPC	-0.146 (-2.111)	-0.137 (-2.964)	-0.159 (-3.751)	-0.130 (-3.086)	-0.168 (-3.901)	-0.168 (-2.487)	-0.177 (-4.385)	-0.139 (-3.053)
REALGR	-0.258 (-1.413)	-0.285 (-1.615)	-0.278 (-1.760)	-0.350 (-1.921)	-0.316 (-1.701)	-0.292 (-1.732)	-0.291 (-1.780)	-0.325 (-2.028)
REALEX	-0.129 (-4.395)	-0.117 (-4.141)	-0.123 (-5.234)	-0.123 (-3.612)	-0.133 (-4.229)	-0.131 (-4.204)	-0.130 (-4.709)	-0.120 (-4.060)
OPEN	—	-0.127 (-1.978)	—	-0.134 (-2.318)	—	—	—	-0.134 (-2.256)
URBAN	-0.070 (-0.130)	—	—	—	—	-0.080 (-0.149)	—	—
CTOT	0.036 (0.317)	0.030 (0.281)	-0.012 (-0.125)	0.039 (0.371)	0.022 (0.196)	0.013 (0.123)	0.011 (0.098)	0.028 (0.271)
VREALXL	0.228 (2.152)	0.260 (3.273)	0.304 (4.082)	0.282 (3.784)	0.297 (3.782)	0.315 (3.698)	0.309 (4.192)	0.294 (4.293)
VINFL	0.039 (1.555)	0.019 (0.789)	—	—	—	—	—	—
Adj. R2	0.900	0.914	0.910	0.913	0.906	0.905	0.910	0.917
Number of obs.	47	47	48	47	47	47	47	47
Standard Error of Regression	0.044	0.041	0.042	0.041	0.043	0.043	0.042	0.040

Note: INFL is the annual change in the consumer price index. ILLITY is the illiteracy rate for the youth in percent of total population. LHOSPITAL is the log of the number of beds per 1000 people. GDPPC is the log of the GDP per capita (purchasing power parity). REALGR is the annual growth of GDP per capita (purchasing power parity). REALEX is the annual change in the real effective exchange rate index (a rise is depreciation). OPEN is the ratio of the sum of imports and exports of goods and services to GDP (all in nominal terms). URBAN is the log of the urban population in percent of total population. CTOT is the rate of change of the terms of trade. The volatility measures are calculated as the ratio of the standard deviation of a variable for t, t − 1, t − 2 and t − 3 to the average value for the same period. VREALXL is the volatility measure of the real effective exchange rate. VINFL is the volatility measure of the inflation rate.

Table 2. Developing Countries with the number of observations greater than or equal to two: Asymmetric Effects on Poverty (OLS with fixed effects).

	Dependent variable: headcount poverty index				
	(1)	(2)	(3)	(4)	(5)
INFL	0.089	0.136	0.074	0.143	0.077
	(1.821)	(2.771)	(2.062)	(2.670)	(1.956)
ILLITY	0.162	—	—	0.119	—
	(0.582)			(0.351)	
LHOSPITAL	−0.127	−0.179	−0.079	−0.190	−0.128
	(−1.239)	(−2.261)	(−1.214)	(−2.373)	(−1.303)
NEGREALGR	0.804	1.115	0.879	1.040	0.909
	(1.735)	(2.941)	(2.071)	(2.157)	(2.192)
POSREALGR	0.118	0.048	0.135	0.031	0.153
	(0.487)	(0.202)	(0.603)	(0.123)	(0.679)
NEGGDPPC	−0.108	−0.113	−0.141	−0.105	−0.105
	(−1.562)	(−2.637)	(−3.847)	(−2.535)	(−1.518)
POSGDPPC	−0.112	−0.114	−0.144	−0.107	−0.109
	(−1.673)	(−2.695)	(−4.049)	(−2.681)	(−1.619)
REALEX	−0.186	−0.177	−0.183	−0.176	−0.190
	(−5.630)	(−5.983)	(−5.934)	(−5.914)	(−5.552)
OPEN	—	−0.130	—	−0.126	−0.297
		(−2.044)		(−1.826)	(−0.626)
URBAN	−0.175	—	—	—	—
	(−0.360)				
CTOT	−0.024	−0.034	−0.045	−0.022	−0.038
	(−0.251)	(−0.352)	(−0.448)	(−0.229)	(−0.402)
VREALXL	0.292	0.256	0.284	0.253	0.307
	(3.489)	(3.763)	(4.183)	(3.662)	(3.839)
Adj. R2	0.903	0.917	0.911	0.913	0.907
Number of obs.	47	47	47	47	47
Standard Error of Regression	0.044	0.040	0.042	0.041	0.043

Note: INFL is the annual change in the consumer price index. ILLITY is the log of the illiteracy rate for the youth in percent of total population. LHOSPITAL is the log of the number of beds per 1000 people. NEGREALGR (POSREALGR) is equal to 1 times the absolute value of REALGR (growth rate of GDP per capita) when REALGR is negative (positive), zero otherwise. NEGGDPPC (POSGDPPC) is equal to 1 times GDPPC (level of GDP per capita) when GDPPC is lower (higher) than GDPPC(-1) , zero otherwise. REALEX is the annual change in the real effective exchange rate index (a rise is depreciation). OPEN is the ratio of the sum of imports and exports of goods and services to GDP (all in nominal terms). URBAN is the urban population in percent of total population. CTOT is the rate of change of the terms of trade. The volatility measures are calculated as the ratio of the standard deviation of a variable for t, t − 1, t − 2 and t − 3 to the average value for the same period. VREALXL is the volatility measure of the real effective exchange rate.

adversely the poor. A similar result was obtained by De Janvry and Sadoulet (2000) using a more parsimonious regression framework. This asymmetric effect is very important. As noted by De Janvry and Sadoulet (2000, p. 284), to the extent that the growth-poverty correlation results mainly from episodes of negative growth rates and increases in poverty, it may lead to erroneous predictions about the potential of growth-oriented policies to reduce poverty.

Table 3 extends the results of Tables 1 and 2 in two directions. First, a measure of inequality, the Gini coefficient, taken from Dollar and Kraay (2001) is added to the regression. Bourguignon (2000) recently emphasized the importance of including a measure of inequality as a regressor in estimating the impact of growth and standards of living on poverty; the previous discussion also suggests the same approach. Second, to test for possible endogeneity problems with respect to income, both the level and the rate of growth of GDP per capita are lagged by one period. The first set of regressions, (1) to (7), show that, by and large, the previous results remain unchanged. An improvement in health conditions or a higher rate of real exchange rate depreciation tend to lower poverty, whereas inflation, macroeconomic volatility and now a higher degree of inequality, tend to increase it. Furthermore, as indicated in regressions (8) to (10), there is again evidence in favor of an asymmetric effect on the *rate of growth* (not the level) of income per capita when the rate of depreciation of the real exchange rate is dropped out of the regression.[49] In line with the previous characterization of the sources of asymmetry, a possible explanation of the latter result is that the rate of growth acts as a proxy for the rate of return on capital. In recessions (or periods of negative growth), the perceived degree of uncertainty about future profitability increases, which leads firms to adopt a 'wait and see' attitude, as a result of irreversibility effects.

The foregoing results are only suggestive. Data limitations and the relatively small number of degrees of freedom limit their reliability. In addition, there are serious measurement problems. For instance, measured poverty rates in the sample may be overstated to the extent that the estimate of income reflects only market or market-related activities. Expanding the database used here would allow expanding the range of variables to be tested – such as for instance the impact of inequality in assets, as opposed to income. In the same vein, it would be useful to develop a measure of financial openness (in addition to the trade openness index used in the regressions) in order to assess the impact of international financial integration on poverty. Finally, it should be noted that the role of the labor market is only implicit (or indirect) in the regression framework used above. Extending the analysis to account explicitly for labor market variables (such as changes in unskilled unemployment, which are only imperfectly correlated with changes in output growth) would allow a more precise assessment of its importance in the transmission of macroeconomic policy to poverty.

6. Summary and Conclusions

The purpose of this paper has been to examine analytically and empirically the various channels through which stabilization policies affect poverty in developing countries, with a particular emphasis on the role of the labor market. Macroeconomic policies must, of course, be evaluated in terms of their macroeconomic objectives; in addition, however, it is important to understand their impact on

Table 3. Developing Countries with the number of observations greater than or equal to two: Inequality and Asymmetric Effects on Poverty (OLS with fixed effects).

	(1)	(2)	(3)	(4)	(5)	(6)	(7)	(8)	(9)	(10)
	Dependent variable: headcount poverty index									
INFL	0.097	0.100	0.085	0.135	0.130	0.112	0.122	0.117	0.117	0.089
	(2.060)	(2.220)	(2.081)	(3.262)	(3.323)	(3.229)	(3.913)	(1.838)	(1.779)	(2.389)
ILLITY	0.148	—	—	0.192	0.103	0.000	—	0.018	—	—
	(0.576)			(0.469)	(0.374)	(0.001)		(0.044)		
LHOSPITAL	−0.070	−0.189	−0.049	−0.003	−0.054	—	−0.045	−0.129	−0.129	−0.076
	(−0.844)	(−1.558)	(−0.701)	(−0.021)	(−0.854)		(−0.766)	(−1.716)	(−1.696)	(−1.316)
GDPPC(−1)	−0.108	−0.050	−0.118	−0.206	−0.180	−0.183	−0.189	—	—	—
	(−3.091)	(−0.829)	(−4.103)	(−2.029)	(−4.676)	(−4.566)	(−5.568)			
REALGR(−1)	−0.195	−0.332	−0.170	−0.322	−0.374	−0.334	−0.362	—	—	—
	(−1.341)	(−1.637)	(−1.127)	(−1.472)	(−3.778)	(−3.486)	(−3.516)			
NEGREALGR(−1)	—	—	—	—	—	—	—	0.848	0.858	0.882
								(2.125)	(2.394)	(2.127)
POSREALGR(−1)	—	—	—	—	—	—	—	−0.109	−0.104	−0.163
								(−0.508)	(−0.452)	(−0.532)
NEGGDPPC(−1)	—	—	—	—	—	—	—	−0.114	−0.115	−0.144
								(−3.149)	(−2.895)	(−4.111)
POSGDPPC(−1)	—	—	—	—	—	—	—	−0.118	−0.119	−0.147
								(−3.347)	(−2.994)	(−4.443)
REALEX	−0.087	−0.078	−0.088	−0.134	−0.128	−0.137	−0.131	—	—	—
	(−3.269)	(−2.360)	(−3.289)	(−2.936)	(−3.311)	(−3.789)	(−3.503)			
OPEN	—	—	—	—	—	—	—	−0.071	−0.072	—
								(−0.678)	(−0.852)	
URBAN	—	−0.776	—	0.316	—	—	—	—	—	—
		(−1.352)		(0.293)						

(Continued)

Table 3. *Continued.*

| | | | | Dependent variable: headcount poverty index | | | | | |
	(1)	(2)	(3)	(4)	(5)	(6)	(7)	(8)	(9)	(10)
CTOT	0.089	0.059	0.080	0.127	0.098	0.075	0.087	—	—	0.057
	(0.911)	(0.624)	(0.825)	(0.841)	(1.079)	(0.815)	(0.950)			(0.571)
VREALXL	0.303	0.290	0.323	0.205	0.198	0.209	0.205	0.009	0.010	0.053
	(3.170)	(2.761)	(3.557)	(2.276)	(2.320)	(2.610)	(2.492)	(0.118)	(0.133)	(0.602)
GINI	—	—	—	0.454	0.461	0.442	0.473	0.429	0.430	0.464
				(4.474)	(4.830)	(4.843)	(5.406)	(5.653)	(5.786)	(5.372)
Adj. R2	0.895	0.899	0.899	0.913	0.918	0.922	0.923	0.910	0.917	0.914
Number of obs.	47	47	47	42	45	42	42	42	42	42
Standard Error of Regression	0.045	0.045	0.045	0.042	0.041	0.040	0.040	0.043	0.041	0.042

Notes: INFL is the annual change in the consumer price index. ILLITY is the illiteracy rate for the youth in percent of total population. LHOSPITAL is the log of the number of beds per 1000 people. GDPPC(−1) is the lagged value of the log of the GDP per capita (purchasing power parity). REALGR(−1) is the lagged value of annual growth of GDP per capita (purchasing power parity). NEGREALGR(−1) (POSREALGR(−1)) is equal to 1 times the absolute value of REALGR(−1) when REALGR(−1) is negative (positive), zero otherwise. NEGGDPPC(−1) (POSGDPPC(−1)) is equal to 1 times GDPPC(−1) when GDPPC(−1) is lower (higher) than GDPPC(−2), zero otherwise. REALEX is the annual change in the real effective exchange rate index (a rise is depreciation). OPEN is the ratio of the sum of imports and exports of goods and services to GDP (all in nominal terms). URBAN is the urban population in percent of total population. CTOT is the rate of change of the terms of trade. The volatility measures are calculated as the ratio of the standard deviation of a variable for t, t − 1, t − 2 and t − 3 to the average value for the same period. VREALXL is the volatility measure of the real effective exchange rate. GINI is the Gini index.

poverty. This issue has been the subject of renewed interest in studies of economic adjustment in developing countries.

The first part of the paper provided a brief review of the recent evidence on poverty, and highlighted the large differences between and within regions of the developing world. The second part provided an analytical overview of the various channels through which macroeconomic policies affect the poor. It was argued, in particular, that a reduction in government expenditure on transfers and subsidies (measured either as a proportion of GDP or as a share of total spending) does not necessarily hurt the poor if it is accompanied by a better targeting of benefits. It was also pointed out that there are several factors suggesting that macroeconomic adjustment might benefit the poor. If the tradable goods sector is labor intensive, the poor will gain from the relative price shifts associated with a real exchange rate depreciation. At the same time, a reduction in (policy-induced) macroeconomic volatility is likely to lead to an increase in savings and investment rates, and thus be conducive to growth. However, these predictions must be qualified because various other factors may mitigate the positive impact of adjustment on the poor. Structural characteristics (such as the extent of price and wage flexibility, the degree of inter-sectoral mobility of the labor force, the extent to which the poor consume tradable goods, and the extent to which they are directly affected by cuts in public expenditure) vary considerably across countries and make it necessary to address these issues on a case by case basis.

The third part presented an analytical framework that captures some of the main features of the urban labor market in developing countries – a large informal sector, efficiency wages and minimum wage legislation in the formal economy, and imperfect mobility of the unskilled labor force across sectors. Both skilled and unskilled unemployment were shown to emerge in equilibrium, despite wage flexibility in the informal sector. Skilled unemployment emerges because the opportunity cost of leisure is low and/or the reservation wage is higher than the going wage in the informal sector, whereas unskilled unemployment results from 'wait' or 'queuing' considerations in the tradition of Harris and Todaro (1970). The model was used to study the macroeconomic effects of fiscal adjustment, namely, an increase in lump-sum taxes on upper-income households. The analysis suggested that in the long run this policy leads to a real exchange rate depreciation and lower unemployment of both categories of labor. It also lowers poverty (with the poor defined as unemployed workers and those employed in the informal sector). This experiment serves to illustrate the importance of accounting for general equilibrium effects in assessing the impact of macroeconomic adjustment on poverty; whereas the direct, partial equilibrium effect of higher taxes is to reduce aggregate demand and employment, the changes in relative prices and wages that result from the initial response of the economy translate into economy-wide movements in labor demand and output. These movements may operate in opposite direction to the initial effects and may end up being beneficial for the poor.

The fourth part provided a brief overview of some of the existing empirical studies focusing on the effect of macroeconomic adjustment on poverty, and presented some cross-country econometric results focusing on some of the factors identified in the previous sections – such as the level of activity, the rate of output growth, changes in the real exchange rate, inflation, and macroeconomic volatility – as well as structural factors (degree of urbanization, health conditions, illiteracy rate, and the degree of income inequality). Although the results should be treated with some caution given the relatively short sample size and some serious measurement problems, they suggest that higher levels and growth rates of per capita income, higher rates of real exchange rate depreciation, better health conditions, and a greater degree of commercial openness lower poverty, whereas inflation, greater income inequality, and macroeconomic instability (as measured by the degree of volatility of the real exchange rate) tend to increase it. In addition, real output growth per capita was found to have an asymmetric effect on poverty: positive growth rates are not statistically significant, whereas higher negative growth rates are significant and tend to raise poverty. Ignoring this asymmetric effect may lead to an overestimation of the potential of growth-oriented policies to reduce poverty.

The analysis presented in this paper can be extended in various directions. The cross-country econometric results presented here could be extended to explicitly account for the structure of the labor market and the role of labor market variables in the transmission of macroeconomic policy shocks. For instance, labor market regulations, by reducing the demand for unskilled labor in the formal economy, may raise poverty in both the short and the long term. Fallon and Lucas (1993), for instance, found that in Zimbabwe job security regulations (including restrictions on firms' ability to dismiss redundant workers) reduced employment by increasing adjustment costs and reducing efficiency. More generally, the evidence appears to suggest that countries that have managed to reduce poverty dramatically have all typically been able to increase the demand for unskilled labor rapidly. To the extent that labor market imperfections hamper the creation of (unskilled) jobs, there may be a close link between reforms aimed at improving the functioning of the labor market and policies aimed at alleviating poverty.

Another potentially fruitful area of research is related to the degree of inter-sectoral mobility of the labor force. As noted earlier, the speed of labor reallocation plays a crucial role in understanding the impact of shocks on poverty and the labor market. However, the available evidence on the degree of labor mobility across sectors in developing countries remains rather scant. In practice, labor mobility depends on a variety of factors, such as employment protection regulations (most notably administrative restrictions on hiring, plant closure and layoffs of permanent labor, and the generosity of severance payments) and other microeconomic considerations, such as proximity and family ties. Fallon and Riveros (1989) took the fact that wage differentials during the early 1980s tended to widen in favor of expanding (tradable) sectors in the urban sector in Argentina, Chile, Colombia, Mexico, and Uruguay as indicating less than perfect labor mobility. However, differences in the pattern of wage formation across industries may well explain such movements. There is a need therefore to extend research on these issues.[50] One possibility would be to follow the approach of Dickens and Lang (1985), which relies on switching regression analysis.[51] The Dickens-Lang method could be used to test for the presence of non-economic barriers to formal sector employment. Their approach consists in postulating a mechanism for the allocation of workers between the formal and informal sectors in the absence of rationing, based on workers' employment choices. Assuming that workers have perfect information and would behave so as to maximize utility over their lifetime, they would choose formal sector employment if the net present value of their income stream in the formal economy exceeded that of the informal sector. This proposition can be tested by a series of constraints on the switching regression.[52] But in practice, assessing the degree of mobility between the formal and informal sectors in developing countries is difficult because data on migration flows between these sectors are generally not available. However, the model developed earlier suggests that the ratio of formal sector wages (for workers with low qualifications) to informal sector wages can be a useful empirical proxy. The model, in fact, suggests an ambiguous effect of the wage differential on poverty, to the extent that the poor are viewed as consisting of all those employed in the informal sector as well as the openly unemployed in the formal economy.[53] A fall in the formal-informal wage ratio, for instance, increases the flow of unskilled workers to the informal sector. To the extent that these workers were previously unemployed, poverty would not change; but to the extent that they were initially employed in the formal sector, poverty would naturally increase. Similarly, a rise in the wage ratio would have an ambiguous effect on poverty because those workers who move to the formal sector to seek a job there may well be unsuccessful and end up joining the ranks of the unemployed. What the foregoing discussion suggests, nevertheless, is that adding the formal-informal sector wage ratio as an independent variable in the type of poverty regressions presented earlier may be one way to capture, with appropriate auxiliary assumptions, the effect of intersectoral labor flows on poverty rates.

Acknowledgements

This paper dwells on some of my recent work on labor market segmentation and asymmetric shocks. I am grateful to the Editor and two anonymous referees for helpful comments on a previous version, and to Nihal Bayraktar for excellent research assistance. The views expressed in this paper do not necessarily reflect those of the Bank.

Notes

1. Efficiency wage considerations have been much discussed in the recent literature on labor markets in developing countries (see Agénor, 1996). Rationales include better nutrition, incentive and morale factors, adverse selection, turnover costs, and shirking costs. As discussed below, such considerations are particularly important for large, capital-intensive firms, which typically operate in the urban formal economy.

2. See Fields (2001) and Ravallion (1994) for a discussion of this measure of poverty, as well as the poverty gap (discussed later), and their limitations.

3. It should also be kept in mind that measures of rural and urban poverty rates – such as those discussed by Sahn *et al.* – are often made on the basis of expenditure data that are not properly deflated across regions, owing to the lack of appropriate regional deflators. Accounting for the difference between the cost of living between urban and rural areas is nevertheless crucial for poverty assessment, in part because prices are typically higher in urban areas. Mazumdar (1993) for instance estimated that in Kenya in the late 1980s, the nominal income differential between rural and urban areas was as high as 4:1, and the cost of living in urban areas was 60% higher. Without price indices (and thus relative weights) that account for consumption patterns in both areas, the difference between the incidence of poverty in rural and urban areas may be overstated.

4. In Ghana, for instance, the sharp reduction in the rural poverty rate between 1987 and 1992 (from 42% to 34%) was the result of a significant increase in the income generated by the poor from non-farm self-employment. According to Canagarapajah and Mazumdar, (1997, p. 44), the share of such income in total household income increased from 19.5% in 1987–88 to 25.7% in 1991–92. At the same time, the share of income generated from farm self-employment fell during the same period from 60.4% to 53%.

5. Of course, a reduction in the share of marketed agricultural output would also lower cash income and possibly force a reduction in the consumption of non-agricultural goods by the rural poor.

6. By contrast, for the period between 1987 and 1992, Anríquez *et al.* (1998) found that in Chile up to 80% of the reduction of poverty was due to growth, with the rest due to changes in income distribution.

7. Government spending on transfers and subsidies also have an indirect effect on aggregate demand, and changes in public sector prices may have an indirect impact on other prices in the economy, as discussed later.

8. Large reductions in subsidies have often been seen as a reflection of the lack of political influence of the poor and pressures exerted by more powerful interest groups.

9. Conversely, of course, social spending may fall more than proportionately during periods of fiscal consolidation. Ravallion (2000) documents the experience of Argentina during the 1980s and 1990s, when pro-poor social spending fell significantly.

10. Indirect effects through portfolio shifts (and capital gains and losses) are typically limited because the poor hold their assets mostly in the form of noninterest-bearing money or bank deposits. There may, of course, be a large effect on *relative* poverty (that is, income distribution) through this channel, to the extent that upper-income groups hold more diversified portfolios of assets.

11. These effects may be exacerbated in the presence of wage and price stickiness (resulting, for instance, from the prevalence of nominal wage contracts and rigid mark-up pricing rules), which imply larger quantity adjustments in the short run.

12. The evidence favoring the Ricardian Equivalence proposition in developing countries is, however, rather weak; see Agénor (2000, ch. 1)).

13. However, this effect is probably relatively small in practice, due to the fact the savings rates of the poor are low to begin with.

14. For Latin America, see in particular Cardoso (1992) and Morley (1995).

15. However, it is possible (at least in principle) that the inflation tax revenue serves to finance a higher level of public expenditure that benefits the poor directly – thereby mitigating the adverse, partial equilibrium effect of the tax on welfare.

16. See Temple (2000 b) for a comprehensive and critical review of the recent literature on inflation and growth, focusing particularly on methodological issues, including the possibility of nonlinearities.

17. Note, however, that there are possible offsetting effects. For instance, a high and variable inflation rate can lead to higher savings due to precautionary motives, and thus to higher growth rates (see below).

18. Results of household surveys in sub-Saharan Africa suggest that not only do the poor sell agricultural output, but that tradable products, both exports and food crops, constitute a significant share of their agricultural earnings (Sahn *et al.*, 1997, p. 32).

19. In contrast to some other studies, inflation in Bleaney's regressions loses its significance when the indicator of real exchange rate variability is introduced.

20. Londoño and Székely argued that this outcome may be explained in part by the fact that the poor are less well equipped to cope with economic shocks and that incomes of the poor are substantially more sensitive to changes in aggregate income than upper-income groups.

21. As discussed in detail by Agénor (2001*a*), two factors may compound the incidence of a credit crunch induced by information problems: the degree of concentration in the financial system, and the fact that small and medium-size firms tend to be more dependent on bank credit than large firms.

22. In principle, the possibility of binding borrowing constraints in adverse state of nature does not, by itself, result in an asymmetric effect. Households may 'internalize' state-dependent credit constraints by deciding, in response to income risk, to accumulate more assets or engage in precautionary savings in 'good' times in order to shelter consumption in 'bad' times. Recent evidence on this type of *ex ante* risk-mitigating strategy is provided by Agénor and Aizenman (2000) for sub-Saharan Africa.

23. See Agénor (1996) for a detailed overview of the literature, and Bigsten and Horton (1998) for a survey of labor markets in sub-Saharan Africa. See also Horton *et al.* (1994) and the World Bank (1995). Marquez and Pagés-Serra (1998) review regulations governing hiring, firing, overtime work, social security contributions, minimum wages and collective bargaining in Latin America, and examines their impact on labor market outcomes. Edwards and Cox Edward (2000) discuss the case of Chile.

24. The informal sector can be defined in various ways. A common definition is that it includes self-employed workers (except for professionals) unpaid family workers, workers employed in small firms (less than, say, 5 or 6 workers), and those working in the trade and services sector without a proper contract.

25. Demery and Addison (1994) provide a partial equilibrium analysis of the role of the labor market in the transmission process of expenditure-switching policies.

26. The model could be extended, along the lines described in Agénor (2002), to introduce a trade union in the formal sector.

27. The model can be extented to account for the existence of a sector producing importables, but at the cost of greater complexity.

28. Note that the assumed technology implies that skilled and unskilled labor are Edgeworth complements.

29. An alternative way to introduce efficiency considerations in the formal sector would be to assume that production requires (as noted earlier) skilled labor to operate physical capital. Firms would then set wages to minimize turnover costs. Assuming that the quit rate is a function of the consumption wage would yield results that are qualitatively similar to those described below (see Agénor, 2001*b*).

30. The condition that the minimum wage be higher than the informal sector wage is necessary to prevent a corner solution in which unskilled workers have no incentive to seek employment in the formal economy.
31. An alternative approach (at this level of abstraction) would be to assume that *all* unskilled workers, in both the formal and informal sectors, are poor. As noted earlier, the empirical evidence suggests indeed that the average number of years of schooling of the poor tends to be much lower than that of the total workforce. However, the approach adopted here is also consistent with the evidence that suggests a concentration of urban poverty in the informal sector.
32. More generally, it could be assumed that the upper-income household holds, in addition to foreign bonds, domestic assets (such as land). To avoid complicating the analysis further, domestic sources of wealth accumulation are ignored in what follows.
33. Life-cycle models would predict a relationship between consumption and lifetime wealth, rather than with income and current wealth. However, in the presence of liquidity constraints, current income would also affect expenditure. See the evidence for developing countries discussed by Khayum and Baffoe-Bonnie (1994) and Veidyanathan (1993), or the literature reviews in Agénor (2000, Chapter 1) and Agénor and Montiel (1999, ch. 3).
34. Evidence supporting this hypothesis is provided by Hirata and Humphrey (1991) for Brazil, Horton *et al.* (1994), and Banerjee and Bucci (1995) for India. Agénor (1996) provides a review of the evidence on skilled unemployment in developing countries. In general, of course, whether skilled workers who are not successful in applying for a job in the formal sector decide to seek employment in the informal economy depends on factors such as the efficiency of on-the-job search activities, demotivation effects, and the degree of support from relatives.
35. In what follows, all derivatives are evaluated at initial values of wages and the real exchange rate equal to unity.
36. Using (21), the equilibrium condition of the market for informal sector goods can be rewritten as, using (13):

$$(1 - \delta)\left\{\frac{\omega_N(z, n_U^s)z}{\eta}\right\}^{\eta/(\eta-1)} = \delta z\left\{\alpha\left[Y_X^s(z; \omega_m) + i^* B^* - T\right] + \upsilon B^*\right\},$$

which can be solved for z as a function of n_U^s and B^*, as well as the exogenous variables ω_m, and i^*.
37. See Bhattacharya (1993) for a review of the literature on the Harris-Todaro model and, for a more critical view, Stark (1991). Note that in the present setup the Harris-Todaro framework is used to explain migration flows between the (urban) informal sector and the (urban) formal sector, rather than migration between the rural and the urban sectors.
38. In practice, a large proportion of government spending consists of outlays on nontraded goods and services. This is hard to account for in the present setting, because there is only one home good, produced in the informal sector.
39. Appendices A and B are available from the author upon request.
40. Because there is no unemployment benefit scheme in the present framework, unemployed workers in the long run are implicitly assumed to either turn to a subsistence activity (home production) or to rely on relatives for their survival.

41. As indicated in (21), for a given level of n_U^s, ω_N must exactly offset movements in z. However, ω_N depends also on n_U^s; the rise in n_U^s puts upward pressure on informal sector wages.

42. See Cardoso (1992) and Morley (1995). Cardoso, for instance, argued that stabilization worsened poverty in Brazil because fiscal adjustment led to a reduction in social expenditures. The issue, however, is quite complex, as discussed earlier.

43. The index combines fiscal, monetary, and exchange rate policies. The fiscal component of the index, for instance, is based on the overall fiscal balance and total revenue. Scores are applied to performance in each of these areas and then added to arrive at the fiscal component of the index. A similar procedure is followed for the exchange rate and monetary components. The aggregate index is a weighted average of perform-ance in each of these three areas of macroeconomic management, with weights given by the relative importance of each component in determining growth, as captured through cross-country regressions.

44. The evidence is based on household sample surveys covering the 1980s and 1990s. As discussed in the first part of this paper, poverty in these countries is predominantly rural, with much of it occurring among small-scale farmers and among the self-employed.

45. Details about IMMPA applications are periodically updated at www.worldbank.org/ immpa.

46. Cross-country regressions have been the subject of criticism for their *ad hoc* specifica-tion and the fragility of many of the results. See Temple (1999, 2000a) for a detailed discussion of the problems that arise in this context and some reasons why they may be, nevertheless, useful tools.

47. In preliminary regressions, two fiscal variables were included to the list of regressors: subsidies and current transfers as a proportion of GDP, and the relative share of transfers and subsidies in public current expenditure. Both variables have *a priori* an ambiguous effect on poverty. The effect of an across-the-board cut in transfers and subsidies, for instance, may be negative; but to the extent that it is accompanied by better targeting (as noted earlier), there may be no significant effect on the poverty rate. Both variables turned out not to be statistically significant and were thus dropped out from the final results. It is difficult, however, to make much of the fact that public transfers and subsidies are not significant in the regressions; the reason is that the variable may not measure very well what are the subsidies and transfers that actually go to the poor (it includes, for instance, transfers from the government to private and public enterprises).

48. I also tried to interact the degree of openness with the terms of trade indicator, on the ground that in more open economies, changes in the terms of trade may have a larger impact on the poor. The variable turned out to be insignificant.

49. Both the rate of depreciation of the real exchange rate, and the indicator of macro-economic volatility became insignificant when the sample is split to test for asymmetric effects. The latter retained the correct sign, and was kept in the regression.

50. Note that in the analytical framework described earlier, the size of the labor supply seeking employment in the formal economy does not depend on the speed of adjust-ment in the long run; only the transitional dynamics are affected.

51. Leontaridi (1998) provides a more detailed discussion of the Dickens-Lang approach.

52. Essentially, if the hypothesis of workers' free choices of sectors is to be accepted, and tastes for the non-pecuniary aspects of employment are independent of individual characteristics (such as the place of residence, marital status, the level of education,

and so on), then one would expect that the coefficients of the variables describing these characteristics in the switching regression be equal to the coefficients in the two wage equations. Failure to accept this restriction can be viewed as *prima facie* evidence of non-economic barriers to employment in the formal sector.

53. This discussion assumes that the employment probability in the formal economy does not change significantly in the short run.

References

Addison, A. and Demery, L. (1994) The poverty effects of adjustment with labor market imperfections. In S. Horton, R. Kanbur and D. Mazumdar (eds), *Labor Markets in an Era of Adjustment*. Washington DC: World Bank.

Agénor, P. R. (1996) The labor market and economic adjustment. *IMF Staff Papers* 43: 261–335.

———— (1997) *Capital-Market Imperfections and the Macroeconomic Dynamics of Small Indebted Economies*. Princeton Study in International Finance No. 82.

———— (1999) Stabilization policies, poverty, and the labor market. Unpublished, World Bank.

———— (2000) *The Economics of Adjustment and Growth*. San Diego CA: Academic (2nd ed., forthcoming, Harvard University Press).

———— (2001a) Business cycles, economic crises, and the poor: testing for asymmetric effects. Unpublished, World Bank.

———— (2001b) Employment effects of stabilization policies. *European Journal of Political Economy* 14: 853–75.

———— (2002) Fiscal adjustment and the labor market in an open economy. Unpublished, World Bank. *Journal of Development Economics*, forthcoming.

———— and Aizenman, J. (1998) Contagion and volatility with imperfect credit markets. *IMF Staff Papers* 45: 207–35.

———— (1999) Macroeconomic adjustment with segmented labor markets. *Journal of Development Economics* 58: 277–96.

———— (2000) Savings and the terms of trade under borrowing constraints. National Bureau of Economic Research Working Paper No. 774. Forthcoming, *Journal of International Economics*.

————, Fernandes, R. and Haddad, E. (2002) Analyzing the impact of adjustment policies on the poor: An IMMPA framework for Brazil. Unpublished, World Bank.

————, Izquierdo, A. and Fofack, H. (2002) IMMPA: an integrated macroeconomic framework for the analysis of poverty reduction strategies. Unpublished, World Bank.

———— and Montiel, P. J. (1999) *Development Macroeconomics*, second edition. Princeton, N.J: Princeton University Press.

Aghion, P., Caroli, E. and Garcia-Penalosa, C. (1999) Inequality and growth: the perspective of the new growth theories. *Journal of Economic Literature* 37: 1615–60.

Aizenman, J. and Marion, N. P. (1993) Policy uncertainty, persistence and growth. *Review of International Economics* 1: 145–63.

———— (1999) Volatility and investment: interpreting evidence from developing countries. *Economica* 66: 157–79.

Alesina, A. and Perotti, R. (1996) Income distribution, political instability, and investment. *European Economic Review* 40: 1203–28.

Amadeo, E. and Neri, M. (1997) Macroeconomic policy and poverty in Brazil. Working Paper No. 383, Pontificia Universidade Católica do Rio de Janeiro.

Anríquez, G., Cowan, K. and De Gregorio, J. (1998) Poverty and macroeconomic policies: Chile 1987–1994. Working Paper No. 27, Universidad de Chile.

Banerjee, B. and Bucci, G. A. (1995) On-the-job search in a developing country: an analysis based on Indian data on migrants. *Economic Development and Cultural Change* 43: 565–83.

Barro, R. J. (1990) Government spending in a simple model of endogenous growth. *Journal of Political Economy* 98: s103–s25.

——— (2000) Inequality and growth in a panel of countries. *Journal of Economic Growth* 5: 5–30.

Bhattacharya, P. (1993) Rural-urban migration in economic development. *Journal of Economic Surveys* 7: 243–81.

Bigsten, A. and Horton, S. (2001) Labour markets in sub-Saharan Africa. In A. G. Ali and E. Thorbecke (eds), *Poverty in sub-Saharan Africa*. Basingstoke, Macmillan.

Bleaney, M. F. (1996) Macroeconomic stability, investment and growth in developing countries. *Journal of Development Economics* 48: 461–77.

Bourguignon, F. (2000) The pace of economic growth and poverty reduction. Unpublished, World Bank.

Bourguignon, F., de Melo, J. and Suwa, A. (1991) Distributional effects of adjustment policies: simulations for archetype economies in Africa and Latin America. *World Bank Economic Review* 5: 315–39.

Breen, R. and Garcia-Penalosa, C. (1999) Income inequality and macroeconomic volatility: an empirical investigation. Unpublished, European University Institute, Oxford.

Bruno, M. and Easterly, W. (1998) Inflation crises and long-run growth. *Journal of Monetary Economics* 41: 3–26.

Bruno, M., Ravallion, M. and Squire, L. (1998) Equity and growth in developing countries: old and new perspectives on the policy issues. In Vito Tanzi and Ke-young Chu (eds), *Income Distribution and High-Quality Growth*. Cambridge MA: MIT Press.

Bulir, A. (2001) Income inequality: does inflation matter? *IMF Staff Papers* 48: 139–59.

Camargo, J. M. and Ferreira, F. H. (2000) The povery reduction strategy of the government of Brazil: a rapid appraisal. Unpublished, Pontificia Universidade Católica do Rio de Janeiro.

Canagarapajah, S. and Mazumdar, D. (1997) Employment, labor markets and poverty in Ghana: a study of changes during economic declines and recovery. Unpublished, World Bank.

Cardoso, E. (1992) Inflation and poverty. Working Paper No. 4006, National Bureau of Economic Research.

Cardoso, E., de Barro, R. P. and Urani, A. (1995) Inflation and unemployment as determinants of income inequality in Brazil: the 1980s. In R. Dornbusch and S. Edwards (eds), *Reform, Recovery, and Growth: Latin America and the Middle East*. Chicago IL: University of Chicago Press.

Castro-Leal, F., Dayton, J. Demery, L. and Mehra, K. (1999) Public social spending in Africa: do the poor benefit? *World Bank Research Observer* 14: 49–72.

Choi, S., Smith, B. D. and Boyd, J. H. (1996) Inflation, financial markets, and capital formation. Review, Federal Reserve Bank of St. Louis, 9–35.

De Janvry, A. and Sadoulet, E. (2000) Growth, poverty, and inequality in Latin America: a causal analysis. *Review of Income and Wealth* 46: 267–87.

Demery, L. and Squire, L. (1996) Macroeconomic adjustment and poverty in Africa: an emerging picture. *World Bank Research Observer* 11: 39–59.

Dickens, W. T. and Lang, K. (1985) A test of dual labor market theory. *American Economic Review* 75: 792–805.

Dixit, A. and Pindyck, R. S. (1994) *Investment under Uncertainty*. Princeton, NJ: Princeton University Press.

Dollar, D. and Kraay, A. (2001) Growth is good for the poor. Policy Resarch Working Paper No. 2587, World Bank.

Dorosh, P. A. and Sahn, D. E. (2000) A general equilibrium analysis of the effect of macroeconomic adjustment on poverty in Africa. *Journal of Policy Modeling* 22: 753–76.

Duryea, S. and Székely, M. (1998) Labor markets in Latin America: a supply-side story. Working Paper No. 374, Inter-American Development Bank.

Easterly, W. (1993) How much do distortions affect growth? *Journal of Monetary Economics* 32: 187–212.

——— (2001) The effect of International Monetary Fund and World Bank programs on poverty. Policy Research Working Paper No. 2517, World Bank.

Easterly, W. and Fischer, S. (2001) Inflation and the poor. *Journal of Money, Credit, and Banking* 33: 160–79.

Edwards, S. and Edwards A. Cox (2000) Economic reforms and labour markets: policy issues and lessons from Chile. *Economic Policy* 15: 181–230.

Fallon, P. R. and Lucas, R. E. B. (1993) Job security regulations and the dynamic demand for industrial labor in India and Zimbabwe. *Journal of Development Economics* 40: 241–75.

Fallon, P. R. and Riveros, L. A. (1989) Adjustment and the labor market. PRE Working Paper No. 214. World Bank.

Fields, G. S. (2001) *Distribution and Development: a New Look at the Developing World.* Cambridge MA: MIT Press.

Fishlow, A. (1995) Inequality, poverty and growth: where do we stand? In M. Bruno and B. Pleskovic (eds), *Annual World Bank Conference on Development Economics.* Washington DC: World Bank.

Galor, O. and Zeira, J. (1993) Income distribution and macroeconomics. *Review of Economic Studies* 60: 35–52.

Gaviria, A. (2001) Household responses to adverse income shocks in Latin America. Working Paper No 455, Inter-American Development Bank.

Gerson, P. R. (1998) Poverty, income distribution, and economic policy in the Philippines. Working Paper No. 98/20.

Gylfason, T. (1998) Output gains from economic stabilization. *Journal of Development Economics* 56: 81–96.

Grootaert, C. (1992) The position of migrants in the urban informal labour market in Côte d'Ivoire. *Journal of African Economies* 1: 416–45.

——— (1997) The determinants of poverty in Côte d'Ivoire. *Journal of African Economies* 6: 169–96.

Harris, J. and Todaro, M. P. (1970) Migration, unemployment and development: a two-sector analysis. *American Economic Review* 60: 126–43.

Hirata, H. and Humphrey, J. (1991) Workers' response to job loss: female and male industrial workers in Brazil. *World Development* 19: 671–82.

Hoddinot, J. (1996) Wages and unemployment in an urban African labour market. *Economic Journal* 106: 1610–26.

Horton, S., Kanbur, R. and Mazumdar, D. (1994) Overview. In S. Horton, R. Kanbur and D. Mazumdar (eds), *Labor Markets in an Era of Adjustment*, Vol. I. Washington, DC: World Bank.

Infante, R. (1995) Labour market, urban poverty, and adjustment: new challenges and policy options. In G. Rodgers and R. van der Hoeven (eds), *The Poverty Agenda: Trends and Policy Options.* Geneva: International Institute for Labour Studies.

Jaffee, D. and Stiglitz, J. (1990) Credit rationing. In B. M. Friedman and F. H. Hahn (eds), *Handbook of Monetary Economics*, Vol. II. Amsterdam: North Holland.

Kanbur, R. (2000) Income distribution and development. In A. B. Atkinson and F. Bourguignon (eds), *Handbook of Income Distribution.* Amsterdam: North Holland.

Khayum, M. and Baffoe-Bonnie, J. (1994) Intertemporal consumer behavior in developing countries. Unpublished, Pennsylvania State University.

Leontaridi, M. (1998) Segmented labor markets: theory and evidence. *Journal of Economic Surveys* 12: 63–101.

Li, G., Steele, D. and Glewwe, P. (1999) Distribution of government education expenditures in developing countries. Unpublished, World Bank.

Loayza, N. V. (1996) The economics of the informal sector: a simple model and some empirical evidence from Latin America. Carnegie-Rochester Conference Series on Public Policy, 45.

Lofgren, H. (2001) External shocks and domestic poverty alleviation: simulations with a CGE model of Malawi. TMD Discussion Paper No. 71, International Food Policy Research Institute.

Londoño, J. L. and Székely, M. (1997) Distributional surprises after a decade of reforms: Latin America in the nineties. Working Paper No. 352, Inter-American Development Bank.

——— (2000) Persistent poverty and excess inequality: Latin America, 1970–1995. *Journal of Applied Economics* 3: 93–134.

Lora, E. and Olivera, M. (1998) Macro policy and employment problems in Latin America. Working Paper No. 372, Inter-American Development Bank.

Lustig, N. (2000) Crises and the poor: socially responsible macroeconomics. Working paper No. POV-108, Inter-American Development Bank.

Maechler, A. and Roland-Host, D. W. (1995) Empirical specifications for a general equilibrium analysis of labor market policies and adjustments. Technical Paper No. 106, Organization for Economic Cooperation and Economic Development.

Marquez, G. and Lora, E. (1998) The employment problem in Latin America: perceptions and stylized facts. Working Paper No. 371, Inter-American Development Bank.

Marquez, G. and Pagés-Serra, C. (1998) Ties that bind: employment protection and labor market outcomes in Latin America. Working Paper No. 373, Inter-American Development Bank.

Mazumdar, D. (1993) Wages and employment in Kenya. Unpublished, Africa Region's Chief Economist's Ofice, World Bank.

——— (1994) The structure of wages in African manufacturing. Unpublished, World Bank.

Morley, S. A. (1995) *Poverty and Inequality in Latin America: the Impact of Adjustment and Recovery in the 1980s*. Baltimore MD: Johns Hopkins University Press.

Neri, M. and Thomas, M. (2000) Household educational responses to labor-market shocks in Brazil: 1982–99. Unpublished, World Bank.

Ramey, G. and Ramey, V. A. (1995) Cross-country evidence on the link between volatility and growth. *American Economic Review* 85: 1138–51.

Ravallion, M., (1994) *Poverty Comparisons*. Chur, Switzerland: Harwood Press.

——— (2000) Are the poor protected from budget cuts? Theory and evidence for Argentina. Working Paper No: 2391, World Bank.

Rodrik, D. (1998) Trade policy and economic performance in sub-Saharan Africa. Working Paper No. 6562, National Bureau of Economic Research.

Romer, C. D. and Romer, D. H. (1998) Monetary policy and the well-being of the poor. Working Paper No. 6793, National Bureau of Economic Research.

Sahn, D. E. (1996) Economic reform and poverty: an overview. In David E. Sahn (ed.), *Economic Reform and the Poor in Africa*. Oxford: Clarendon Press.

Sahn, D. E., Dorosh, P. A.and Younger, S. D. (1997) *Structural Adjustment Reconsidered: Economic Policy and Poverty in Africa*. Cambridge: Cambridge University Press.

Sarel, M. (1996) Nonlinear effects of inflation on economic growth. *IMF Staff Papers* 43: 199–215.

Sarris, A. H. (1996) Macroeconomic polices and household welfare in Tanzania. In D. E. Sahn (ed.) *Economic Reform and the Poor in Africa*. Oxford: Clarendon Press.

Stark, O. (1991) *The Migration of Labor*. Oxford: Basil Blackwell.

Subramanian, S. (1996) Vulnerability to price shocks under alternative policies in Cameroon. In D. E. Sahn (ed.) *Economic Reform and the Poor in Africa*. Oxford: Clarendon Press.

Székely, M. (2001) The 1990s in Latin America: another decade of persistent inequality, but with somewhat lower poverty. Working Paper No 454, Inter-American Development Bank.

Temple, J. (1999) The new growth evidence. *Journal of Economic Literature* 37: 112–56.

—— (2000a) Growth regressions and what the textbooks don't tell you. *Bulletin of Economic Research* 52: 181–205.

—— (2000b) Inflation and growth: stories short and tall. *Journal of Economic Surveys* 14: 332–426.

Veidyanathan, G. (1993) Consumption, liquidity constraints and economic development. *Journal of Macroeconomics* 15: 591–610.

Wodon, Q., Castro-Fernandez, R., Lee, K., Lopez-Acevedo, G., Siaens, C., Sobrado, C. and Tre, J. P. (2001) Poverty in Latin America: trends (1986–1998) and determinants. Unpublished, World Bank.

World Bank (1995) *Workers in an Integrating World*. Washington DC: World Development Report.

—— (1997) Poverty in Côte d'Ivoire: a framework for action. Unpublished, World Bank.

—— (1998) *Attacking Poverty*. Washington DC: World Development Report.

—— (2000) *Attacking Poverty*. New York: Oxford University Press.

7

THE ASYMMETRIC EFFECTS OF MONETARY POLICY

Anna Florio
Politecnico di Milano

1. Introduction

It is widely recognised that monetary policy has real effects on the economy over short horizons. The idea that these real effects are asymmetric is, by contrast, less well established in the literature. In particular, the reduction in output following a negative monetary policy shock appears larger than the expansion induced by a positive shock of similar size. The limits of an expansionary monetary policy have been known at least since Keynes introduced the idea of a *liquidity* trap, where interest rates are so low that they could not be lowered further in order to improve economic conditions. In 1967 Milton Friedman had in mind this kind of asymmetry when he compared monetary policy to a string that you can pull but not push.

More recently, the seminal work by Cover (1992) has drawn attention to an apparent asymmetric effect of monetary policy on aggregate output for the USA, with monetary contractions having a greater effect on output than equally sized monetary expansions. This (relatively) new strand of literature consists mainly of empirical studies that test for the existence of an asymmetry in the response to monetary policy; very little literature has been devoted to the various channels through which such an effect may arise.

The analysis of such an asymmetry presumes the existence of a causal relationship between money and output. Friedman and Schwartz's monetary history of the USA (1963) highlights such a relationship and the link between money and business cycle fluctuations.[1] The authors find that all the six periods[2] of severe economic contraction which took place in the USA from 1867 to 1960 were accompanied by a big decline in the stock of money, with the most severe contraction (1929–33) accompanied by the most severe decline. More recently the aggressive interest rate cuts by the Federal Reserve, following September 11 2001, and their apparent ineffectiveness in stimulating an output recovery, provide a topical illustration of asymmetry.

This paper reviews the literature on the asymmetric effects of monetary policy. The first section provides a brief narrative overview of the effectiveness of monetary policy in the USA, Japan and Italy. The choice of these three countries is motivated by, respectively: the focus of most of the empirical literature on the USA; Japan providing a recent example of a "liquidity trap"; while Italy is of interest because, during the 1960s, it experienced a very effective tight monetary policy and an ineffective easy one. Sections 2 and 3 are devoted respectively to the empirical studies assessing asymmetry and to its possible theoretical explanations; section 4 concludes.

2. Asymmetric Effects of Monetary Policy: Tales from Three Countries

2.1 *The USA*

The possibility of an asymmetric effect of monetary policy that is, the idea that a tight monetary policy could check a boom while an easy one would not be able to bring the system out of a recession, was first considered during the Great Depression.

Up until the end of the 1920s monetary policy was believed to be perfectly symmetric. After the creation of the Federal Reserve System, in fact, the economic stability that characterized the USA was ascribed to the System's ability to use monetary policy both to slow down and to stimulate the economy.

The belief in the effectiveness of easy monetary policy faded during the Great Depression. During the Depression, the three month treasury bill rate fell from almost 5% in 1929 to just under 1% in 1932 and monetary policy was thought to be expansionary. The inability of the (presumed) easy monetary policy to stimulate the recovery led to the opinion that, as Milton Friedman claimed in his presidential address to the American Economic Association in 1967, 'monetary policy was a string. You could pull on it to stop inflation but you could not push on it to halt recession. You could lead a horse to water but you could not make him drink' (Friedman, 1968, p. 1). That is to say, an expansionary monetary policy could be undertaken but there was no way to force people to borrow and invest if they were not willing to do so. The economic system seemed to be in a liquidity trap: low interest rates accompanied by low investment.

This notion of asymmetry was widespread until it was highlighted by Friedman and Schwartz in the 1960s that monetary policy during the Great Depression had, in fact, been tight and not easy as previously believed. During the period 1929–33 one third of the banks failed or merged and the quantity of money in the USA fell by one third. This reduction in the monetary aggregate was not ascribed to the reluctance of firms and households to borrow but to the behaviour of the Federal Reserve that didn't provide the banking system promptly with the needed liquidity.

In that period, despite the fall in nominal interest rates, prices were falling, so real interest rates were actually very high. The downturn was so severe and lasting because the banking crisis in 1930–31 disrupted the credit system and this prevented the public from borrowing the funds they needed to invest.

A peculiar case of asymmetric monetary policy seems present in the USA in the years following World War II. During that period, the fiscal deficit associated with the War made the government the main borrower of the banking system, which was forced to hold a substantial proportion of its assets in government securities. In such a setting the Federal Reserve was seen as a mere executor of the Treasury's needs and the efficacy of monetary policy was compromised. In particular, an easy monetary measure was thought to be ineffective while a tight one was judged effective but undesirable.

In the sixties and at the beginning of the eighties (at the end of 1982) there are examples of effective monetary easing. In both cases, however, monetary policy measures were matched with fiscal ones (the war in Vietnam and Reaganomics respectively) thus it is not easy to distinguish fiscal policy effects from monetary policy ones.

A more recent episode that casts doubts on the efficacy of an easy monetary policy is the difficulty encountered by monetary authorities to cope with the 1990–92 recession in the USA. During this period there were tight credit conditions. Banks were reluctant to lend and, particularly, they reduced real estate lending both because of the increased credit risk associated with these loans and to increase their capital to assets ratios to meet the standards of the Basle Accord. Faced with this situation, the Federal Reserve decided to ease monetary policy to prevent a credit crunch.

The Federal Reserve was, however, very cautious in cutting interest rates – 'in the two years between December 1990 and December 1992 the Federal Reserve cut the discount rate an average of 57 basis points on seven separate occasions, with an average of three months separating each decision' (Caplin and Leahy, 1996, p. 690). This policy proved ineffective in stimulating economic activity because the public- who were aware that, if the recession had persisted, interest rates would have been cut further, decided to wait for the lowest interest rates to undertake their investment and this delay in investment translated into a prolonged recession. What is more, the new regulatory guidelines adopted at the beginning of 1991 by the Federal Reserve to reduce impediments to lending turned out to be ineffective and credit values remained weak throughout the year.

The latest episode that casts doubt on the efficacy of an easy monetary stance in the USA is the response of the economy to the interest rate cuts in the years 2001–02. In that period, the Federal Reserve cut the funds rate in a gradual way to avoid the possible deflationary impact of the financial bubble bursting. This policy, however, did not appear to succeed in affecting spending that was instead depressed by accounting and corporate scandals.

2.2 *Japan*

Japan, the world's second largest economy, is another fertile ground for examples of ineffective expansionary monetary policy. As Paul Krugman pointed out in a number of articles, Japan seems to represent the textbook case of a Keynesian liquidity trap (see e.g. Krugman, 1998).

During the years 1953–73 sustained growth propelled Japan into the group of the most advanced economies in the world. The process of growth was character-ized by the strong influence of government in the management of the economy and the peculiar link between banks and firms. The distortions that these anomal-ies induced, already evident at the end of the 1980s, gave rise to the so called 'bubble economy'. When the financial bubble exploded in 1991, Japan fell into a recession. At the time of writing, Japan has not succeeded in escaping recession despite money market interest rates below one per cent. The economy experienced a disinflation which brought inflation down from between 2 and 3% to below zero by 1995 and deflation coupled with the zero bound on interest rates limited the Bank of Japan's flexibility to engineer further reductions in real short term rates (see Yates, 2004, for a broader discussion of the zero bound).

Given the constancy of the ratio of consumption to GDP in the 1990s it seems that the liquidity trap is the outcome of declining investment demand rather than rising saving supply. The bursting of the bubble removed the equity market as a source of firms' funds, and the fall in asset prices caused a reduction in the value of the collateral used to secure new loans. Both of these features contributed to reduce investment demand. The fall in investment demand did not materialize earlier because of the financial bubble that made most of the investment projects appear profitable.

The effectiveness of easy monetary policy was probably hindered by the weak-ness in the financial sector affected by the balance sheet problems associated by the collapse of asset prices. The deterioration in loan performance and the weakening of the banking system, which failed to write off bad loans and to maintain capital adequacy ratios, has limited its ability to make new loans to support economic recovery.

2.3 *Italy*

In the monetary history of Italy at least two meaningful episodes of asymmetric monetary policy can be found. The first is the post World War II period which includes the year 1947 when an extremely tight monetary policy was undertaken – with large depressing effects on real activity- by the Central Bank headed by Luigi Einaudi. The second (1963–69) is even more relevant for our analysis because it can be split into two sub-periods (1963–64 and 1969) of monetary policy restric-tions, with great effects on output, separated by the years 1964–65 when an easy monetary policy failed to boost investment.

During World War II there was a situation of repressed inflation. Inflation began to rise in 1944 when the government decided to abolish the controls on goods and financial markets. The growing liquidity injected into the system, due to the expansion of credit to firms, pushed up inflation.

In the first half of 1947 the government realized that it could not go on ignoring high inflation[3] and, in September 1947, the first restrictive monetary measure was undertaken under the supervision of Einaudi to whose name this policy has remained associated. A ceiling was imposed on bank deposits in order to limit the amount of credit extended by the banking system. This policy succeeded in stopping inflation but the country suffered from a severe recession. Firms lacking liquidity cut back on investment and this, in turn, hindered the already slow post-war reconstruction.

Turning to the 1960s, in 1962 there was an increase in wages that was soon translated by firms into higher prices, which in turn induced a deficit in the trade balance. Policy makers faced a trade off: they wanted to reduce inflation and to improve the balance of payments but they wanted to avoid stopping the process of economic growth that took off in the 1950s.

Initially, during 1962 and the first half of 1963, the monetary authorities gave more importance to the goal of full employment and economic development and began to allow credit expansion to firms to stimulate investment but this worsened inflation.

During the second half of 1963 the authorities changed their policy stance, introducing a severe monetary contraction: the monetary base that in the spring of 1963 was 1200 billion lire was reduced to 150 billion in 1964. This contraction can be compared in magnitude to that of 1947 by Einaudi. The reduced demand for consumption goods caused a slow down of industrial production that brought Italy into a deep and long economic depression.

The asymmetric aspect of monetary policy can be highlighted by comparing the period just described with the one immediately following it (from October 1964 to 1965) when an easy monetary policy was undertaken to move the economy out of depression. This easy monetary policy failed to achieve its aim. Despite the increased liquidity the banking system failed to expand credit – easing monetary policy did indeed appear comparable to 'pushing on a string'. At the end of 1965 an expansionary fiscal policy was undertaken to stimulate production. This fiscal stimulus had little time to affect real activity because in 1969, to reduce inflation, monetary policy was again severely tightened.

3. Empirical Methodology and Evidence

While the previous section was devoted to the detection of cases of an asymmetric effect of monetary policy in different countries, this section reviews the work that looks for that evidence in the data. The discussion is organised in terms of the measures used by different authors to identify the stance of monetary policy. The first subsection analyses the effect of a change in monetary aggregates on production and the problems with this procedure, which induced others to use the federal funds rate (subsection 3.2), the yield spread (3.3) or indices based on policy makers' statements (3.4).

3.1 Monetary Aggregates

The work by Cover (1992) can be considered the seminal one of this stream of economic literature. Cover, identifying money supply with M1 and using a two-step OLS procedure,[4] tests for the presence of an asymmetric effect of monetary policy on output using quarterly US data for the period 1951–87.

He estimates a system comprising a money equation and an output equation. The first equation describes the money supply process:

$$m_t = \alpha_0 + \sum_{i=1}^{N} \alpha_i^m m_{t-1} + \sum_{i=1}^{M} x'_{t-1} \alpha_i^x + u_t$$

where m_t is the money growth rate (using the aggregate M1), x_t is a vector of other relevant variables, such as the lagged growth of the monetary base, the lagged first difference of the treasury bill rate, the lagged unemployment rate, and the lagged growth rate of real GNP. The terms in α are coefficients, and the error term u_t represents the money supply shock. From this residual series of shocks from the money process Cover constructs two distinct series of money supply shocks. He identifies easy money supply shocks with:

$$u_t^+ = \max(u_t, 0)$$

and the tight money supply shocks by:

$$u_t^- = \min(u_t, 0)$$

The second equation is that for output:

$$y_t = \beta_0 + \sum_{i=1}^{P} \beta_i^r y_{t-i} + \sum_{i=0}^{Q} \beta_i^r r_{t-i} + \sum_{i=0}^{S} (\gamma_i^+ u_{t-i}^+ + \gamma_i^- u_{t-i}^-) + v_t$$

where y_t is the output growth rate in period t and r_t is the change in the three-month Treasury bill rate. As before, the terms in β and γ are coefficients and v_t is the output shock.

Verifying the presence of an asymmetry means to compute tests on the coefficients γ of the money supply shocks in the output equation.

Cover finds that negative monetary innovations affect output in a large and statistically significant way. By contrast, positive innovations to the money supply do not have such effects on output.

De Long and Summers (1988) extend Cover's analysis[5] using annual data and considering the pre-war and pre-Depression periods in addition to the post-war period. Unlike Cover they use the broader monetary aggregates M2 and M3 but they find very similar results in all the periods considered.

Karras (1996a) adopts a methodology very similar to Cover's two step procedure to test whether the asymmetry in the effects of monetary policy is a European phenomenon too, using annual data for 1953–90 for 18 European countries. He finds that in Europe negative money supply shocks have a larger impact on output than positive ones.

The results of Cover (1992) thus seem robust both to changes in the period and in the countries considered. However, all the work reviewed above employs a monetary aggregate as a measure for money supply shocks. Using a monetary aggregate gives rise to an identification problem; a change in monetary growth might, in fact, reflect a change in the demand for money and not in the supply. What is of interest is the effect that changes in policy have on output and not the reverse (the impact that output has on money growth) but the two-step procedure does not succeed in distinguishing these two effects. This identification problem, together with the structural instability of money demand in some of the periods considered, has induced researchers to use the federal funds rate as a measure of the stance of monetary policy.

3.2 *The Federal Funds Rate*

Bernanke and Blinder (1992) emphasize the role of the federal funds rate as an indicator of the stance of monetary policy at least when the period 1979–82 is excluded (during 1979–82 the Federal Reserve explicitly abandoned use of the Federal funds rate as intermediate target).[6]

The identification problem with monetary aggregates, mentioned above, remains present with the federal funds rate. As emphasized by Kakes (1998), the 'use of the level of the federal funds rate as an indicator of monetary policy stance could, in fact, reflect endogenous responses of monetary policymakers to events – e.g. oil price shocks – that have real effects by themselves or which can be anticipated and should therefore be ineffective' (p. 16).

To solve the identification problem Morgan (1993) uses a two-step procedure where, in the first stage, the federal funds rate is regressed on its own lagged values, on current and lagged values of both output growth and inflation, on a constant and a trend variable. The residuals of this regression are hence used to identify the policy stance: positive (negative) residuals identify a monetary tightening (easing). In the second stage output growth is regressed on lagged values of these residuals of the funds rate as well as on its own lagged values, a constant and a trend variable. In the sample period 1963–1992 the regression provides evidence of an asymmetric effect of negative and positive shocks to the federal funds rate. In particular, tight monetary policy has a large and highly significant effect on output while easy policy has a small effect on real activity, which is not significantly different from zero. When the author excludes from the sample period the years 1979–1982, when the Federal Reserve did not use the federal funds rate as a policy target, the evidence of asymmetry is still present but weaker.

3.3 *The Yield Spread*

The yield spread – the difference between long term and short term interest rates – is generally considered as a very good predictor of future output changes.[7]

The relationship between the slope of the term structure (the yield spread) and real economic growth can be explained by the expectations hypothesis of the term structure. Monetary policy induces changes in short term rates and affects long term rates insofar as it can influence inflation expectations. Assume, for instance, the central bank tightens by raising short term rates; if long term rates decrease, it means that this kind of policy is expected to reduce future inflation. Such expectations lead to a downward-sloping term structure that is likely to be associated with future recessions if expectations are correct on average. The slope of the yield curve reveals what financial markets expect to happen to short term rates in the future too. In the example above the expectation of lower inflation induces the public to expect a reduction in the future short term rates.

The yield spread is a good candidate as an indicator of the monetary policy stance since it can be observed immediately and is not subject to measurement errors. Macklem *et al.* (1996) use the yield spread[8] as an indicator of monetary stance in Canada for the period 1958–1994 to assess the asymmetric effects of monetary policy. They use a methodology very close to the one used by Cover (1992) and divide the negative innovations to the spread, that are leading indicators of recessions, from the positive ones that, instead, precede expansions. The growth rate of GDP is then regressed on its lagged values and on the negative and positive monetary shocks. The empirical finding is consistent with an asymmetric effect of innovations in the yield spread on output: while positive shocks have no significant effect on output, negative shocks seem to reduce it.

3.4 *The Narrative Approach*

An alternative methodology to identify the stance of policy is the narrative approach: Romer and Romer (1989) read through the minutes of the Federal Open Market Committee to identify the so called 'Romer dates' in which Federal Reserve policy switched toward a tougher stance against inflation.

Boschen and Mills (1993) provide a monthly index of the Federal Reserve's intentions based on the Record of Policy Actions of the Federal Open Market Committee from 1953 to 1991. Their index ranges from −2, which identifies a very easy stance of policy, to +2 identifying a very tight policy.

Morgan (1993), after a reminder that this measure is subject to the same problems of identification as those reviewed above, uses this index to find evidence of the asymmetric effect of monetary policy employing a two-stage procedure. In the first stage, as with the approaches described above, the index is regressed on its own lagged values and on current and lagged values of output and inflation. The second stage is devoted to the regression of output growth on positive and negative residuals which result from the first regression. This second regression is estimated again for two sample periods: one that includes the period 1979–82 and one that excludes it. Using this measure of policy, researchers have found a strong asymmetry in the full sample case. Moreover, in contrast to the results based on the Federal funds rate, the evidence is stronger when the period 1979–82 is dropped from the sample.

4. Explanations of Asymmetry

The literature about the asymmetric effects of monetary policy is largely devoted to empirical evidence of such an asymmetry and there is limited treatment of the reasons why a tight monetary policy is more effective than an easy one. In this section four main explanations are proposed.

4.1 Changing Outlook

This explanation hinges on the change in the state of confidence of the private sector about the phase of the business cycle. During a recession pessimism induces firms not to invest and consumers not to spend in spite of low interest rates. This is precisely what happened during the Great Depression and what is happening in Japan at present.

Our focus, however, is not on the ineffectiveness of easy monetary policy *per se* but on its failure compared with the effectiveness of tight monetary policy. The theory mentioned above only explains the poor performance of an expansionary policy. In order for this to explain asymmetry, the pessimism during a recession needs to be greater in intensity than the optimism during a boom. Otherwise a tight monetary policy action undertaken to check a boom, could be ineffective if the public is sufficiently optimistic and goes on investing and consuming despite the increasing interest rates.

Another reason for the asymmetric effects of monetary policy related to the private sector's expectations is again suggested by Keynes, who links the relevance of expectations to the concept of the marginal efficiency of capital. In Chapter XI of *The General Theory* (Keynes, 1936) he wrote:

> The schedule of the marginal efficiency of capital is of fundamental importance because it is mainly through this factor (much more than through the rate of interest) that the expectation of the future influences the present. (p. 145) [and again] This is the factor through which the expectations of changes in the value of money influences the volume of current output. The expectation of a fall in the value of money stimulates investment . . . because it raises the schedule of the marginal efficiency of capital . . . ; and the expectation of a rise in the value of money is depressing, because it lowers the schedule of the marginal efficiency of capital (p. 142).

Figure 1 illustrates the problem. On the vertical axis we measure the marginal efficiency of capital and the interest rate, on the horizontal axis the quantity of investment. Starting from point E in the figure, the expectation of a fall in the value of money (an increase of the price level) shifts the equilibrium – for a given rate of interest i_E- from point E to point A, pushing up investment. To bring investments back to I_E, interest rates could be increased to the level i_A (where equilibrium A' is reached). This argument holds for every outward shift of the schedule of the marginal efficiency of capital. If, instead, the marginal efficiency of capital schedule shifts inwards, it gives, at an interest i_E, a level of investment equal to I_B. In this case it may not be possible for investment to be brought back to the previous (larger) value I_E because the interest rate that would achieve this is negative (i_B). While a tight policy would manage to reach the desired level of

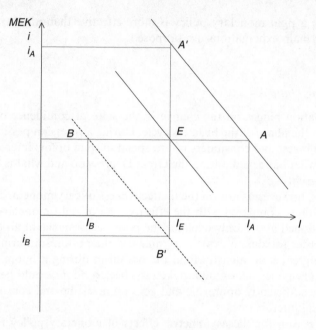

Figure 1. Asymmetric Effects and the Marginal Efficiency of Capital.

investment, an easy policy may not succeed in that task, hence monetary policy's effects on output are asymmetric.

4.2 *Expected Inflation and the Term Structure of Interest Rates*

While authorities use short term rates to implement monetary policy, aggregate spending decisions depend on long term interest rates. Hence monetary policy will be effective if and only if it succeeds in affecting longer term interest rates too.

According to the expectations theory of the term structure we have:

$$i_{n,t} = \frac{1}{n+1} \sum_{i=0}^{n} E_t i_{t+i} \tag{1}$$

That is, the n-period interest rate is equal to an average of the current short term rate and the future short term rates expected to hold over the n-period horizon. Keeping in mind Fisher's identity, the nominal interest rate on an n-period bond can be written as:

$$i_{n,t} = \frac{1}{n+1} \sum_{i=0}^{n} E_t r_{t+i} + \frac{1}{n+1} \sum_{i=0}^{n} E_t \pi_{t+i} \tag{2}$$

where $E_t r_{t+i}$ is the one period interest rate expected at t to prevail at $t+i$ and the last term is the expected change in log price from t to $t+n$.

From the relation above we can infer that fluctuations in the long-term rate will be caused both by a component connected with short maturity rates and by a component driven by expectations of inflation.

The analysis of the co-movement of long and short term interest rates (see Good-friend, 1998) provides another explanation for the asymmetric effects of monetary policy. An aggressive policy action not only would change short term rates but would also affect the market expectations of inflation and could cause a perverse effect on long term rates. An aggressive reduction in the policy rate to encourage real growth might fail to decrease long-term rates because of inflation expectations.

By contrast, an aggressive increase in the policy rate, undertaken to bring down the trend rate of inflation, could immediately increase long term rates and affect output. An increase in the policy rate shifts both components of the long rate: the short term rates unambiguously rise while the behaviour of expected inflation is uncertain. A monetary policy tightening will decrease expected long run inflation if disinflation is credible. In the absence of credibility, the last term on the right hand side of equation (2) may remain high or rising. This would lead to an immediate and significant upward shift of the long rate and so to a large effect of the policy stance on output. If there is no similar effect in periods of easy monetary policy we have the asymmetry we are looking for.

Another possibility for an asymmetric effect of monetary policy occurs in a deflationary environment. In such a situation, with a negative term for inflation expectations, a reduction in the nominal rate of interest can increase (and not decrease) the real interest rate. As a consequence, the long term interest rate rises and the easy monetary policy stance can turn out to be ineffective. On the other hand, a deflationary environment would allow a stronger impact of increasing short term rates on long term ones and so it would lead to a more effective tight monetary policy.

4.3 *Asymmetric Price Adjustment*

Both the Keynesian models of downwardly rigid and upwardly flexible wages and prices and the usual assumption of factors' decreasing marginal productivity generate a convex aggregate supply curve in the (Y,P) plane. This curve can be obtained by 'smoothing' an inverted L shaped aggregate supply curve that is horizontal (as in the Keynesian case) up to full employment and vertical (as in the neoclassical case) at full employment.

It is not difficult to realize that, in the presence of a convex aggregate supply curve, monetary policy will have asymmetric effects on real output. Shocks of the same magnitude but different sign to aggregate demand will have different effects on the price level and output. A positive money supply shock will result in a larger change in prices and a smaller change in output than a negative shock.

The models aimed at microfounding this theoretical explanation of the asymmetric effects of monetary policy rely on the existence of trend inflation and small menu costs. In the presence of these costs it is expensive for firms to continuously adjust prices to their desired level. In this sticky price model, monetary policy will have asymmetric effects because positive trend inflation makes price reductions less likely than price increases so, after a negative shock, the firm is less likely to change its price and the shock is therefore more likely to have real effects while after a positive shock there is more likely to be a price and not a quantity adjustment.

This explanation of asymmetry has been formalized in various models,[9] all based on the three assumptions of costly price adjustment, state-dependent pricing and positive trend inflation. The common prediction of these models is that at higher rates of inflation the downward price rigidity result becomes stronger and that without the presence of positive trend inflation adjustment will be symmetric.

Caballero and Engel (1992) using annual data from 37 countries with moderate inflation for the period 1960–82 find empirical support for the prediction that as inflation rises the output reaction to aggregate demand shocks decreases and its asymmetric reactions to positive and negative shocks increases.

Ball and Mankiw (1994) calibrate their model and find that monetary shocks have asymmetric real effects if inflation is positive and, in particular, they find a distribution of output skewed to the left – 'a deep recession is more likely than an equally large boom'(p. 255). Furthermore they note that monetary policy shocks of the same size yield a bigger output loss when the rate of inflation prevailing in the economy is higher.[10] This result is consistent both with the findings of Bullard and Keating (1995), who claim that permanent shifts in the rate of money growth have a zero or negative effect on output for countries with a high rate of inflation, and with Barro (1995), who finds an inverse relation between growth and inflation at high rates of inflation.

4.4 *Credit Market Imperfections*

Theories based on imperfections in the credit market predict that asymmetries are caused by the different size of effects that easy and tight monetary policy have on aggregate demand. In particular, negative monetary policy shocks affect aggregate demand more than positive shocks of a corresponding magnitude and consequently, if the aggregate supply curve is linear, they have larger effects both on output and, contrary to the prediction of Keynesian convex aggregate curve theories, on prices (Figure 2).

We can imagine that immediately after the monetary policy contraction the shift of the aggregate demand curve (AD') is of the same magnitude as that following a monetary policy easing (AD_{easy}). The credit channel approach to monetary policy suggests that a further inward shift of the AD curve after a tight policy (to AD_{tight}) may arise due to the macroeconomic ramifications of bank failures or to the increase of the external finance premium. The credit view of the monetary policy transmission mechanism is based on the idea that credit market imperfections make external funds more expensive than internal ones because of agency costs which are reflected in the external finance premium (see, e.g., Bernanke and Gertler, 1995). Inside the credit view we can distinguish two different approaches: the *lending channel* and the *balance sheet channel* (or financial accelerator approach). According to the lending channel, formalised by

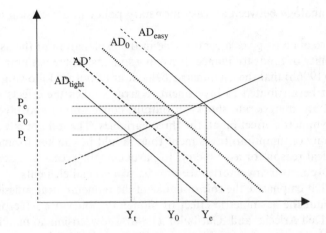

Figure 2. Asymmetric Effects and the Credit View.

Bernanke and Blinder (1988), after a monetary tightening there is a reduction in the supply of credit: if banks deny credit to firms that do not have alternative sources of funds (usually the smaller or the younger firms). These firms will be forced to cut back on investment and this will cause a reduction in output.

In the balance sheet channel (see, e.g. Bernanke and Gertler (1989, 1990); Greenwald and Stiglitz (1988, 1993)), agency costs are inversely related to borrowers' net worth, which moves pro-cyclically. A rising interest rate lowers the present value of firms' net worth and so decreases the value of firms' collateral to the lender, who will ask for a larger premium to continue financing the firms' investment. It follows that the effect of a monetary contraction is magnified through its impact on the external finance premium, which thus provides another explanation for the larger shift of the aggregate demand curve to the left in figure 2

The effectiveness of both the lending and the balance sheet channel increases when borrowers strictly depend on external finance. In this case monetary policy effectiveness depends on the phase of the business cycle.[11] In periods of boom, since the economy is growing, there are more possibilities to undertake investment and the demand for credit is high. When investment opportunities are good relative to liquid assets, firms may be constrained by the amount of internal funds available. In such a framework a monetary tightening, increasing interest rates and the risk of bankruptcy, can make banks less willing to lend to some borrowers (the lending view approach) or can deteriorate borrowers' balance sheets inducing a rise in the external finance premium (the balance sheet channel. In this situation a credit constraint would be binding and would lead to a reduction in production.

A monetary expansion undertaken to move out of a recession would not be so effective. During a recession it is highly likely that the sluggish economy leads to a smaller demand for credit. If this is the case the credit constraint is not binding and an easy policy that reduces interest rates won't have a large effect on output.

Hence the analogy between an easy monetary policy in a recession and pushing on a string.

The above analysis gives a central role in the explanation of the asymmetry to the availability of funds to finance firms' investments. There is empirical evidence by Karras (1996b) that the asymmetric behaviour of output following a monetary shock must be attributed to investment. Karras studies the effects of a money supply and an interest rate shock on output, consumption and investment. He finds an asymmetric effect on all the three variables. The mildest effect, however, is the one on consumption. Investment thus should be the key to understanding the theoretical reason for asymmetry. In particular the access to external finance and the movement in inventories seem to be two crucial elements.

Models that emphasize the role of banks in the monetary transmission mechanism to explain the asymmetric effect of monetary policy are widespread in this literature. Dell'Ariccia and Garibaldi (1998) show, using a matching model (developed by Mortensen and Pissarides, 1994), that if banks can quickly recall existing loans but are unable to expand credit so quickly (because it is difficult to find good investments, the screening is time consuming etc.), the bank credit reaction to monetary policy could be asymmetric. They support their model with empirical evidence for Mexico and the USA and find that bank lending responds asymmetrically to an increase and a decrease in money market rates.

5. Conclusions

The studies on the asymmetric effects of monetary policy developed to date and surveyed in this paper shed light on an issue often raised by policy makers but not covered widely in the economic literature: the greater effectiveness of tight policy compared to easy policy. As already stressed, the major part of the literature has been devoted to detecting asymmetry in the data; with most studies finding evidence of asymmetry. This evidence, backed up by policy-makers' observations, calls for a theoretical explanation. A variety of reasons were put forward in the preceding section, in brief:

a) the nominal interest rate can be raised without end but it has a lower bound that equals zero;
b) investment depends on the comparison between the marginal efficiency of capital and the interest rate: if expectations get worse there may be no reduction in interest rates that can compensate for a very low marginal efficiency of capital;
c) in order to invest firms need finance that can be scarce as a consequence of a tight monetary policy which reduces external funds and compels (some) firms to reduce investment.

Theories that hinge on expectations and on the importance of credit markets seem more useful to explain the observed asymmetry. The ineffectiveness of easy monetary policy in all three countries discussed in section 2 stems from the inadequacy of low interest rates to stimulate credit demand in the presence of bad expectations about the future while the extreme effectiveness of a tight monetary policy is generally associated with a deterioration in borrowers' balance sheets that induces a rise in the external finance premium and limits firms' ability to borrow in order to invest.

The main drawback of the current approaches to the study of the asymmetric effects of monetary policy is the literature generally studies the effects on output of an easy and a tight monetary shock starting from the same point of the business cycle. In both Keynesian convex aggregate supply curve theories and in models based on credit market imperfections opposite movements in the aggregate demand curve (that lead to the asymmetric result) are considered as starting from the same point of the business cycle. A more accurate description of reality should not neglect the fact that monetary policy acts counter-cyclically. A tight monetary policy is undertaken to check a boom and an easy one is undertaken to move out from a recession. Therefore, a more interesting approach would be that of conditioning the effectiveness of monetary policy to the stage of the business cycle.

Theories based on the balance sheet channel can be useful for this purpose because easy and tight monetary shocks can have different effects according to the stage of the business cycle when they occur. In particular, the effectiveness of easy and tight monetary policy can depend on firms' balance sheets and, given that firms' net worth is strongly linked to the stage of the business cycle, it is easier to understand how effectiveness varies when real activity varies. What is more, a shock that hits lenders' balance sheets could modify the responsiveness of loan interest rates to money market rates. Banks are more reluctant to decrease their loan interest rates immediately after an easy monetary policy stance than to raise them after a tight monetary policy. Moreover, the responsiveness of loan rates to money market rates could be linked to changes in borrowers' net worth. During a boom net worth is high, banks' loan supply curve is almost flat and equilibrium loan rates change almost one to one with money market rates. During a recession, by contrast, the low net worth and the very steep loan supply curve makes loan rates almost insensitive to money market rates. This suggests that tight monetary policy in booms works better than easy monetary policy in recessions. Future research on monetary policy asymmetry should, therefore, put greater emphasis on the balance sheet channel of monetary policy transmission.

Furthermore, although there are some empirical papers that use the term structure to find evidence of asymmetry, there are not, at present, theoretical models that use the term structure to consider monetary policy asymmetry explicitly. Given the central role played by agents' expectations of future inflation in determining long term interest rates this seems another fertile ground for future research.

Notes

1. According to the conventional wisdom, changes in money growth rates cause changes in real activity. On the other hand, changes in output might cause changes in money growth if the reverse causation argument discussed in King and Plosser (1984) holds.

The latter view is based on the fact that most monetary policy actions consist of smooth responses to the state of the economy rather than exogenous policy shifts.

2. These contractions took place in the following years: 1873–79*, 1893–94*, 1907–08*, 1920–21, 1929–33* and 1937–38. The starred periods were characterised by major banking or monetary disturbances.

3. The price index, base 1938 = 100, was 5159 in 1947.

4. The same procedure was employed by Barro (1977, 1978) and Mishkin (1982) to study whether unanticipated changes in money supply did have real effects on output.

5. In 1988 De Long and Summers already knew Cover's results because his paper circulated as a working paper of the University of Alabama in the same year.

6. The use of monetary aggregates to identify a shift in monetary policy has been disputed by Sims (1980) who discovered that interest rates had a better predictive power for real activity: 'when a short interest rate is added to the vector autoregression...the central role of the money stock surprises evaporates' (p. 250).

7. See, among others, Bernanke and Blinder (1992), Estrella and Hardouvelis (1991), Bernard and Gerlach (1996).

8. The spread used is given by the difference between the yield of 10-year and over Government of Canada bonds less the interest rate on 90-day corporate paper.

9. Caballero and Engel (1992), Tsiddon (1993), Ball and Mankiw (1994).

10. Rhee and Rich (1995) make an empirical study of the relation between the level of inflation and the asymmetric effects of money on output fluctuations. Assuming that the size of the effects of monetary shocks varies in response to movements in average inflation, they find evidence of asymmetric effects of monetary policy.

11. A different stream of economic literature links monetary policy effectiveness to the phase of the business cycle. Recognising that small firms are more financially constrained during recessions than during expansions, Garcia and Shaller (1995) and Kakes (1998) stress that monetary policy- either tight or easy – should be more effective during recessionary than during expansionary periods of economic activity.

References

Ball, L. and Mankiw, N. G. (1994) Asymmetric price adjustment and economic fluctuations. *Economic Journal* 104, March, 247–261.

Barro, R. (1977) Unanticipated money growth and unemployment in the United States. *American Economic Review* 67, 101–15.

Barro, R. (1978), Unanticipated money, output, and the price level in the United States. *Journal of Political Economy* 86, 549–580.

Barro, R. (1995) Inflation and economic growth. National Bureau of Economic Research, Working Paper no. 5326.

Bernanke, B. (1983) Nonmonetary effects of the financial crisis in the propagation of the Great Depression. *American Economic Review* 78, 3, 257–276.

Bernanke, B. and Blinder, A. (1992) The federal funds rate and the channels of monetary transmission. *American Economic Review* 82, 901–921.

Bernanke, B. and Gertler, M. (1995) Inside the black box: the credit channel of monetary policy transmission. *Journal of Economic Perspectives* 9, 4, 27–48.

Bernanke, B. and Gertler, M. (1990) Financial fragility and economic performance. *Quarterly Journal of Economics* 105, 1, 87–114.

Bernanke, B. and Gertler, M. (1989) Agency costs, net worth, and business fluctuations. *American Economic Review* 79, 1, 14–31.

Bernard, H. and Gerlach, S. (1996) Does the term structure predict recessions? The international evidnce. Bank for International Settlement, Working Paper no.37.

Boschen, J. and Mills, L. O. (1993) The narrative approach to evaluating monetary policy: consistency of interpretation and the relation to monetary activity. Mimeo, Federal Reserve Bank of Richmond.

Bullard, J. and Keating, W. (1995) The long-run relationship between inflation and output in postwar economies. *Journal of Monetary Economics* 36, 477–496.

Caballero, R. and Engel, E. (1992) Price rigidities, asymmetries, and output fluctuations. NBER Working Paper, No.4091.

Caplin, A. and Leahy, J. (1996) Monetary policy as a process of search. *American Economic Review* 86, 4, 689–702.

Cover, J. P. (1992) Asymmetric effects of positive and negative money-supply shocks. *Quarterly Journal of Economics* 107, 1261–1282.

De Long, B. and Summers, L. (1988) How does macroeconomic policy affect output. *Brooking Papers on Economic Activity* 2, 433–494.

Dell'Ariccia, G and Garibaldi, P (1998) Bank lending and interest rate changes in a dynamic matching model. IMF Working Paper

Estrella, A. and Hardouvelis, G. (1991) The term structure as a predictor of real economic activity. *Journal of Finance* 66, 2, 555–576.

Friedman, M. (1968) The role of monetary policy. *American Economic Review* 58, 1, 1–17.

Friedman, M. and Schwartz, A. (1963) *A Monetary History of United States, 1867–1960.* Princeton NJ: Princeton University Press.

Garcia, R. and Schaller, H. (1995) Are the effects of monetary policy asymmetric?. *Cyrano* n. 95s–6.

Goodfriend, M. (1998) Using the term structure of interest rates for monetary policy. *Federal Reserve Bank of Richmond Economic Quarterly* 84/3, 13–30.

Graziani, A. (1972) Problemi di politica monetaria in Italia (1945–1970). In *Lezioni sulla olitica economica in Italia a cura di Valerio Balloni*, pp. 290–345.

Greenwald, B. and Stiglitz, J. E. (1993) Financial market imperfections and business cycles. *Quarterly Journal of Economics* 108, 77–114.

Greenwald, B and Stiglitz, J. E. (1988). Imperfect information, finance constraints and business fluctuations. In: Kohn, M. and Tsiong, S. C. (eds), *Finance Constraints, Expectations and Macroeconomics.* Oxford: Oxford University Press.

Hubbard, G. (1998), Capital market imperfections and investment. *Journal of Economic Literature* 36, 193–225.

Kakes, J. (1998) Monetary transmission and business cycle asymmetry. Groningen University Working Paper

Karras, G. (1996a) Are the output effects of monetary policy asymmetric? Evidence from a sample of European countries. *Oxford Bulletin of Economics and Statistics* 58, 267–278.

Karras, G. (1996b) Why are the effects of money-supply shocks asymmetric? Convex aggregate supply or 'pushing on a string'? *Journal of Macroeconomics* 18, 605–619.

Karras, G. and Stokes, H. (1999) Are the output effects of money-supply shock asymmetric? Evidence from prices, consumption and investment. *Journal of Macroeconomics* 21, 713–728.

Kato, R., Ui, T. and Watanabe, T. (1999) Asymmetric effects of monetary policy: Japanese experience in the 1990s. Working Paper, Bank of Japan.

Keynes, J. M. (1930) *A Treatise on Money.* London: Macmillan.

Keynes, J. M. (1936) *The General Theory of Employment, Interest and Money.* London: Macmillan.

Kim, J Ni, A and Ratti, R. A. (1998) Monetary policy and asymmetric response in default risk. *Economic Letters* 60, 83–90.

King, R. G. and Plosser, C. (1984) Money, credit, and prices in a real business cycle. *American Economic Review* 74(3), 363–80.

Krugman, P. (1998) It's baaack: Japan's slump and the return of the liquidity trap. *Brookings Papers on Economic Activity* 2, 137–204.

Macklem, T., Paquet, A. and Phaneuf, L. (1996) Asymmetric effects of monetary policy: evidence from the yield curve. CREFE Working Paper.

Mishkin, F. (1982) Does anticipated policy matter? An econometric investigation. *Journal of Political Economy* 90, 22–51.

Morgan, D. P. (1993) Asymmetric effects of monetary policy. *Federal Reserve Bank of Kansas City Economic Review*, 21–33.

Mortensen, D. T. and Pissarides, C. A. (1994) Job creation and job destruction in the theory of unemployment. *Review of Economic Studies* 61, 397–415.

Ravn, M. and Sola, M. (1997) Asymmetric effects of monetary policy in the US: positive vs. negative or big vs. small? Universitat Pompeu Fabra Working Paper.

Rhee, W. and Rich, R. W. (1995) Inflation and the asymmetric effects of money on output fluctuations. *Journal of Macroeconomics* 17, 4, 683–702.

Romer, C. and Romer, D. (1989) Does monetary policy matter? A new test in the spirit of Friedman and Schwartz. *NBER Macroeconomic Annual* 4, 121–170.

Sims, C. (1992) Interpreting the macroeconomic time series facts: the effect of monetary policy. *European Economic Review* 36, 975–1011.

Sims, C. (1980) Comparison of interwar and postwar business cycles: monetarism reconsidered. *American Economic Review* 70(2), 250–7.

Spinelli, F. and Fratianni, M. (1991) Storia Monetaria D'Italia. L'Evoluzione del Sistema Monetario e Bancario. Mondadori.

Tsiddon, D. (1993) The (mis)behaviour of the aggregate price level. *Review of Economic Studies* 60, 889–902.

Yates, T. (2004) Monetary policy and the zero bound to interest rates: a review. *Journal of Economic Surveys* 18(3), 427–81.

8

MONETARY POLICY AND THE ZERO BOUND TO INTEREST RATES: A REVIEW[1]

Tony Yates

Bank of England

1. Introduction and Overview

Researchers and central banks[2] have debated openly whether the zero bound to nominal interest rates means that low inflation, aside from the benefit it brings, may imply a cost in terms of higher inflation and output variability.[3] The concern is that at low inflation rates central banks will be less able to counteract the effect of large deflationary shocks, since the zero bound constrains the amount by which they can cut nominal, and therefore real interest rates. Or worse, that a large enough shock could push the economy into a 'deflationary spiral', where inflation and expected inflation fall, nominal interest rates at some point come up against the zero bound, real interest rates rise, aggregate demand and expected inflation fall even further, real rates rise by yet more, and so on.[4]

Whether there is a trade off between inflation on the one hand and inflation and output variability on the other will depend on whether there are substitutes to conventional interest rate policy at the zero bound. In the absence of policy alternatives, this trade-off will depend on the properties of interest rate rules and of the disturbances that those rules are designed to stabilise. The significance of this trade-off (if there is one) for optimal policy will depend on how costly inflation is relative to inflation and output variability.

This paper evaluates what the literature to date has had to say on these questions. In short, I conclude the following:

Quantitative studies suggest that the risks of encountering the zero bound are quite small – in the region of 5% – when policy aims at inflation rates similar to the objectives pursued by many central banks, and moreover that the risks of succumbing to a deflationary spiral are negligible. This said, studies tend to show that those same risks increase a great deal as average inflation rates fall toward zero.

The risks of hitting the zero bound appear to be demonstrably smaller still if central banks commit to inducing persistence in interest rates, which increases the central bank's leverage over real rates and reduces the need for nominal rate cuts.

The menu of alternatives to cutting interest rates includes: more active fiscal stabilisation; taxes on money to lower the zero bound to interest rates; money 'rains' or transfers to the private sector; using open market operations to buy up long government bonds, or private sector assets, or even to buy assets denominated in foreign currency in the hope of devaluing the exchange rate; or, finally, writing options that promise to hold interest rates at the zero bound for a definite period of time.

How much comfort should central banks with explicitly quantified low-inflation objectives draw from this work? On the one hand, taken at face value, the work so far provides some reassurance. Yet on the other there is the preoccupation with the experience of Japan, which many argue is indeed an economy 'trapped' at the zero bound, if not yet one in a deflationary spiral.

The risks of hitting the zero bound – however small – are in one important respect overstated in the literature. They are calculated studying economies when the central bank is committed and believed to be committed to interest rate rules that in practice no central bank implements (or would ever implement). Ad hoc deviations from the rules that studies use would almost certainly reduce the apparent risks of hitting the zero bound. Such deviations, since they are rational, would be expected.

On the other hand, estimates of these risks depend critically on estimates of the shape of the distribution of shocks that are likely to hit the economy and be propagated into changes in desired interest rates. This distribution is a key unknown. The logical approach is for policy to take out insurance in the form of higher average inflation to cope with the possibility that the estimates are based on distributions that are too narrow.

Higher inflation looks even more attractive a policy choice when we consider how uncertain is the efficacy of the policy alternatives (discussed at length in the paper). As Fuhrer and Sniderman (2000, p. 845) put it 'prevention is likely easier than cure'.

However, this is not to say that those central banks that have quantified inflation objectives are following 'targets' (or whatever one should call them) that are too low. Insurance carries with it a premium: in this case the welfare costs of inflation itself. The amount of insurance central banks should therefore take out depends on a careful analysis of the benefits that come with lower outcomes for inflation and output variability, relative to the costs of the higher associated inflation. Central banks could never hope to reduce the chance of avoiding the zero bound *to zero*. And the costs of inflation would make it undesirable to try. It is perfectly conceivable, therefore, that the objectives that typify modern monetary regimes already have more than enough insurance built into them to accommodate the problem of the zero bound to interest rates.

The rest of the paper is set out as follows: section 2 describes a stylised version of the monetary policy problem in which the implications of the zero bound for optimal policy become clear. Section 3 recapitulates the literature that explains what brings about the zero bound to nominal interest rates, and what could make the floor differ from zero. Section 4 reviews the studies that have examined what the risks of hitting the zero bound are at different inflation rates (accompanied by an Appendix which sketches the studies in a little more detail), or have identified 'perils' of following interest rate rules. Sections 5–10 go through the alternatives to interest rate policy so far suggested: Gesell money or a 'carry tax' (5); money 'rains' (6); exploiting the home economy portfolio balance channel by buying long bonds or shares (7); stimulating the economy via a devaluation of the exchange rate (8); selling options to the private sector that embody a promise not to raise rates in the future (9); and stimulating the economy through conventional debt financed reductions in taxes or increases in spending (10).

2. The Zero Bound: Where Does It Come from and Is It Really Zero?

Suppose there are only two assets: money and default-risk-free government bonds. Money yields some service.[5] Suppose that the extra service you get from an extra unit of money declines as you accumulate more real balances. Suppose too that the only cost to holding money is that you forego the chance to earn interest on government debt. The lower the interest rate foregone, the larger are optimal real balances of currency. The Government could try to offer less than zero interest rates on its debt, but no-one would swap money for that debt. Money pays a certain and zero nominal interest rate stream, and carries with it no other costs.

Imagine instead that holding real balances does involve some cost: for example, that the only currency is gold, and storage space and security guards are costly. In this circumstance, as real balances got larger and larger, and the transactions costs reducing service yield of an additional gold bar fell, the storage cost would start to dominate. If the marginal costs of managing gold balances were constant, then the central bank would be able to lower interest rates to a negative number equal to this cost. Once the transactions reducing benefit had fallen to a point where it was negligibly small, I would be willing to hold bonds instead of gold, even at a negative interest rate, since by doing so I could avoid paying for storage and security.

The floor to nominal interest rates is therefore given by the costs of holding currency. Can we say anything about the shape of this cost function in a modern economy? In the limit, we could think of infinite levels of real balances as infinitely costly to handle, monitor and store. If this is the limiting case, then it seems equally plausible to believe that the marginal cost of managing real balances must at some point rise from a quantity that is negligible at levels of real balances held at inflation rates typical of modern developed economies, to something significant. It seems plausible too to think that the costs of handling real balances are larger in economies with more primitive financial systems. (It is cheaper to store paper money than gold bars). Beyond that it is hard to say more. McCallum (2000) is sceptical that the marginal costs of managing real balances would amount to something that could lower the floor to interest rates by more than a few basis points.

Another possibility is that bonds may provide a service to holders not captured by the interest rate, perhaps a form of liquidity service not perfectly substitutable for that provided by cash. If there were any benefit to holding bonds of this sort then (leaving aside the costs of holding cash for a moment) the observed interest rate could fall to a level equal to minus the benefits from holding bonds. At this below-zero interest rate, I'd still be willing to hold bonds, as the 'liquidity service' would compensate me for the payments I have to make to the Government for the privilege (the negative interest rate).

Yet another possibility is that some of the benefits from holding *cash* do not asymptote to zero as real balances increase, that there might be some portion of the returns to real balances that are constant, and not diminishing. This could be true for those who hold cash to facilitate criminal economic activity, or to engage in legitimate activity that requires complete anonymity to make it attractive.[6] The benefit of holding the €1 millionth in cash for this purpose could be no less than the benefit from holding the tenth. Both provide the same anonymity service.[7] The more important is anonymously financed activity in the economy, the larger the portion of cash holdings that will be held with these benefits in mind, and the higher will be the floor to nominal rates.[8-10]

So the zero bound will be *lower* than zero to the extent that there are, at some point, significant costs of managing real balances, and to the extent that there are non-pecuniary benefits of holding bonds. And it will be *greater* than zero to the extent that there are, for the average economic participant, some significant (e.g. anonymity) benefits from holding cash that do not diminish as real balances rise.

Note that the bound to interest rates, which occurs at the point where the marginal net benefits to holding money flatten out, also generates the 'optimum quantity of money' in the sense of the Friedman rule. In an economy where there are no frictions, and no need for stabilisation policy, positive interest rates constitute a tax on money, and since money is socially productive by assumption, this erodes welfare. So the zero bound is the fulcrum of two competing objectives of policy. One drives inflation towards the Friedman rule, to preserve the value of money; the other drives inflation up above it, because the central bank needs to use interest rates stabilisation to make the inflation rate stationary about its optimal rate.

This model of the zero bound is the foundation for our analysis of the risks and welfare consequences of hitting a zero bound and the efficacy of policies to escape it. Wallace (2000), in his comment on McCallum (2000), questions whether the metaphors used in these models are adequate enough to capture what he sees as the real motivation for individuals holding money: namely, that exchanges conducted with money can be done 'without knowledge of individual histories.' The models he comments on do not describe the imperfections in monitoring credit histories that could give money some value, and are, he argues, therefore internally inconsistent.[11]

I make the following remarks by way of a defence of the literature. First, is the money metaphor any less adequate or internally consistent than other parts of the story modern macroeconomics tells about the world? Wallace singles money out for special attention because the interest-rate floor puts the properties of money and other assets under the spotlight. But macroeconomics (and the use to which we put it in our study of the zero bound) is built out of a house of such cards, (or internal contradictions) not just one.[12] Second, regardless of where our macroeconomic house of cards is weakest, what does the applied theorist and policymaker do about it anyway? Without an alternative workhorse model, perhaps the best we can do is to proceed, but with a degree of caution, noting that our models and our conclusions built on them will be fraught with imperfections. In order for us to find some other way forward, we would need for it to be shown conclusively that an alternative model of the zero bound would invalidate policy analysis based on existing monetary foundations.

3. Computing the Risk of Hitting the Zero Bound

3.1 *Quantitative Estimates of the Risk of Hitting the Zero Bound*

One strategy for assessing the risk of hitting the zero bound is to use historical or cross-country experience and look at how often the zero bound is encountered. But I am going to largely ignore this approach. Inferring anything useful from historical evidence is difficult. Relevant historical episodes (like the USA in the 1930s) were the product of an economic environment and a regime that differs from today's in ways it is hard to be precise about. This complicates the task of replaying history with today's monetary policy, which is the relevant counterfactual. Looking at other countries is fraught with the same difficulty. Japan's nominal interest rates have been close to zero for some time. But what that tells us about optimal policy in the USA or in Europe is not obvious. It is plausible to argue that Japan's monetary institutions differ in many ways from the arrangements that surround, for example, the policy of the euro area, or the Bank of England. And there are those that argue that Japan's monetary conjuncture is the result of many factors other than the design of monetary policy.[13]

An alternative is to construct a model of the monetary policy problem and imagine the consequences of policy targeting different inflation rates, and conjecture further that there is no alternative to interest rate stabilisation.[14] This is an approach that has been followed by Cozier and Lavoie (1994), Fuhrer and Madigan (1997), Black *et al.* (1998), Orphanides and Weiland (1998), Wolman (2000), Reifschneider and Williams (2000), Hunt and Laxton (2002).[15] It is an approach that I will argue is also open to criticism, but the one I will concentrate on here. Results from these studies are compiled in Figure 1.

The consensus emerging from these studies,[16] which use different models and different policy rules, suggest the following: that targeting inflation rates of 2% or above implies a small risk of hitting the zero bound. A ballpark figure is that the central bank might expect rates to be held at zero for between 1% and 5% of the time at a 2% inflation target. They imply very small risks indeed of the economy entering a deflationary spiral. Hunt and Laxton (2001), the only ones to report this explicitly, report that at 2% there is virtually no chance of the economy entering such a spiral. But the median study also suggests that the risk is significant at inflation rates lower than that, and that the chance of the zero bound binding increases exponentially as the inflation target is lowered. Estimates of the length of time rates are likely to spend held at zero when the central bank pursues a zero inflation target range from about 15–30%. If such a target is followed, Hunt and Laxton report that the central bank can expect to endure a deflationary spiral for around 10% of the time.[17]

The conclusions in these studies, and indeed our conclusions more generally about the risks of hitting the zero bound, are going to depend on many factors. But we might single out the following; an assumption about the variance of shocks in the future; an assumed equilibrium real interest rate; what we suppose about the rule the central bank follows (if any) in setting monetary policy; and of course on a particular representation of the economy, which propagates the shocks into distributions for desired interest rates.

3.2 *The Distribution of Shocks*

The shape of the distribution of shocks hitting the economy that policymakers wish to stabilise will be crucial in determining how the likelihood of hitting a zero

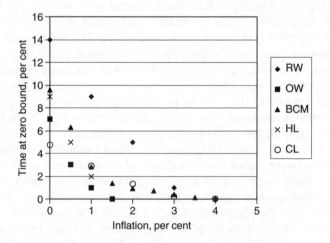

Figure 1. The Risks of Hitting the Zero Bound.

bound to interest rates rises as the mean inflation rate falls. We can conduct thought experiments where we imagine that the costs of an inflation policy are given by the portion of the distribution of desired nominal interest rates which turns out, for the distribution of the shocks in the economy, to be negative and, therefore, infeasible.

Think of a linear, static economy subject to shocks that are uniformly distributed between two values. In this kind of economy the distribution of desired interest rates would also be uniform. Policymakers could choose a range of inflation outcomes above a certain point for which there was no sacrifice in terms of the variability of inflation or output since the shocks would never be large enough to prompt an interest rate likely to hit the zero bound. Below a certain point, the uniformity of the distribution of shocks would mean that the cost in terms of variability (of output and inflation) of reducing inflation by each extra amount would be some constant positive number.[18] Each one percentage point move down in the inflation target would shift an equal portion of the probability of desired interest rates into 'negative territory'.

The larger the variance of this uniform distribution of shocks, other things equal, the higher the inflation rate at which positive costs of inflation reduction would start to kick in. If the shocks were normally distributed, then the marginal cost in terms of variability of a unit of inflation reduction would itself be normally distributed, rising from zero at some infinitely high mean inflation rate, (when a negligible part of the distribution of desired rates crosses the zero bound) up to a maximum, and then asymptoting to zero again at infinitely negative inflation (where since almost all the distribution of desired rates is negative anyway, there is no cost to reducing inflation further). Suppose we begin from a point where we imagine that the mean interest rate is 5% and the mean, target inflation rate is 2%. A reduction in the target of one percentage point will put some portion of the distribution of desired rates below zero; a further reduction will put an even larger portion of the distribution below zero. And so on.

A simple qualitative example is set out in the four panels of Figure 2. The vertical axis of the first three panels shows the frequency; the shape plotted in the top left panel is the density function for desired interest rates when the inflation target is π. The top right panel shows how the density function of desired interest rates shifts to the left when the inflation target is reduced by $\Delta\pi$. The shaded area A is the frequency that the central bank, free of the zero bound, would like to choose negative nominal interest rates. This is not possible, but this area will determine the cost of reducing inflation by $\Delta\pi$ from π. Reducing inflation by another $\Delta\pi$ from a target of π- $\Delta\pi$ will involve a cost related to the shaded area B in the bottom right hand panel. The cost of inflation reduction at different inflation rates (or rather, the determinant, the mass of the density function of desired rates less than zero) is plotted out in the bottom right hand panel.

So, in short, the dispersion of the distribution of shocks (which will be a sufficient statistic for the dispersion of interest rates under active monetary policy in this linear static world) will determine the portion of the distribution of desired rates that is negative, at some inflation rate. It will therefore determine the cost of

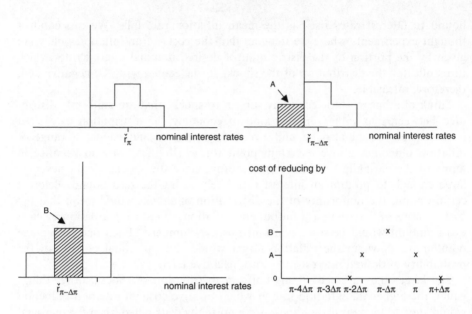

Figure 2. The Cost of Reducing the Inflation Target.

a given inflation rate. And the shape of the distribution – how fast the tails thin out – will determine the shape of the schedule that plots the marginal cost of inflation reduction against inflation.

3.3 *Equilibrium Real Interest Rates*

The higher the equilibrium real interest rate, the higher the equilibrium nominal interest rate associated with an inflation objective, and, for a given distribution of shocks, the lower the probability of interest rates hitting the zero bound for a given size of shock. A higher equilibrium real interest rate therefore lowers the cost of a given inflation rate. If the distribution of shocks is normal, an increase in the equilibrium real interest rate would reduce not only the cost of a given inflation rate, but also the marginal cost of a unit of inflation reduction.[19] Alternatively, if the distribution of shocks were uniform, the marginal cost of inflation reduction would not depend on the equilibrium real rate, (although the average cost of a given inflation rate would). Contemplating the effect of a change in equilibrium real rates is analogous to contemplating a change in the inflation target. Both change the equilibrium nominal interest rate, of course.

Not all changes in the equilibrium nominal interest rate make more room for interest rate cuts. An increase in an inflation risk premia would raise the equilibrium nominal interest rate, but that premia would be built into nominal rates at all times, and raise the floor to interest rates by the same amount.

To recall, optimal policy will equate the marginal benefits of steady-state inflation reduction with the marginal costs coming from hitting the zero bound and impairing inflation and output stabilisation. Clearly, the interaction of two sources of ignorance – the shape of the distribution of shocks, and the equilibrium real interest rate, both of which we will expect to influence the marginal cost of inflation reduction – are going to make this calculation extremely uncertain. The dispersion (variance), symmetry (skewness) and the thickness of the tails (kurtosis) of the distribution of shocks are all important unknowns in this calculation.

The studies cited at the beginning of this section typically assumed normal distributions for shocks, calibrated to have variances in line with the variance of past, estimated disturbances. These assumptions are probably the only convenient benchmark to use in evaluating the risk of hitting the zero bound. But there is no reason to expect assumptions like this to be reliable. For example, if the normality of residuals is (and it surely often is) used as a criterion for choosing good models from bad, we can't tell much from discovering, at the end of the process of model-building, that we have 'shocks' that appear to have been normal in the past. We would need other evidence independent of the model to do that. Even if we had such evidence, we could not guarantee that any information we get about the shape of the distribution in the past is going to be a reliable guide to the shape of the distribution in the future. None of our theories tell us that.

To repeat, knowing something about the shape of the distribution of shocks is the key to assessing the risk of hitting the zero bound, and the marginal cost of inflation reduction at a given inflation rate. Uncertainty about those distributions is going to lead to uncertainty about the optimal inflation rate. Ideally, the design of a policy that aims to balance the costs of inflation against the risk of hitting the zero bound would take account of the inherent uncertainty about the shape of the distribution of shocks.[20]

The equilibrium real interest rate may itself be related to the choice of the average inflation rate. This can be rationalised in a 'money in the production function' model. In such a world, money provides firms with a transactions service analogous to the benefit the McCallum-Goodfriend (1983) 'shopping-time' model tells us money confers on consumers. (Money can help firms save time 'shopping' for inputs, just as it can help individuals 'shopping' for consumption goods. High inflation changes the relative price of real balances and other factors, and induces firms to substitute out of real balances into, say, capital. This lowers the marginal product of capital and, in a closed economy, lowers real interest rates.[21]

McCallum (2000) attempts to calibrate this effect. His results are, in his own words 'unlikely to provide much reassurance to policymakers' (p. 879): his calculations suggest that reducing the inflation rate from 10% to zero increases the real rate by only 7 basis points.[22]

3.4 From a Distribution of Shocks to a Distribution of Desired Nominal Interest Rates

Anything that shrinks the variance of desired rates relative to the variance of shocks will reduce the cost of a given inflation rate and reduce the costs of inflation reduction, at least for distributions with thin tails and fat middles. The ingredients that do this are the model of the economy and the policy rule. So it is natural to organise our questions about the risk of hitting the zero bound around these two factors.

3.4.1 *Policy Rules and History-dependence*

In rational expectations models central banks that announce (and can commit to) interest rate rules embodying history-dependence can reduce the amount by which they need to move the nominal interest rate to bring about a given change in real interest rates. In so doing they can therefore reduce the variance of desired nominal interest rates for a given variance of shocks. This in turn implies reducing the chance of hitting the zero bound at a given inflation rate.

Woodford (1999) explains the case where interest rates are set as a function of lagged interest rates.[23] When the central bank lowers interest rates today, (say, in response to a demand shock), private agents will expect interest rates to be lower tomorrow too. This will have two beneficial effects. The first is that expected future inflation will be higher because policy will be looser for longer. The second is that long nominal rates will be lower. Both effects lower real rates, relative to a normal policy rule, for a given change in nominal rates. And this in turn implies that the amount by which the central bank needs to reduce rates to offset the demand shock will be lower.

But interest rates are not special in this regard. The beneficial effects through expectations can be got by setting interest rates as a function of the history of any variable. Moreover, research in this area has yielded up two forms of commitments. Not only can we can think of promises to follow particular interest rate rules with historical arguments in them (what we might call 'interest rate rule history-dependence'), we can also conceive of a commitment that the central bank will find an optimal rule subject to an objective that itself has historical terms in it ('objective or contractual history-dependence'?); or more precisely, one that weights historical terms more than does the underlying social objective function.[24] Central banks subject to a contractual history-dependence will find themselves, of course, behaving like central banks with interest rate rule history-dependence.

Reifschneider and Williams (2000) illustrate the benefits of two types of related history-dependence. One takes the form of adding to a conventional simple interest rate rule involving inflation and output gap deviations, terms in lagged inflation and lagged output gaps (and then searching for the optimal coefficients on all of them). Another 'turns on' only when the zero bound constraint binds.[25] While the interest rate is at the zero floor, the central bank accumulates a gap between the actual and desired level of rates. If the central bank commits to leaving rates low (in proportion to this cumulated gap) once the recession is over, then the expectations channel works in the way described above. Future inflation will be higher, and real rates lower during the recession, etc. etc.

Similar beneficial results have been obtained by those who have studied interest rate rule or contractual history-dependence that focuses on a concern for a price-level target.[26] A price-level target requires that policy commit to reversing the effects of past shocks that have lead prices to deviate from target. A demand shock that leads to prices being below target will cause agents in the future to expect inflation to be higher. And this will bring about a reduction in real rates that acts to reverse the effect of the demand shock.

If the distribution of shocks is such that a normal-like (thin tails, fat middle) shape is imparted to the distribution of nominal interest rates, history-dependence is likely to reduce the cost of inflation reduction at a given inflation rate. To recall, the cost of inflation reduction is going to be given by the height of the density function of interest rates at zero interest rates. And shrinking the variance of nominal interest rates will lower the height of that density function at zero interest rates.

For example, Reifschneider and Williams' (2000) simulations show that the cost of reducing inflation by two percentage points is greatly reduced by introducing history-dependence into the interest rate rule, both in terms of inflation and output variability.[27] Although the authors don't say so, this is an artifice, in my view, of (quite reasonably) using shock distributions with tails that thin out. To stress again a point I made earlier, it seems likely that *any* policy that shrinks the variance of interest rates relative to some other policy will reduce the marginal cost of inflation reduction[28] at the starting inflation rate, provided that the distributions of shocks involve tails that get thinner away from the mode.[29] And the reasoning here is the same as the reasoning I used in the simple example above when contemplating the effect of a change in the variance of shocks. The thought-experiment that contemplates shrinking the variance of interest rates relative to the variance of shocks by improving the policy rule is the same as a thought experiment where we hold the rule constant and shrink the variance of the shocks. Both shrink the variance of desired interest rates.

The benefits of 'interest rate rule' or 'contractual' history-dependence will depend on how closely the process by which expectations are formed resembles the model-consistent version so far assumed; and, to the extent that expectations are forward- looking, how credible a strategy history-dependence is.

There are an unlimited number of ways that expectations formation can differ from the rational, model-consistent expectations that are at work in the way the benefits of history-dependence have so far been described. So it is difficult to make general statements about how the net benefits of history dependent policy rules will change once we depart from the model-consistent variety. But with this caveat in mind we could hazard two predictions by way of an illustration.

First, the less forward-looking are expectations, the weaker will be the effect on future expected nominal rates and expected inflation of committing to a price level target, for example. To be more specific, we could imagine a (very particular) spectrum of expectations formation processes. At the one extreme, we have model consistent expectations, where the effect of price level (and other history-dependent) targets is as I have described it here. At the other is an economy where expectations are set purely as a distributed lag of past inflation rates. In the middle are economies where expectations are set as weighted sums of the model-consistent and past inflation rates.[30] For economies with a high weight on past inflation in expected inflation, a low inflation rate which causes an undershoot of a price level target will generate only a weak boost to expected future inflation, and therefore, other things equal, the nominal interest rate cut required in the first place will have to be large.

Second, and in contrast, to the extent that backward-lookingness in expectations informs nominal contracts, a given stimulus to future inflation could have a larger effect on aggregate demand, (by reducing real factor prices) and, therefore, require less history-dependence in the first place.

Turning to the issue of credibility. Suppose a central bank really faces an inflation target, but commits to a price-level target in order to gain extra stabilisation power. The benefits of history-dependence following a deflationary shock (say, when there is a price level target) come about because agents expect policy to be loosened, and therefore expect future inflation to be higher, which in turn reduces real rates now, and therefore reduces the amount by which the central bank needs to cut nominal rates to bring about the real rate stimulus it needs. However, when the time comes to loosen policy and generate the inflation agents expected when the deflationary shock hit, central banks who really face an inflation target, (and where the price level target is just a device to reap stabilisation gains) will have an incentive to renege on their commitment. If this incentive is large enough, agents will expect the commitment to be reneged upon, and the beneficial stabilising effects of the history-dependent rule with a price level target in will not be reaped in the first place.

The key question, therefore, to repeat, is how large these incentives are likely to be.[31] If the framework in which the central bank operates is such that it is sufficiently long-sighted, it will compute the present value of history dependent policies in the way that Woodford (1999) shows us and stick to them. If not, it won't. One argument is that central banks will need to establish a reputation for keeping their history-dependent promises before they will work. In which case the version of history-dependence in Reifschneider and Williams (2000)[32] that only 'turns on' when the zero bound bites is likely to be less beneficial. Since at other times this kind of history-dependence will be observationally equivalent to policies that aren't history dependent at all. Central banks that intend to stick to history-dependent promises will look no different from those that don't. To the extent that writing contracts for the central bank can provide a device that guarantees commitment more effectively than announcing a rule for the interest rate, then contractual forms of history-dependence may also be more desirable.

If history dependent policies that only turn on when the zero bound bites are beneficial (relative to those that operate all the time), and yet the private sector need to learn that the central bank would stick to its history dependent promise at the zero bound, there may be an incentive to target lower average inflation, at least initially, to induce episodes from which the private sector can learn. (Or periodically, if the private sector not only learns, but forgets). In this scenario, ironically, the strength of the motivation to target positive inflation – the costs of the impairment to stabilisation policy imposed by the zero bound – would be precisely what determined the incentive to push inflation low to create these learning opportunities.

3.4.2 Interest Rate Rule 'Pathologies': Do They Bear on the Choice of the Inflation Objective?

Some researchers have discussed the possibility that there are compelling and less benign influences on the risk of hitting the zero bound that emerge from the interaction of private sector expectations and the policy rule. Benhabib et al (2000, 2001), Buiter and Panigirtzoglou (1999), Bullard and Cho (2002), Christiano and Rostagno (2001), Alstadheim and Henderson (2002) have all studied what Christiano and Rostagno call 'pathologies' associated with central bank commitments to interest rate rules. These pathologies can include multiple equilibria, indeterminate or explosive equilibria. And amongst them can be equilibria dubbed a 'liquidity trap' where interest rates are zero and 'trapped' at zero.

The likelihood of the economy finding itself on one of these trajectories, and subsequently hitting the zero bound to rates, is, we might conjecture, typically not going to be affected by the choice of the average inflation rate. That has instead to do with the interaction of central bank commitments to a particular type of policy rule and private sector expectations.[33] These studies point to there being many equilibria, some appealing, stable, determinate, some not. They raise questions about what would determine which of the many possible equilibria a central bank might find itself in to begin with. There are questions too about what might cause the economy to switch from one equilibrium to another, and what the dynamics of the economy might look like in transition. But choosing high rather than low inflation does not seem likely to serve the role of a beneficial equilibrium selection device, nor to influence the chance of the economy moving from one to another.

A reasonable assumption, therefore is that studies of interest rate pathologies do not tell us anything about the cost of a given inflation rate in terms of inflation and output variability, but tell us instead about the risk of hitting the zero bound at *any* inflation rate when the central bank commits to a particular types of interest rate policy.[34] They suggest, therefore, that there is a component of the risk of hitting the zero bound for which choosing high inflation would not be any sort of reliable protection. More inflation may be neither a necessary nor a sufficient remedy.

These analyses of interest rate rules do serve to illustrate, however, that the mapping between the distribution of disturbances and the distribution of interest rates will not be as trivial as in the linear, static case we started out with. But in economies with these unattractive pathologies the mapping (however complex or discontinuous) between the distribution of shocks and interest rates is likely to be preserved as we move around the mean interest/inflation rate up or down. So, for example, it should therefore not undermine the statements we have already made about how the costs of inflation reduction vary with the variance of the distribution of shocks.

Some have questioned whether the 'pathologies' associated with interest rate rules have any economic significance at all. McCallum, since he advocates a rational expectations solution method that allows the economist to rule out equilibria of the sort discussed above, thinks them to be little more than a mathematical curiosum.[35,36] His criterion involves conjecturing solutions that involve the minimum number of what he calls the 'relevant' state variables (MSV), and of course imagining that private agents do the same. The authors in the pathology literature implicitly find this solution elimination criterion 'arbitrary' (otherwise they wouldn't list more than one solution); McCallum (2002) finds doing anything else equally so.

Evans and Honkapohja (1999, 2001) advocate an alternative method for selecting amongst multiple solutions that involves examining which of the multiple solutions would be converged on in an economy where agents learned the coefficients in the model: this is not always the MSV case. McCallum concedes this, but argues that all economically plausible (or in his words 'well formulated') models are indeed cases where the MSV solution would be converged on by agents who learned in the way Evans and Honkapohja illustrate. So arbitrary it might be, but it is a short-cut to selecting a learnable solution, and one that means that there are no economically meaningful 'perils' associated with interest rate rules.

Whether the real world is likely to be infected by the 'pathologies' that infect special cases of metaphors meant to describe it (RE models above) of course depends on what agents actually do (to form expectations), not whether an equilibrium is learnable under very specific models of learning.[37] Resolving that debate is the subject of an ongoing and likely inconclusive research program. Resolving the debate by inspecting economic outcomes would be just as uninformative. There can be multiple equilibria that might exist without an economy ever moving from one to the other.

One type of interest rate rule pathology that does bear on the choice of the inflation target is the 'instability' to which Reifschneider and Williams (2000) draw our attention. They observe that 'extreme' shocks can push the FRB/US model into a deflationary spiral (p942). Higher inflation rates would reduce the risk of such extreme shocks inducing a spiral like this. This observation tells us that the choice of the inflation target will be influenced by the width of the region within which the model can be restabilised once interest rates have hit the zero bound. If immobilising interest rates for even short periods of time – or with respect to even very small desired cuts in rates – results in unstable oscillations policymakers will choose a higher inflation target than if the dynamics are such that the system has more tolerance of constant rates.

The parameter space in Reifschneider and Williams (2000) is such that it takes a large shock to tip the economy into such a state. But we must surely be uncertain about the 'shock tolerance' of the unknown parameter space in the real economy facing policymakers. This is a key uncertainty in our knowledge about how the distribution of shocks in the economy (which we of course also don't know) would translate into costs of low inflation.

3.4.3 *History-dependent Rules and Deflationary Spirals*

These circumstances highlight an important feature of the mechanics of the signalling benefits of history-dependent policies that is worth returning to. History-dependent policies work to mitigate either the chance of hitting the zero bound in the first place, or the length of time interest rates are held there (and the accumulated deviation from desired rates suffered while at the bound) provided the shock experienced is not so large or protracted as to push the economy into a deflationary spiral (or a 'liquidity trap'). In such a spiral, history dependent commitments are ineffective. The commitment to keep rates lower at some point in the future when a tightening would be warranted does not affect future inflation expectations, because those expectations are formed in the knowledge that the economy is beyond stabilisation. So the signalling inherent in these policies is a useful device for improving stabilisation performance, but it is not a device for escaping from this form of zero bound trap. This is why the proposals of Krugman (1998) have been criticised. He proposed that the solution to Japan's problem was to make a credible announcement of future inflation. The leverage over the economy in normal times through history dependent policies is via making a credible commitment to higher future inflation: it is credible because the private sector expects the central bank to have a lever to generate that inflation (the nominal interest rate will still work). The circumstances that Krugman's Japan finds itself in are such that that the conventional interest rate lever no longer exists (although others might, of course, as this paper aims to explore).

3.4.4 *Interest Rate 'Pathologies' and Credibility*

The conclusion about the benefits of history-dependence resting on the credibility of the rule also applies to what we make of the analysis of some of the undesirable properties or 'pathologies' of interest rate rules. My view of this family of studies – the Reifschneider and William/Hunt and Laxton/Cozier and Lavoie/Black *et al.* pieces – is that it gives us some very specific information about the risks of hitting the zero bound. It tells us something about the risks of hitting the zero bound when central banks are credibly committed to pursuing certain interest rate rules in a forward looking model and for some assumed distribution of shocks. However, if the zero bound were to bite, or threaten to, there are grounds for thinking that policy could and would be expected to deviate from the interest rate policies assumed in these studies, and that therefore the risks of hitting the zero bound are overstated.

   Consider the following scenario. Policymakers follow some simple interest rate rule. They commit to doing so. The private sector believes them, up to the point where they think it is still in the central bank's interest. And up to a point, it *is* rational to stick with the rule: central banks get some leverage over long rates by sticking to their commitments. But in some circumstances they will break that commitment. For example, if there is a large shock, one large enough that threatened to put the economy in Reifschneider and Williams' (2000) 'region of instability', or a shock that threatened to send the economy on one of the 'pathological' trajectories in the other studies, a rational private sector agent would likely re-evaluate the costs and benefits of the central bank following such a rule and rationally foresee that it will follow some other kind of policy. (If there is another kind of policy).

One reading of these studies is that they tell us about the dynamics of an economy where the central bank commits to and is judged by the private sector as likely to follow policies it has no interest in following.[38] We could construct a model of an exchange rate peg, for example, whereby we studied how, under some circumstances, there was a risk that the central bank not only exhausted its foreign exchange reserves defending the peg, but the government subsequently bankrupted the economy by raising taxes continuously to fund an ongoing and hopeless defence, right to the point where all economic activity ceased. But in doing so we would be identifying the 'perils' of a policy that no central bank or government would or could follow, nor would ever be expected to follow. And so with the perils of interest rate rules.

If we can argue convincingly that the equilibrium dynamics of the economy in reality (under 'discretion', or under commitments that will be believed to the point where it is rational to stick to them) are likely to be the same, or at least similar to those under commitment, then we can take estimates of the 'risk' of hitting and/or being trapped at the zero bound at face value. But to do this we would need to believe that there was no alternative policy available to the central bank in the face of a disturbance that threatened to send the economy onto a disastrous path. (Where an alternative policy would bring with it both a cost of being seen to break a previously held promise and some stabilisation benefit). In the example of the exchange rate peg, Governments have a viable alternative, (to dump the peg early), and are expected to follow it, and so the self-destruct scenario is not very informative. So to in the interest rate case. And this does not mean we need to posit an effective alternative to using interest rates to stabilise the economy (although I will indeed discuss the alternatives to interest rate stabilisation in later sections of this paper): setting interest rates according to some other procedure would do.[39]

One factor that might make a pathological scenario plausible is the speed with which the economy heads to the Reifschneider and Williams (2000) 'region of instability', relative to the time it would take for the consequences of sticking to the current rule to become apparent, and for an alternative plan to be put into action. If such trajectories are 'fast', then we can take them seriously. If they are 'slow' enough for policymakers to make sense of them, then we need not.

A more constructive way of interpreting the results of studies in the vein of Reifschneider and Williams (2000) and others is that they tell us about the benefits of actual regimes, which do not embody commitments to any particular policy rule and provide therefore a positive explanation (although not the only explanation) for central banks' reluctance to make such commitments.[40]

None of this is really a criticism of the family of studies mentioned here. Rather it is a word of caution about what we should make of the results. The authors have to posit a rule of some sorts for interest rates. And they posit one that has been shown to both provide a reasonable empirical description of *ex post* movements in official interest rates and to provide a reasonable approximation to optimal rules in normal times. But herein lies the limit of these studies. Had normal times involved shocks that risked tipping the economy into a zero-rate trap, the empirical content of the Taylor like rules would have broken down temporarily. And the approximation to optimal policy (under discretion or commitment) of such rules must likewise become worse and worse the more telling is the zero bound constraint.

3.4.5 *The Economy and the Risks of Hitting the Zero Bound: Inflation Persistence*

So far I have discussed how features of the policy rule affect the mapping from the distribution of disturbances to the distribution of desired interest rates. Equally important will be structural features of the economy that propagate shocks into variations of things that policy would like to stabilise (inflation, output) and thereby feed into the variance of desired nominal interest rates for a given variance of the shocks hitting the economy.

Other things equal, the more swift and strong is the transmission of policy changes into inflation and output, the smaller are the risks of hitting the zero bound at a given inflation rate, since the smaller and less sustained are implied variations in desired interest rates. Moreover, the more strong and swift is the transmission mechanism, the larger the benefits to committing to history-dependent rules. At this point I could digress to review innumerable literatures on various components of the transmission mechanism. One example to pick out here is the degree of inflation persistence.[41] When inflation is not sticky, the policymaker can credibly commit to inducing large variations in future inflation for a given change in interest rates, and therefore generate significant movements in real rates for a given change in nominal rates. Wolman (1998, 2000) makes just this observation, and this feature of his model informs his optimism about the risks of hitting the zero bound at low inflation.[42]

On the other hand, if the factors that mean that the transmission of monetary shocks into inflation and output is strong also mean that the propagation of other shocks into inflation and output is strong, the variance of desired interest rates will be larger, and the costs of a given inflation rate larger too.

There is nothing special about structural inflation persistence that warrants us picking that out: were there space to do justice to it, I could digress at this point to review innumerable literatures on various components of the transmission mechanism.[43]

3.5 *Linear Rational Expectations Models in the Face of a Non-Linearity*

There is one final, technical caveat, but an important one, to bear in mind when trying to draw policy conclusions from estimates of the risk of hitting the zero bound. These models are solved (and generate series for expectations) conditioning on the linearity of the model, but are simulated in response to shocks with the zero bound constraint binding. Ideally, they would be solved under the assumption that the private sector would factor in the chance that it might bind. The lower the inflation target, and the lower the equilibrium nominal interest rate, and therefore the more likely the zero bound constraint is going to bind for a given distribution of shocks, the more inaccurate is a model solution conditioned on the notion that it will never bind. So the closer to the origin, the less well measured are the points in Figure 1. Reifschneider and Williams (2000) and Orphanides and Weiland (1998) attempt to correct for the bias that this introduces, but can do so only in an ad-hoc way. Klaeffling and Lopez (2002) use non-linear solution methods and are therefore immune from this problem. The other studies are subject to this criticism and make no adjustment.

Absent any adjustment, the probabilities of hitting the zero bound are probably too low. Before a shock hits, expectations of future interest rates will be based on distributions that assume a symmetric response to shocks; such distributions put too much weight on interest rate cuts relative to the agent that correctly anticipates the zero bound. This itself will imply a monetary stimulus that would not be there in reality, and imply a commensurately lower probability of hitting the zero bound in the first place.

4. Gesell Money, or the Carry Tax

Thus far we have discussed the zero bound as though it were a binding constraint, and as if there were no alternative to moving interest rates to stabilise output and inflation. Sections 4–10 discuss other policies that it has been suggested central banks can follow.

Recall that the zero bound on short term interest rates on Government debt comes about because investors can always hold cash, which pays a guaranteed zero return. Any mechanism that seeks to lower the return to cash below zero would therefore lower the zero floor to interest rates. Goodfriend (2000) and Buiter and Panigirtzoglou (1999) propose mechanisms to lower the returns to holding cash.[44] These proposals amount to levying a tax on cash, and, as with all taxes, its efficacy depends on the feasibility of enforcement. Cash is anonymously held and there is no incentive for an anonymous bearer to present his cash liabilities for the levy.

Buiter and Panigirtzoglou (1999) describe a scheme where the legal tender status of notes would be conditional on bearers presenting them periodically to be re-issued, or stamped or clipped. Buiter and Panigirtzoglou and Goodfriend (2000) discuss taxing cash reserves held by clearing banks at the central bank. This second proposal seems the most plausible, since central banks arguably already tax banks in the way they regulate interactions with the central bank for settlement purposes (e.g. by compelling them to deposit with the central bank interest-free) and so the significance of crossing the zero bound is not great.

Either way, the tax could be manipulated to make room for interest rate cuts below zero either permanently, or when implied desired nominal rates are (or look likely to be) negative. Permanent measures would familiarise the authorities and the private sector with the system and the phenomenon of negative rates, but would carry with them larger social costs: just as it is wasteful to tax cash with inflation, so would it be to tax it directly, assuming that cash itself is a socially productive thing. A one percentage point carry tax would be equivalent to increasing inflation by 1%. A variable or a temporary tax on money that fluctuated precisely to equal the desired level of (negative) interest rates would not interfere with portfolio decisions (the returns on cash and money would be equal, just as they are at the Friedman rule when nominal interest rates are zero).

It seems unlikely that taxes could be moved in perfect synchronicity with the desired negative rate on bonds. (If this were a possibility, then *negative* taxes – or money subsidies – could surely be used to equalise returns on cash and bonds even at positive interest rates, eliminating the (shoe leather) costs of inflation at a stroke!) A more plausible alternative would be to lower the interest rate floor by some discrete amount, ahead of a recession, and by enough to provide 'room for' some anticipated interest rate cut below the old zero floor. To the extent that this is the case, then regardless of whether the tax is a constant or temporarily invoked but constant when levied, the tax would generate an expected stream of social costs.

The costs and benefit analysis of a permanently lower floor or of planning in advance to lower the floor for some periods, is very similar to the cost-benefit analysis of raising the inflation target.[45] The costs are the shoe-leather costs of inflation in each case: the benefits are those of avoiding the floor to rates.[46] To figure out the socially optimal tax on money of this sort, we still have to compute the rate of transformation of a unit of inflation reduction into inflation and output variability, and the rate at which society prefers to substitute between them, even if by lowering the zero floor via the money tax we are positing that we can shift all of the curves in 'inflation space' (and achieve higher welfare).

To repeat, the shoe-leather costs that would come with a money tax come from not being able to move that tax in synchronisation with the negative interest rate. Taxes adjusted precisely to match the desired negative rate would present no wedge between the costs of holding money or bonds. So the more synchronous is the tax with the desired interest rate, the better in welfare terms it is compared to levying the tax by aiming for higher inflation.

A policy of temporary money taxes to lower the interest rate floor is, in modern times, untested.[47] Although inflation and 'money taxes' are perfect substitutes in principle, in practice, therefore, the returns to increasing inflation are better understood than the benefits of money taxes. We typically advise risk averse policymakers to invest less in policies that are uncertain, holding mean returns constant. This is a theme treated more explicitly in the literature on using monetary policy to exploit portfolio balance effects,[48] which I will discuss below.

5. Money 'Rains', Real Balances

Another option for policy is to engage in money 'rains'.[49] In open market operations, the central bank trades money for short-term debt. At zero interest rates, money and debt become perfect substitutes. Open market operations will change the composition of private sector portfolios, but will not affect private sector wealth. When interest rates are positive, offering individuals more real balances gives them something they still value for reasons other than their usefulness for storage. But at zero interest rates, swapping money for bonds does nothing for them.

The central bank could instead give money to the private sector without taking debt in exchange. Some call this a money 'rain'.[50] A money rain will increase wealth and boost consumption and aggregate demand, temporarily raise equilibrium real rates (lowering actual real rates relative to equilibrium) and increase expected inflation, lowering real rates and boosting aggregate demand via this route too.

There are several points of debate about the usefulness of such a measure: some practical, some theoretical.

Practical objections raised by Goodfriend (2000) and Bryant (2000) centre on whether money transfers that did not generate other costs would be administratively feasible. My own view is that modern financial economies with welfare states already have systems that could implement transfers. Most individuals have bank accounts. Those that do not are likely to be in regular receipt of benefit payments. Both involve automated systems that could surely, at some feasible cost, or rather some cost that is comparable to the alternatives available be used to distribute money.

A more significant difficulty is that money transfers would have to be designed so as not to interfere with initial wealth distributions (supposing that the fiscal authority had already sorted out redistributive policy as best it could via conventional taxes and benefits). Approximate information on the distribution of wealth would be available from information collected in the course of levying many types of wealth-related tax (capital gains, interest income, property, inheritance taxes, for example). But this approximation would undoubtedly mean that the money rain would generate redistributive effects (and, compounding this, be expected to). The key question is how costly the approximation would be relative to the social costs of not stabilising the economy, and relative to other policy options at the zero bound.

The closest substitute to monetary transfers would be for the central bank to print money to finance tax cuts. Governments that engage in ongoing spending could have that spending financed by central bank money rather than taxes. Goodfriend (2000) and Bryant (2000) both argue that monetised tax cuts would be more practical. My own view is that both would involve financial exchanges via the same route (bank accounts or benefit offices) and are therefore close substitutes. The distortionary implications of literal money transfers or monetised tax cuts are likely to be very similar. Both require the same information about initial wealth holdings, and to the extent that that information is imperfect, both policies will involve allocative costs.

A second question is how strong the aggregate wealth effects of money transfers would be. Money transfers that were not to be repeated would be spent only to the extent that private sector agents are credit constrained or not perfectly forward-looking: else consumers would consume only the annuitised value of the addition to permanent income.

Goodfriend (2000) debates further how, in his words, 'a central bank must be prepared to reverse monetary injections after the economy recovers in order to maintain price stability' (p. 1026). He rightly points out that any transfer that agents expect to be reversed at some point (by whatever means) would have no wealth-stimulating effects on a private sector that faced no credit constraints. But in general, the costs and benefits of reversing the money transfer, vis-à-vis the likely threat to 'price stability' depend on the circumstances at hand. For example, one scenario is that a central bank that, in the course of experiencing a shock that pushes nominal interest rates to zero, has undershot either a price level or an inflation target, and will therefore be looking for ways to generate both expected and actual inflation, (expected inflation to lower real interest rates and boost aggregate demand, and actual inflation to keep to its target) *in order to meet its price stability objective*. For a central bank in this situation, a money transfer could help and not threaten the credibility of the target.

Promising to reverse a monetised tax cut in these circumstances would be counter-productive, and, if the private sector understands the authorities object-ive, perhaps not even credible. Note too that if the money rain brought about a larger increase in the price level than was thought consistent with the inflation objective, the central bank has got the option of raising nominal interest rates too. Reversing the monetary injection might not be necessary, nor even sufficient.

A caveat here is that money rains may have a second effect, aside from the wealth effect, by increasing liquidity in the economy (Goodfriend, 2000). This effect is described in more detail in the next section, since it underpins a proposal for the central bank to buy illiquid bonds, and stimulate the economy that way. At the risk of pre-empting that discussion, adding money to the average agent's portfolio gives them more assets that they can use to borrow against for the purposes of avoiding external finance premia. This effect will not be so wholly undone as the wealth effect of the money rain if the rain is to be reversed: the provision of liquidity even for a temporary time provides a service that is useful. It relaxes credit constraints for the duration. An analogy would be if the central bank were to give out cars to the private sector, and promise to take them back in the future. There would be little wealth effect from the car loan. But while the private sector had extra cars, they could, if they wanted, make extra journeys, which they might value.[51] But readers will find this paragraph more comprehen-sible after they have read the next section.

However, a private sector that either saw a central bank rain money, or under-stood that it was prepared and clearly administratively capable of raining money on the private sector when interest rates hit the zero bound might suspect that it would rain money on them at other times too. In this sense Goodfriend (2000) has a point in that he identifies that the facility to engage in and reputation for engaging in money rains would threaten the credibility of *future* policy. Unfortu-nately, committing to reversing the money rain in the future, either in good times, or while interest rates are zero, would undo some of the benefits of the money rain itself.[52]

Money rains work by increasing the value of real assets, albeit temporarily. But it is worth noting two things here. First, this mechanism is different from the 'real balance effect' identified by Ireland (2001), McCallum (2000) and Nelson (2002), and invoked by Meltzer (1999), and probably others too. As Woodford (1999) notes, *that* real balance effect is that at positive interest rates, when interest rates are lowered, and the new equilibrium involves the private sector having agreed to swap bonds for increases in real balances, it gains something with transactions-facilitating benefits that it still values and is therefore better off, and aggregate demand increases as a result. But at zero interest rates, interest rates *are* zero precisely because the transactions-cost-reducing benefits of real balances have been exhausted. So any further bonds-for-money trades that the central bank does leave it no better off. Bonds and money are just identical means of storing wealth at zero interest rates. Increases in real balances at this point that are offset through open market operations leave the private sector no wealthier than it was before. It is therefore not correct to believe that the real balance effect allows for conventional open-market-operations monetary policy to stimulate the economy.

Second, it is worth pointing out that if the economy experiences deflation, real balances will increase in the way intended in a money rain automatically. As the price level falls, nominal balances of money and outstanding nominal bonds will become worth more in real terms: consumers and firms will experience increases in wealth, and aggregate demand may rise as a result.[53] How strong this automatic stabiliser is is unclear. As an aside, I quote Sims (2000), who remarks that 'real balance effects can be important to guaranteeing stability, even if they are seldom or never important over the course of ordinary business cycle fluctuations' (p. 969). He implies that the past, when there might not have been a deflationary spiral, may therefore not be a good guide to the future importance of channels like this. We do have empirical evidence of real balance effects at work in normal times, but, as we have observed already, that effect will contain the real balance effect described here, and the effect of increasing consumers' wealth via adding to their store of transactions-improving real balances. That channel won't be working at the zero bound, as we have observed, so we must presume that the real balance effect would be weaker than that picked up in studies like that of Ireland (2001).

Short Term Debt Rains

A related option is for the central bank to 'rain' down short-term debt on the private sector. At zero interest rates, the private sector will be indifferent between a money and a debt rain. A debt rain that will be made good by future taxation will have a 'wealth effect' like a money rain to the extent, of course, that agents either ignore those future taxes or feel that they will not fall on them. It will also have a similar 'liquidity effect' to the money rain (which will obtain even if agents factor in expected future taxes needed to repay the debt) since short term debt, like money, will be more liquid than the representative asset already on the private sector's balance sheet. A debt rain that is to be made good by printing money in the future ought to be a close substitute for a policy that gets money directly into the hands of the private sector today: to repeat, money and short term bonds are perfect substitutes at zero interest rates.

6. Monetary Policy and the Portfolio Balance Channel[54]

Some, (for example Meltzer (1999a,b), Friedman and Schwartz (1982) and Goodfriend (2000))[55] reject the notion that the current and expected future setting of risk-free interest rates is a necessary and sufficient description of the monetary stance of the central bank.[56] On these grounds they therefore reject the notion that the monetary authorities are impotent at the zero bound simply because interest rates cannot fall now, and therefore will not be expected to fall in the future.

Goodfriend (2000) argues that the central bank can increase the volume of 'broad liquidity services' in the economy by conducting open market operations that exchange money for long-term bonds. An asset that offers broad liquidity is something that enables its holder to 'minimise one's exposure to the external finance premium in the sense of Bernanke and Gertler (1995)' (p. 1019). As the quantity of broad liquidity in the economy rises, so the cost of finance falls.[57] Open market operations in short term bonds involve trading assets that serve just as well as devices for avoiding external finance premia. Both money and short-term bills or bonds can be borrowed against, since they are both default-risk-free and easily verifiable as such. But trades of money for some long-term bonds can increase liquidity. Liquidity in bond markets is highly discontinuous and concentrated in particular (e.g. 10 year) instruments. Bonds that are not traded in such large volumes will be less liquid than the cash the central bank offers to trade them for. So the central bank can increase the volume of liquidity services available in the economy in this way.

Other things equal, the private sector as a whole will try to rid itself of this excess liquidity (it was chosen optimally, for the conditions that prevailed before the open market operation). But it will be unable to do so in aggregate. The effect of trying will be to bid up asset prices (reduce yields) in less liquid assets and durable and even non-durable goods.

Central banks could of course increase the amount of this form of 'broad liquidity' available in the economy by purchasing not just long term government bonds, but any private sector asset, and perhaps any foreign-currency denominated asset that was likewise less liquid than the cash offered in exchange. And to recall from the previous section, the broad liquidity exploited here by these money for long bond swaps would also be at work if the central bank were instead to engage in a 'money rain' of the sort we have already described.[58]

Note that the portfolio rebalancing will very likely result in an increase in the price level. This in turn would burn off the increase in nominal broad liquidity that the central bank wrought in the first place. On the other hand, to the extent that portfolio rebalancing does increase the price level, and is anticipated to do so, the increase in expected inflation will reduce real interest rates and stimulate real spending through this route too.

Policies of this sort are clearly open to central banks conducting open market operations at *any* interest rate, not just at zero interest rates. To the extent that cash and even very short term bonds and bills do not have identical liquidity characteristics, central banks may in fact be operating through this channel unavoidably at all times. The difference between normal operations in short-term markets and the policies that Goodfriend and others advocate at zero interest rates must surely be one of degree. In principle, some clue as to the effectiveness of the policy could be uncovered in data from regimes at positive rates. In practice, however, portfolio balance effects are likely to be highly non-linear, and only manifest and exploitable when the central bank deals in very large quantities (near zero interest rates) or in very imperfect substitutes for its cash.[59]

The most obvious side-effect of this kind of policy (discussed by Goodfriend (2000) and others) is the consequence for fiscal policy of having less than perfectly liquid, risky assets on the central bank balance sheet. Central banks buying either long dated government bonds or private sector assets expose themselves to capital (or even default) risk. Whether or not losses are realised, the central bank takes on risk by engaging in these activities, which is an economically costly activity. In forward looking models we would expect that the effect of market interventions like this would be muted by the effect on aggregate demand of future taxes to make up capital losses, or of the ongoing costs of insuring against them. In fact, it would seem to me that the risk of a loss is quite high. And, perhaps even the inevitable consequence of the outcome sought for monetary policy. If the stabil-isation works, the economy will return at some point to a situation where interest rates are higher and bond prices therefore lower across the board.[60]

There must be doubts too about how stable the patterns of liquidity differences between assets that the central bank exploits would be once the private sector understands what the central bank is trying to achieve. For example, suppose that to some degree, the liquidity concentration in certain government bonds is not related to 'fundamentals', (the correspondence of the asset maturity with the maturity characteristics of liabilities of investors?...) but is due instead to the fact simply that because everyone thinks everyone else wants to deal in those bonds, everyone does. Equilibria like this will be self-reinforcing. The marginal market maker is forced to deal in those bonds because the fixed costs of dealing in other bonds will force it to charge higher bid-ask spreads for those trades, which in turn discourages marginal investors from trading in them, and so on.

However, the announcement that the central bank will systematically deal in non-standard illiquid bonds will immediately make such a bond more liquid. Before, the non-standard bond would have been held on the expectation that it could be sold in a market with a few private sector participants. Now the non-standard bond can be sold in a market that, in the event of the economy hitting a zero bound, will be contain a central bank willing to buy them: and precisely at a time when the prices of bonds as a whole are likely to be high (because the nominal interest rate component of the price is low) which is precisely the time investors are likely to want to sell.

In practice, the private sector must expect that the chance of hitting the zero bound is pretty low. And so the chance of having a central bank to deal with on the other side of the market for the non standard bonds is also low. So a 'fundamentals based' expectation of the change in the liquidity of that market, due simply to the expected participation of the central bank, might be small. Moreover, the central bank could sell back not the illiquid bonds it bought in the first place, but more liquid shorter-term debt: this would reduce the expected 'fundamental' change in liquidity arising from a systematic policy of this sort even further. But if the liquidity concentrations are due in large measure to the kinds of self-reinforcing, expectational mechanisms described above, then a small shift in the 'fundamentals' could induce a significant shift in the patterns of liquidity concentration. This would not make a liquidity injection impossible, but it would make it more difficult to pull off repeatedly, or pull off with predictable affects.

If there are special characteristics of assets – either government bonds or private sector assets– that the central bank can reliably exploit then it is important to note too that the efficacy of policy will depend not only on current open market operations but expected future operations too. The effect of increasing broad liquidity today will be less if it is expected that the central bank will reverse any large-scale purchase in the future. (And at some point, it surely must reverse these purchases, otherwise its balance sheet will continue expanding indefinitely.) But this is no different from the limit on the effectiveness of interest rate policy in normal times, which the private sector knows will be reversed.

Intervening in public and private sector asset markets[61] will likely risk inducing a host of microeconomic distortions. Any policy that interferes with the informativeness of relative asset prices would be socially wasteful. Private sector purchases would risk either moral hazard, or bring with them the burden of devising procedures to avoid it.

Aside from microeconomic distortions, if there are portfolio balance effects coming from the imperfect substitutability amongst public and private sector assets, any intervention by the central bank will disrupt and frustrate private sector attempts to arrive at optimal portfolios with respect to their own liabilities and risks. And the private sector will be worse off as a result.[62] The usefulness of this channel relies on there being imperfect substitutability amongst assets. Without it, government purchases would be useless, dwarfed by the infinite supply of near perfect substitutes for whatever it buys. But the more imperfectly substitutable for others are the assets the central bank buys, the more the private sector suffers from the intervention.

But these distortions must be compared to the welfare consequences of not intervening. The motivation for active monetary policy in the first place comes, presumably, from the lack of cheap enough forms of insurance against business cycle fluctuations, or the inequitable access to insurance of this kind.

A final comment about this kind of policy is familiar from thinking of the other options at the zero bound. Since what Goodfriend calls 'quantitative policy' is somewhat untested, the returns to this kind of policy are uncertain. The key uncertainty is the elasticity of the schedule of asset prices to central bank purchases, and how stable this elasticity would be over time. As we have noted already: the more uncertain a policy, the less a risk-averse policymaker should rely on it in its contingency planning.[63] (The problem is even worse to the extent that we don't know how uncertain the returns are.[64] But this issue I will return to in section 10.) A central bank already trapped at the zero bound will not be deterred by the uncertainty surrounding the effects of a liquidity injection of this sort. But a central bank planning in advance how to substitute between higher inflation and relying on liquidity injections would invest less in this strategy and more in inflation, other things equal.

Some – for example Meltzer (1999b) – have inferred from historical experience that quantitative policy is both effective and exploitable. Meltzer makes, in my view, inferences which more cautious logic would avoid. He and others observe that in the USA, following the Great Depression, despite interest rates being at or near zero for the duration, aggregate demand and inflation stabilised. This argument then goes on to infer that there must therefore have been advantageous, systematic, non-interest-rate stabilisation at work (and therefore available to policy-makers today). This observation is consistent with the Fed having usefully exploited a portfolio balance effect (or having conducted some other policy). But it is also consistent with them having been entirely helpless, or having made matters worse by doing whatever they did.

By way of illustration, recall the results of Hunt and Laxton (2002). They observe that the probability of entering a deflationary spiral is very much smaller than the probability of interest rates reaching and staying at the zero bound. They illustrate therefore that the economy may experience periods where, although stabilisation policy is impotent, and nominal rates are at the zero bound, eventually the economy recovers without the help of the central bank. The experience of the 1930s may not provide the comfort it is intended to. Quite the opposite. That experience could suggest that even eventually self-correcting recessions could be devastating in the mean time.[65]

The evidence of Hanes (2002) is evidence in favour of one leg of Meltzer's hypothesis. Hanes finds that positive shocks to the supply of reserves lowered 3–5 year yields on Treasuries during the 1934–39 period, when short term rates were at or near the zero bound. But this evidence is not enough. We would need to establish further that the reduction in long term rates was, first, the successful consequence of an intended monetary loosening, and second, that it contributed significantly to the subsequent economic recovery, (rather than perhaps being simply a consequence of it).[66]

Goodfriend argues that quantitative policy is not 'logically harder' than interest rate policy. This is true, in the sense that the story he tells about how the central bank injects liquidity into the economy is no more mysterious than the stories we tell normally about how interest rate policy works. However, this begs the question as to why interest rate policy is the option so many central banks have chosen as their instrument for normal times. Is the reason that the fiscal worries about quantitative policy are so compelling that an otherwise adequate substitute for interest rate policy is *never* worth exploiting away from the zero bound? This seems unlikely. Surely there must be something 'harder' about this policy. Either that or central banks should be doing more of it regardless of whether they are at the zero bound or risk hitting it.

7. Exchange Rate Intervention

Some (for example, Meltzer (1999b), Svensson (2001) and McCallum (2000)) have suggested that central banks could intervene in foreign exchange markets to bring about an exchange rate devaluation and stimulate aggregate demand and inflation and increase inflation expectations, even when the nominal interest rate is at the zero floor.

There are two classes of policy envisaged. McCallum (2000) envisages that the central bank have a time-varying exchange rate target, (in the same way that under normal conditions it used a time-varying interest rate target) to stimulate the economy. Svensson (2001) envisages a one-off devaluation and thereafter a defence of an exchange rate peg, until such time as the economy is lifted out of the zero bound trap. But the efficacy of both policies relies on central banks either actually exploiting or credibly promising to exploit a portfolio-balance channel in foreign exchange.

Svensson's (2001) proposal is as follows. The central bank announces a devaluation of the nominal exchange rate such that the real exchange rate is below equilibrium (which is possible when prices are sticky). It announces a commitment to peg the exchange rate at the lower level. On top of this the central bank announces a rising target path for the price-level.[67] The central bank should commit to a peg for the nominal exchange rate that corresponds to the difference between the price level target path, and expected foreign inflation. (So, if the two are equal, then they commit to an exchange rate peg.) The first effect is for short term nominal rates to rise above the zero floor: this has to happen to compensate investors for any expected nominal depreciation of the exchange rate.[68] The deflationary effect of rising short term rates is offset by three factors. First, an expected long run real appreciation (which must obtain if the real exchange rate is pushed below equilibrium) will be accompanied by a fall in long-term real interest rates. Second, the fall in the exchange rate will boost foreign demand for domestic output (which, since the output gap is negative at the start can be supplied). Third, expected inflation will increase. With the nominal exchange rate pegged, inflation faster than foreign inflation will be associated with the real appreciation. The central bank announces it will follow this policy until the price level target is met. After which, the exchange rate peg will be abandoned, and the central bank will adopt a more conventional monetary policy.

A large literature has discussed the efficacy of exchange rate targeting via foreign exchange intervention, though the focus there is typically on the difficulty of sustaining exchange rate targets that are meant to anchor an otherwise inflationary currency rather than the reverse (are, in other words, 'too high'). Many of the potential problems associated with using the home-asset portfolio-balance effect – its uncertainty, instability, especially once exploited – we can carry over to our study of foreign-exchange based policies. We can profitably concentrate on the Svensson proposal here, and I do so noting that a number of potential problems with his policy have been exposited by Svensson himself.[69]

One obvious problem, remarked on by many, is that these policies clearly rely on the cooperation of foreign monetary authorities. The exposition above takes the actions of foreign authorities as given. The efficacy of intervention is going to depend on the trade-weighted objectives of other monetary authorities. If the trade weighted policy objectives are the same as the home country, and the trade weighted shocks (and therefore desired monetary stabilisation) are perfectly negatively correlated, then a devaluation will suit everyone. If not, it won't. In other words, if other countries are looking for a relative monetary contraction they will accept the exchange rate appreciation sought by the home country's intervention. However, if other countries are looking for a contraction, it is likely that a devaluation would occur anyway through normal channels as expectations of movements of future foreign rates worked through. But in the more likely case that these conditions do not hold, other countries may 'fight' using their own monetary instrument; or be expected to fight; or 'fight' passively using other automatic fiscal stabilisers, or be expected to do so. All of which would undo the stabilising effects of the peg, and or be expected to do so!

Alternatively, pessimism about the reactions of foreign monetary authorities might be overdone. The short term costs of a temporary monetary contraction in their economies associated with an appreciation of their currencies may be more than offset by the discounted benefits associated with lifting a major trading partner out of the liquidity trap, and eventually boosting that economy's demand for the foreign economies' exports. The studies of the forces that will bring about monetary policy coordination rather than competition typically study stationary economies. The cost-benefit analysis of a foreign country competing against a devaluation (by loosening policy at home) in times when neither country is threatened with a deflationary spiral may not be that informative about the likelihood of competition when one country faces just such a situation.

Svensson addresses the most compelling problem in his own analysis. It relates to the effectiveness of the promise to defend the peg, and, in turn, to the nature of the portfolio balance channel itself.

A central bank that is prepared to print unbounded quantities of money to buy foreign currency will force other sellers of the home currency to exchange at the rate the central bank desires. Central banks trying to push *up* the exchange rate have limited foreign exchange reserves to use to buy home currency, and therefore cannot credibly commit to buying unlimited quantities. Central banks trying to push a currency *down* have 'reserves' limited only by the capacity of the currency printing presses multiplied by (discretionary) currency denominations![70] If the central bank can credibly promise to print unlimited quantities of home currency to defend the peg, then, in equilibrium, it may not have to purchase anything at all, or only very small quantities of currency. If, however, printing unlimited quantities of the home currency is likely to conflict with, rather than support central bank objectives, then this promise will not be credible. And a likely equilibrium will be that the market pushes the central bank to print currency up to the point where it is not optimal to do it any more, and the exchange rate peg fails.[71]

Svensson argues that a crucial comparison will be where this limit is, relative to the point at which portfolio balance effects – where massive purchases of foreign assets, because of the imperfect substitutability of those foreign assets relative to currency movement adjusted home assets, bid up their relative price – begin to bite. Provided the central bank can print currency and buy foreign assets without harming its interests beyond the point where portfolio balance effects begin to manifest themselves, then the peg could be defendable. Otherwise, it won't be.

The point at which printing money to defend the peg becomes harmful and therefore, *ex ante*, not credible, is going to be related to the price stability objectives held by the central bank (or even more diffuse aims that we might express in words like 'currency integrity', or 'maintaining a reliable means of exchange'). A central bank entirely unconcerned with the potential costs of infinite volumes of paper currency outstanding relative to the supply of goods (or at least believed to be entirely unconcerned) will be able to commit to those unlimited currency issues. Central banks that either are not indifferent to these costs, or are thought not to be by the private sector will not be able to make such promises.[72] Surely all central banks fall into this latter category.

Arguably, there is a contradiction between the price-level target component of the Svensson policy proposal, and the implicit promise to debase the currency (or nearly so) to defend the currency peg. If the price level leg of the strategy is believed, then the exchange rate leg may not be. Yet if the exchange rate leg of the target is believed, it may be because the price-level objectives of the central bank are not credible, and won't be. (Though at least in this case, the expected inflation will bring with it a short-term benefit).

The Svensson proposal (like most monetary policies) relies on expectational channels to generate the stimulus needed to lift the economy out of the zero bound trap. In this case: the expected fall in long real rates that accompanies the real appreciation and the expected inflation. The less credible is the policy in the first place, or the more backward-looking are expectations, (and the more, therefore, that expectations of the future are based on the event that the economy stays trapped at the zero bound), the weaker these effects will be, and perhaps the larger the exchange rate devaluation needed in the first place.

Suppose this prediction is correct. Suppose too that we combine it with a second speculation, that the larger the exchange rate devaluation needed, the more likely it is to prompt a counterproductive response from the foreign monetary authorities. In this case the efficacy of the expectational channel may well dictate whether the policy is feasible in the first place or not.

Finally, and rather obviously, as Svensson and others who have commented on his proposal have noted, the usefulness of the foreign exchange portfolio-balance type policies hinges on the degree of openness of the economy. This was cited by some as a reason to be sceptical that it would be a feasible policy option for Japan;[73] and the same logic would apply to the US and the Euro area, where trade forms a similar percentage of GDP.

8. Options and Signalling

Tinsley (1999) suggested another way for the central bank to reduce rates further out along the term structure. He proposed that the central bank sell options to the private sector that would, should future short rates turn out higher than whatever is stipulated in the option, lead the central bank to incur financial losses. Long interest rates may be higher than (zero) short interest rates either because the market puts some weight on the hypothesis that the economy will lift itself with or without the help of the central bank out of the liquidity trap such that at some point a monetary contraction is warranted, or because of uncertainty about future rates. This in turn may constrain aggregate demand undesirably. Writing options that embody a financial commitment to zero rates (for example) could, the argument goes, lower long rates, and therefore lower real interest rates and boost aggregate demand. The private sector would consider that the central bank would want to avoid penalising itself and therefore consider it more likely that interest rates would not rise; this same effect would reduce the private sector's uncertainty about future rates. Both the first and second moment effects of selling the options would lower long rates.

The policy was suggested as a self-standing action by central banks, but in principle selling options of this sort could be a device to bolster the credibility of all policies we have discussed so far that benefit from being able to commit to future values of the interest rates; for example, the type of 'constant' history-dependence advocated by Woodford (1999) and Reifschneider and Williams (2000); or the history-dependence that 'turns on' when rates hit the zero bound suggested by Reifschneider and Williams (2000).

But my own view is that these kinds of options are likely to be at best, wholly ineffective, and at worst, ineffective and costly. Suppose agents are rational and forward looking. And that the economic situation is such that any increase in short rates over the foreseeable future is likely to be harmful to the interest of the central bank, (e.g. if it is in the interests of the central bank to commit to history-dependence), no such increase would be expected, and long rates will be low without writing options. Alternatively, suppose that economic circumstances were expected to be such that an increase in rates was warranted in the future. In which case the welfare benefits of increasing rates at that time would dwarf all but the most enormous financial penalties levied on the public sector. If the penalties were not large enough, the private sector would understand that and the writing of options would have no effect on expected future short rates.

For the same reason, such options may have no discernable effect on the uncertainty component of long rates. The distribution of possible future short rates would depend on the distribution of shocks hitting the economy over the future, and central bank responses to those shocks. Only extremely large financial penalties would make it rational for a central bank to factor them in when deciding the optimal setting of interest rates, and since the private sector will expect this, the risk of future interest rates rises will not be affected. To the extent that expectations are not as model-consistent as the world described above, the motivation for options trades diminishes anyway.

Indeed, long rates could even increase. If the penalties embedded in the options were very large, it is conceivable that there would be a range where long rates increased, as uncertainty about the central bank balance sheet increased, or increased later on, as speculation about whether or not the central bank would stick to its promised grew more intense.

9. 'Fiscal Policy'

An obvious alternative to interest rate stabilisation at the zero floor to rates is for the government to manipulate conventional fiscal (spending and taxation) tools to boost aggregate demand. Reifschneider and Williams (2000) conduct their experiments assuming fiscal stabilisation policy is as active as it has been historically in the USA. It is plausible that there might be more active fiscal policies than the one they study which lower the risk of hitting the zero bound without bringing with them extra costs.[74]

Our discussion of fiscal stabilisation necessarily focuses on how good a substitute fiscal policy is likely to be for monetary policy, when interest rates are held at zero.[75,76]

First, a familiar argument is that moving tax and spending instruments is a slow and imprecise business, so much so that it makes fiscal policy a very poor substitute for monetary policy: one of the reasons that objectives currently assigned to central banks *are* assigned to central banks. Many capital and current spending liabilities do not lend themselves to high frequency variations (health, education, defence . . .).

So-called 'automatic stabilisers' – like spending on unemployment related benefits and income, expenditure and profit taxes – could be amplified, *ex ante*, to provide an immediate stimulus that did not require any administrative or policy change.

But the authorities would need to offset the benefits of any stimulus that fiscal policy could provide against the costs of tax and expenditure variations. The distortions that come from predictable tax liabilities are less than those that come from uncertain ones.[77] Amplifying automatic stabilisers would involve increasing distortions and reducing welfare.[78] Any welfare-enhancing effects of government current or capital spending could be eroded by inducing (extra) pro-cyclicality in that spending. There is nothing to say that the optimal spending plans for transport or health provision infrastructure, for example, are likely to be coincident with the cycle.

Of course, fiscal stimuli injected by a government when the economy is at the zero bound to interest rates will be saved by consumers and firms who anticipate future taxes levied to pay for it and who are already on their desired consumption and investment plans. On the one hand, a systematic stabilisation rule (in the event of a zero bound) would, to the extent that stabilisation is effective, bring with it expected future inflation and a fall in real rates that reduced the necessary stabilisation needed in the first place, following the same logic as our discussion of history-dependent interest rate policies. On the other, systematising this kind of stabilisation will be less effective precisely *because* it is understood that the fiscal stimulus will be reversed at some point. Which effect would be the stronger is unclear.

Fiscal Dominance, Monetary Policy Rule-based Fiscal Dominance

So far we have talked about what initiatives a fiscal authority could take to stimulate the economy. It is possible that, *in extremis*, events might be taken out of the hands of the fiscal agent by the private sector. A live debate in the literature is under what circumstances, inflation may become a 'fiscal phenomenon' in the long as well as the short run.[79] 'Fiscal dominance' occurs when agents come to expect that taxes will not be levied to finance expenditures: or vice-versa, that deficit plans will, holding the price level constant, not be set to finance expenditure plans. In which case the real value of deficits is eroded by a jump in the price level to the point which equalises the present value of asset (tax) and liability (current expenditure plus interest payments plus debt redemption) streams.

Arguably, what Woodford termed 'fiscal dominance' is more likely to come about when the economy is trapped at the zero bound to interest rates than otherwise. During these times, the fiscal authority might find itself less able to reconcile streams of expenditure and taxes, and be expected by the private sector to find it harder to do so. And for two reasons. First, in a situation where the nominal rate is trapped at zero, it is possible that either the tax base might be shrinking and/or the pressure for higher government spending is likely to be higher. The political economy problems of levying extra taxes to stabilise public finances in either case are likely to be acute. (The economy is in recession, and no-one wants contractionary fiscal policy).

If the price level becomes 'fiscally' determined in this way then the economy will be hit by an actual and expected inflation. Since nominal rates are held at zero, this will bring about the monetary stabilisation the central bank was unable to provide by conventional means.

Could the mechanisms that give rise to fiscal dominance be exploited by a policymaker concerned about stabilisation? Would such a policy be desirable if it could? Sims (2000) appears to state that it is, when he urges that '... policymakers understand that under some circumstances budget balancing can become bad policy.' (p. 970).

A deliberately induced 'fiscal dominance' could implement a cut in real rates, but would risk arbitrary transfers of wealth either too or from those who hold existing nominal government debt. Sims seems to propose that the fiscal dominance be calibrated to rule such transfers out when he argues that a successful policy will come from 'assuring the public that deflation-generated increases in the real value of government debt will not be backed by increased future real taxation.' (p. 969) Sims implies therefore that the government should make it clear it will plan to levy taxes to pay back debt accrued from times of rising prices. But that other real debt incurred as a result of unplanned periods of falling prices will not be factored into future tax plans.

A general 'rules-based-fiscal-dominance' in theory could announce financing shortfalls of different sizes to match the amount of stabilisation needed. Such an amount chosen could seek to trade off wealth transfers to or from existing debt holders against the stabilisation benefits thereby obtained. This kind of policy would involve overlaying the 'fiscal-dominance' with 'monetary dominance'. The promise to 'default' would be guided by underlying price and output stability objectives.

Though the idea is logically coherent, it seems to me to be far-fetched as a proposal for systematic policy. Moreover, would a government that was prepared to manipulate an expectation of fiscal dominance to escape a deflationary spiral be able to re-establish conditions for monetary dominance in normal times?[80] The thought experiment is similar to that underpinning the exchange rate peg proposal that Svensson advocated. There, we are to believe that the central bank can devalue the currency by threatening to debase it, but is able to resume credible inflation-concerned policy again in normal times. Here, we need to believe that somehow the government could announce a partial default on its debt, but will be able to resume credible bookkeeping once the economy recovers.

Credibility and Fiscal Policy

In economies where fiscal stabilisation is effective the reliance on fiscal policy of this sort would confront policymakers with a similar set of time-consistency problems regarding inflation stabilisation that motivated governments to delegate monetary policy to an independent central bank. The problem would not be identical, (and therefore would not require an identical remedy), since those fiscal authorities that have delegated monetary policy to a central bank left themselves with a policy instrument that is a very imperfect substitute for monetary policy, for all the reasons we have suggested above.[81]

On the other hand, though fiscal stabilisation may involve credibility problems, they afflict fiscal authorities regardless of whether they are at the zero bound. It is not clear that announcing a transparent pro-cyclical fiscal stimulus in the event of a severe negative shock would measurably erode the (already imperfect) credibility of the overall government 'inflation and output stabilisation' policy (the collection of institutions that govern both fiscal and monetary policy). In fact, it may not be credible to establish fiscal rules that promise *not* to indulge in this kind of stabilisation when there is a risk of hitting the zero bound. Or at least, the more likely is the economy to hit the zero bound, the more likely agents are to expect governments to break any fiscal promises they have made that deprive them of a useful instrument.

For example, Reifschneider and Williams' simulations involve a fiscal rule that embodies the degree of activism in fiscal policy observed over the past (during which time the zero bound was not encountered). This kind of rule may not be credible if the economy either hits or risks hitting the zero bound. More active fiscal stabilisation may be desirable (it may better serve the stabilisation objectives that the government and central bank share) and, as a result, be anticipated.

Optimal Mixes of Monetary and Fiscal Stabilisation
This section digresses to consider three related propositions: (i) 'policies that are 'fiscal' should not be in the province of the central bank; (ii) policies that happen to be in the province of the central bank, but are 'fiscal' should not be pursued by it; and (iii) policies that are not in the province of the central bank, and are 'fiscal' should not be used by the fiscal authority in the pursuit of objectives delegated to the central bank.

Propositions (i) to (iii) do not seem at first blush to be such a bad description of modern, developed economy regimes. And some papers, by so conspicuously avoiding discussion of fiscal policy, imply them.[82] But I am going to draw out three points that I think are clear from the original contributions to the zero bound literature.

First, propositions (i) to (iii) are problematic given that monetary and fiscal policies interact so intimately. Given this, proposing that fiscal policy substitute for monetary policy in the case of a zero bound is not so radical: relative to what happens in modern regimes in normal times, it is merely a quantitative, not a qualitative change.

To illustrate, it has been clear throughout that 'fiscal' policies have clear 'monetary' consequences, and vice versa. Beginning with the fiscal consequences of 'monetary policy':[83] taxes on cash to bring about negative nominal rates will boost central bank revenues while they are in force. Intervening in either long bond or private sector asset markets will expose the central bank balance sheet to potential (in fact highly likely) capital losses that the fiscal authority will have to underwrite, (and the private sector will expect will be underwritten) or capital gains that it will have to redistribute; writing 'Tinsley' options likewise.

And the monetary consequences of 'fiscal policy': money rains will increase prices, of course. And conventional fiscal stabilisation affects the setting of real rates for a monetary regime that is concerned about stabilising inflation. (Which is precisely why it is a potential substitute for monetary policy at the zero bound).

To repeat my first point in this section: proposing that fiscal policy substitutes for monetary policy when interest rates hit the zero bound is not so radical when we see how intimately they are mixed during normal times.

My second point here is this: that the optimal mix of monetary and fiscal policy for a regime that never hits the zero bound is very likely to be different from the optimal mix in an economy that may, or has already hit the zero bound.

Third, the institutional arrangements that divide monetary and fiscal policies should be designed to facilitate as close an approximation to that optimal mix, placing due weight on time-consistency problems that may impair both monetary and fiscal policies when these policies are not isolated from day to day political imperatives. If the optimal mix of monetary and fiscal policy differs for an economy that is susceptible to hitting or hits the zero bound, then so will the optimal institutional framework that is needed to support them. In other words, if the zero bound calls for more fiscal policy, then institutions should reflect that fact, rather than be designed in spite of it.

Return to propositions (i) to (iii), and they now look problematic. To repeat, they were: (i) 'policies that are 'fiscal' should not be in the province of the central bank; (ii) policies that happen to be in the province of the central bank, but are 'fiscal' should not be pursued by it; and (iii) policies that are not in the province of the central bank, and are 'fiscal' should not be used by the fiscal authority in the pursuit of objectives delegated to the central bank. But, if all monetary actions open to a central bank have direct and predictable fiscal consequences, only in a semantic sense (distinguishing between actions and known consequences) can we fulfil (i) and (ii). And if the reverse is true, that all fiscal actions have direct and predictable 'inflation' consequences, (iii) is likewise impossible.

10. Optimal Policy When Interest Rates Are Bounded at Zero

What would a close reading of the literature suggest about an optimal policy that takes account of the zero bound? A useful place to begin to take stock is the benchmark suggested by the consensus in the simulation studies of the 'risks' of hitting the zero bound at inflation rates close to those pursued by prominent central banks. The consensus, as we have observed, seems to be as follows. First, at inflation rates around the levels of those quantified by some central banks, the risk of hitting the zero bound is small. Second, the risk of hitting the zero bound and being trapped at it – of entering a 'deflationary spiral' – is very small indeed at these inflation rates. Third, this risk seems to increase a great deal as the central bank starts to pursue inflation rates that fall towards zero.

Beginning from this benchmark, there are reasons why we might think that they offer too much comfort to central banks right now: but there are also reasons why they may overstate the costs of the current regimes.

The key unknown for policymakers in choosing an inflation rate is the dispersion of desired interest rates, which in turn depends on the dispersion of the shocks hitting the economy and how the economy and the policy rule combined propagate these shocks into a distribution for desired rates. The consensus about the risks of hitting the zero bound is based on assuming that these are normal, symmetric, and, in the case of some studies, resemble those shocks seen in the past. The question is how accurate these historical distributions will be in guiding a policy choice, and how large are the consequences of making a mistake (in particular, being too optimistic about the dispersion of shocks to desired rates).

The assumptions made by the authors about the distribution of shocks (normality, symmetry, congruence with past) are as good as any other. But the problem is what to do about the possibility that these assumptions may be wrong, either too pessimistic or too optimistic. 'What policy should do about the uncertainty it faces in gauging the extent of uncertainty' is a question that those who have written on 'robust' policies have addressed. Those authors (for example, Hansen and Sargent (1999)) were read as making a comment more directly about what might be good rules for stabilising variables central banks care about (for example, but not exclusively, inflation) about a *given target*, when the distribution of shocks about that target was itself, in some well defined sense, subject to some uncertainty. But that literature focused on how the concern for robustness might influence the choice of parameters in the rule for *any* inflation (or more complex) target. In the face of the zero bound constraint, the choice of the *inflation objective itself* is an exercise that could benefit from a concern for robustness. If we are uncertain about the probability of hitting the zero bound, and the difficulties that would pose for policy, we may be better off assuming that our estimates of that probability are too small, than too large (or assuming that our estimate of the dispersion of desired nominal interest rates is too narrow). This would imply choosing a higher mean inflation rate than otherwise. Suppose the mistake we make is in underestimating the variance of shocks hitting the economy. Here the costs of underestimating the downside portion of the distribution exceed those on the upside. Larger than expected upside shocks to desired interest rates can be stabilised with conventional policy. Larger shocks on the downside cannot.

The more difficult question is how much insurance it would be worth buying to reduce the risk of hitting the zero bound. Answering this involves evaluating the relative social costs of inflation versus inflation and output variability. This is firmly beyond the scope of this paper. But it is worth noting one thing: it is conceivable that central banks have already 'bought' enough by choosing the inflation rates they have. Studies that warn against choosing inflation rates below 2% do so implying that the benefits in terms of lower inflation would be outweighed by the costs of extra variability. But this is an unfounded conjecture in my view. Those same studies have models that do not allow us to uncover rigorous measures of welfare. Evidence that the 'risks' of hitting the zero bound increase below 2% is not by itself enough to warrant such a conjecture. All we can say is that the inflation rate should be higher, other things equal, if the zero bound is a problem. Nothing more.

(Studies that work with micro-founded models that do allow us to make statements about welfare – for example Wolman (1998, 2000) – would even suggest that inflation objectives quantified by central banks are too high, as we have already observed in section 3. But, arguably, those studies buy access to sound welfare analysis at the expense of realism. Making inferences for policy from the zero bound literature is fraught with the same trade-off as with any other macroeconomics literature in this respect.)

So much for the reasons why the literature gives us perhaps too much comfort. On the other hand, there are two clear possibilities that suggest that a simple reading of the 'risks' of hitting the zero bound as they have been computed may lead us to be too pessimistic about the welfare consequences of the current low inflation rates chosen by central banks.

First, the simulation studies necessarily do not consider many of the alternative policy options that researchers in the field have suggested are open to central banks to follow. Some studies do not consider fiscal alternatives to monetary stabilisation. Those that do consider only stabilisation as active as policy has been in the past, when more active stabilisation policies may be an option.

Again, most necessarily exclude some of the other policy options we have discussed here (money rains, taxing money, buying other assets, writing options...) They therefore exaggerate the risks of hitting the zero bound, (and the risks of a 'deflationary spiral') and the costs in terms of impaired stabilisation of remaining there.

This said, the returns to using these policies must be considered highly uncertain (including fiscal policy, where previous estimates of the efficacy of fiscal stimulus may, as we have suggested, be unreliable in novel situations like the one we are considering here). And that would make them less valuable insurance policies compared with the insurance of choosing a higher inflation rate. (It does not make them less valuable when choosing a higher inflation rate may not be an option, in other words, when the economy is already or thinks itself already trapped at the zero bound to interest rates. In this situation, however uncertain the returns may be, the authorities may have no option but to engage in unconventional policies.)

By way of qualification, there is perhaps a danger in drawing too stark a contrast between the 'known' performance of interest rate policies and 'unknown' nature of the other policy options. There are many discrepancies between the kind of rules studied in evaluations of monetary policy and the policies followed by actual central banks: policymakers themselves are reluctant to describe their policy as following a procedure as mechanical as those portrayed in the academic literature. Empirical descriptions of interest rate policies include features that are, to some degree, theoretically puzzling (like the excess autocorrelation of interest rates, or movements in discrete steps). Simulation studies therefore give us an assessment of *an* interest rate policy in a particular model, but cannot reliably taken as providing certain estimates of *interest rate policy in general* against which we can contrast entirely uncertain alternatives policy.

A second and related point is that, as we have already discussed above, the risks of hitting the zero bound and the costs of enduring periods there are calculated assuming that central banks credibly commit to policy rules which (i) none are currently credibly committed to and (ii) would not be credible under the circumstances under which they are studied (severe negative shocks). Central banks could and indeed would be expected to deviate from such rules once the circumstances they faced became clear, and perhaps indulge in more active conventional stabilisation (a larger, earlier cut in rates than warranted by the simple rules under study?) and it is conceivable that the risks as calculated are thereby overstated.

11. Conclusions and Summary

To recap:

A large literature evaluating the performance of alternative interest rate rules or alternatives to interest rate based stabilisation has grown up as central banks have pursued low rates of inflation. The views expressed in this paper could be summarised in the following set of statements.

The bound to nominal interest rates is given by the value to which the marginal utility of real balances tends. The zero figure comes from thinking that the transactions benefits to holding extra real money balances eventually diminish to nothing. But the bound may be higher than zero if there are anonymity benefits to holding cash that don't diminish to zero; or lower than zero if there are either significant costs of storing or managing real balances that kick in at some point, or non-pecuniary benefits to holding the other riskless alternative, bonds.

In the absence of perfect alternatives to interest rate stabilisation, policy faces the task of choosing an inflation rate to balance the costs of inflation and output variability against the costs of inflation itself.

The consensus in the literature on the risks of hitting the zero lower bound seems to be that the risk is small down to inflation rates close to those currently pursued by central banks, but gets much larger below that. The risk of a deflationary spiral seems to be very small indeed. The distinction is important. Many shocks that will force interest rates down to the zero bound will not be large enough to tip the economy into a deflationary spiral.

A key unknown in the calculation of the risks is the shape of the distribution of shocks that hit the economy and are propagated into shocks to desired interest rates. This must temper the comfort we draw from the studies so far carried out. Optimal policy would probably argue for a choice of inflation rate that is 'robust' to making mistakes about that distribution, and point to higher inflation than otherwise.

But computing the risks of hitting the zero bound doesn't tell us about optimal policy until we evaluate the benefits of avoiding the zero bound, as against the costs of inflation. Those central banks that have either privately or publicly quantified inflation objectives may already have taken out enough insurance in this regard. (Or even too much).

Studies of the risks of hitting the zero bound (and diagnoses of 'pathologies' associated with interest rate rules) are hampered by the fact that they study commitment to rules that no central bank does, or, under the circumstances considered, could commit to. They therefore overstate the risks. Moreover, studies of the 'perils' or 'pathologies' of interest rate rules do not tell us about the risk of hitting the zero bound at some inflation rate: choosing higher inflation would not provide an insurance against these catastrophes. But to repeat, these catastrophes again come out of simulating the pursuit of interest rate policies that are not credible. They are therefore either curiosities or a positive explanation for why central banks don't commit to policies of this form.

The central bank could engage in 'money rains' or monetary financing of the fiscal deficit. On the one hand, it would be counter-productive to commit to reversing money rains ('money drains'?) in the future. But on the other, the central bank might find it hard, once it has rained money in this way, to convince the private sector that it would not rain money (in whatever form) in normal times.

'Tinsley' style options that penalise the central bank for breaking a commitment not to raise interest rates in the future are likely to be ineffective at best, and harmful at worst. Financial penalties on the central bank and the public purse would have to be enormous to persuade the private sector that it was no longer in the interest of the central bank to raise rates. It is plausible to think that long rates could even increase, rather than fall, if penalties embedded in these options were large enough.

The central bank can clearly opt to exploit portfolio balance effects in markets for longer-term government, private sector, or even foreign assets. The most persuasive argument here is Goodfriend's argument that such purchases would increase broad liquidity in the market and reduce real rates. If these effects exist, they may already be at work anyway in normal times, and would certainly be open to policymakers to exploit at any interest rate, not just zero. The drawbacks are that the effects of interventions like this are very uncertain, may be unstable, and actions like this will expose the central bank to significant fiscal losses that the private sector as a whole will have to underwrite; they may also distort price signals in the market for risk.

A related proposal advanced by Svensson is to commit to an exchange rate depreciation, underpinned by portfolio balance effects in foreign exchange, and a rising path for the price level. How effective the exchange rate peg is will depend on how much intervention the central bank would have to engage in (relative to an amount that would be consistent with stabilisation objectives) before the point at which portfolio balance effects start to kick in is reached. A central bank understood to be committed to some notion of price stability may either not have or not wish to seek the option of credibly committing to debasing its currency. McCallum's proposal for a time-varying exchange rate target is subject to an analogous set of problems.

Conventional fiscal stabilisation carries with it many familiar costs: of implying larger microeconomic distortions from stronger automatic stabilisers; of interfering with the ongoing time consistency of monetary and fiscal policy. 'Fiscal dominance' may be more likely to occur in a deflationary spiral than in normal times, but is more likely to be a consequence of policy failure, rather than an option for systematic policy. This said, the burden of pursuing monetary policy objectives is already shared out between monetary and fiscal policies, by virtue of the fact that fiscal instruments have monetary policy consequences, so a further step in the fiscal direction may not be so radical.

Commitments to history-dependence in interest rate rules can help reduce the risk of hitting the zero bound, but do not provide a means of escape from it. Whether such commitments can be credible depends on whether you think central banks can 'just do it' (as Woodford, (1999) and McCallum, (1998) clearly believe) or will be expected to be susceptible to changes of heart (as Svensson, (1999) believes). Commitments that 'turn on' when the zero bound bites (as suggested by Reifschneider and Williams (2000), and simulated by Hunt and Laxton (2002)) are likely to be less effective in so far as they don't allow the central bank to build a reputation for sticking to its history-dependent promises.

Overall, the risks of being trapped at the zero bound to interest rates are probably small, and probably overstated. But the returns to policy alternatives are decidedly uncertain as most of their proponents have recognised. Given the uncertainties around the estimates of the risk of a 'deflationary trap', as Fuhrer and Sniderman (2000, p. 845) put it 'prevention is likely easier than cure', or, in the words of Ueda, of the Bank of Japan board: 'Don't put yourself in the position of zero interest rates'.[84] Alternatives to 'prevention' are of course more interesting for monetary authorities for whom prevention is too late. But how much 'preventative' medicine to take depends on evaluating the social preferences for inflation and output variability, relative to inflation. It's conceivable that the inflation objectives that typify modern monetary regimes have already prescribed more than enough of this kind of medicine.

Acknowledgements

The work underlying this review was undertaken while on secondment at the ECB.

This paper has benefited a great deal from conversations, comments and email communications with Ignazio Angeloni, Peter Andrews, Charles Bean, Claus Brand, Willem Buiter, Gunter Coenen, Spencer Dale, Paola Donati, Marvin Goodfriend, Alex Jung, Hans-Joachim Kloeckers, Klaus Masuch, Roberto Motto, Massimo Rostagno, Stuart Sayer, Frank Smets, Peter Tinsley, Jan Vlieghe and Michael Woodford. This paper has also benefited from insightful comments from three anonymous referees, for which I am grateful. I thank these individuals without implicating them in any of the views or errors remaining in this paper, which are my responsibility alone. Importantly, the views in this paper should not be taken to be those of the ECB, the ESCB, the Bank of England nor any of their respective monetary policy or other decision-making bodies.

Notes

1. There are many excellent reviews of the literature already, from which this paper has benefited. See, for example, Amirault and O'Reilly (2001), Goodfriend (2000), Johnson *et al.* (1999), McCallum (2000), Svensson (2001), Finicelli *et al.* (2002).

2. See, for example, the minutes of the January 2002 FOMC meeting, which include the following reference, and are worth quoting at length: '... members discussed staff background analyses of the implications for the conduct of policy if the economy were to deteriorate substantially in a period when nominal short-term interest rates were already at very low levels. Under such conditions, while unconventional policy measures might be available, their efficacy was uncertain, and it might be impossible to ease monetary policy sufficiently through the usual interest rate process to achieve System objectives. The members agreed that the potential for such an economic and policy scenario seemed highly remote, but it could not be dismissed altogether. If in the

future such circumstances appeared to be in the process of materialising, a case could be made at that point for taking pre-emptive easing actions to help guard against the potential development of economic weakness and price declines that could be associated with the so-called 'zero-bound' policy constraint.' And see a speech by Kazuo Ueda, (2001) member of the Board of the Bank of Japan, (at http://www/boj.org.jp/en/ press/] where he says, for example, that 'The BOJ has been groping for policy options that are valid near a liquidity trap. Life would have been very easy for the BOJ had simple increases in the monetary base led to a significant rise in the general price level. Instead the BOJ has been thinking very hard and carried out a variety of policy measures, attempting to over come the difficulty generated by the liquidity trap.'

3. Of course there may be other costs of pursuing low inflation not connected with the risk of hitting the zero bound, associated, for example, with downward nominal rigidities in prices or wages, or with the possible overstatement of true inflation in published measures. But I am going to say nothing about those issues in this paper.

4. Analogous to the scenario painted by Wicksell.

5. It could cut transactions costs, or help with 'shopping time' (McCallum and Goodfriend, 1987); it could be required 'in advance', in a manner originally suggested by Clower (1969). Or we can think of it providing some other unmodelled utility (Sidrauski, 1967).

6. Dreheman *et al.* (2002) cite examples like gambling or legal sex-related industries.

7. In fact, if I were a cash-holding criminal, the costs of my criminal activity being detected by my deciding to hold my wealth in interest-bearing, but more visible assets would not only not decline, they may even be increasing in real balances if all my real balances were confiscated as a result! If I have a million ill-gotten pounds, and contemplate putting that million into interest bearing assets, I risk being found out and losing a million pounds. If I have two million, and contemplate putting those into bonds, then I risk losing two million if I am found out.

8. Drehemann *et al.* (2002) and Rogoff (1998) have suggested that holdings of notes and coins by those engaged in criminal activity may be significant, especially if the prevalence of very high denomination notes is used as an indicator. High-denomination note holders might distinguish criminals from those who engage in activity they simply don't want to disclose, even though it is legal, since high denominations would be inconvenient as a medium of exchange for those activities.

9. But of course, the more important are criminals in cash holding, the higher is the socially optimal inflation rate, since inflation serves as a tax on criminal activity, and would bring with it the social benefits associated with reducing crime.

10. There are, of course, bearer bonds, where the owner is not identified. But bearer bonds are still surely more likely to lead to identification since they will be exchanged amongst a smaller group than will cash, and, by virtue of that, will not serve as a medium of exchange for anonymously engages in or criminal activity.

11. See also Wallace (2001) where he describes his disquiet with workhorse monetary models – and the unsoundness not just of zero bound analysis but other monetary questions – in more detail.

12. For instance: our model includes firms, although we say nothing about why firms exist; our model includes Governments and public monetary authorities, though we say nothing about why they exist either; we assume markets, yet ignore the delicate equilibria that underpin the property rights that create them; and agents trade, although there is nothing generating an incentive to specialise and exchange. . . .

13. For a recent commentary on Japan's monetary policy, see Ahearne *et al.* (2002) and the references therein.
14. Some (but not all) of these studies do allow for automatic fiscal stabilisers to work in the absence of monetary policy.
15. Some of the results in Hunt and Laxton (2001) are also presented in a box authored by Hunt in Chapter 2 of the IMF *World Economic Outlook*, May, p93, entitled 'Can inflation be too low?', within the essay 'Monetary Policy in a low inflation era', by Terrones and Sgherri.
16. A brief summary of each study appears in the Appendix. The numbers behind Figure 1 appear in Table 1 at the end of the paper. Note that these numbers are approximate and based on my own estimates from what is presented in the papers cited. The most important change I have made is an adjustment to the assumed equilibrium real interest rate to make the studies as comparable as possible. (They take different positions on this issue).

Table 1. Estimates of the Risk of Hitting the Zero Lower Bound (per cent of time interest rates at zero).

	Assumed inflation objective (per cent)								
	0	0.5	1	1.5	2	2.5	3	3.5	4
RW	14		9		5		1		<1
OW	7	3	1	<1					
BCM	9.6	6.3	2.8	1.4	0.9	0.7	0.4	0.1	
HL	9	5	2		1				
CL	4.8		2.9		1.3		0.2		0

Notes: OW: Authors own rough calculations from Figure 6 on page 45 of OW 1998. They assume a value of 1 for the steady state real interest rate. I add 1.5 to make that comparable with RW, and present the Taylor rule results.
BCM: Authors own calculations from BCM, taking the results they have assuming that the interest rate floor is zero (they experiment with different levels of the floor) and subtracting 1.5 from their reported inflation rates in Table 3 on page 325) to get results for a real rate that is equivalent to Reifschneider and Williams. BCM assume 4% real rates.
HL: Hunt and Laxton simulate the Japan block in MULTIMOD. They assume a real rate of 2.2%. These figures are taken, unadjusted, from Table 7 on page 26. HL describe these figures as underestimating the risk of hitting the zero bound, relative to RW, for a variety of reasons.
CL: The assumed real rate in this paper is not transparent. Figures approximate, taken from a chart with no exact numbers.

17. Calculating the 'risk' of hitting the zero bound in this way is more of an art than a science. But it gives a flavour of two more compelling statistics in a way that is comparable across studies: the portion of the *ex ante* desired interest rate distribution that is ruled out by the zero bound; and the increase in the variability of inflation and output.
18. Up to the point where the mean inflation rate is so low that every value of the uniformly distributed shocks is expected to imply zero interest rates, after which point there is no extra variability implied by choosing even lower inflation.
19. Unless the mean inflation target is such that the mean interest rate is less than zero, in which case the cost of reducing inflation from that point will be higher, the higher is the equilibrium real interest rate.

20. One complicating factor is that the distribution of shocks to desired interest rates may be related to the choice of the average inflation rate. It is hard to find a coherent economic argument for a mechanism like this. One plausible rationale for why the variance of shocks might increase as the inflation target falls might be that the degree of nominal stickiness may increase as the inflation rate falls. See, for example, Ball, Mankiw and Romer (1988). This would increase the short impact of a given change in interest rates on real variables, but reduce the impact of interest rates on nominal variables, but at any rate would change the distribution of desired interest rates for a given set of shocks. Note that Klaeffling and Lopez (2002) contemplate the opposite case, that high inflation implies a larger variance of demand shocks. They cite the widely documented correlation between the level and variance of inflation in support of the idea. (Although in my view there is some way to go before we interpret the increased variance of inflation as an increased variance of shocks. I would conjecture that this phenomenon is more likely to reflect either an actual or perceived lack of concern for inflation variation on the part of those policymakers that tolerate higher inflation, rather than a higher variance of shocks to which policymakers in high inflation rate countries have to respond.)

21. Another route by which inflation could affect real rates is very loosely described by the following: if inflation affects growth, and growth itself is related to the real rate, then lower inflation could raise the real rate.

22. However, I would add this qualification to McCallum's gloomy assessment. The amount of 'reassurance' (or the amount by which a rise in the real rate might translate into a fall in the risk of hitting the zero bound) 7 basis points could provide depends on the shape of the distribution of shocks (and therefore of desired nominal interest rates). If the economy is already at a point where the density function of desired interest rates is high (or thick) at the zero bound, then 7 basis points will lower the risk of hitting the zero bound a good deal. If the density function is very thin at the zero bound, then shifting up the real rate by 7 basis points will have very little effect on the risk of hitting the zero bound. By extension, think of the effect on the optimal inflation rate. If shocks were uniformly distributed, and the economy was already at the point where the marginal benefit of inflation-reduction equalled the marginal cost, then neither a 7 basis point, nor a 100 basis point rise in the real rate would change the optimal inflation rate. Recall from the above that the optimal inflation rate equates the marginal benefit with the marginal cost of a unit of inflation reduction. And that the marginal cost of a unit of inflation-reduction is given by the slope of the density function of desired rates. However, if the slope of the density function of the shocks at the current optimal inflation rate was quite steep, then contemplating even a small rise in the real rate could imply a significant change in the optimal inflation rate.

23. He attributes the original argument to Goodfriend (1991).

24. Batini and Yates (2003) dwell on these two types of commitments, and present history-dependent examples of both in the course of discussing price level targeting. But expositions of this kind of policy pre-date this paper.

25. Hunt and Laxton (2001) consider a similar type of price-level target rule, that they class as a 'one-off intervention': an amendment to a Taylor rule that only takes effect if the zero bound constraint binds (see page 17).

26. See Batini and Yates (2003), Ditmar et al. (2000), Gaspar and Smets (2000), Svensson, (1999), Vestin (2000), Wolman (1998, 2000).

27. See, for example, Figure 9, page 961.

28. And provided that the initial inflation target is one that involves a mean desired nominal interest rate that is positive.

29. Another example is in the same Figure 9 of Reifschneider and Williams, which shows that the marginal cost of inflation reduction is lower for Henderson-Mckibbin (HM) rules than for Taylor rules. Comparing like for like, HM rules generate lower inflation and output variability than Taylor rules. HM rules also imply a lower cost of reducing inflation from 2 to zero.

30. This is of course not meant to define a spectrum along which we might locate all possible expectations formation processes. It is just meant to make more concrete some notion of 'backward-lookingness' in expectations that would weaken the benefits of (a given degree of) history-dependence.

31. This is a debate that researchers had when they discussed the material significance of the 'average inflation bias': whether central banks needed to be endowed with legislative independence to remove the incentive to inflate, or could, as McCallum (1995) suggested 'just do it', or, as Woodford (1999) (and perhaps others) suggested, did in fact just do it. And the debate about the 'stabilisation bias', the incentive to renege on interest rate rules even when there is no incentive to try and raise average inflation in the economy, takes the same form. Svensson (1999) has argued that interest rate rules in general, and therefore by implication history dependent rules in particular, are 'incentive incompatible', i.e. could not be committed to. Woodford takes issue with him in a comment, claiming that this belief 'is tantamount to an argument that rational persons are... incapable of self-control or ethical behaviour' (p. 24), and cites Blinder (1999, p. 49) who wrote that time-inconsistency problems are a feature of many areas of economic life and are dealt with 'by creating and then usually following norms of behaviour by building reputations and by remembering that there are many tomorrows. Rarely does society solve a time-inconsistency problem by rigid pre-commitment or by creating incentive-compatible schemes for decision-makers.'

32. And more recently by Hunt and Laxton (2001).

33. I say 'typically', here, since Bullard and Cho (2002) is an exception. In their world temporary low inflation states are brought about by periodic clusters of shocks convincing the private sector that the central bank has lowered its inflation target. Since the central bank moves its target in part in line with what the private sector expects (perhaps because of a desire to avoid the output fluctuations that would come with expectational errors), the target then does indeed shift down, and the process is, for a while, self-reinforcing. In these circumstances, choosing a higher inflation rate would indeed reduce the chance of a temporary low inflation state brought about in this way forcing interest rates against the zero bound.

34. McCallum, for example, notes: 'if one is inclined to doubt the stabilising properties of Taylor rules, or interest-instrument rules for inflation targeting, then this doubt should logically exist without any regard to ZLB considerations.' (p. 901).

35. As did the anonymous referee of this paper.

36. See McCallum (2000) for his application of this point with respect to the literature on the zero bound trap, and McCallum (2002) for a full exposition of his position on the debate about appropriate criterion for eliminating equilibria when there are multiple such solutions.

37. My reading of Buiter and Panigirtzoglou in a 2002 revision of their 1999 paper is that they appear to sympathise with this view.

38. This is a comment I conjecture applies just as much to the literature on 'perils', (Christiano and Rostagno (2001), Benhabib *et al.* (2001), Buiter and Panigirtzoglou (1999) etc.), as it does to the literature on the risks of hitting the zero bound and entering a deflationary spiral. But since those papers arguably do not bear on the cost of inflation reduction, the narrative focuses on the studies that do.

39. Christiano and Rostagno (2001) illustrate just such an alternative – hinted at in Sims' (2000) comments on Reifschneider and Williams – to avoid the 'perils' and 'pathologies' identified in their and other studies, but in a subtly different context. They propose that the central bank could commit to an interest rate rule, but also commit to deviate from it should the money supply breach some pre-announced bounds. However, the argument here is that no such commitment would be needed. Central banks would in fact not be expected to follow the interest rate rule in the first place. The commitment to the money growth exemption from the Taylor rule is surely superfluous. Alstadheim and Henderson (2002) consider an asymmetric policy rule that commits the central bank to reducing interest rates in response to a 'negative' shock by more than in response to a 'positive' shock. And Hunt and Laxton (2002) and of course Reifschneider and Williams (2000) study alternative interest rate procedures from the Taylor rule that they use to compute the risks of hitting the zero bound. These are alternatives that are studied under 'commit-ment'. They are therefore subject to the same observation I make about Christiano and Rostagno: namely, that the point (for our inquiry) is not that there is an alternative *commitment*, but that since there is an alternative policy to the plain vanilla Taylor rule, discretionary policy will follow it, and be expected to follow it. But, nevertheless, these simulations serve to illustrate that there *are* alternatives to the rigid interest rate rules, whether they are options to be committed to or 'just done'. All of these alternatives are shown to yield benefits over their benchmark, more Taylor-like competitors. Bryant (2000) too discusses how a central bank could announce that it would depart from conventional interest rate rules if the conjuncture justified it.

40. Other arguments for not committing to 'rules' for setting interest rates have been made in public by central banks. That, for example, rules could not summarise the complex array of information that policymakers want to take into account when setting interest rates. Or that it may not be practical to commit to any procedure for setting rates in the presence of continual structural change.

41. Specifically, the degree of inflation persistence embedded in structural features of aggregate supply, not the autocorrelation of inflation itself, which will depend on the regime. Though of course it's possible that nominal rigidities that give rise to inflation persistence are themselves a function of steady state inflation. Higher inflation could lead to less persistence and hence to more powerful expectational effects from credible policy commitments.

42. Hunt and Laxton (2002) make the same point, arguing that if inflation is more persistent in the euro area than in the USA, then, other things equal, that would support targeting a higher inflation rate in the euro area than the USA. However, we would be completely mistaken to infer from this that the Euro area inflation objective should be higher *than it already is*. That conclusion would depend on evaluating the relative social costs of inflation, and inflation and output variability, as I have already described. For that reason, there is nothing in the Hunt-Laxton study that can support the view that the ECB should increase its definition of price stability. On the contrary, we could just as well use it to argue that the Fed should lower its implicit inflation objective to something below the ECB's.

43. Instead, see the many papers reviewed by Angeloni *et al.* (2001).
44. The intellectual pedigree of this idea is traced by Goodfriend (2000) in a helpful footnote on page 1008 of his paper. He refers us to Keynes (1936, ch. 17, p. 234 and ch. 23 pp. 353–358); Dahlberg (1938, chs 7 and 8) and Hart (1948, ch. 20, pp 443–47). Both Buiter and Panigirtzoglou (1999) and Goodfriend point out that Keynes credits Gesell with the original idea.
45. Of course, when the time arrives such that circumstances generate a need for a lower floor to interest rates, raising the steady state inflation target is not a feasible short-term policy option.
46. Taxing money directly, rather than through inflation, differs to the extent that there are 'unit of account', 'menu' or relative price variability, or imperfect tax indexation type costs associated with positive inflation.
47. Buiter and Panigirtzoglou (1999) point out that Gesell-like schemes had been tried, for reasons not connected with the zero bound, in Alberta in Canada, and in Austria in the 1930s.
48. Formalised by, for example, Orphanides and Weiland (1999).
49. See Goodfriend (2000), Clouse *et al.* (2002), Wolman (1998).
50. Equivalent to one of Friedman's 'helicopter drops'!
51. A money rain that was not reversed would probably still generate a stronger liquidity effect than one that was. A ten year loan of cash to the private sector relieves credit constraints for ten years, but without perfect certainty that some other form of collatoral would come along in ten years, or the need for borrowing would have passed, a ten year loan is still a poor substitute for an infinite period loan.
52. Although as I have already said, and just as with other 'fiscal' policies discussed later, if credit constraints are severe, a money rain that was accompanied by an announcement that it would be reversed in good times might still boost aggregate demand.
53. This is the 'real balance effect' identified with Haberler (1946), Pantinkin, (1965) Pigou, (1943) and de Skitovsky (1941).
54. This section relies heavily on Goodfriend (2000).
55. This from Meltzer, (1999): 'They claim that the lower bound was in effect during the 1930s, so monetary policy was inflexible for part of that decade. For this claim to be true, the short term interest rate must be the principal or only means by which monetary actions are transmitted from the central bank, through the market, to the economy. As my old friend Karl Brunner often said: we know this is false. Monetary actions are effective and powerful ... where there is no money market ... relative prices respond to monetary impulses in countries without central banks, and without money markets. There is more to the transmission process than the models recognise.' (p. 5). And this, (also cited in Nelson (2000, p. 15): 'Monetary policy works by changing relative prices. There are many, many such prices. Some economists erroneously believe... monetary policy works only by changing a single short-term interest rate.' See also this quote from Friedman and Schwartz, (1982), cited in Nelson (2000, p. 15): 'Keynesians regard a change in the quantity of money as reflecting in the first instance 'the' interest rate, interpreted as a market interest rate on a fairly narrow class of financial liabilities... We insist that a far wider range of marketable assets and interest rates must be taken into account... [We] interpret the transmission mechanism in terms of relative price adjustment over a broad area rather than in terms of narrowly defined interest rates.' (pp. 57, 58).
56. Meltzer makes two arguments. The first is that there is a 'real balance effect' of the kind investigated by McCallum (2000), Ireland (2001) and Nelson (2001). The second

is that money, govt debt and private sector assets are all imperfect substitutes and that open market operations can affect their relative prices. This second argument is what we focus on here. The real balance effect of the first kind, as we have already discussed in the previous section, does *not* provide policymakers with leverage over the economy at zero interest rates.

57. I can do no better than quote Goodfriend (2000) at this point: 'when the stock of outside bonds is small and the marginal implicit liquidity services yield is high, the explicit premium on equity relative to bonds is large, because the implicit marginal liquidity yield on bonds is large. As the per capita inventory of bond holdings increases, individuals are better protected against having to smooth consumption by paying large transactions costs to sell other assets. The required explicit bond return rises as the marginal implicit liquidity services yield falls, that is, the explicit equity premium falls' (p. 1021).

58. Finally, note that the central bank could conduct open market operations by swapping short-term debt for the illiquid long term debt. Money and bonds are perfect substitutes at zero interest rates, of course, and therefore could be used interchangeably in an operation like this.

59. Less optimistically, the more these effects are operating in normal times, the more will our surmises about the performance of 'interest rate policies' be contaminated by portfolio balance transmission effects. The comparison in such a world would be between an 'interest rate plus small portfolio balance effect' at positive interest rates, and a 'portfolio balance effect only' policy at the zero bound.

60. Goodfriend, in addition, worries that 'if the public thinks that the central bank is unwilling to take losses on its long bonds, then the central bank's ... policy will lack credibility' (p. 1027). I am less sure that there is a problem central banks can do anything about. My surmise is that there would be no difference between the expectations of future policy, and of the future net worth of the public sector between a central bank that engaged in long bond purchases but did not want to take capital losses, and a central bank that engaged in these purchases but was prepared to accept them. Both would have little choice but to take those losses. And central bank purchases, whatever announcements accompanied them, would prompt a rational private sector to expect them. The only alternative is for the central bank to sell back the bonds when the price is high again. But that would conflict with the objectives of stabilisation policy that would prevail at the time.

61. And here I lump together all such assets, including making direct loans to private sector companies.

62. If there are two goods, apples and oranges, and they are imperfect substitutes, and in fixed supply, then not only will government intervention by buying up apples change the relative price of apples, it will also reduce welfare possibilities achievable with a given income. So too with exploiting portfolio balance effects. Buying up a large enough fraction of a particular asset or class of assets to affect their price will reduce the amount of hedging that is achievable for a given income.

63. Orphanides and Weiland (1998) present a model with a portfolio balance effect in that incorporates the extra uncertainty surrounding the use of this kind of 'quantitative' monetary policy at the zero bound, in the same way as did Brainard (1967) in the case of only one policy instrument.

64. Of course strictly speaking, we don't know how uncertain the returns to any policy are, but our knowledge about the portfolio balance channel would seem to be even less well developed than our understanding of other aspects of the transmission mechanism.

65. We could make a related comment on Meltzer's inference that there is something that monetary authorities do in countries where there are no money markets that suggests there is something monetary authorities could do in countries where there are money markets but where they are stuck at the zero bound (in the quote cited in footnote 39). Monetary authorities in these countries may well do something useful that could be mimicked by other central banks. Or they may equally well be doing something that is worse than doing nothing.

66. Hanes himself makes it clear that he does not consider his empirical study one that evaluates a Meltzer-type argument of this kind (in footnote 1 on page 5 of his paper, he says 'a related but distinct question, which I do not address in this paper, is whether a central bank can boost real activity through channels other than a decrease in interest rates on liquid debt'), so readers should be clear that I am arguing against an interpretation of his work that Hanes himself does not put on it. Hanes in fact advances a separate argument. In normal times, when interest rates are positive, banks worried about interest rate risk can purchase short-dated assets and still earn positive interest. However, when short-dated interest rates are zero, this option is not available to them, so they may seek instead to buy longer-dated assets, taking into account the interest rate risk that goes with them. This would generate a downward sloping demand for those assets that the central bank could exploit.

67. The central bank announces a rising path for the price level in preference to a positive inflation target to eliminate the potential costs that some saw with the Krugman proposal, namely, that by announcing a commitment to increase inflation, it might be difficult to convince the private sector that it would not at some future date announce a further increase in the inflation target, or renounce inflation control altogether. These concerns were expressed by, amongst others, the Bank of Japan.

68. Svensson has the exchange rate determined in part, but not only by uncovered interest parity. Provided the exchange rate peg is credible, *ex post* the exchange rate will have appeared to move in line with uncovered interest parity. If the peg had come under attack and the central bank had been involved in a defence, via exploiting portfolio balance effects in foreign exchange, UIP would, after the event, appear to have been violated.

69. See his 2001 paper. Finicelli *et al.* (2002) also evaluate the Svensson proposal. Some of the points made here draw on these two papers.

70. This from Meltzer (1999): 'Suppose, now, with a short term interest at zero, the Bank of Japan announces that it wants the dollar exchange rate to fall by 50% and that it is prepared to print yen to buy dollars until that occurs. Is there any doubt that the yen would depreciate or that the depreciation would affect spending, output and prices in Japan?' (p. 4).

71. The mechanism here would no doubt have 'self-fulfilling' properties of the sort discussed in the literature that developed to explain how commitments to keep nominal exchange rates 'high' failed, begun by Krugman (1979) and evolving through the work of Obstfeld (1996) and others.

72. Printing currency to the point where portfolio balance effects bite may involve interferences with foreign monetary policy beyond the effect imposed by the exchange rate peg. Massive purchases of foreign government assets could, for instance push up prices and reduce rates on those assets: this could, however, offset the contractionary effect on the foreign economy brought about by the exchange rate devaluation, and, therefore, be an advantage.

73. Indeed, others (McKinnon and Ohno, 2000) suggested that political economy pressures from the USA lay behind the 'high' value for the yen and, therefore, contributed to the problem Japan found itself in the first place.

74. Klaeffling and Lopez (2002) solve for optimal policy when fiscal stabilisation is a substitute for monetary policy. They therefore envisage a fiscal policy that would indeed be more active than a policy that had been observed during a history of higher inflation rates (when the zero bound was not encountered, or encountered less frequently). Fuhrer and Madigan (1997) note how active fiscal policy improves the response of the economy to shocks when interest rates are constrained.

75. It is worth noting for completeness that if either public consumption is a perfect substitute for private consumption in individuals' utility functions, and or public investment is a perfect substitute for private investment in firms' production functions, then fiscal stabilisation will be ineffective. A point stressed in this context by Buiter and Panigirtzoglou (1999).

76. Klaeffling and Lopez (2002), amongst others, raise this concern.

77. More realistically, we are contemplating the welfare costs of adding to expenditure and tax uncertainty through the use of more active fiscal stabilisation, rather than comparing interfering with currently certain interventions by the government.

78. For example, unemployment-related benefits would have to increase to provide a larger stimulus when unemployment increased. Higher unemployment benefits would mean a higher natural rate of unemployment. The rise in benefits accompanying a rise in the natural rate would involve an associated increase in average tax burdens and therefore an additional distortion from this source.

79. See, for example, Woodford (1999), Buiter (2002) and Christiano and Fitzgerald (2000).

80. It is possible that such a policy would also increase long-term rates. If the current 'inflation' risk premia in nominal debt factors in a small possibility of a deflation, then ruling out taxation to repay the portion of debt incurred through deflation would make the bet for the private sector, in terms of prices, one-sided.

81. For instance, the credibility problem in monetary policy has at its heart the knowledge that agents who have to set nominal contracts before a shock arrives know that a central bank will not only have an incentive but will also have the ability to break its promise on monetary policy once contracts are set, to deflate real prices and boost output and employment. A fiscal authority which finds it either more costly or more time-consuming to change the fiscal stance in response to high frequency news on the economy will find that its promises not to move fiscal policy are more readily believed by the private sector.

82. See, for example, Clouse et al. (2000) and Buiter and Panigirtzoglou (1999).

83. Of course, monetary policy choices in normal situations, leaving aside monetary policies that we would consider only when the zero bound to nominal interest rates has become a constraint, have 'fiscal' consequences. Conventional monetary policy at positive inflation rates involves seigniorage revenues. The choice of the inflation rate will influence the natural rate of output, and clearly, therefore, outcomes that are relevant for the 'fiscal' authority. (Not only because of the usual 'costs of inflation' but because of the zero bound itself, of course).

84. Cited by Fuhrer and Sniderman (2000, p. 846).

85. Induced by quadratic costs of adjustment rather than Fuhrer-Moore style contracting.

References

Ahearne, A., Gagnon, J., Haltmaier, J., Kamin, S., Erceg, C., Faust, J., Guerrieri, L., Hemphill, C., Kole, L., Roush, J., Rogers, J., Sheets, N. and Wright, N. (2002) Preventing deflation: lessons from Japan's experience in the 1990s. *Board of Governors of the Federal Reserve System (U.S.)* in its series *International Finance Discussion Papers* number 729.

Amirault, D. and O'Reilly, B. (2001) The zero bound on nominal interest rates: how important is it? Bank of Canada Working Paper no 01–6.

Alstadheim, R. and Henderson, D. (2002) Price level determinacy, the zero bound on the interest rate, and the liquidity trap. Mimeo, Georgetown University.

Angeloni, I., Kashyap, A., Mojon, B. and Terlizzese, D. (2001) Monetary transmission in the Euro area: where do we stand? ECB Working Paper no 114.

Ball, L., Mankiw, N. G. and Romer, D. (1988) The new Keynsian economics and the inflation-output trade-off. *Brookings Papers on Economic Activity* 19, 1: 1–65.

Batini, N. and Yates, A. (2003) Hybrid price level and inflation targeting. *Journal of Money, Credit and Banking* 35(3): 283–300.

Benhabib, J., Schmitt-Grhoe, S. and Uribe, M. (2003) The perils of Taylor Rules. *Journal of Economic Theory* 96: 40–69.

Bernanke, B. and Gertler, M. (1995) Inside the black box: the credit channel of monetary policy transmission. *Journal of Economic Perspectives* 9 (Fall), 27–48.

Black, R., Coletti, D. and Monnier, S. (1998) On the costs and benefits of price stability. In *Price Stability, Inflation Targets and Monetary Policy*. Proceedings of a conference held by the Bank of Canada, May 1997, 303–42.

Blinder, A. S. (1999) *Central Banking in Theory and Practice*. Cambridge: MIT Press.

Blinder, A. (2000) Monetary policy at the zero lower bound: balancing the risks. *Journal of Money, Credit and Banking* 32 (4): 1093–99.

Brainard, W. (1967) Uncertainty and the effectiveness of policy. *American Economic Review* 57 (2): 411–425.

Bryant, R. C. (2000) Comment on 'Overcoming the zero bound on interest rate policy' by Marvin Goodfriend. *Journal of Money, Credit and Banking* 32, 4: 1036–1051.

Buiter, W. (2002) The fiscal theory of the price level: a critique. *Economic Journal* 112 (July), 459–480.

Buiter, W. and Panigirtzoglou (1999) How to avoid them and how to escape them. NBER Working Paper no 7245.

Bullard, J. and Cho, I. K. (2002) Escapist policy rules. Federal Reserve Bank of St Louis Working Paper 2002–2.

Christiano, L. and Fitzgerald, T. (2000) Understanding the fiscal theory of the price level. NBER Working Paper no 7668.

Christiano, L. J. and Rostagno, M. (2001) Money growth monitoring and the Taylor rule. NBER Working Papers 8539, National Bureau of Economic Research.

Clouse, J., Henderson, D., Orphanides, A., Small, D. and Tinsley, P. (2000) Monetary policy when the nominal short term interest rate is zero. International Finance and Economics Discussion Paper No 2000–51.

Clower, R. (1967) A reconsideration of the microfoundations of monetary theory. *Western Economic Journal* 6, 1: 1–9.

Cozier, B. and Lavoie, C. (1994) Is there a floor to nominal interest rates? Evidence and implications for the conduct of monetary policy. Paper presented at Canadian Economic Association Meetings, Calgary University, June.

Dahlberg, A. (1938) *When Capital Goes on Strike*. New York: Harper.

Dittmar, R., Gavin, W. T. and Kydland, F. E. (1999) Price level uncertainty and inflation targeting. *Review of the Federal Reserve Bank of St Louis*, 81 (4): 23–34.

Drehmann, M., Goodhart, C. A. E. and Krueger, M. (2002) The challenges facing currency usage: will the traditional transaction medium be able to resist competition from the new technologies? *Economic Policy*, April, 195–27.

Evans, G. and Honkapohja, A. (1999) Learning dynamics. In Taylor, J. and Woodford, M. (eds), *Handbook of Macroeconomics*. Amsterdam: North-Holland.

Evans, G. and Honkapohja, A. (2001) *Learning and Expectations in Macroeconomics.* Princeton, Princeton University Press.

Finicelli, A., Pagano, P. and Paterno F. (2002) Monetary policy when the short-term nominal interest rate is 0%. Mimeo, Bank of Italy.

Friedman, M. and Schwartz, A. (1982) The effect of the term structure of interest rates on the demand for money in the United States. *Journal of Monetary Economics* 90, 1: 201–12.

Fuhrer, J. C. and Madigan, B. F. (1997) Monetary policy when interest rates are bounded at zero. *Review of Economics and Statistics* 79: 573–85.

Fuhrer, J. C. and Sniderman, M. S. (2000) Conference summary. *Journal of Money, Credit and Banking* 32 (4): 845–867.

Gaspar, V. and Smets, F. (2000) Price stability: some issues. *National Institute Economic Review no. 174.*

Goodfriend, M. (1991) Interest rates and the conduct of monetary policy. *Carnegie-Rochester Conference Series on Public Policy* 34: 7–30.

Goodfriend, M. (2000) Overcoming the zero bound on interest rate policy. *Journal of Money, Credit and Banking* 32(4): 1007–35.

Goodfriend, M. and King, R. (2001) The case for price stability. In Herrero, Gaspar, Hoogduin, Morgan an Winkler (eds), *Why Price Stability?* European Central Bank.

Hanes, C. (2002) The liquidity trap, the supply of reserves and US interest rates in the 1930s. Mimeo, Federal Reserve Board of Governors.

Hansen, L. and Sargent, T. (1999) Wanting robustness in macroeconomics. Mimeo, University of Chicago.

Haberler, G. (1946) *Prosperity and Depression: a Theoretical Analysis of Cyclical Movements*, 3rd edn. United Nations: New York.

Hart, A. G. (1948) *Money, Debt and Economic Activity*. New York: Prentice-Hall.

Hunt, B. and Laxton, D. (2001) The zero interest rate floor (ZIF) and its implications for Japan. IMF working paper 01/186.

IMF, (1999, 2002) *World Economic Outlook.*

Ireland, P. N. (2001) Money's role in the monetary business cycle. NBER Working Papers 8115, National Bureau of Economic Research.

Johnson, K., Small, D. and Tyron, R. (1999) Monetary policy and price stability. International Economics and Finance Discussion Paper no 641.

Keynes, J. M. (1936) *The General Theory of Employment, Interest and Money.*

Klaeffling, M. and Lopez, V. (2002) The optimal inflation target in the face of a liquidity trap. Mimeo, European Central Bank and University of Bonn.

Krugman, P. (1979) A model of balance of payment crises. *Journal of Money, Credit and Banking* 11 (August), 311–25.

Krugman, P. (1998) It's Baack: Japan's slump and the return of the liquidity trap. *Brookings Papers on Economic Activity* 49(2): 137–206.

McCallum, B. T. (1995) Two fallacies concerning central bank independence. *American Economic Review Papers and Proceedings* 85, 2: 207–211.

McCallum, B. T. (2000) Theoretical analysis regarding a zero lower bound on nominal interest rates. *Journal of Money, Credit and Banking* 32(4): 870–904.

McCallum, B. T. (2002) Consistent expectations, rational expectations, multiple-solution indeterminacies, and least-squares learnability', Mimeo, Carnegie-Mellon University.

McCallum, B. and Goodfriend, M. (1987) Theoretical analysis of the demand for money. *The New Palgrave: a Dictionary or Economic Theory and Doctrine*. New York: Stockton Press.

McKinnon, R. and Ohno, K. (2000) The foreign exchange origins of Japan's economic slump in the 1990s and low interest liquidity trap. IMES Discussion Paper Series 2000-E-19. Tokyo: Bank of Japan.

Meese, R. A. and Rogoff, K. (1983) The out-of-sample failure of empirical exchange rate models: sampling error or misspecification? In Frenkel (ed.), *Exchange Rates and International Macroeconomics*. Chicago IL: University of Chicago Press.

Meltzer, A (1999a) The transmission process. Mimeo, Carnegie-Mellon University and American Enterprise Institute.

Meltzer, A (1999b) A liquidity trap? Mimeo, Carnegie-Mellon University.

Nelson, E. (2000) Direct effects of base money on aggregate demand: theory and evidence. Bank of England Working Paper no 122.

Nelson, E. (2002) Direct effects of base money on aggregate demand: theory and evidence. *Journal of Monetary Economics* 49, 4: 687–708.

Obstfeld, M. (1996) Models of currency crises with self-fulfilling features. *European Economic Review* 40 (April), 1037–48.

Orphanides, A. and Weiland, W. (1998) Price stability and monetary policy effectiveness when nominal interest rates are bounded at zero. Working Paper 1998–35, Finance and Economics Discussion Series, Federal Reserve Board.

Orphanides, A. and Weiland, W. (1999) Efficient monetary policy design near price stability. Working Paper no 1999–67, Board of Governors of the Federal Reserve Board.

Patinkin, D. (1965) *Money, Interest and Prices*, 2nd edn. New York: Harper and Row.

Pigou, A. C. (1943) The classical stationary state. *Economic Journal* 53, (December), 343–351.

Reifschneider, D. and Williams, J. C. (2000) Three lessons for monetary policy in a low inflation era. *Journal of Money, Credit and Banking* 32(4): 936–66.

Rogoff, K. (1998) Blessing or curse? Foreign and underground demand for euro notes. *Economic Policy* (April), 263–303.

Sidrauski, M. (1967) Rational choice and patterns of growth in a monetary economy. *American Economic Review* 57 (2): 534–544.

Sims, C. A. (2000) Comment on 'Three lessons for monetary policy in a low-inflation era' by David Reifschneider and John C. Williams, pp. 967–79.

Skitovsky, T. De (1941) Capital accumulation, employment and price rigidity. *Review of Economic Studies* 8 (February), 69–88.

Summers, L. (1991) How should long term monetary policy be determined? *Journal of Money, Credit and Banking* 23: 625–31.

Svensson, L. E. O. (1999) Price level targeting versus inflation targeting: a free lunch? *Journal of Money, Credit and Banking* 31(3): 277–95.

Svensson, L. E. O. (2001) The zero bound in an open economy. A foolproof way of escaping from a liquidity trap. *Monetary and Economic Studies* 19 (February), 277–312.

Tinsley, P. (1999) Short rate expectations, term premiums, and central bank use of derivatives to reduce policy uncertainty. Mimeo, Federal Reserve Board of Governors.

Vestin, D. (2000) Price level targeting versus inflation targeting in a forward-looking model. Svierges Riksbank Working Paper no 106.

Wallace, N. (2000) Comment on 'Three lessons for monetary policy in a low inflation era' by Reifschneider, D. and Williams, J. C., *Journal of Money, Credit and Banking* 32(4): 973–978.

Wallace, N. (2001) Whither monetary economics? *International Economic Review* 42(4): 847–869.

Wicksell, K. (1898) *Interest and Prices*. London, Macmillan, 1936 edition, translated by RF Kahn.

Wolman, A. L. (1998) Staggered price setting and the zero bound on nominal interest rates. *Federal Reserve Bank of Richmond Economic Quarterly* 84(4): 1–24.

Wolman, A. L. (2000) Real implications of the zero bound on nominal interest rates. Mimeo, Federal Reserve Bank of Richmond.

Woodford, M. (1999) Commentary: how should monetary policy be conducted in an era of price stability? In *New Challenges for Monetary Policy*. Symposium sponsored by the Federal Reserve Bank of Kansas City.

Appendix: Short Summary of the Main Studies on the Effects of the Zero Lower Bound

Cozier and Lavoie (1994)

Calibrated model: backward looking aggregate demand; 'expectations-augmented Phillips Curve'; monetary policy rule described as 'forward looking monetary policy rule with an inflation target' by Amirault and O'Reilly. Stochastic simulations.

Record that the probability of interest rates being at the zero bound is 3.5% when the inflation target is 1%, and 5% when the inflation target is reduced to zero.

Fuhrer and Madigan (1997)

Model: backward looking aggregate demand; variant on Taylor (1980) overlapping contracts in aggregate supply (i.e no inflation persistence). Interest rate reaction functions: one Taylor type rule with interest rates responding to deviations of nominal income growth from.

Compare the impulse response of aggregate demand to IS shocks at an inflation rate of 4% compared to zero. The differences between the responses are quite small for short-lived shocks, and for rules that incorporate some dependence on past values. For longer lived shocks, or for rules that involve aggressive responses, the differences are larger.

Hunt and Laxton, also reported in IMF World Economic Outlook (2002)

Simulations using IMF multi-country model 'MULTIMOD', imagining a hypothetical Japanese policymaker conducting policy with a Taylor rule. Report that the probability of hitting the zero bound is 4% at 2% inflation. (Slightly lower than Reifschneider and Williams, therefore). But this rises non-monotonically as inflation falls. For example, the probability of hitting the zero bound is reported to be 13% at 1% inflation, and 31% at zero inflation. (This compares with the Taylor rule results of Reifschneider and Williams of a 14% chance of hitting the zero bound at zero inflation.) Also report the probability of entering a 'deflationary spiral', the same as Reifschneider and Williams' 'region of instability'. This is 0% at 2% inflation, but rises to 11% at zero inflation. Considers the effect of increasing the aggressiveness of the Taylor rule (increases likelihood of hitting the zero bound). And of interventions once the zero bound is hit: committing to reversing price level target declines suffered at the zero bound (induces a faster escape); and a fiscal stimulus (also induces a faster escape); and also a Svensson style depreciation plus price level target (induces a faster escape). But the success of these policies is really given by assumption in the model, (price level/depreciation targets believed, fiscal stimulus assumed to generate extra aggregate demand ...).

Orphanides and Wieland (1998)

Model: estimated Fuhrer-Moore (1995) model with overlapping contracts and a forward looking aggregate demand side (with future income terms in a consumption equation, and backward looking investment and stocks). Taylor and Henderson-Mckibbin rules. (HM rules include coefficients of 2 on lagged output and 1 on lagged inflation-target deviation). Find that effects of zero bound are negligible at inflation rates down to 2%. But at targets between 0 and 1% the zero bound affects inflation and output variability significantly. For example: interest rates never at zero with target inflation at 3%. Interest rates at zero 30% of the time with an aggressive HM rule, or 15–20% of the time with a Taylor rule.

Wolman (1998)

Calibrated, optimising theoretical model embodying price rather than inflation stickiness: optimising model enables welfare comparisons of regimes to be made, unlike other studies. Price level targeting regime optimal, and negligible risk of hitting the zero bound due to the ability to credibly induce large fluctuations in future inflation.

Reifschneider and Williams (2000)

Model: FRB/US forward looking aggregate demand, inflation persistence in aggregate supply.[85] Study performance under a Taylor and a HM rule (as above). With a Taylor rule, effect of zero bound negligible down to inflation targets of 2%. Effect increases markedly towards zero. For example, percentage of time interest rate bounded at zero is 5% at 2% inflation, but 14% at zero inflation. The HM rule, which implies more aggressive responses of rates, (but lower inflation and output variability on average), implies hitting the zero bound more often: 17% of the time at 2% inflation, 31% of the time at 0% inflation. Cost of zero bound in all cases felt more in terms of output than inflation variability. Assume steady state real rate is 2.5%.

Black, Coletti and Monnier (1999)

Bank of Canada QPM. Calibrated forward-looking aggregate demand, some sluggishness in inflation process. Inflation forecast based interest rate rule. For a level of the real rate that is 0.5 pp above that assumed in Reifschneider and Williams, they have nominal rates at the zero floor 0.9% of the time at 2% inflation (p. 325, Table 3); and at 0% inflation at the floor about 10% of the time.

INDEX

Note: Page numbers in *italics* refer to figures and those in **bold** refer to tables.

DATE DUE

GAYLORD			PRINTED IN U.S.A.